MADNESS

Madness: A History is a thorough and accessible account of madness from antiquity to modern times, offering a large-scale yet nuanced picture of mental illness and its varieties in western civilization.

The book opens by considering perceptions and experiences of madness starting in biblical times, ancient history and Hippocratic medicine to the Age of Enlightenment, before moving on to developments from the late eighteenth century to the late twentieth century and the Cold War era. Petteri Pietikainen looks at issues such as eighteenth-century asylums, the rise of psychiatry, the history of diagnoses, the experiences of mental health patients, the emergence of neuroses, the impact of eugenics, the development of different treatments and the late twentieth-century emergence of anti-psychiatry and the modern malaise of the worried well. The book examines the history of madness at the different levels of micro, meso and macro: the social and cultural forces shaping the medical and lay perspectives on madness, the invention and development of diagnoses as well as the theories and treatment methods by physicians, and the patient experiences inside and outside the mental institution.

Drawing extensively from primary records written by psychiatrists and accounts by mental health patients themselves, it also gives readers a thorough grounding in the secondary literature addressing the history of madness. An essential read for all students of the history of mental illness, medicine and society more broadly.

Petteri Pietikainen is a professor of the History of Science and Ideas at the University of Oulu in Finland. His publications include *C.G. Jung and the Psychology of Symbolic Forms* (1999), *Alchemists of Human Nature* (2007) and *Neurosis and Modernity: The Age of Nervousness in Sweden* (2007).

MADNESS

A History

Petteri Pietikainen

LONDON AND NEW YORK

First published 2015
by Routledge
2 Park Square, Milton Park, Abingdon, Oxon OX14 4RN

and by Routledge
711 Third Avenue, New York, NY 10017

Routledge is an imprint of the Taylor & Francis Group, an informa business

© 2015 Petteri Pietikainen

The right of Petteri Pietikainen to be identified as author of this work
has been asserted by him in accordance with sections 77 and 78 of the
Copyright, Designs and Patents Act 1988.

All rights reserved. No part of this book may be reprinted or reproduced
or utilised in any form or by any electronic, mechanical, or other
means, now known or hereafter invented, including photocopying and
recording, or in any information storage or retrieval system, without
permission in writing from the publishers.

Trademark notice: Product or corporate names may be trademarks
or registered trademarks, and are used only for identification and
explanation without intent to infringe.

British Library Cataloguing-in-Publication Data
A catalogue record for this book is available from the British Library

Library of Congress Cataloging-in-Publication Data
Pietikainen, Petteri.
  Madness : a history / Petteri Pietikainen.
    pages cm
  Includes bibliographical references and index.
  1. Mental illness—History.   2. Mental illness—Social aspects—
History.   3. Mental illness—Treatment—History.   4. Psychiatric
hospitals—History.   5. Psychiatry—History.   I. Title.
  RC438.P54 2015
  616.89—dc23
  2014045449

ISBN: 978-0-415-71316-0 (hbk)
ISBN: 978-0-415-71318-4 (pbk)
ISBN: 978-1-315-70896-6 (ebk)

Typeset in Bembo
by Apex CoVantage, LLC

CONTENTS

List of figures	*vii*
Publisher's acknowledgements	*viii*

1 Introduction to madness and its history	1

PART I
Madness from Antiquity to the Age of the Enlightenment
13

2 Madness in ancient and medieval times	15
3 Madness, folly and religion in early modern Europe	38
4 From the devil's temptation to wrong thinking: madness in the seventeenth and eighteenth centuries	57

PART II
The great transformation: medicalization of madness in the long nineteenth century
75

5 The Age of the Asylum	77
6 The medical management of madness	106

vi Contents

7 Living and dying in asylumland 134

8 Naming the mad mind 158

PART III
Naming and managing madness in the Golden Age of Asylums 183

9 Mental maladies in the twentieth century 185

10 Mental treatment from magnetism to psychoanalysis 211

11 War and madness 228

12 Shocks and surgeries: somatic treatments of
the twentieth century 242

PART IV
Madness in the Cold War era and beyond 267

13 Mind control, political psychiatry and human rights 269

14 The psychopharmacological revolution 287

15 Madness between sanity and normality 312

Epilogue *333*
Index *337*

LIST OF FIGURES

3.1	An exorcist casting demons out of a woman who has killed her child and her parents.	45
5.1	Bethlem (Bedlam) depicted in William Hogarth's *A Rake's Progress* (1732–5).	86
6.1	Théodore Géricault's 'Portrait of a Woman Suffering from Obsessive Envy' (*Monomane de l'envie*), 1822.	118
6.2	Experiences relating to spasms provoked in hysterical patients at the Salpêtrière in Paris.	119
6.3	Cover of *American Phrenological Journal*, 1848.	122
7.1	A patient in a restraint chair at the West Riding Lunatic Asylum, Wakefield, Yorkshire, ca. 1869.	139
7.2	Method of coercion for violent lunatics, particularly used in Germany.	142
7.3	Hatanpää Mental Hospital in Tampere, Finland, in the early 1920s.	148
8.1	Jean-Martin Charcot giving a clinical demonstration at the Salpêtrière.	174
9.1	Vaslav Nijinsky in Stravinsky's ballet *Petrouchka*, ca. 1910.	197
11.1	A Nazi (NSDAP) Party poster showing how disabled people cost money and promoting eugenics and euthanasia of the disabled.	233
12.1	A male nurse gives glucose to a patient undergoing insulin shock therapy at Runwell Hospital in Essex, England, in 1943.	246
14.1	Thorazine advert (1962).	297

PUBLISHER'S ACKNOWLEDGEMENTS

The publishers would like to thank the following for giving permission to reproduce copyright material: Alamy; Helsinki University Museum; The Imperial War Museum; Museum of Fine Arts, Lyon; New York Public Library; Steiermärkisches Landesmuseum Joanneum, Alte Galerie, Graz; Wellcome Library, London.

1

INTRODUCTION TO MADNESS AND ITS HISTORY

Psychiatrist C.G. Jung claimed that the difference between the sane and the insane is a matter of scale: in madness, we can see the same traits that can be found in sanity. The only difference is that these traits or characteristics, such as hearing voices or talking to oneself, are more distinguishable in madness (Jung 1977, 35). Behind psychological definitions, medical diagnoses and social labels there is a whole kaleidoscope of human experience – all possible variations of normality and deviance, familiarity and strangeness. In a mode of thinking that emphasizes the unity of human nature, madness is not so much otherness as sameness, even if a somewhat exaggerated and unusual kind of sameness. There is often a continuum between normal and abnormal behaviour, and between good or ill health. This idea can be illustrated by a little story of an unusual encounter between a physicist and a physician.

In 1946 the US Army was drafting men for the occupation of Germany. The Selective Service Board called up Richard Feynman (1918–88), who later was awarded the Nobel Prize in Physics. After a check-up of his physical health, he saw a psychiatrist. As told by Feynman,

> 'Do you think people talk about you?' he asks, in a low, serious tone.
> I [Feynman] lit up and said, 'Sure! When I go home, my mother often tells me how she was telling her friends about me.' [. . .]
> 'Do you think people *stare* at you?'
> I'm all ready to say no, when he says, 'For instance, do you think any of the boys waiting on the benches are staring at you now?'
>
> (Feynman 1992, 157)

'How many guys are staring at me at the moment?' Feynman did some mental arithmetic and replied: 'Yeah, maybe two of them are looking at us.'

He turned around and looked:

> Sure enough, two guys are looking. So I point to them and I say, 'Yeah –
> there's *that* guy, and that guy over *there* looking at us.' Of course, when I'm
> turned around and pointing like that, other guys start to look at us, so I
> say, 'Now him, and those two over there – and now the whole bunch.' He
> [psychiatrist] still doesn't look up to check. He's busy writing more things
> on my paper.
>
> (Feynman 1992, 157–8)

More questions follow: 'Do you ever hear voices in your head? Do you talk to
yourself? I see you have a deceased wife – do you talk to her?'

The last question annoyed Feynman, but he contained himself and said: 'Sometimes, when I go up on a mountain and I'm thinking about her.' He also mentioned that he had an aunt in an insane asylum.

At the end of the interview, the psychiatrist becomes friendly again:

> 'I see you have a Ph.D., Dick. Where did you study?'
> 'MIT and Princeton. And where did *you* study!'
> 'Yale and London. And what did you study, Dick?'
> 'Physics. And what did *you* study?'
> 'Medicine.'
> 'And *this* is *medicine*?'
>
> (Feynman 1992, 159)

Feynman's 'innocent' question irritated the psychiatrist, who told him to go
back to the benches and wait. Soon he was called over to see another psychiatrist.
This one was older and more distinguished. He asked about the voices in Feynman's head, and about Feynman's deceased wife:

> 'What do you say to her?'
> I got angry. I figure it's none of his damn business, and I say. 'I tell her I love
> her, if it's all right with you!'

The tone of the interview became more tense. After an argument about the
reality of the 'supernormal', the psychiatrist asked:

> 'How much do you value life?'
> 'Sixty-four.'
> 'Why did you say "sixty-four"?'
> 'How are you supposed to measure the value of life?'
> 'No! I mean, why did you say "sixty-four", and not "seventy-three", for
> instance?'
> 'If I had said "seventy-three", you would have asked me the same question!'
>
> (Feynman 1992, 160–1; see also Gleick 1992, 223–5)

The interview ended when the psychiatrist handed papers to Feynman. While he was waiting in the line, he looked at the papers and noticed that he had received 'D' (*deficient*) in the psychiatric section. 'What does that mean?' Feynman wondered. When it was Feynman's turn, he handed his papers to the officer, ready to explain everything. But the officer did not look up. He saw the 'D' in the psychiatric section, reached for the rejection stamp without asking any questions and stamped Feynman's papers 'REJECTED'. Uncle Sam did not want Richard Feynman (Feynman 1992, 161–3).

Feynman's anecdote illustrates the key-idea that there is ambiguity regarding the definition of madness. Is talking to your deceased loved one a symptom of madness? What about hearing voices or talking to oneself? Or, the belief that people talk about you?

The relativity and historicity of madness, including the variability of the criteria for madness, form one major theme that runs through the pages of this book. As this book demonstrates, madness has many faces, and they are constantly changing. Still, they are recognizable faces throughout history, because people who have been perceived and treated as mad have behaved in ways that deviate from the so-called average behaviour more than the strictures of normality allow. Feynman's 'auditory hallucination' does not sound too serious, but if he had talked about the devil giving him orders through a radio, he might have been taken straight from the draft office to the nearest asylum. Madness can be understood only in terms of degree, and of the prevailing medical and cultural beliefs about human nature, normality and deviance. And these beliefs change when we move from one historical period to another, and from one place to another. For example, our current infatuation with individualism and self-assertion would have been perceived as conceited and presumptuous by medieval Europeans whose modes of thinking and acting were strongly influenced by the Catholic Church and religious precepts. Similarly, modern secular Europeans would be inclined to categorize people who hear voices or claim to be possessed by the devil as mentally disordered, whereas medieval Europeans could have thought that individuals hearing voices had a privileged line of communication with God, and that those who claimed to be possessed, or who behaved as if they were possessed, actually were so. This book shows that there have not been, and there will never be, universal and timeless rules regarding how madness manifests itself.

Another theme of this book is the rise of the medical management of madness. Psychiatrists who interviewed Feynman represented a medical profession that is specialized in the naming, explaining and classifying of 'mental illnesses', as various forms of madness began to be called in the nineteenth century. From Part II onwards, psychiatrists occupy the centre stage in this book as managers of madness. Jack Pressman, the late historian of psychosurgery, has defined psychiatry as the management of despair (Pressman 1998, 438). This is aptly put: since the nineteenth century, mental health professionals have tried to manage human despair, mental confusion and suffering by various methods of treatment, diagnoses and preventive work. The task has been daunting, because the spectrum of mental suffering is very wide, ranging from full-blown psychosis with delusions

4 Introduction

and catatonic exclusion of outer reality to various neuroses, phobias and mood swings. Some of us are completely crazy, others completely sane, but most of us occupy the grey zone where we are mad at some times, neurotic at other times and, most of the time, not so sure whether our minds are truly in order or not.

The third major theme of this book is also related to Feynman's experiences in the draft office: I give the mad or the mentally ill a larger role and louder voice than they have had in any other general history of madness or psychiatry to date. More precisely, my book moves back and forth between the different levels of micro, meso and macro. At the macro level, I discuss the social and intellectual forces shaping medical and lay perspectives on madness; at the meso level, I examine the invention and development of diagnoses, theories and treatments. Finally, at the micro level I focus on the shop floor practices and the patient experiences inside and outside the prevailing mental health care system. My goal is to establish both a large-scale historical narrative and a detailed medical and patient-centred context. This means that I do not lose sight of the *Lebenswelt* (the lived reality) of the individual and the ideas and deeds of the 'mad-doctors', psychiatrists and other managers of madness. The present book is a human-centred history of madness, which makes it different from previous histories: I will observe madness in the wards of the asylums, in the clinics and, to some extent, in communities. In my view, this concretization of madness is crucially important, even though it can be difficult to find the patient's own voice behind medical diagnoses, patient records and case histories in the ocean of medical books, articles and other published documents. Fortunately, subjective experiences and the lived reality of the mentally afflicted can be seen in the letters, diaries, notes and autobiographical texts they have written, as well as in interviews and oral histories.

My book provides an overall picture of madness, but I do not attempt to include everything from early antiquity to the early twenty-first century in this book. Rather, I will lead the reader on a walk through the history of madness, or the 'path of madness', and stop when I see developments and events worthy of closer observation and examination. I will focus on 'European madness', including its North American variant, but I will also shortly discuss madness in the Islamic Near East and the asylum system in Argentina, Australia and New Zealand as well as French colonial psychiatry in North Africa. Within Europe, I will mostly travel in the Nordic countries, Britain, France and Germany. Modern psychiatry developed in this part of Europe, as well as in the Netherlands and Italy, and there were many medical and economic similarities in common between these countries. There are also several first-class historical studies examining the history of madness and mental illness in different parts of Europe, and during different periods. I have used these studies as well as medical publications and patient records of the Oulu District Mental Hospital in Finland.

Since the early 1960s, historical scholarship on mental illness has steadily increased and deepened. My own ambition is to offer a large-scale, yet historically nuanced picture of madness and its varieties in the western cultural sphere. While the present book 'tells the whole story', so to speak, it will say more about the developments between the late eighteenth and late twentieth century than about the previous two millennia. A book such as this one has not been published since 1961, when Michel Foucault's classic (even if historically less than convincing) *History of Madness* (*Histoire de la folie à l'âge classique*) was published. An abridged English translation of Foucault's book appeared in 1964, and a complete translation was published in 2006 (Foucault 2006). The only comparable book to Foucault's magisterial work is the medical historian Edward Shorter's more recent *A History of Psychiatry* (1997). Shorter's fine book examines developments in psychiatry and medical science, and his strong belief in biological psychiatry gives a somewhat biased picture of mental medicine. Moreover, neither Foucault nor Shorter pays much attention to the mental patients and their point of view, as I do.

My book owes most to the late historian Roy Porter, a veritable one-man publishing house of high-quality books on a wide variety of topics. Porter combined patient-centred and socio-cultural perspectives, displayed a sceptical attitude towards over-generalizing and opinionated explanations and entertained his readers with his story-telling gifts and his ability to see essential details in the larger canvas of historical development. Like Porter, I strive to avoid the pitfalls of partisanship or the narrow view from a committed ideological mindset. At the same time, my book aims to be wider in scope and more exhaustive than works that are focused on limited themes, isolated materials and narrow questions published for professional audiences. In today's academic world of specialized studies, more informative histories that take a broader view on the human condition are badly needed.

In the first part of the book I give an overview of madness from ancient times to the Age of the Enlightenment. In this section, we will meet melancholics, dancing maniacs, the possessed, court fools and murderous religious fanatics. In Part II, my pace slows down as I focus on the great transformation in the management of madness in the nineteenth century. I describe the 'great confinement' of the mad, the professionalization of 'mad-doctors' and the classification of madness into distinct diagnostic entities. Part III deals with the multifarious ways in which the mentally ill have been treated and mistreated by their physicians and other caretakers from the late eighteenth to the late twentieth century, including hypnotism, psychoanalysis and psychosurgery. I also examine the history of major twentieth-century disease entities (schizophrenia, manic-depression and psychopathy) and the 'war neuroses' of the two world wars in Part III. In the fourth and last part of the book, I first investigate the more sinister developments during the Cold War era, including the CIA's mind control programme and political psychiatry in the Soviet Union. Then I move on to the so-called psychopharmacological revolution of the 1950s, and in the final chapter I explore developments since the 1960s, focusing on anti-psychiatry and its legacy, the revival of biological psychiatry and the late twentieth-century 'deinstitutionalization' of mental health care.

I am convinced that there is a need for a synthetic overview of the history of madness that brings together the rich scholarship of many decades and incorporates

6 Introduction

archival material and primary sources into the story. This is what I aim to do in the present book.

Madness and the human condition

Charles Chaplin, a great comedian and a great moralist, once said that life is a tragedy when seen in close-up but a comedy in long shot. I suggest that Chaplin's observation of the life in close-up is correct with regard to the mentally ill. I am less certain about his long shot. In this history of madness, sometimes I focus on the close-up and discuss the destiny of a single individual. At other times I stand back to look at and describe large-scale phenomena, such as the Age of the Asylum, changes in the explanations of madness and the convoluted development of mental medicine. In this fashion, my goal is to create a history of madness in the western world without neglecting the significance of human experience. By experience I mean a sampling of the continuum and variety of being mad, sad, strange, deviant, eccentric, mysterious and yet . . . also, familiar. In the chapters to follow, we come across melancholics who are descended into the abyss of doom and gloom. We meet schizophrenics visiting heavenly spheres, restless maniacs in straitjackets and people in the grip of a fugue or nostalgia. We meet neurotics absorbed in their misery, and men and women consumed by obsession. There are theatrical hysterics and individuals tormented by demonic possession.

But why do I talk about the history of 'madness', and not, for example, the history of 'psychiatry' or 'mental illness'? The reason is simple: I want to go beyond the confines of medicine and psychology and look at the spheres of culture, society and ideas. Moreover, I want to de-medicalize madness and emphasize the situational and cultural aspects of derangement. For most of human history, what we call mental illness has been understood in vernacular terms as madness, lunacy, obsession, spiritual affliction, nervousness and so forth. As a socially oriented intellectual historian, I am sensitive to concepts and their changing meanings. The word 'madness' itself is a very ambiguous term. In the course of history many different social, medical, judicial and religious meanings have been attached to it, and these various meanings have determined the 'use-value' of madness. In sixteenth-century Germany, for example, confused and disordered people avoided the label 'madness' (*Unsinnigkeit*) for social and judicial reasons. This was because the term implied a lack of reason, which could have meant that the afflicted were declared incompetent to manage their affairs. As incompetent, people were in danger of losing their property, as well as their status in the community, indeed their status as human beings. Consequently, Germans preferred to be regarded as temporarily confused due to a physical illness, adverse circumstances or even possessed by demons (Lederer 2006, 154–8). On the other hand, in the Nordic countries, 'madness' does not have such a negative connotation. The word has been used as a common vernacular term to refer to a behaviour deemed strange, extreme or ridiculous, but not necessarily insane. In general, in western culture, madness has been tossed around spontaneously when someone has said or done something unusual or peculiar (for an argument about great historical continuity in the ways of speaking about madness, see Thiher 2004).

Until the twentieth century, the popular terms employed to denote mental illness in the Anglo-American world were 'madness', 'lunacy', 'insanity,' 'hurry of the spirits' and 'demoniac possession'. Of these terms, 'possession' was clearly religious in tone, while 'lunacy' originally referred to the belief that intermittent phases of mental derangement were causally related to phases of the moon (the Old English equivalent was *monaðseocnes*; literally 'month-sickness'). 'Madness' in turn suggested manic restlessness, wildness and loss of self-control. Even today, we may describe an angry or enraged person as 'mad'. When madness was turning to a clinical disease entity in the nineteenth century, the early psychiatrists began to use the more medical term 'insanity' as a contrast to 'sanity' or 'healthy' (and 'clean'). Through medical diagnosis and explanation, it is instructive to see how everyday madness gradually changed into mental illness and psychiatric disorder.

When we study madness we simultaneously study human nature. Definitions of and criteria for madness change temporally and locally. Through studying violations of the boundaries of normality and sanity we can illuminate the mysteries of the human condition. The starting point of my book is the assumption that culture shapes madness, but I also subscribe to the view that madness shapes culture by impacting the ways in which we understand ourselves, our fellow humans and the surrounding reality. For this reason, to study madness historically is to study the intellectual and the socio-cultural changes that constitute varieties of human experience.

As a historian I believe in situational explanations of behaviour: the explanation for much of our behavior is linked to our social context. People live within the institutions and social structures that organize their lives. This includes parents, relatives, friends, members of the community, authority figures, religion, economy, educational institutions and the political system. Prevailing cultural beliefs shape our world views and our self-understanding. This does not necessarily mean that we are totally determined by this environment. Human beings are also biological creatures shaped by evolutionary adaptations. As individuals we have innate traits and inclinations that are manifest in our basic temperament, moral emotions, fears and hopes.

The kind of situational explanatory model I subscribe to is definitively *not* inspired by environmental determinism that sees the human mind as a blank slate or *tabula rasa*, which the social environment colonizes and directs. Evolution has probably designed some of our minds in a way that is not always optimal in today's 'knowledge economy'. Some phobias, obsessive compulsive disorders, anxieties and even depression may be partly explained by our evolutionary past as hunter-gatherers (Nesse & Williams 1996; McGuire & Troisi 1998). Fortunately, in recent years the human sciences have begun to pay some attention to the interdependencies of genetic and environmental factors in cultural evolution.

8 Introduction

The question of the co-evolution of biology and culture is exemplified in our understanding of schizophrenia, the 'cancer of the mind'. To what extent can schizophrenia be explained as a biological illness? And, conversely, to what extent can it be explained by adverse environmental influences that may damage the mind so badly that the result is psychosis? In fact, such dichotomies are most probably misguided, because a gene-centred approach to mental illness does not exclude social factors, and vice versa. Focusing on environmental factors does not mean that one omits biological discoveries and theories of human malfunctioning. If we are to believe some radical cognitive researchers and philosophers, the whole idea of the dualism of mind and body, or culture and biology, is erroneous. The American neurophilosopher Alva Noë even disputes the basic assumption that consciousness is located in the brain. He contends that consciousness expands from the brain to the other parts of the body and even to the external environment. To Noë, the sense of consciousness is more than brain activity; it is a dynamic product of wide-ranging interactions between the body and the world it inhabits. Metaphorically, consciousness is like dance, for our ability to dance depends not only on our inner or mental functioning, but also on our attunement to the people and the world around us (Noë 2010). This view is an imaginative hypothesis that is difficult to confirm (or refute), but as such it challenges the human sciences and especially the neurosciences – should we have a broader, less individual and brain-centred approach to the human being?

Social scientists have often seen madness as a form of deviance, 'deviance' denoting a more or less consistent habit of breaking social norms. In this view, criteria such as norm-following and adjustment to the environment in general are used to denote mental illness. Sociologists are interested in social order and *disorder*, exemplified in criminality, rebelliousness, sectarian religiosity, sexual promiscuity and madness. According to the moderate sociological view, social structures and processes influence the outbreak and representation of mental illness, whereas an extreme 'sociologism' claims that mental illness is *produced* by social structures and processes. Because the mentally ill have caused social disorganization by deviating too much from the accepted rules, they have been stigmatized – their identity is 'spoiled', as the Canadian-American sociologist Erving Goffman put in the 1960s (Goffman 1963). According to this explanation, the negative attitude of community members and prejudices towards deviancies paved the way for the increasingly common practice in which oddly behaving individuals are seen as mentally deranged. A prominent representative of this view is the American sociologist Thomas Scheff, with his labelling theory (Scheff 1999).

Historical explorations of the cultural factors of madness are often illustrative and important. For example, for a person publicly to declare one's religious atheism or anti-racism was certainly a form of deviance in the southern United States in the early days of the civil rights movement. In this book, we shall meet one such 'madman', who spent time in a mental hospital as a schizophrenic and who later became a civil rights activist. However, I am not contending that, for the most part, people have been pronounced mentally ill because their behaviour has been deviant or unacceptable. There must have been some sort of radical change in the personality of individuals before they were regarded as clinically insane. Moreover, it seems quite obvious that in severe mental illnesses, such as schizophrenia or manic-depression, there are biological components involved in the onset of illness. Mental illness is not a social construction, which could be eradicated if the structures, values and norms of society changed. Behind the culturally varying signs and symptoms of madness there is biology, the reality of nature.

Research on the history of madness and mental illness

There are three distinct phases in the historiography of madness and mental illness. The first phase started in the early twentieth century, and it was characterized by the internalist history of medical progress, in which rational, scientific and humane psychiatry replaced superstitious beliefs and unscientific explanations of madness, and in which the rise of modern mental asylums put an end to the mostly inhumane treatment of the mad. In this edifying story of increasing enlightenment, psychiatrists appeared on the scene of madness as knights in shining armour, slaying the dragon of superstition and irrationality. The first knight in this tale has usually been the French physician and pioneer psychiatrist Philippe Pinel, who in 1793 unchained the patients of the Bicêtre Mental Hospital in Paris, thereby opening a new chapter in the history of madness. This story of the origins of psychiatry was usually told by medical professionals themselves. It focused on prominent physicians and the progressive development of mental science, culminating in whatever period the author happened to live in. (A typical representative of such an approach to the history of psychiatry was the esteemed Swedish psychiatrist Bror Gadelius; see Gadelius 1933.)

In the 1960s, this 'Whiggish', optimistic and unproblematic historical take on madness began to be challenged by the socially oriented historians and 'antipsychiatric' critics, who portrayed psychiatry as a form of social control. The representatives of this second phase began critically to investigate the broader historical and social forces that shaped the practices as well as the public understanding of madness. In their writings and public presentations, they questioned the inordinately progressivist views of the former psychiatric historians and placed madness and psychiatry in the framework of large-scale socio-political, economic and cultural developments. Influential thinkers in this genre were the French philosopher and 'archaeologist of knowledge' Michel Foucault, sociologist Erving Goffman and psychiatrist Thomas Szasz. In the radicalized intellectual and cultural atmosphere of the 1960s, there was ample room for iconoclastic approaches to the management of madness.

During the last two decades of the twentieth century a new and more versatile 'research programme' emerged. Scholars began to study mental hospitals, patients and treatment methods, and new research topics, such as psychopharmacology, medicalization and therapeutic culture, have enriched the field. Nowadays, madness and mental health care are studied from the perspectives of, for example,

10 Introduction

gender studies, post-colonialist studies and microhistory. The research scope is now wider than ever, and different approaches, methods and contexts bring new knowledge about and insights into the theory and practice of mental health care. I have myself learned the 'trade' by studying history of psychiatry, psychology and psychoanalysis for two decades. As a medical *and* intellectual historian, and as someone who is keen on looking at the fates of people facing new and unexpected situations, I aim to place madness in larger contexts without losing sight of the individual experiences. I have rehearsed this approach in my classes at the Universities of Helsinki and Oulu, where I have received valuable feedback from my students. My own historical consciousness is the result of my social interactions with students, colleagues and friends.

* * *

Nobody is born insane. The mad, the mentally ill, the insane were, in most cases, not destined to lose their minds. If their lives had taken different paths, most of them might not have been burdened with mental illness. In fact, throughout history many people with mental afflictions have recovered or learned to live with their affliction. To study madness historically is important precisely because it helps us understand how madness appears and makes itself visible at different times and in different places. It may also help us see how mental health is created. As the philosopher Ludwig Wittgenstein put it, madness 'need not be regarded as an illness. Why shouldn't it be seen as a sudden – more or less sudden – change of character?' (Wittgenstein 1980, 54e). It is instructive to keep this question in mind when you turn the pages of this book and encounter madness in all its rich varieties.

Bibliography

Feynman, R. (1992) *'Surely You're Joking Mr. Feynman!' Adventures of a Curious Character*, 1st edn 1985, London: Vintage.

Foucault, M. (2006) *History of Madness*, ed. J. Khalfa, trans. J. Murphy and J. Khalfa, orig. French edn 1972, London: Routledge.

Gadelius, B. (1933) *Human Mentality in the Light of Psychiatric Experience*, Copenhagen: Levin & Munksgaard.

Gleick, J. (1992) *Richard Feynman and Modern Physics*, London: Abacus.

Goffman, E. (1963) *Stigma. Notes on the Management of Spoiled Identity*, New York: Simon & Schuster.

Jung, C.G. (1977) *Tavistock Lectures* (1935), *Collected Works*, Vol. 18, Princeton, NJ: Princeton University Press.

Lederer, D. (2006) *Madness, Religion and the State in Early Modern Europe*, Cambridge: Cambridge University Press.

McGuire, M. and Troisi, A. (1998) *Darwinian Psychiatry*, Oxford: Oxford University Press.

Nesse, R.M. and Williams, G.C. (1996) *Why We Get Sick: The New Science of Darwinian Medicine*, New York: Vintage.

Noë, A. (2010) *Out of Our Heads: Why You Are Not Your Brain, and Other Lessons from the Biology of Consciousness*, New York: Hill & Wang.

Pressman, J.D. (1998) *Last Resort: Psychosurgery and the Limits of Medicine*, Cambridge: Cambridge University Press.

Scheff, T. (1999) *Being Mentally Ill: A Sociological Theory*, 1st edn 1966, New York: Aldine Press.

Shorter, E. (1997) *A History of Psychiatry*, New York: John Wiley & Sons.

Thiher, A. (2004) *Revels in Madness: Insanity in Medicine and Literature*, Ann Arbor: University of Michigan Press.

Wittgenstein, L. (1980) *Culture and Value*, ed. G.H. von Wright, trans. P. Winch, Chicago: The University of Chicago Press.

PART I

Madness from Antiquity to the Age of the Enlightenment

2

MADNESS IN ANCIENT AND MEDIEVAL TIMES

In this chapter, I will explore the question of how aberrant, odd and crazy behaviour was defined and treated in Europe from antiquity to the late medieval times. I start with myths and religious stories and focus on the descriptions of madness in the Bible. Then I move on to the golden age of ancient Greece, when the mythical and supernatural explanations of madness were contested by rational and naturalistic approaches to health and disease. This intellectual change from *mythos* to *logos* was best exemplified in the rationalism of Hippocratic medicine that emerged in the fifth century BCE. Hippocratic medicine had an enormous influence on the theories and treatment of madness up until the eighteenth century, although during the Middle Ages it co-existed with the religious understanding of madness. I will also describe how the Islamic Near East perceived madness; how 'spiritual physick' was practised in Christian Europe during the Middle Ages; and, finally, how the Black Death (plague epidemic) devastated fourteenth-century Europe and produced economic, spiritual and cultural chaos, an example of which was the religious madness of a group of fanatical pilgrims called 'flagellants'. The Black Death and its aftermath represented a transformation of Europe, and, concurrently, a transformation of the medieval world view and the sense of self.

Madness in ancient mythology and the Bible

Is madness as old as humanity itself? This is what the historian Roy Porter has claimed (Porter 2002, 10). Archaeologists have discovered human skulls, at least 7,000 years old, in which they have found tiny round holes made by stone tools. The rationale for these early 'psychosurgical' operations may have been to help obsessed people – or people with painful headaches – by releasing evil spirits out of the holes in the skull. Unfortunately, due to the lack of sources, madness of the pre-historical humans is out of our reach. What we can say for certain is that all

16 From Antiquity to the Enlightenment

known cultures have distinguished between 'normal' and 'abnormal' behaviour, and in all known languages there are words to describe people who act crazy or who are out of their minds. Understood as a breakdown of behaviour, madness can be seen as a human universal (Brown 1991).

Myths and religious stories are the oldest written sources that refer to madness. In Babylonian and Mesopotamian texts we can see the religious and magical world view of the early historical period (ca. 3000–500 BCE). In this ancient world, reality was populated by gods, demons and spirits, and specific diseases – such as epilepsy – were seen to be caused by supernatural beings, by magic or as a consequence of breaking of a taboo. Evil spirits in particular haunted people and caused disturbances of behaviour, thinking and mood. Spirits of the dead could also punish people by making them ill. The Hebrews and other ancient peoples attributed diseases and misfortunes to the divine punishment for disobedience of God's (or gods') commandments or violation of divine laws.

Judaism, Christianity and madness are closely intertwined. In the Old Testament, there are numerous references to madness, which is *shiggayon* in Hebrew (*meshugga* is the word for 'madman'). In Deuteronomy the Lord threatens to strike his chosen people, if they do not obey him, 'with madness, blindness, and stupefaction' (28:15, 28), and in Proverbs a man who deceives another is compared to 'a madman shooting at random his deadly darts and lethal arrows' (26:18–19). In the First Book of Samuel, David feigns madness while visiting the fearsome King Achish of Gath: 'So he altered his behaviour in public and acted like a madman in front of them all, scrabbling on the double doors of the city gate and dribbling down his beard' (21:13). In the Second Book of Kings, the officers of King Jehu ask him 'what did this crazy fellow [a young prophet who anointed Jehu king over Israel] want with you?' (9:11).

Especially interesting is the story of the Saul (ca. 1020–1000 BCE), the first king of Israel, in the First Book of Samuel. In the story, Saul changes from a shy young man to a megalomaniac ruler who defies God's will. This act of impudence makes the 'spirit of the Lord' leave Saul, and in its place comes an evil spirit from God. Following the instructions of his servants, Saul sends for David, a skilful player of the lyre, whose music soothes the king's possessed soul 'so that relief would come to Saul; he would recover and the evil spirit would leave him alone' (16:23). Saul, however, becomes jealous of David, and, when an evil spirit from God seizes on him, he hurls a spear at David. Later, the spirit of God makes Saul fall into a prophetic frenzy. In the end, severely wounded in a fight against the Philistines, he commits suicide (18:10–12; 19:23–4; 31:4).

In the Old Testament, we come across other mad rulers. Self-satisfied, power-crazy Nebuchadnezzar, king of Babel (Babylon), lost his mind when he had a vision telling him to leave his people and 'share the lot of the beasts in their pasture'. 'His mind', the heavenly voice continued, 'will cease to be human, and he will be given the mind of a beast' (Daniel 4:4–16). So Nebuchadnezzar was banished from human society, and he spent seven years living in the fields with animals, eating grass like oxen, 'and his body was drenched with the dew of heaven,

Madness in ancient and medieval times **17**

until his hair became shaggy like an eagle and his nails grew like birds' claws'. At the end of the appointed time, Nebuchadnezzar was restored to his right mind (Daniel 4:32–4). In the Bible, God has a tyrannical power over people. Especially in the Old Testament, God is constantly intervening in people's lives and minds. The spirit of God makes people fall into religious ecstasy, while evil spirits, sent by God, obsess people and fill their hearts with fury, as in the case of King Saul. God of the Old Testament was wrathful and vengeful.

In the New Testament, there are references to ecstatic madness, foolishness and possession. The most well-known story is the one about Jesus' acts of exorcism. In the Gospels, Jesus is described as casting out demons when he goes through Galilee, healing a crippled woman 'whom Satan bound for 18 years', as well as a demoniac who lived in tombs, and roamed the hills, crying and cutting himself. When Jesus asked the man's name, he was told by the man (or the devils) that his name was Legion, 'for there are so many of us'. The devils themselves asked to be expelled into a large herd of pigs nearby. Jesus allowed this to happen, and thereafter the 'unclean spirits' came out of the man and went into the pigs, which then rushed over the edge into the lake and drowned (Matthew 8:28–32; Mark 5:1–13; Luke 8:26–33).[1] He also cast seven devils out of Mary Magdalene (Mark 16:9; Luke 8:2). Even Jesus himself was considered mad. Once, when he was in the countryside with his disciples, his relatives believed he had gone mad, and they set out to take charge of him. Meanwhile, Jesus was having a discussion with his disciples and the scribes in a crowded house. Apparently taken aback by Jesus' teachings, the scribes proclaimed, 'He is possessed by Beelzebul', and 'He drives out demons by the prince of demons', as if weaker madmen would take fright at stronger madmen (Mark 3:20–2).

In Jesus' time, to be a holy man meant that one could forgive sins, and to forgive sins was to heal. Hence 'to forgive sins', 'to expel demons' and 'to heal' were interchangeable terms (Dols 1992, 187). In early Christianity, madness was believed to be demonic possession. The early Church Father Origen (Origen Adamantius, ca. 185–254) confirmed the belief that was to become decisive for Christian theology until the early modern times: madness meant intrusive possession.

Madness in antiquity

Madness has a visible role in Greek mythology. As in ancient Near East and Egypt, in Homeric and archaic Greece (700–500 BCE) the cause of madness was attributed to gods or evil spirits. Gods who were angry or dissatisfied with people were especially willing to drive them crazy. As the Greek proverb went, 'those whom the gods wish to destroy they first make mad'. A good example of this is the story of Hercules, who is driven mad by the goddess Hera. In a state of frenzy, the mad

---

1 There are some discrepancies about this particular exorcism; in the Gospels of Mark and Luke, only one man was possessed, whereas Matthew saw two men whom Jesus freed from demoniac possession.

18 From Antiquity to the Enlightenment

Hercules kills his own and his brothers' children. In Sophocles' (ca. 496–406 BCE) play *Ajax*, the warrior Ajax slaughters sheep in a state of madness because he imagines them to be his enemies, the Greek leaders. In ancient Greece, madness had a strong tragic dimension, which was closely related to the god Dionysus. Among the gods of Olympus, Dionysus was an outsider, the god of the grape harvest, wine, ritual madness and ecstasy. Some forms of Greek madness were distinctly Dionysian in their violent impulsiveness, obsessions and intoxication. Other forms were more restrained and Apollonian, as they could be manifested in holy visions and dreams, which testified to the communication between humans and gods. A corresponding dichotomy between 'Dionysian' and 'Apollonian' forms of madness can be seen in the Christian Middle Ages.

In the Greek myths and stories of the Classical era (480–323 (death of Alexander the Great) BCE), humans are not individuals with individual egos. Rather, subjected to divine forces, they are marionettes whose motives for action are external to themselves. Individuals who monitor themselves and reflect on their own states of mind emerged in a later period when the Homeric person of the Archaic era changed into the Socratic person of the Classical era. Socratic persons are 'modern' in the sense that they think about the relationship between self and the world and express their thoughts in rational rather than supernatural terms. Archaic humans of the Old Testament, Greek mythology and the Babylonian and Mesopotamian religions were different from the Socratics of the naturalistic and rationalistic era, or from the playwright Euripides (n. 480–406 BCE), a pioneer in the psychological portraits of humans. Hence, Greek madness in the Archaic, mythological era was quite different from what it was in the later age of Classical antiquity: in the Classical era, people (usually) lost their minds for natural reasons, not because gods or demons intervened in their lives.

Classicist Ruth Padel argues that the foundation for the grammar of the western language of madness is in ancient Greece in general and in Greek tragedies in particular. In Padel's interpretation, there are three fundamental images in the Greek explanations of madness: darkness, wandering and damage. *Darkness* refers to the darkness of the mind, to the black bile as well as to anger. Madness is the darkness of both mind and intestines, and it isolates individuals from their communities, thereby shrinking their world. Next, the idea that *wandering* is associated with madness is based on the belief that madness makes people go off the rails and drives them to wander aimlessly from place to place. Wanderers have become strangers to their communities – and to themselves. The external wandering of the madmen corresponds with the interior wandering of their minds. Madness makes people 'err' ('error' is Latin for 'wandering'), and it also punishes 'error'. Finally, madness causes destruction when the inner *damage* leads to damaging outward acts. In its extreme form, madness causes self-damage when people defy their gods or kill their own children. This sort of link between murder and mania is often presented in Dionysian cults and tragedies. At the same time, madness in Greek tragedies was seen as a temporary and acute state, not as a permanent condition or disease. Madness was visible action caused by external forces; it was something that *happened* to people rather than existed in them. Madness was a tragedy precisely because it was *not* a part of human nature but something that happened to a person and caused darkness, wandering and damage (Padel 1995).

The change from *mythos* to *logos*, from mythical to rational thinking, in ancient Greece is the great dividing line in western culture. To simplify, an animistic world view based on the interventions of supernatural beings changed into naturalistic and rationalistic assumption according to which everything was composed of natural entities and explainable by human reason. Socratic persons were in possession of reason and will, and the source of their thinking and action was in themselves, not in gods or other supernatural beings. When humans became conscious agents of their own lives, they also became responsible for their deeds and acts. In consequence, they began to be troubled by *inner* conflicts. This can be seen in Sophocles' *Oedipus Rex* as well as in Euripides' *Medeia*. What was also transformed was madness, which in the Socratic or Classical era was no longer an instrument of divine punishment but an illness caused by natural reasons.

Hippocratic medicine

In medicine, the most enduring legacy of Greek naturalism was the birth of Hippocratic medicine in the fifth and fourth centuries BCE. It was during this period that the idea of madness as a *mental* illness emerged for the first time. This momentous innovation is commonly attributed to Hippocrates, a Greek physician from the island of Cos who lived between 460 and 370 BCE. It is not altogether clear how much the real-life Hippocrates contributed to what is known in its Latin name as *Corpus Hippocraticum*, a collection of Hippocratic writings consisting of 72 books and more than a thousand pages, so it is more accurate to regard 'Hippocrates' as a collective pseudonym. During a century and half, different Greek authors contributed to a remarkable 'paradigm shift' in which medicine became naturalistic. In Hippocratic medicine, the brain began to be seen as a centre of mental activity, and diseases were treated as pathological states of the human organism.

At the heart of Hippocratic medicine was the doctrine of four humours or bodily fluids. This doctrine had its natural matrix in the world view of ancient Greece, in which material reality was made up of earth, wind, fire and water. Correspondingly, the humoral doctrine accounted for the physical anatomy and physiological phenomena, such as diseases and mental illnesses, on the basis of four essential elements or humours. These humours were black bile (*melan chole*), yellow bile (*chole*), phlegm (*phlegma*) and blood (*haima*). Both physical and mental health depended on the balance or *eukrasia* between these bodily fluids. In this view, the state of imbalance (*dyskrasia*) was a consequence of an excessive amount of a certain humour in the human body. For example, fever, pneumonia and diarrhoea were seen to be caused by an excess of yellow bile, while an excess of blood caused hemoptysis (coughing up of blood or blood-stained sputum). The excess of black bile caused, for example, tetanus (lock-jaw), paresis, headaches and melancholy. The excess of phlegm in turn caused attacks of vertigo, epilepsy,

20   From Antiquity to the Enlightenment

fainting, consumption, diabetes and swelling. When a person was struck with mania, the affliction was attributed to the excess of either phlegm or yellow bile. Those whose mania was caused by phlegm were quiet and decent, while those whose mania was caused by a cerebral overflow of yellow bile were frenzied and mischievous. In short, madness was caused by the state of humoral imbalance (Lloyd 1983, 249).

When diseases were explained within the framework of humoralism, the standard methods of treatment followed the logic of *eukrasia* or balance. Thus attempts were made to relieve patients of the specific bodily fluid that had caused the disease. Bloodletting, emetics and purges were among the methods employed to expel a harmful surplus of a humour. Various herbs, drugs, proper diet as well as hot and cold baths were also used in the belief that they would restore health by stabilizing the humoral balance. Herbs and drugs often made patients sweat, and they also caused vomiting and diarrhoea, which was taken as a sign that they worked. In the 'crisis' or turning point of the disease, the patient either died or recovered. Based on the course of the disease, physicians aimed to make a *prognosis* (i.e. a prediction of the probable course and outcome of a disease) at this point. If the prognosis was bad, there was no point in continuing treatment. Hippocratic therapy emphasized the healing power of nature, and the physician's duty was to reinforce this power. Hippocrates' son-in-law Polybus, who lived on the island of Cos in the fourth century BCE, consolidated the humoral doctrine by writing medical treatises on, for example, 'the nature of man' (*De Natura Hominis* in Latin) and 'the healthy way of life' (*De Salubri Victus Ratione* in Latin). *De Natura Hominis* is the earliest known work to advance humoral theory.

In the history of madness, the birth of Hippocratic medicine was a crucial turning point not only because of its naturalism, but also because it led to the classification of the various forms of madness as well as to the development of new methods of treatment. The naturalization of madness also meant its *somatization*: mental illnesses were now seen as bodily illnesses, and they were described together with other somatic afflictions. In Hippocratic medicine, two forms of madness became major illnesses. One was mania, the other melancholy. According to the humoral doctrine, *raging* mania was caused by the surplus of yellow bile, while *quiet* mania was caused by the excess of phlegm. Melancholy in turn was caused by the surplus of black bile (*melan chole*), and its distinct symptoms were sadness, fear and despair. The Hippocratic treatment of mania and melancholy included proper diet and ways to make patients sweat, vomit or suffer from diarrhoea. Perhaps the wretched physical condition caused by powerful drugs and herbs made maniacs and melancholics forget their wretched mental condition, at least for a little while.

In addition to the Hippocratic corpus, Greek medicine was influenced by thinkers such as Democritus (c. 460–c. 370 BCE), who formulated an atomic theory of the universe. Democritus' theory inspired Asclepiades (ca. 124–40 BCE), the most famous physician of the Hellenistic era, who lived and worked in Rome. Asclepiades claimed that diseases were caused by the irregular or non-harmonic movements of the bodily 'atoms' or particles. He prescribed his manic and melancholic patients pleasant baths, massage, exercise and a healthy diet. He admonished his contemporaries for putting their patients in dark rooms in their erroneous belief that darkness soothes the mind. Asclepiades himself ordered his patients to stay in light and sunny rooms, because he believed that clear perceptions of concrete reality had beneficial effects on patients (Deutsch 1949, 9). He also prescribed wine as a medicine. Asclepiades stands out in the history of madness in his humane treatment of patients. As we shall see later in this book, when physicians have treated patients as fellow human beings deserving sympathy and compassion, it has generally improved their health and increased their well-being. Asclepiades probably understood better than many of his psychiatric colleagues 2,000 years later that physicians do not just offer diagnoses and prescribe treatment; they also interact with human beings who have their own personalities, thoughts and feelings.

During the Hellenistic era (323–ca. 30 BCE), Hippocratic medicine was promoted especially by the medical school of Alexandria. In late antiquity, Hippocratic medicine was further developed by Claudius Galenus or Galen (129–ca. 200). Like Asclepiades, Galen was Greek but practised his profession in Rome. In his early career, he worked as a physician to the gladiators in Pergamon, his home town, and later he worked as a court physician to the Emperor Marcus Aurelius. In his dissertation *De Temperamentis*, Galen created a hugely influential typology of human temperaments based on humoral theory and his understanding of the four elements and their qualities (hot, cold, dry and wet). Together with the so-called *pneuma* (air, breath), the fundamental principle of life, the balance between these qualities determined one's temperament (or complexion). A *sanguine* temperament was dominated by the paired qualities of hot and wet, a *phlegmatic* temperament by cold and wet, a *choleric* temperament by hot and dry and a *melancholic* temperament by cold and dry. Each temperament described both mental traits and physiological and bodily features. Individuals with sanguine temperaments were social, pleasure-seeking and impulsive. Choleric people were energetic and passionate, even aggressive and prone to dominate. Melancholics were thoughtful, considerate and cautious, and phlegmatics were relaxed, calm and observant. Temperaments predisposed individuals to specific diseases so that the short-tempered and ambitious choleric was inclined to become a raging maniac, while the sensitive and contemplative melancholic tended to become . . . melancholic (Jackson 1986, 41–5)!

Galen's doctrine of temperaments became an essential part of western medicine, and in its psychophysiological classification it influenced psychological thinking and descriptions of human characteristics. In late antiquity, his writings and ideas spread widely across the Roman Empire, supported by the dissemination of the Latin language. Galen became the most important medical authority in Europe, and his doctrines were in use for about 15 centuries. As late as the early nineteenth century, Galen's doctrine of *dyskrasias* or pathological conditions provided the theoretical foundation for the studies of many renowned physicians. Galen also increased the understanding of the human anatomy with his dissections of (mainly) monkeys and pigs, because Roman law had prohibited the dissection of human cadavers from about 150 BCE (Hankinson 2008).

The doctrine of humours was one of the foundation stones of western medicine for two millennia. It was only the final breakthrough of experimental medicine at the turn of the nineteenth century that sounded the death toll for Hippocratic medicine. The longevity of Hippocratic tradition says more about the persistent weakness of experimental science in Europe than about the soundness of the doctrines themselves. Despite its naturalism and rationalism, there was very little progress in Hippocratic medicine through the centuries, simply because it lacked the experimental method, the very backbone of empirical science. Due to its 'anti-empirical' stance, western medicine suffered from insufficient knowledge about anatomy, physiology and pathology until the Age of the Enlightenment. Dissections of human cadavers were prohibited, and medical practice was enslaved to opinions, beliefs and assumptions presented in the writings of traditional medical authorities. As the medical observations were so theory-laden, medicine as a clinical practice made very little progress for two millennia. On the other hand, Hippocratic medicine had a very strong sense of ethics, with its strong emphasis on the value of human life and the professional integrity of the doctor. This ethical basis of medicine was an important legacy of Greek medicine both to the medieval Christian era and to modern times (Dols 1992, 46).

Divine madness and the madness of a multitude

The rich mythology of ancient Greece and the naturalism of Hippocratic medicine were not mutually exclusive. Mythical and naturalistic world views might seem like odd bedfellows, but a Greek living in the Classical era did not see reality through antagonistic either-or lenses. This avoidance of dichotomy between *mythos* and *logos* is evident in Plato's (427–347 BCE) philosophy. Obviously, *logos* or reason occupies a dominant position in Plato's thinking, but occasionally he expresses his thoughts in a metaphoric or poetic form. Such a selective use of *mythos* can be seen in some of his dialogues, including *Phaedrus*. There, Plato lets Socrates declare that 'there are two kinds of madness, one produced by human illness, the other by a divinely inspired release from the normally accepted behaviour' (Plato 1997, 265a). For Plato's Socrates, madness can be explained either as a natural (illness) or supernatural (act of divinity) phenomenon. Socrates says nothing more about naturalistic madness but elaborates on the notion of the divine kind of madness. As Plato writes in the dialogue,

> we also distinguished four parts within the divine kind and connected them to four gods. Having attributed the inspiration of the prophet to Apollo, of the mystic to Dionysus, of the poet to the Muses, and the fourth part of madness to Aphrodite and to Love, we said that the madness of love is the best.
>
> (Plato 1997, 265b)

In *Phaedrus*, Plato's Socrates refers to men of ancient times who assumed that 'the best things we have come from madness, when it is given as a gift from the god'. Socrates also points out that the god-sent form of madness 'is given us by the gods to ensure our greatest good fortune. It will be a proof that convinces the wise if not the clever' (Plato 1997, 244a–245c). Prophetic madness, ecstatic madness, madness inspiring poetic imagination and, on top of it all, madness of love are all gifts of gods. Can one talk about madness in a more poetic way?

What about the other, more mundane kind of madness? Apparently, Plato was not too enthusiastic about madness as a naturalistic illness; it lacks the glow of love madness. In the ancient world, there were very few free and affluent individuals, such as Plato. The great majority of people in Mediterranean Europe and elsewhere lived in poverty, many as slaves. For the common people, there were no benevolent doctors *à la* Asclepiades around who would have prescribed baths, massage and wine to their patients.

There were other kinds of treatments for the madness of a multitude. For instance, the learned man and master of medical knowledge, Aulus Cornelius Celsus (25 BCE–50 CE), recommended chains and whipping as well as starving the patient as a proper treatment for the mad. It was also helpful to instigate fear and terror in madmen. Celsus was probably the first to describe paranoia – perhaps his patients started to show signs of paranoia when, in the name of therapy, they were subjected to whipping or put in irons. To the common people of ancient Greece and Rome, and especially to slaves, Celsus' recommended treatments were rather common experiences, whether or not they were mad. When slaves and the poor became ill, usually their only hope was that they would be cured by the healing powers of nature, as the Latin phrase *vis medicatrix naturae*, derived from the Hippocratic medicine, proclaims. There is some circumstantial evidence that, in antiquity, the mentally ill from the lower classes were sometimes killed (Deutsch 1949, 11).

On a lighter note, in antiquity 'madness' was used in humorous and satirical contexts as well. The Roman lyric poet Horace (Quintus Horatius Flaccus, 65 BCE–8 CE) wrote about 'the follies of mankind' in his *Satires* (ca. 30 BCE). In a dialogue between the poet and a certain Damasippus, a bankrupt speculator and dealer in works of art, the conception of madness is examined. The starting point for the satirical dialogue is the Stoic view that everyone save the wise man is mad. After discussing the four phases of madness in the sermons of the Stoic sage Stertinius – avarice, ambition, self-indulgence and superstition – Horace turns the laugh against himself by asking Damasippus:

Horace:	And what is my madness? I think I am sane.
Damasippus:	So Agave [Goddess in Greek mythology] thought, when she was carrying in her hands the head of her unfortunate son.
Hor.:	Well, what is my madness?
Dam.:	You are aping the great, like the frog in the fable. You write verses, you have a bad temper [. . .]

Hor.:	Stop now!
Dam.:	Your style beyond your means –
Hor.:	Mind your own business, Damasippus.
Dam.:	Your thousand passions for lads and lasses.
Hor.:	O greater one, spare, I pray, the lesser madman! (O maior tandem parcas, insane, minori!)

(Horace 2005, 150–1, 181)

Perhaps the most exhaustive description of madness in antiquity can be found in the texts of Soranus (first–second century CE), who was a Greek physician from Ephesus (Gerdtz 1994). His major work, *On Acute and Chronic Diseases*, has survived as a complete Latin translation (*De morbis acutis et chronicis*). Soranus distinguished between three different kinds of madness, which were phrenetis, mania and melancholy. I have already briefly discussed mania and melancholy, but *phrenetis* is a new illness to the reader. It referred to some kind of acute fever or toxic symptom, in which the pulse was in turn rapid and slow, and which made bodily movements confused and groping. Phrenetis was clearly a form of madness that was caused by a somatic illness. *Mania*, on the other hand, was an archetypal *mental* illness to Soranus: mania denoted chaotic thoughts, frenzy, anger and delirium without fever. As we know, loud or raging mania was also caused by a somatic or physiological affliction, namely a surplus of yellow bile (while the excess of phlegm caused quiet mania). The third form of madness, *melancholy*, had some resemblances to modern depression, since its symptoms included sadness, fear and despondency. But melancholy was more than that; it referred, for example, to states of paranoia and to a kind of catatonic stupor that we now associate with schizophrenia, as its main symptom was the patient's withdrawal from external reality to the impenetrable inner world. We should be on our guard when comparisons are made between ancient melancholy and today's depression – over the centuries, melancholy has referred to such complex multilayered states of mind that it is unhelpful and futile to reduce it to something as 'flat' and medicalized as today's clinical depression (Jackson 1986).

Melancholy remained a 'classic' illness in the Christian Middle Ages and beyond to the age of industrialism. This is how one of the most popular poems in the history of both medicine and literature, 'A Salernitan Regimen of Health' (*Regimen sanitatis Salernitanum*, written some time during the twelfth or thirteenth centuries), describes a melancholic:

There remains the sad substance of the black melancholic temperament,
Which makes men wicked, gloomy, and taciturn.
These men are given to studies, and little sleep.
They work persistently toward a goal; they are insecure.
They are envious, sad, avaricious, tight-fisted,
Capable of deceit, timid, and of muddy complexion.

(Joutsivuo 2014, 35)

Signs, symptoms and images of madness have changed considerably from antiquity to the modern age, but mania and melancholy have remained 'diagnostic evergreens'.

The Middle Ages: the Dark Age?

The Mediterranean world changed after the Hellenistic period (323–30 BCE) as the Roman Empire first became larger and larger and then went down in the fifth century CE. The Emperor Constantine gave Christianity a legal status in the Roman Empire in 313, and gradually the Christian (Catholic) Church became a great power first in the southern Europe and then in the central and northern parts of the continent. The Catholic Church managed to strengthen its hold in western Europe because of the fall of the Roman Empire, which created a power vacuum in (western) Europe. The Roman Empire divided into east and west between the fourth and sixth centuries, and the eastern part began to be known as the Byzantine Empire. It was regarded as the continuation of the Roman Empire, because it survived the fifth-century fragmentation and collapse of the western Roman Empire. The eastern Roman Empire – Byzantium – continued to thrive, existing for an additional thousand years until it fell to the Ottoman Turks in 1453. Its capital city was Constantinople (modern-day Istanbul, originally known as Byzantium) and the population was predominantly Greek-speaking and Greek-Catholic or Orthodox Christian. During most of its millennium-long existence, the Byzantine Empire was the most powerful economic, cultural and military force in Europe, and it kept the Muslims from expanding across Asia Minor and the Dardanelles into Europe (Herrin 2008).

When Europe entered the Middle Ages, it signified a return to the supernatural world view that had once been successfully challenged by Greek rationalism and naturalism. This time the supernatural reality was advocated by Christianity in general and the Catholic Church in particular. In this sense, the Middle Ages meant a regression to a mythical-religious thinking that denied the primacy of reason and natural explanations and instead looked at natural and social phenomena in supernatural and superstitious terms. In recent decades, medievalists have tried to correct the widespread and largely prejudiced assumption that the Middle Ages were dark, chaotic and primitive by emphasizing, for example, the twelfth-century 'Renaissance', the return of classical intellectual culture, as well as the early beginnings of political and legal administration. In an important rebuttal to the conventional historical view of the Middle Ages as the Dark Age, a group of medievalists remind us that, when we look into the apparently strange and terrifying medieval world, we are easily led astray by our own unrecognized misconceptions and prejudices, such as the 'medieval Church was corrupt', 'medieval medicine was irrational', 'everybody in the Middle Ages believed in God and flat earth and was superstitious' and 'medieval peasantry were hopelessly exploited and powerless'. None of these sweeping, simplistic assertions is true, especially when the period under discussion covers a whole millennium (500–1500) (Harris &

Grigsby 2008). It would be equally absurd to claim that our modern age (ca. 1500 onwards) is characterized by witch-hunting (peaking in the seventeenth century), strict sexual morality (peaking in the Victorian era of the nineteenth century), extremely violent ideologies (exemplified by twentieth-century fascism and communism) and rampant superstition (more people believe in astrology today than in medieval times).

At the same time, it is clear that the oppressed masses were governed not only by individual lords, but also by the Church and the religious fear of damnation. Especially during the High Middle Ages (ca. 800–1200) the world view of Europeans was dominated very concretely by sin, Hell and redemption, Satan and Jesus, demons and the Holy Ghost, the great and unchanging chain of being as well as eschatological expectations of the end of the world. In the European collective consciousness, if one can speak of such, the older layer of pagan beliefs lived side by side with Christianity, whereas remnants of the great cultural tradition of Greek and Roman civilization survived in a few monasteries here and there. Dormant intellectual culture began slowly to revitalize at the end of the first Christian millennium when the first universities were founded in Italy (Bologna and Padova) and France (Paris and Montpellier).

Madness in medieval Islamic culture

During the Early and High Middle Ages, the most learned and civilized part of Europe was in the Iberian peninsula (in today's Spain and Portugal). By 714, the Islamic Empire had expanded to Europe, and Muslim forces controlled much of Iberia, a region they called Al-Andalus. In the tenth century, Al-Andalus became the Emirate (later Umayyad Caliphate) of Córdoba, which lasted until 1492. Especially during the heyday of the Caliphate (between 929 and 1031), the Islamic kingdom experienced a large expansion of trade and culture. The tenth-century library of Al-Hakam II in Córdoba, the cultural and intellectual centre of Al-Andalus, was one of the largest libraries in the world, housing at least 400,000 volumes. A university was founded in Córdoba at the end of the tenth century, more than a century before the first university in Christian Europe was established in Bologna. Compared to Europe, the level of medical learning was much higher in Al-Andalus. Throughout the period of Muslim civilization in the Iberian peninsula, Jewish and Christian communities survived in the kingdom, and Jews and Arabs lived in relative harmony (Jews had been persecuted in the Christian Iberia since 589, when the Visigoths converted to Catholicism). It was not until the fall of the 'Spanish Moor' in 1492 that the incoming Christians banished the Jews from Spain (Lewis 2008; Fletcher 1993). Muslims had a higher social standing than 'infidels', but the cosmopolitan towns of Al-Andalus were populated by Arabs, Berbers, Visigoths, Jews, Slavs and Christians, many of whom converted to Islam. In comparison, the Christian kingdom of Charlemagne (742–814) and his successors was distinctly uncivilized: there were very few urban centres, very little trade, no major libraries and even the elite groups of society were illiterate.

Moreover, some leaders of the increasingly powerful Catholic Church were fanatical about religious dogmas, while others were at least as greedy power-mongers as the secular lords and princes. The fourteenth-century Italian Renaissance humanist and poet Petrarch famously coined the term 'Dark Age' to emphasize the value of Greek and Roman antiquity by contrasting this 'golden age' with the 'cultural degeneration' of medieval Europe (Nauert 2006).

All through the medieval period the most enlightened approach to madness can be found in the Islamic cultural sphere, where the Hippocratic tradition survived via Galenic texts (Dols 1987, 1992; Miller 1985). Just as in the Greek and Roman cultural sphere, madness did not have a precise meaning in Muslim societies. Michael W. Dols, the late great historian of Islamic medicine, decided to use the word *majnūn* ('madman' or 'possessed'), which was the most widely used designation for a 'mad' or oddly behaving individual in Arabic during the Middle Ages (Dols 1992, 3). Islamic health care was generally governed by the moral imperative to treat both the rich and the poor. The hospitals were largely secular institutions, many of them open to all regardless of sex, age, status or religion. The first Islamic hospitals were modelled on the East Christian charitable institutions (*xenodocheion*), which had been mainly monastic infirmaries in Syria, Persia and Iraq (Baghdad). The eminent Persian-Turkish physician-philosopher Ibn Sina (Avicenna, 980–1037) explained mental illnesses naturalistically and, as a follower of Galenic medicine, treated the mad as if they were in need of medical cure, not as sinners possessed by demons. Facilities for the treatment of the mad were probably first established in the Islamic world, more precisely in Egypt and in Baghdad.

A Jewish traveller, Rabbi Benjamin, visited Baghdad around 1170 and described a hospital founded by the caliph:

> There is [. . .] a large building, called Dār al-Māristān [insane asylum], where they keep charge of the demented people who have become insane in the towns through the great heat in the summer, and they chain each of them in iron chains until their reason is restored to them in the wintertime. Whilst they abide there, they are provided with food from the house of the caliph, and when their reason is restored they are dismissed, and each one of them goes to his own house. Money is given to those that have stayed in the hospices on their return to their homes.
>
> (Dols 1992, 119)

In Aleppo, Syria, a new hospital was built in 1354 by the order of the Mamlūk sultan. There were two courts in the hospital, probably for the male and female patients. In order to cheer the insane, music was played to them, and flowers were planted along the walls of the court and around the pools. On the other hand, in the Islamic town of Fez in Morocco, the insane were bound in iron chains, and the 'person [who] was in charge of them constantly carried a whip, and when he saw an agitated patient, he administered a good trashing' (Dols 1992, 121, 127). In medieval Islamic societies, there were no public institutions

28 From Antiquity to the Enlightenment

or governmental services for the mad, the poor and the disabled. This meant that the direct personal charity of individual Muslims played a crucial role in Islamic mental health care. And Muslims were inclined to charity, because a moral imperative towards human kindness has been part and parcel of Islam since its inception (Stillman 1975).

In the Qur'ān, the holy book of Islam, there are references to madness (*māniyā* or *junūn*). In the book, madness is presented as self-torment, verbal and physical violence, degradation of religion, talking to oneself as well as a constant state of over-excitement (Suras 2:169, 17:64). Madness is caused by Satan, whose voice confuses people to the extent that they start to regard it as their own voice, and so they go astray in believing Satan's will to be their own. Satan's power in Islam is comparable to that of the Olympian gods in Greek tragedies. In order to be cured, an ill person has to develop an insight into the true cause of madness, Satan, who cunningly tries to hide himself and make people believe that their satanic or mad ideas have sprung from their own heads (Sura 7:200). But those who follow the right way will not be tempted by the Satanic madness. Just like Jesus in the New Testament, the prophet Muhammed was accused of being merely mad, and not God's messenger. Sura 68 deals with this accusation:

> By the pen! By all they write! Your Lord's grace does not make you [prophet] a madman: you will have a never-ending reward – truly you have a strong character – and soon you will see, as will they, which of you is afflicted with madness.
>
> (Sura 68:2–6)

In pre-Islamic Arabia, the belief in supermundane spirits was common, and Muslims continued this religious tradition, including spiritual healing. Early Muslims were influenced particularly by eastern Christians living in Egypt and Syria. Islamic culture also recognized the possibility that madness was not a condition that needed to be treated or exorcised. Madness could as well be the wisdom of the fool, the divine love of the mystic or the 'love madness' of the otherwise sane. In general, harmless lunatics were sometimes venerated as saints, whose reason was in heaven while the body was on earth (Dols 1992, 12, 417). In his magisterial work on the history of madness in the Islamic world, Michael Dols states that Islamic society 'permitted a much wider latitude to the interpretation of unusual behaviour than does modern western society and much greater freedom to the disturbed, non-violent individual' (Dols 1992, 4). What about western conceptions of madness in medieval times?

Christian madness in the Middle Ages

In the early Christian era, religious people, be they pagans, Jews or Christians, easily attributed both the cause and the cure for madness to supernatural forces, gods and deities. In miracle collections and other medieval texts, various forms

Madness in ancient and medieval times **29**

of mental disorders can be found. These include epilepsy, mental impairment, mania and demonic possession. They were typically listed among diseases curable by heavenly remedy. An important influence on the medieval understanding of madness in Christendom was St Augustine (354–430). He divided illnesses into two groups, those that have natural causes and those that are caused by demonic possession. No prizes for guessing to which category the venerable Church Father placed mental illnesses? In Augustine's view, patients who are suffering from demonic possession can only be cured by religion. What the mad needed were prayers or miracle-working saints and their relics.

In early Christianity, the most fiendish of the demons were *succubi*, demons in female form who tempted men to sexual intercourse, and *incubi*, male demons who did the same for women. An *incubus* may have pursued sexual relations in order to father a child, as in the legend of Merlin: Merlin's father was said to be an *incubus* in Geoffrey of Monmouth's *Historia Regum Britanniae* (written ca. 1136) and many later tales. Christian tradition claimed that repeated intercourse with an *incubus* or *succubus* may result in the deterioration of health, or even death (Stephens 2002). There was even a disease called *incubus*, which was caused either by a sexual demon or by a superabundance of black bile or some other physiological disorder. Some medieval authors dismissed *incubi* and *succubi* altogether and attributed the whole phenomenon to dreams and imagination (Katajala-Peltomaa 2014, 108–9).

Augustine's ideas on madness were sanctioned by the Church, and they seem familiar to those who know about the supernatural world view of the pre-Christian cultures. In the medieval world, the fight between the Holy Spirit and the devil over the soul of the Christian was understood not metaphorically but concretely. In this supernatural cultural framework, belief in malevolent spirits was seen as the immediate cause of illness. The typical Christian method of treatment was to cast out demons by exorcism or by such robust physical means as whipping. In Christian theology, paganism itself was demonic, and, from the early third century onwards, the healthy converts needed to be exorcised as a necessary preparation for baptism. Beliefs in demonology and in exorcism, magic spells and rituals as forms of healing permeated all levels of Christian societies. As Michael Dols has noted, 'it may even be said that demonology became a way of defining reality; it shaped the way an afflicted person could describe his inner experiences and others could account for his outward behaviour' (Dols 1992, 191). The Church, however, had an ambiguous attitude towards madness. In addition to the possessed mad, there were holy fools, who were deemed to have a privileged connection to God – they were fools for Christ's sake.

A famous example of a holy fool in western Christianity is St Francis of Assisi (ca. 1181–1226), founder of the Franciscan Order. St Francis is said to have talked with birds, and preached in the streets and villages to the common people. He was known for his joyful spirit, and in his humour and laughter he was a typical medieval holy fool. In eastern Orthodox Christianity, there were holy fools who deliberately acted foolish in the eyes of the people. The Orthodox Church claimed

30 From Antiquity to the Enlightenment

that holy fools voluntarily took up the guise of insanity in order to conceal their perfection from the world, thereby avoiding praise (Otto 2001; Feuerstein 1990). Prophecies, falling in ecstasy, speaking in tongues and seeing visions might have been seen as 'blessed foolishness', as signs that God was in contact with His children. It helped if the fool's visions and revelations could be integrated into the religious symbolism of the Church, because it saved him from being branded a dangerous madman or, which was probably worse, a heretic (Jung 1981). Also in the Islamic world there were holy fools and wise fools, and 'prophetic medicine' emphasized divine causation and spiritual healing. Muslim hospitals were visited by mystics and intellectuals who wanted to interview the insane in the belief that they might serve as the mouthpiece for spiritual truths. The holy fools 'often articulated the frustrations of the silent majority – the poor, the sick, and the crazed' (Dols 1992, 13).

Medieval Europeans lived partly in the material world, partly in the spiritual world, and the connection between these two was more real and concrete than it is for modern westerners. Socio-cultural reality included astrology and alchemy, which ostensibly revealed the secrets of nature. Still, what should be borne in mind was that madness was not seen exclusively in a supernatural framework. On the contrary, it was quite common to explain madness as an unfortunate result of natural phenomena, such as accidents, human temperament and strong desires and passions. In the medieval world view, the universe was divided into sublunar and celestial (or superlunar) spheres. The sublunar sphere was a corruptible and imperfect region of the cosmos from moon to the earth, while the celestial sphere was a region of the unchanging spirit world, an incorruptible dwelling place of angels, demons and spirits. Medieval people were affected by both spheres, and for this reason their conception of madness was twofold: madness was supernatural *and* natural. 'Supernatural' did not mean the Christian spirit world only; in most European countries and especially in the countryside, pagan beliefs about the spiritual world often lived side by side with Jesus and the saints. For example, the animistic world view made villagers in sixteenth-century Germany believe that vexatious spirits 'might frighten the cattle, spoil the beer, and keep butter from forming in the churn' (Midelfort 1999, 53).

In the everyday life of medieval people, death was present in a much more concrete and tangible way than it is today. A firm belief in the afterlife, either in Heaven or Hell, was commonplace. Due to the uncertainty of earthly pilgrimage, people were inclined to find consolation in their faith in the immortality of the soul. This faith had a frightening side as well, because there was no guarantee that the soul would ascend to Heaven at physical death. Depending on the heavenly judgement, the soul might also descend into Hell. No wonder the gatekeepers of the afterworld – the Church and the clergy – had such a prominent position in medieval society and in communities. The thoughts of medieval people, provided that they were religious individuals, were directed at the afterlife to an extent that is hard to comprehend in our own (relatively) secular age.

'Spiritual physick' and medical practitioners

In medieval Europe, attitudes towards the mad changed from place to place, but reactions to the madness of the lowest social groups – serfs and farmhands – appeared to be generally rather straightforward. The mad were excluded from their communities, chained or locked in caves. In the High Middle Ages, religious orders started to establish shelters for the sick and the crippled. These shelters – called Hospices of the Holy Spirit in northern Europe – sometimes provided basic care for the mad. Because their important mission was to save the sinful souls of the inmates, the 'care ideology' of the shelters was emphatically religious and moralistic. A belief in miracle cures was widespread. Until the early modern period (the sixteenth and seventeenth centuries) it was commonplace all over Europe and especially in Catholic countries to take madmen on pilgrimages to shrines, healing springs, temples, monasteries and churches. They provided cure and consolation to the physically and mentally ill. Some shrines specialized in alleviating spiritual anguish (Midelfort 1999, 277–321; Lederer 2006, 99–144). People went there to pray, seek consolation and find a miraculous cure by staying close to relics. Another reason for going on pilgrimages was to fulfil a publicly made vow or promise – *votum* – to visit a shrine after one has recovered from the illness or ailment.

In France, approximately 10 per cent of those who went on a pilgrimage were deemed to be afflicted by madness at the end of the first millennium. In the Nordic countries between 1350 and 1500, more than a quarter of pilgrims were considered mad (Krötzl 2004, 327–8). For the ill, pilgrimages offered the mad a chance to temporarily leave behind problems in their communities and to strengthen their self-esteem by the often unique opportunity to experience something that was larger-than-life, maybe even the purifying presence of God or a saint, in these shrines and temples. Shrines may have had therapeutic effects occasioned by the strong faith of pilgrims, coupled with the power of self-suggestion – pilgrims were predisposed to have strong religious experiences in sacred places. Pilgrimages were also considered an effective cure against demonic possession. Once demons were successfully cast out of the pilgrims, they were then deemed cured in the eyes of the community and no longer tainted by moral stigma. As a bonus, pilgrims enjoyed greater respect in their communities. In Bayern, the two most popular shrines attracted Germans up until the early twentieth century. To local communities, shrines were often a significant source of income (Lederer 2006, 124, 142). The most well-known shrine offering 'spiritual physick' was located in Gheel in what is now Belgium. From the seventh century onwards, thousands of madmen were brought to Gheel, and the legend goes that many of them were miraculously cured in the shrine. Later, the village of Gheel became a famous colony for the mentally ill as townspeople began to take some of the patients into their own homes. For centuries, Gheel has successfully provided family and community care to mental patients and set a fine example of an effective and admirably humane treatment. This fine tradition is still alive in Gheel (Roosens 1979).

32 From Antiquity to the Enlightenment

In the Middle Ages, there were no hospitals in the modern sense, and the classical medicine of late antiquity had largely degenerated into religious spells and magical recipes. The social prestige of physicians had declined, while that of the clergy had increased. The centre of medical practice from the mid-tenth century to the thirteenth century was Salerno in southern Italy, where the practitioners, including women, were known for their practical skills in learning (Siraisi 1990, 13). Beginning in the thirteenth century, the first medical schools were established in the university towns in Italy (Bologna and Padua) and France (Montpellier and Paris). University studies took six years for a Master of Arts degree, and grammar, logic and rhetoric were the most important of the seven liberal arts for medieval students. Later, the curriculum came to include physics, metaphysics and moral philosophy, the three Aristotelian philosophies. Students who held Master's degrees were allowed to study law (canon and civil), medicine or theology, which was the most important discipline and the most respected faculty. Following the Arab-Islamic model, the medical curriculum was divided between theory and practice (Porter 1999, 113–18). When Aristotle's writings became available in Latin during the twelfth and thirteenth centuries, Aristotelian philosophy and physical science began to dominate European intellectual culture. However, Aristotelian natural philosophy had only a limited impact on medicine, which continued to rely heavily on Hippocratic and Galenic writings, on one hand, and practical skills, techniques and magical 'secrets', on the other. Medical practice was often combined with astrology, especially in the princely courts, where the university-educated physicians used 'astronomical tables to draw up general forecasts for the coming year or to cast horoscopes of princely employers' (Siraisi 1990, 68). Until the early modern era, only a minority of medical practitioners in Europe were trained in universities.

The practitioners of medicine in medieval Europe were both laymen and members of the clergy, and secular and religious healing existed side by side. The lay-practitioners either attended universities or joined a medical guild, which began to be formed from the thirteenth century onwards. Especially in the countryside the practitioners were usually folk healers whose skills were based on traditional beliefs and practices. In northern Europe, the professionalization of medicine was a slower process than in southern Europe, and regulations were more lax, or ignored; almost half of the medical practitioners in late sixteenth-century London worked without official endorsement of any kind (Siraisi 1990, 20). There were all sorts of practitioners from surgeons and barber-surgeons to barbers, apothecaries, empirics and professional midwives. Family members, neighbours, priests and mendicants (members of any of several Roman Catholic religious orders who assume a vow of poverty and support themselves by work and charitable contributions) could also serve as casual healers.

From the perspective of modern medicine, it is easy to ridicule medieval medicine and what looks like bizarre or irrational cures and remedies. But it should be borne in mind that there are only a few similarities between medieval and modern medicine, especially with regard to the theoretical and socio-cultural framework

Madness in ancient and medieval times **33**

through which each approaches illness (Harris & Grigsby 2008). All through the Middle Ages, physical illnesses, impairments and mental afflictions were intertwined and the mental – and the moral – could not be separated from the physical. This meant that 'the theories and practices concerning human body and soul were often inseparable or, at least, mingled with each other in various ways' (Katajala-Peltomaa & Niiranen 2014, 2–3).

The Black Death and an epidemic of religious madness

Throughout the Middle Ages, mortality, especially infant mortality, was very high, and the average lifespan very low. Epidemics reaped a deadly harvest; malnutrition was widespread and the more local infectious diseases were often perilous. Probably the most well-known pandemic in world history is the Black Death, which killed at least a third of the European population in the short time span of five years (1347–52). ('Black Death' was not the term used in the Middle Ages; it was apparently coined by Danish and Swedish chroniclers in the sixteenth century.) Perhaps as many as 200 million people perished, with many more victims in southern Europe than in northern Europe and Britain. There have been several competing theories as to the etiology of the Black Death, but a recent (2010) analysis of DNA from victims in different parts of Europe indicates that the pathogen responsible was the *Yersinia pestis* bacterium. The virulent plague bacillus was injected into its human host by a flea's bite, and the bacilli probably caused several forms of plague, some variants of which may no longer exist (Haensch et al. 2010).

The Black Death ravaged Europe for over a century, during which time the people had to learn to live with plague – and to die with it (Platt 1996, vii). Most sufferers died of heart failure, internal haemorrhage or exhaustion. If they did not succumb to the disease within about a week of the appearance of buboes, they had a chance of surviving. Especially in crowded towns the plague overwhelmed all efforts to check it, and churchyards were full of unburied corpses. The origins and symptoms of the Black Death are memorably described in the Italian poet and Renaissance humanist Giovanni Boccaccio's *The Decameron*, written between 1348 and 1353 (see Boccaccio 2011). Boccaccio and his contemporaries were horrified not only by the manner of the deaths, but also by their sum – bodies were here, there and everywhere in his home town, Florence. Whole families died, and there was often nobody to honour the dead. One man who lost his children lived in the town of Siena:

> Father abandoned child; wife, husband; one brother, another [. . .] And none could be found to bury the dead for money or friendship [. . .] And in many places in Siena great pits were dug and piled deep with the multitude of dead [. . .] And I, Agonolo di Tura, called the Fat, buried my five children with my own hands.

> (Platt 1996, 5)

34 From Antiquity to the Enlightenment

To contemporaries, the Black Death, or the Great Death, was widely regarded as God's scourge to people living in sin, and another popular belief was that *miasma* or 'bad air' had caused the plague. The epidemic also led to persecutions against Jews, particularly in German-speaking Europe, because Jews, 'poisoners of wells', were a convenient scapegoat for all sorts of crises and catastrophes (Trachtenberg 1983; Herlihy 1997, 67–8).

The years of the Black Death were also an era of violent religious madness. In particular, there was one fanatical religious movement that was a real danger to the Jews in Germany and the Netherlands. The members of the group were called *flagellants*, and they wandered around central Europe, whipping themselves in the belief that disciplining oneself was a way to seek atonement for the sins of humanity, and to show contempt for mundane reality. The flagellants were famous for including flamboyant public flagellation in their rituals. It was not a rare practice among the more fervently religious during the High and Late Middle Ages. The first recorded incident was in 1259 in Perugia, from where the mania for flagellation spread across northern Italy and into Austria. Not coincidentally, this happened one year after severe crop damage and famine throughout Europe. There are reports on how the flagellation mania in Perugia 'infected' almost everybody in the town. Other incidents are recorded in 1296 and a number of times in the fourteenth century. The popularity of the movement was based on the general inclination to religious fervour as well as on the growing dissatisfaction with the Church's control. Thousands of people gathered in processions, singing, carrying crosses and banners and marching throughout the town whipping themselves. This was not all: one chronicler wrote that anyone who did not join in the flagellation was accused of siding with the devil.

When the Black Death devastated the Continent, flagellant groups arose across central Europe in late 1348 and early 1349. Flagellants wore white robes with a red cross and marched across Germany and the Rhine valley in dramatic campaigns of penance. It was especially in Germany where flagellant groups were organized as a movement that turned vehemently against the Church and the Jews. German flagellant bands, varying in size from 50 to 500, were each commanded by a leader whose orders had to be obeyed without hesitation. The bands moved in a procession, the duration of which was mysteriously set to 33½ days. Flagellants camped in fields near towns and held their standardized rituals twice a day. In the ritual, the flagellants would strip to the waist, fall to their knees and scourge themselves with knotted cords, gesturing wildly to indicate their sins and striking themselves rhythmically to songs, known as *Geisslerlieder*, until blood flowed. Sometimes the blood was soaked up in rags and treated as a holy relic. Although flagellants apparently imagined that they contributed to the collective healing from the plague with their rituals, some town councils began to notice that sometimes they brought plague to towns where it had not yet appeared – bloody wounds spread plague. When they were denied entry to towns, the flagellants responded with increased physical penance. To many laymen, flagellants appeared to embody virtues such as asceticism and godliness that they could not easily find among the clergy (Cohn 2004, 131–5).

Although mostly consisting of peasants and artisans, there were more and more vagabonds, outlaws and criminals of all kinds in the flagellant bands. In a Messianic fervour, the German flagellants would occasionally provoke the populace to stone the clergy, but those who suffered most were the Jews, who were burned to death in Basel and Bern. In Strasbourg, the whole Jewish population – 2,000 Jews – was hanged or burned in its own cemetery in February 1349. When the flagellants entered Frankfurt in July, they rushed straight to the Jewish quarter and exterminated the entire Jewish community. The town authorities were appalled, but the townsfolk joined in the massacre. A month later the same tragic fate befell the Jews in Mainz and Cologne. Mainz had the largest Jewish community in Europe, and there the townsfolk lost their mind during a flagellant ceremony and fell upon the Jews. In Brussels too, the approach of the flagellants whipped up mob passions against the Jews, with the result that the whole community of 600 Jews was murdered. The Jewish community was also exterminated in Antwerp. In many areas of the Low Countries the 'flagellants, aided by the masses of the poor, burnt and drowned all the Jews they could find, "because they thought to please God in that way"' (Cohn 2004, 139). After the massacres of 1348–9, the Jewish communities in Germany and the Low Countries were all but wiped out, and the whole European Jewry was devastated both by the plague and by this late medieval Holocaust.

Pope Clement VI issued a bull against the flagellants in 1349, and although its effect was immediate, in those desperate times the movement was too popular to be easily suppressed even by papal decrees. Such was the power of the Church, however, that the flagellant groups disbanded, and both the Church (Inquisition) and the secular authorities started to persecute the flagellants as dangerous heretics and troublemakers, hanging or beheading them and burning many at the stake. Still, the movement lingered on here and there for another century. All in all, the flagellant groups were part of the European cultural, spiritual and bloodthirsty landscape for more than two centuries (Cohn 2004, 127–47). They are exemplary representatives of religious madness that has devastated Europe, especially in times of crisis.

* * *

The economic and social consequences of the Black Death and the following plagues were remarkable (Byrne 2004, 57–72). Because of the drastic depopulation, there was more social mobility and liberated land, as a result of which there was not only a surplus of arable land for new farmers, but former wheat fields could also be turned to pasturage and forest. A sudden shortage of labour improved the condition of serfs and workers in western Europe, and it may have been a driving force behind a more diversified economy and technological development as Europeans tried to create labour-saving devices. Indirectly, the great plague probably had an influence on general cultural evolution, which, however, only gained momentum in the fifteenth-century Renaissance. What is beyond doubt is that during the century and half after the Black Death, feudalism was on the decline

36 From Antiquity to the Enlightenment

in western Europe, while urbanization, a more developed division of labour as well as rudimentary forms of capitalism gave new impetus to European societies. In short, Europeans had to rebuild their society along different lines. According to the late medievalist David Herlihy, the Black Death 'assured that the Middle Ages would be the middle, not the final, phase in Western development' (Herlihy 1997, 38). In Herlihy's intriguing view, the Black Death signified the 'transformation of the West', a transition from medieval to modern 'systems of behaviour'.

In many ways, what Europeans experienced in the early modern period was not so much an enlightened march to freedom and affluence as another dark age of European history tainted by religious and political conflicts, wars, economic chaos and the persecution of 'witches'. In the next chapter I will examine eruptions of madness in the early modern Europe.

Bibliography

Boccaccio, G. (2011) 'A description of the plague from *The Decameron*', in K.R. Bartlett (ed.) *The Civilization of the Italian Renaissance: A Sourcebook*, Toronto: University of Toronto Press.

Brown, D.E. (1991) *Human Universals*, New York: McGraw-Hill.

Byrne, J.B. (2004) *The Black Death*, Westport, CT: Westwood Press.

Cohn, N. (2004) *The Pursuit of the Millennium*, 1st edn 1957, London: Pimlico.

Deutsch, A. (1949) *The Mentally Ill in America*, New York: Columbia University Press.

Dols, M.W. (1987) 'The origins of the Islamic hospital: myth and reality', *Bulletin of the History of Medicine*, 61: 367–90.

Dols, M.W. (1992) *Majnun: The Madman in Medieval Islamic Society*, ed. D.E. Immisch, Oxford: The Clarendon Press.

Feuerstein, G. (1990) *Holy Madness*, New York: Penguin Group.

Fletcher, R. (1993) *Moorish Spain*, Berkeley: University of California Press.

Gerdtz, J. (1994) 'Mental illness and the Roman physician: the legacy of Soranus of Ephesus', *Hospital & Community Psychiatry*, 45: 485–7.

Haensch, S., Bianucci, R., Signoli, M., Rajerison, M., Schultz, M. et al. (2010) 'Distinct colones of Yersinia pestis caused the Black Death', *PLoS Pathogens* 6(10): e1001134. doi: 10.1371/journal.ppat.1001134

Hankinson, R.J. (ed.) (2008) *The Cambridge Companion to Galen*, Cambridge: Cambridge University Press.

Harris, S. and Grigsby, B.L. (eds) (2008) *Misconceptions about the Middle Ages*, London: Routledge.

Herlihy, D. (1997) *The Black Death and the Transformation of the West*, Cambridge, MA: Harvard University Press.

Herrin, J. (2008) *Byzantium: The Surprising Life of a Medieval Empire*, Princeton, NJ: Princeton University Press.

Horace (2005) *Satires, Epistles and Ars Poetica*, trans. H.R. Fairclough, 1st edn 1926, Cambridge, MA: Harvard University Press.

Jackson, S.W. (1986) *Melancholia and Depression from Hippocratic Times to Modern Times*, New Haven, CT: Yale University Press.

Joutsivuo, T. (2014) 'How to get a melancholy marquess to sleep?', in S. Katajala-Peltomaa and S. Niiranen (eds), *Mental (Dis)Order in Later Medieval Europe*, Leiden: Brill.

Jung, C.G. (1981) 'Brother Klaus' (1933), in *Collected Works*, Vol. 11, London: Routledge & Kegan Paul.

Katajala-Peltomaa, S. (2014) 'Demonic possession as physical and mental disturbance in the later medieval canonization processes', in S. Katajala-Peltomaa and S. Niiranen (eds) *Mental (Dis)Order in Later Medieval Europe*, Leiden: Brill.

Katajala-Peltomaa, S. and Niiranen, S. (2014) 'Perspectives to mental (dis)order in later medieval Europe', in S. Katajala-Peltomaa and S. Niiranen (eds) *Mental (Dis)Order in Later Medieval Europe*, Leiden: Brill.

Krötzl, C. (2004) 'Pyhimysten vai lääkärien avulla? Keskiajan ihmeparantumiset', in Andreo Larsen (ed.) *Antiikin lääketieteen perintö*, Helsinki: Yliopistopaino.

Lederer, D. (2006) *Madness, Religion and the State in Early Modern Europe*, Cambridge: Cambridge University Press.

Lewis, D.L. (2008) *God's Crucible: Islam and the Making of Modern Europe, 570–1215*, New York: Norton.

Lloyd, G.E.R. (ed.) (1983) *Hippocratic Writings*, trans. J. Chadwick and W.N. Mann, Harmondsworth, Middlesex: Penguin Books.

Midelfort, E. (1999) *A History of Madness in Sixteenth-Century Germany*, Stanford, CA: Stanford University Press.

Miller, T. (1985) *The Birth of the Hospital in the Byzantine Empire*, Baltimore, MD: Johns Hopkins University Press.

Nauert, C.G. (2006) *Humanism and the Culture of Renaissance Europe*, Cambridge: Cambridge University Press.

Otto, B.K. (2001) *Fools Are Everywhere: The Court Jester Around the World*, Chicago, IL: University of Chicago Press.

Padel, R. (1995) *Whom Gods Destroy. Elements of Greek and Tragic Madness*, Princeton, NJ: Princeton University Press.

Plato (1997) *Phaedrus*, in J.M. Cooper (ed.), *Complete Works*, trans. A. Nehamas and P. Woodruff, Indianapolis, IN: Hackett Publishing Company.

Platt, C. (1996) *King Death: The Black Death and Its Aftermath in Late-Medieval England*, London: UCL Press.

Porter, R. (1999) *The Greatest Benefit to Mankind*, New York: Norton.

Porter, R. (2002) *Madness. A Brief History*, Oxford: Oxford University Press.

Roosens, E. (1979) *Mental Patients in Town Life: Geel, Europe's First Therapeutic Community*, Beverly Hills, CA: Sage Publications.

Siraisi, N.G. (1990) *Medieval & Early Renaissance Medicine*, Chicago, IL: University of Chicago Press.

Stephens, W. (2002) *Demon Lovers*, Chicago, IL: University of Chicago Press.

Stillman, N.A. (1975) 'Charity and social service in medieval Islam', *Societas*, 5: 105–15.

Trachtenberg, J. (1983) *The Devil and the Jews: The Medieval Conception of the Jew and Its Relation to Modern Antisemitism*, Philadelphia, PA: Jewish Publication Society.

3

MADNESS, FOLLY AND RELIGION IN EARLY MODERN EUROPE

This chapter focuses on four distinct phenomena that indicate how madness was intertwined with religion, power and cultural beliefs and customs in early modern Europe (ca. 1500–1700). These four rather extraordinary phenomena are dancing mania, demonic possessions and exorcisms, witchcraft, and folly. It is tempting to be judgemental when one is delving into practices, beliefs and behaviour patterns of past peoples that to us seem strange and bewildering, even outrageous. But it advances historical understanding not one iota if one does not make an honest attempt to respect the integrity of the past. When reading this chapter it is important to remember that we need to investigate past practices and belief systems on their own terms, not from our allegedly enlightened and at least implicitly superior perspective. In other words, we have to be sensitive to the reality in which peoples of the past lived and acted. What to us may seem utterly irrational, incomprehensible or erroneous may very well have been rational, understandable and justifiable to the people who lived in a different age than our own. We do not need to go back and condemn, say, sixteenth-century Strasbourgian dancing maniacs for being unlike us today, for acting in ways that we find puzzling or even terrifying. It is much more advisable to seek to understand early modern Europeans as they may have understood themselves. Instead of assuming that the past is inferior to the present, the task of historians is to comprehend why epidemics of dancing mania occurred or why the majority of Europeans considered demonic possession a real threat.

The waning of the Middle Ages

It was during the sixteenth and seventeenth centuries that the relatively stable world of the Middle Ages disintegrated and modern Europe went through painful birth pangs. Reformation and Counter-Reformation, the Thirty Years' War, population growth, increased poverty, social unrest and bad harvests due to the cooling of the climate roughly between the sixteenth and the nineteenth centuries (called the 'Little Ice Age') brought dire consequences to many Europeans. At the same time, growing commerce and trade and nascent capitalism increased the affluence of some social groups, such as merchants, bankers and slave traders (Goldthwaite 2008). This socio–economic polarization and the build-up of tensions and grudges found one outlet in witch-hunting, which was aggravated by the spiral of revenge and a search for scapegoats. Social mobility, poverty and epidemics weakened social cohesion, exacerbated conflicts and created a crisis-ridden mentality and cultural atmosphere. In the early modern age, Europe did not exactly become more tolerant and peaceful, power more dispersed and basic human rights more respected; in fact, a fight for religious, political and economic power occupied the centre stage in Europe. In Florence, historian, politician, diplomat and philosopher Niccolò Machiavelli (1469–1527) wrote *The Prince* (*Il principe*, 1513), an audacious prescription for power that almost single-handedly transformed political philosophy and created a stir among educated elites in Europe. As for the changes in the general world view of Europeans, the cosmology of the essentially unchanging great chain of being was broken during the early modern age (Lovejoy 1936).

On the threshold of the new era, European collective consciousness was still governed by traditional modes of thinking. This is how the great Dutch cultural historian Johan Huizinga describes the transition period, the 'waning of the Middle Ages':

> To the world when it was half a thousand years younger, the outlines of all things seemed more clearly marked than to us. The contrast between suffering and joy, between adversity and happiness, appeared more striking. All experience had yet to the minds of men the directness and absoluteness of the pleasure and pain of child-life. Every event, every action, was still embodied in expressive and solemn forms, which raised them to the dignity of a ritual. [. . .] [A]ll things in life were of a proud or cruel publicity. Lepers sounded their rattles and went about in processions, beggars exhibited their deformity and their misery in churches.
>
> (Huizinga 1972, 9)

The language of madness in the autumn of the Middle Ages was rich and colourful, reflecting the 'heated pathos' described by Huizinga. For example, Martin Luther (1483–1546), a seminal figure in the Protestant Reformation and well-known for his impetuousness, made several references to madness, using such terms as *furor, insania, mania, dementia, stultitia* and *Narrheit* (foolishness). For Luther, madness and sin were interconnected, as madness could be a form of sin, and sinfulness in turn could be so senseless as to become indistinguishable from madness. Luther saw the devil himself as mad, because the Prince of Darkness could not help feeling the constant wrath of God, and so he was 'filled with blind rage and unreasoning, uncontrollable fury at the ever-advancing progress of God's plan for his Creation' (Midelfort 1999, 85–92).

40 From Antiquity to the Enlightenment

During this period, central Europeans often avoided the term 'madness', because it was also used as a legal term, and as such it was associated with mania (*Raserei*). Mania was defined as senselessness or lack of reason (*Unsinnigkeit*), which in turn implied a potential for violence. For example, seventeenth-century Bavarians who were legally identified as mad could face serious consequences, such as losing their property, their autonomy and their impunity. Hence, 'mad' Bavarians preferred being identified as melancholics, because 'melancholy' indicated a condition in which an afflicted person was in possession of reason and common sense. Bavarians would also rather be suffering from tribulation, confusion, despair or demonic possession than madness, which was associated with legal as well as social control (Lederer 2006, 143, 154–6). Spiritual afflictions of Bavarians were often related to sexual relationships. Bavarian women, especially, appeared to suffer from complications of pregnancy, childbirth, infant mortality and illegitimate children, as well as from marital difficulties and courtship. Among the afflicted there were also victims of 'love magic'. According to the historian David Lederer, the great majority of those suffering from spiritual afflictions in early modern Europe were women (Lederer 2006, 183–7, 288).

Dancing mania

Dancing mania (*choreomania*) constitutes one of the most extraordinary chapters in the history of madness.[1] This socio-psychological epidemic appeared a few times in different parts of central Europe between the fourteenth and eighteenth centuries. Dancing mania refers to a phenomenon, in which groups of people – men, women and children – were overwhelmed by an urge to dance collectively in a state of disorientation and without any self-control. This strange mania was contagious, infecting people across towns and villages and at times taking hold of thousands of people. The two main characteristics of this mania were that the dancers did not feel any joy and they could not control themselves. Sometimes they continued moving their limbs uncontrollably, hopping and leaping until they were foaming at the mouth and so exhausted that they collapsed with blistering wounds on their legs. To the observers watching this ghastly spectacle, it looked as if the dancers were possessed by the devil. One chronicler, referring to eye-witness accounts, reported an outburst of this malady in Germany in 1463:

> These dancers jumped about in circles, always separately, thinking that they could by exertion and body movement drive out the pains they felt in their heart and viscera. But not getting any better, and thoroughly exhausted, they called upon St. John the Baptist, whose disease [*plagam*] they said this was.
>
> (Midelfort 1999, 32)

---

1 Dancing mania should not be confused with Huntington's disease (*chorea*), a neurodegenerative genetic disorder that affects muscle coordination and causes dementia as well as abnormal involuntary writhing movements called *chorea*.

Madness, folly and religion   **41**

This strange sort of mania probably started in Aachen, Germany, on 24 June 1374. On that day, townspeople began to dance wildly on the streets, screaming and hallucinating, twisting and jerking, until total exhaustion put an end to this bizarre drama. From Aachen, dancing mania spread to the Netherlands, north-eastern France and Rhineland. People were infected through the senses of sight and hearing: bystanders watching the dancers joined them. It was not a question of a local incident but a rather widely spread phenomenon across central Europe. This extraordinary epidemic seemed to follow the pilgrim routes.

The most well-preserved record of dancing mania concerns the 'dancing plague' of 1518 in Strasbourg in today's France. According to contemporary chroniclers, the first to dance was a certain Frau Troffea, who started to move her limbs and her body one July day. As far as we know, her dancing was not accompanied by music, and she did not show any signs of joy or pleasure, quite the contrary. When the warm day turned into evening, she still kept on dancing. It was clear to her worried husband that she just could not stop. Finally, after long hours of obsessive dancing, Frau Troffea collapsed, bathed in sweat and with muscles twitching. After sleeping a few hours, she continued her solitary dancing. She danced all through the following day, and the day after that. Townspeople gathered around her and wondered aloud whether God or the devil had taken control of the frenzied woman, whose shoes were now soaked with blood. They came to the agreement that St Vitus had sent out a scourge to punish sinners. Interestingly, St Vitus could be seen as both the cause and the cure of this disease. Therefore, maniacs were taken to the shrine of St Vitus near Saverne. Without further ado, they lifted Frau Troffea up to a wagon and transported her to a nearby shrine to receive St Vitus' blessing and to find a cure for her ailment. Dancing mania became known in the late medieval times as St Vitus' dance.

This was not the end of the story. In the following days, more than 30 men and women, infected by the same mania, took to the streets of Strasbourg, dancing, hopping and leaping. In August, there were at least 100 manic dancers, maybe as many as 400. Dancing mania lasted for more than six weeks, with a tragedy at the end of July when some of the totally exhausted dancers died (Waller 2008, 1–4). Uncontrollable, insatiable dancing took people to the limits of their endurance and beyond to the state of unconsciousness and, in some cases, to death. One woman kept on dancing for six days in a row. Some people never recovered from the mental and physical torment. Physicians in Strasbourg, wary of spreading hysteria and superstition, explained the mania as a natural illness caused by an overheated blood. Their naturalistic explanations clashed with moral explanations favoured by many churchmen and common people (Midelfort 1999, 33–7).

Epidemics of dancing mania continued until the end of the seventeenth century. Occasionally, mania struck the same individuals repeatedly. A physician in the town of Ulm recorded cases in which the same women had bouts of dancing mania annually on the same day for two decades or more. One possible explanation for such regular mania is the dancers' belief that these bouts of wild dancing would spare them from worse manifestations of the saint's malice (Waller 2008,

42 From Antiquity to the Enlightenment

168–9). In that case, it was a question of a sort of sacrifice offered through dancing. If saints, in this case St Vitus, were not adequately venerated, they might punish the imprudent mortals – Madonnas maimed as well as cured people (Midelfort 1999, 37; Waller 2008, 71). The double role of saints was a typical late medieval Catholic phenomenon.

Excluding the well-recorded 1518 dancing mania in Strasbourg, outbursts of frenzied dancing were mostly very poorly recorded. Therefore, we need to be careful in our modern assessment of this strange phenomenon. What seems to be a valid observation is that, compared to us, medieval Europeans may have been more inclined to get carried away by events and incidents that aroused their passions and enlivened their imagination. Historian John Waller has studied dancing mania in Strasbourg, and in his view the phenomenon can be seen as a collective stress reaction of the lower social classes to physical and spiritual anguish and despair. In other words, people escaped their unbearable condition by dancing themselves into a state of trance, which gave them a fleeting relief from their torment. To be sure, dancing away the misery was anything but easy, and contemporaries spoke of sufferers whose misfortunes were too severe to be danced away. The years preceding dancing mania had been particularly hard for the Strasbourgians: they had been struck by famine, diseases and adverse weather conditions that had ruined their harvests. On top of these physical misfortunes, people were disillusioned by the gluttony, greed and cruelty of the corrupted clergy. Indeed, Martin Luther nailed his 95 theses against the clerical abuses on the door of the Castle Church of Wittenberg in 1517, a year before the outbreak of dancing mania in Strasbourg. The general atmosphere in Strasbourg at that time was probably tense and anxious, and people's minds may have been filled with fear of God's wrath against sinners. Sixteenth-century Europeans in general may have been inclined to express themselves in body language and give physical forms to their feelings. The cultural norm of self-control was probably not as strong in the early modern age as it was in the following centuries. To some extent, dancing mania could be seen as an illustration of the historicity and situation-boundedness of psychosomatic afflictions. In the western cultural hemisphere, equivalent psychosomatic 'epidemics' were the reappearance of hysteria in the late nineteenth century, and the sudden outbreak of multiple personality disorder in the late twentieth century.

Dancing mania disappeared in the eighteenth century, but our 'enlightened age' has its own share of equivalent 'collective manias' or 'hysterias'. In the Nuremberg rallies of the Nazi Party in the 1930s, there were similar 'hysterical' scenes and a sort of herd mentality. In Tanzania (then Tanganyika), a laughter epidemic broke out at a mission-run boarding school for girls in 1962. The laughter had started quite innocently with three pupils, but then it spread throughout the school, affecting 95 pupils, aged 12–18. In some cases, symptoms lasted for more than two weeks. The school was forced to close down temporarily, but the epidemic spread to a nearby village, where 217 people had laughing attacks. A little later, the laughing epidemic spread to another girls' school. All in all, 14 schools were shut down and thousands of people were affected to some degree before the phenomenon died out. In addition to uncontrollable laughter, symptoms included fainting, rashes, attacks of crying and screaming (Rankin & Philip 1963). Closer to home, less severe versions of 'mass hysteria' and social delusions can be seen in rock concerts, sports events and in the meetings of revivalist movements of Protestant Christianity. Sociologist Robert E. Bartholomew has recorded and analysed a number of such outbreaks, including dancing mania, and his general conclusion is that medically labelling such phenomena 'mass hysteria' or 'psychogenic illnesses' is not very helpful. Instead, we need to study and understand cultural assumptions and belief systems that shape our varying expressions of anxiety, panic and fear, and, on a more general level, our perceptions of reality (Bartholomew 2001). If Chinese men start to panic because they fear that they are losing their penises, it may seem absurd to westerners, but in the context of Chinese folk beliefs it can be seen as a real threat. Expressions of physical, psychological and spiritual malaise represent prevailing world views and understanding of the self in different cultures and historical periods. Dancing mania and similar expressions of seemingly collective madness also illustrate the basic idea that human behaviour can be strongly affected by the behaviour of others, especially those that are emotionally close to us.

Possession and exorcism

Another phenomenon characterizing madness in the late Middle Ages and the early modern age was demonic possession. It was related to dancing mania, because sometimes compulsive dancers claimed to be possessed by evil spirits. This happened, for example, in the Rhineland in the 1370s, when the maniacs shouted out names of devils and demons. In Italian towns, water was commonly associated with possession, and wells were especially dangerous: many water fetchers appeared to have fallen victim to demons when they drank from a well (Katajala-Peltomaa & Niiranen 2014, 19). Although demons and other malign spirits were spiritual creatures, they could enter the body by eating or drinking. When demons entered the human body, they took up residence amidst the entrails and filth, but they could not enter the human *soul*; only a divine spirit was able to do that. An external sign of possession could have been an abnormal swelling of the body (Katajala-Peltomaa 2014, 114–15).

In the medieval world, madness was not necessarily attributed to demonic possession, hence the possessed were not, as a rule, considered mad. Contemporary authorities distinguished between organic mental disorders and disorders due to the demonic intervention in the soul of the afflicted, and demons were not the primary explanation for madness in late medieval times. Historian Erik Midelfort has demonstrated in his excellent study of madness in German-speaking Europe how demonic possessions increased rapidly in the latter half of the sixteenth

44 From Antiquity to the Enlightenment

century, attaining near-epidemic proportions (Midelfort 1999). Theologians, lawyers and physicians typically theorized that, just like madness, demonic possession was a spiritual or mental disturbance without a physiological basis. Indeed, Christian culture has for centuries maintained the idea of spiritual illness or affliction, and provided spiritual physick (*medici spirituali*) to the afflicted. This tradition of spiritual physic has continued up to modern times (Lederer 2006). The most well-known German physician of this period was Paracelsus (Theophrastus Philippus Aureolus Bombastus von Hohenheim, 1493–1541), an eccentric medical reformer who was also a natural philosopher and alchemist. He regarded mental illnesses (*Geisteskrankheiten*) as diseases of the soul (or spirit) and introduced the idea that there could be specific remedies available to cure specific conditions – for example, music for melancholics and a chemical-astrological shield for lunatics to protect their minds from the detrimental influence of the moon. Probably referring to the feebleminded, Paracelsus also claimed that those insane from birth were the product of their parents' sexual carelessness: 'If parents had intercourse in the midst of passion, their temporary insanity might well be transmitted to the fetus' (Midelfort 1999, 9, 117).

Compared to witch-hunting, the phenomenon of possession was probably less gender-specific in Germany. Erik Midelfort's analysis of sixteenth-century German documents indicates that there were an equal number of men and women among the possessed, but in the seventeenth-century Bavarian documents utilized by David Lederer the number of possessed women was much higher than that of men (Midelfort 1999, 7; Lederer 2006, 175). What appears to be the case is that it was more common to attribute aggressive and agitated behaviour to possession if the violent persons were women; if men acted violently, they were often categorized as raving mad. Women were also more vulnerable to external influences, such as demons, because their bodies were more open than men's bodies (Katajala-Peltomaa 2014, 14–15). As for England, many of the possessed people who were taken to the shrine of Thomas Becket in Canterbury were described as violent, but in the case of one woman the demon caused her to speak Latin and German. This was not a unique case: there are similar accounts of demoniacs who spoke foreign languages they had not known before, or they could answer complicated philosophical questions, predict the future or reveal the sins of other people (Caciola 2003, 48–9). Demonic possession was a plausible explanation in such cases, because it was hard to find natural reasons for these special abilities (Rider 2014, 47). Pondering on the cultural meaning of possession for ordinary people, Midelfort wonders whether, for the victims, the experience of possession signified 'a painful liberation from the piety to which they aspired'. In Midelfort's plausible interpretation, 'diabolic possession gave vent to the agonized religious frustrations, fears, and yearnings of the would-be pious' (Midelfort 1999, 76).

There was no question about the proper remedy for possession: demons had to be cast out by exorcism (Caciola 2003, 225–73). In the Christian tradition, exorcism has been the most powerful weapon in the battle against the devil. Until the mid-seventeenth century, it was part of the official religious policy of the Catholic Church (Lederer 2006; Schott & Tölle 2006, 22–5). One of the official ritual works of the Catholic Church, *Rituale Romanum*, created official rules for the rite of exorcism in 1614. The Roman Ritual also listed the four cardinal symptoms of possession: 'Repulsiveness exhibited toward the application of holy objects, the ability to speak in previously unknown languages, superhuman strength and knowledge of facts hidden or secret' (Lederer 2006, 175). Notably, unlike witchcraft, it was no crime to be possessed. Whereas theologians, jurists and physicians deliberated on the judicial and religious aspects of witchcraft, possession was more of an interest of the common people. Erik Midelfort argues that cases of demonic possession were in large part the product of collective imagination, of popular fears, images and fantasies of the devil or other evil spirits. This realm of popular imagination was partly or wholly inaccessible to the literate magisterial classes of Europe (Midelfort 1999, 70).

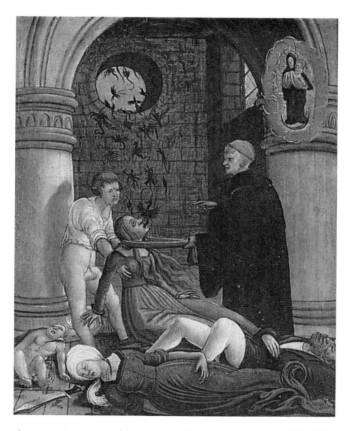

FIGURE 3.1 An exorcist casting demons out of a woman who has killed her child and her parents. Part of a large painted altarpiece, the so-called 'Miracle Altar' (*Großer Mariazeller Wunderaltar*), 1519 (author unknown). The Miracle Altar has 47 panels, and today it is kept in Styrian Universalmuseum Joanneum in Graz, Austria.

Source: Reproduced with permission of Alte Galerie – Universalmuseum Joanneum GmbH

46   From Antiquity to the Enlightenment

To drive out demons was a very concrete act: it could happen through application of relics, which resulted in the departure of the demon or demons through vomiting black blood, coals and other black items, or demons made an exit through armpits or in the form of an insect. Before leaving the sufferer's body, demons often announced their presence by cursing, screaming and raving frantically (Lederer 2006, 175, 189, 235; Katajala-Peltomaa 2014, 124–5). In addition to relics, exorcists used many kinds of spells and incantations. Some exorcists appeared to have great powers over demons. One French bishop forced demons to sign a contract that bound them to leave their victim in peace in the future. In Vienna in 1583, some churchmen declared that they had cast out no fewer than 12,652 demons during the year.

To be sure, there were also sceptical physicians who regarded demons as hallucinations or delusions brought on by melancholy (black bile). Melancholy was associated with possession, because fear and sadness were regarded as dangerous and detrimental sentiments – dangerous because they weakened the mental immunity of people, which in turn could expose them to the influence of malignant spirits (Kanerva 2014, 231–2). Other sceptics dismissed the role of demons by arguing that they were conjured up by ignorant people who misunderstood the true causes of their mental conditions (Rider 2014, 57). But sometimes even the academic physicians were caught off guard by the phenomenon. The Swiss physician Felix Platter (1536–1614) observed a case of possession in his early medical career. His father, Professor Platter, had sent Felix to the house of a 'professional' exorcist in the hope of putting an end to his 'godless' calling. The exorcist made his living by casting out demons, but his work was not officially sanctioned by the Church. After entering the house, young Felix witnessed something he would never forget:

> [A] robust demoniac was brought in, stiff as a board, and was dumped on the floor. There he lay, deaf and dumb with twisted legs and hands for several days without eating or drinking and without emitting any bodily substance. Most extraordinary was his head, which was so twisted that it faced exactly backward. Felix Platter was so horrified that he left.
>
> (Midelfort 1999, 175)

In a book he wrote later (*Praxis*, 1602), Platter, a 'modern physician', had to admit that there were both natural and supernatural forms of 'mental consternations'. The cause of supernatural consternation was the devil.

Possession can be seen as a manifestation of a sort of madness-as-alienation from the normative precepts of a society oppressed by severe religiosity. Many Germans lived in agony, because behind the facade of Christian piety they were haunted by sinful lusts, desires and suspicions. Some parishioners – both Catholics and Protestants – broke down under the pressure of rigid moral demands and relieved their anxieties by succumbing to the demonic temptations. In the words of Erik Midelfort, the 'history of demonomania, of diabolic obsession and possession, is the dark side of the history of piety' (Midelfort 1999, 76–8). This explanation of possession is corroborated by David Lederer's remark about the responsibility of the Christian sufferers for their spiritual afflictions: if confession and penance failed to bring mental relief, the sufferers were on their own, tormented by guilt and angst. Such a desperate state of mind could find an outlet in diabolic possession (Lederer 2006, 97–8).

Excluding the relatively small group of learned men, Europeans of the early modern age adopted a strong magico-religious world view. Small wonder, then, that they easily interpreted madness and despair as the wages of sin and as demonic possession. This can be seen in the records of Richard Napier, an English clergyman and astrological physician who treated over 2,000 mentally disordered patients between 1597 and 1634 (all in all, he treated tens of thousands of patients for every kind of affliction). Napier became a famous healer in and around Buckinghamshire, and most of his patients were ordinary men and women, to whom he offered 'spiritual physick' based on the synthesis of magic, religion and science.

Napier's patients had no doubts about demons causing mental and physical diseases. In their mental universe, spiritual beings, witches and malevolent spirits were real, and all of them could intervene in people's lives. Not surprisingly, then, Napier exorcised his possessed clients. He used either Catholic formulas or his own texts that harmonized better with the tenets of the Anglican Church. This is how he addressed spirits possessing a certain Edmund Francklin:

> Behold, I God's most unworthy minister and servant, I do charge and command thee, thou cruel beast, with all thy associates and all other malignant spirits in case that any of you have your being in the body of this creature, Mr. E. Fr., and have distempered his brain with melancholy and have also deprived his body and limbs of their natural use, I charge and command you speedily to depart from this creature and servant of God, Mr. E. Fr.
>
> (MacDonald 2008, 215)

Many of Napier's patients believed that exorcisms and amulets protected them against mental torment. Magical beliefs had a therapeutic function in that they helped the insecure English men and women to deal with the mysterious and potentially dangerous forces that affected their health and sanity. Religion offered consolation, but it could also produce anxiety: almost 300 of Napier's mentally troubled patients suffered from spiritual malady or religious anxiety. Nearly 100 men and, especially, women told Napier that they were doubtful of salvation. Such anxieties could have been aroused by the Puritan clergy, whose sermons created threatening images of damnation and stressed the terrifying consequences of a sinful life. As historian Michael MacDonald notes in his book on Napier and his patients, 'instead of strengthening the people against the psychological miseries of

48 From Antiquity to the Enlightenment

the sinful life, they [the clergy] shattered the mental composure of their audiences'
(MacDonald 2008, 224).

Demand for exorcism increased from the mid-sixteenth to the mid-seventeenth
century, after which it slowly started to decrease. An important reason for this
gradual decline was the secular authorities' and reformist churchmen's opposition
to exorcism. The public authorities wanted to have more complete control over
the citizens' lives, while the younger members of the clergy felt uncomfortable
with such popular manifestations of the devil's existence; it smacked of extravagant
superstition. The art of exorcism was carried on by some Jesuits and profit-seeking
'popular exorcists', and to a small extent it has continued to the present day, not
only in the Catholic Church but throughout the world (Lederer 2006, 198–201).

Witchcraft

Possession has a complex relationship with witchcraft, the most well-known outbreak of 'mass hysteria' in the western world. Witchcraft appeared in different
parts of Europe at the end of the fifteenth century, assumed epidemic proportions in the mid-seventeenth century and continued more sporadically until the
eighteenth century. In several cases witchcraft and diabolic possession were connected; the main difference between them appeared to be in the form of demonic
encounter. Those accused of witchcraft had willingly entered a pact with the devil,
while the possessed were more passive victims of the devil's power – or, of witchcraft. In German-speaking Europe, there was a widespread assumption that
demon possession could be caused by witchcraft.

One impetus for the witch-hunts was the *Malleus maleficarum* ('Hammer of the
Witches'), a malicious treatise on the prosecution of witches (Kramer & Sprenger
2011). Authors of this 'handbook' were two German members of the Inquisition,
Jacob Sprenger and Heinrich Kramer alias Henricus Institoris, and the latter was
most probably mainly responsible for the contents of the book. The motive for writing the book is not clear, but it seems that it was not originally commissioned by the
Pope. Instead, in 1484 Kramer and Sprenger managed to receive a papal bull *Sum-
mis desiderantes affectibus*, which was included as part of the preface of the *Malleus*, as
it seemed to give full papal approval for the Inquisition, and Kramer and Sprenger
specifically, to prosecute witchcraft. It replaced the rule of the old canonic treatise
Canon episcopi, which had defined witchcraft as a pagan religion, hence practitioners
of witchcraft were outside the jurisdiction of the Inquisition. Until the late Middle
Ages, the Church was more concerned about sorcery than the far more serious crime
of witchcraft (Bailey 2001, 960–1). But in the new bull, witchcraft was defined as
Satan worship, an extremely serious sin and crime. However, only three years after
it was published, the Catholic Church condemned *Malleus* as false.

Malleus is a misogynistic and cruel treatise. It was meant to be used in witchcraft
trials and, more generally, to propagate the view that witchcraft exists and that it
is mostly practised by women. It was also read by 'laymen', who were titillated by
descriptions of the various ways in which the devil seduces his female victims into

sexual intercourse. The authors asserted that women were more inclined to witch-craft than men, because they were weaker in faith and more carnal than men, and therefore more susceptible to demonic temptations:

> [S]ince they are feebler both in mind and body, it is not surprising that they should come more under the spell of witchcraft. For as regards intellect, or the understanding of spiritual things, they seem to be of a different nature from men; a fact which is vouched for by the logic of the authorities, backed by various examples from the Scriptures. Terence says: Women are intel-lectually like children [. . .] But the natural reason is that she is more carnal than a man, as is clear from her many carnal abominations. And it should be noted that there was a defect in the formation of the first woman, since she was formed from a bent rib, that is, a rib of the breast, which is bent as it were in a contrary direction to a man. And since through this defect she is an imperfect animal, she always deceives [. . .] To conclude. All witchcraft comes from carnal lust, which is in women insatiable.
>
> (Kramer & Sprenger 2011, 101–14)

The authors of the *Malleus maleficarum* were themselves efficient witch-hunters, finding 48 witches in one diocese. All of them women, presumably. *Malleus* was not the only book dealing with witches, demons and sorcerers in late medieval Europe. An earlier treatise that inspired Kramer and Sprenger was the German Dominican theologian Johannes Nider's treatise *Formicarius*, written in the 1430s and printed in 1475, ten years before the publication of *Malleus*. It was Nider who introduced (in Book Five of the treatise) three ideas that would play a leading role in the witch-hunts: first, witches operated as members of an organized sect; sec-ond, anybody, and not just learned men, could become a witch; and, third, witch-craft was an especially feminine crime. Nider's book helped spread the belief that an archetypal witch was an uneducated, ordinary woman, and that anybody could attain magical powers simply by entering a pact with the devil (Bailey 2003).

The assumption that witches and especially female witches entered a pact with the devil started to gain ground in central Europe at the end of the fifteenth cen-tury. This pact was supposedly sealed in the regular nocturnal gatherings known as Sabbaths, where lascivious witches worshipped the devil and 'in exchange for his promise on magical power, forswear Christ, the church, and the entire Chris-tian faith. They would also murder and devour babies, engage in sexual orgies, and perform other sinful and abominable rites' (Bailey 2001, 962). These outra-geous ideas about witches were not disseminated by superstitious peasants but by the learned men of Europe, especially theologians and jurists. What characterized European witchcraft was that it was originally not a bottom-up phenomenon but a fantasy of the learned, which had little appeal among the 'ignorant' people in the countryside. Secular authorities usually conducted witch trials, but clerics were instrumental in shaping the concept of witchcraft, the principal context of which was ecclesiastical and inquisitorial (Bailey 2001, 962).

Victims of witch-hunts

It has been said that the victims of witch-hunts were often the mad, whose strange behaviour was attributed to demonic possession. Certainly some mad women were persecuted as witches, but historical records show that witchcraft trials aimed to differentiate clearly between witches and the mad. Rather than being the devil's allies, the mad were victims of external forces or their own disease, either possessed or driven crazy by physical diseases, losses or adversities.

What made witchcraft trials so nightmarish for the victims was the reintroduction of ancient techniques of torture in European legal trials in general and witchcraft trials in particular. Since torture was used to obtain evidence, the accused were driven to admit their alleged crimes. Sometimes 'witches' were publicly executed by burning, and sometimes they were hanged. In England, they were often first hanged and then burned. In Germany, unrestrained torture was widely practised, which naturally resulted in a large number of confessions. In Germany and Denmark (where about 1,000 people were executed), the use of torture led to a chain reaction, in which those accused of witchcraft denounced others as witches, who in turn denounced others, and so forth. What disgraced these trials was that 'confessions' were often taken at face value despite the fact that the accused were subjected to torture. No wonder witch-hunts and death sentences were less common in areas where torture was not practised. Another restraint was a judicial system in which the higher court supervised the lower courts. Such supervision often resulted in the mitigation of conviction in the lower courts. Little by little, the virus of witch-craze started to infect local communities, where accusations often arose from conflicts between villagers – especially women – and where witchcraft was understood in the context of the practical advantages that could be obtained from men and women who had supernatural powers (Briggs 2002, 264–82).

The number of executions for witchcraft is based on rough estimates. What has become evident in the more recent scholarship is that rather than there being millions of victims, the probable number of total executions is somewhere between 40,000 and 60,000. About 20 or 25 per cent of the victims were men. Regional differences were striking, and for this reason it is difficult to make sweeping statements about 'European witchcraft'. Persecutions were most intense in western and central Europe, especially in Germany, Switzerland and France. These were the regions where the Protestant Reformation weakened or – in Switzerland – almost wiped out the Catholic Church. In Germany, perhaps as many as 26,000 people were killed, whereas in Ireland, a thoroughly Catholic country, there were fewer than ten victims. Also Spain and Portugal, the strongly Catholic countries of southern Europe, were virtually devoid of witch-hunts. From central Europe, witch-hunts spread to the Baltic countries, Scandinavia and Russia. Regarding the question of gender, in Germany about 80 per cent of the alleged witches were women, whereas in Finland more than half of the accused in the sixteenth and seventeenth centuries were men (Nenonen & Kervinen 1994, 247). In Germany, the accused were often unmarried elderly women (more than 50 years of age), who were thus deviant, 'useless' and rather defenseless against persecution. Due to their age, they were regarded as 'dry' (infertile) and therefore more potential prey to the devil's lures than the younger and healthier women who could satisfy their sexual desires with men.

Most people were convicted in local, secular courts, but there is no doubt about the predominance of the religious element in witch-hunts – it is not much of an exaggeration to call early modern Europe a continent ruled by 'theocracy' or 'ecclesiocracy' (rule by a church). Perhaps the single most important factor that had a restraining effect on the witch-craze was the religio-political peace agreement reached in Westphalia in 1648. The peace in Westphalia signified the end of the Thirty Years' War (1618–48), and it also initiated a new political order in central Europe, creating a basis for national self-determination and a confirmation of the principle of *cuius regio, eius religio* ('whose the region, his the religion') of the Peace of Augsburg of 1555. This principle dictated that a local sovereign would have the right to determine the religion of his own region, the options being Catholicism, Lutheranism or Calvinism. As the first international peace of modern times, the Treaty of Westphalia codified the new secular political order and put an end to doctrinal issues that had torn Europe apart for more than a century.

Avoidance of doctrinal approach to witchcraft was not an invention of the Treaty of Westphalia. By the end of the sixteenth century, the learned men of Europe had started to look at witchcraft with a more sceptical eye. The renowned Dutch physician Johann Weyer (1515–88), who was well-versed in the Roman tradition of civil and canon law, published a book 'On the Deceits of the Demons' (*De praestigiis daemonum*) in 1563 (the book was published in English in 1991 with the title *Witches, Devils, and Doctors in the Renaissance*; see Weyer 1991). Based on his empirical investigations of 'weird events', Weyer presented in his widely read book a ground-breaking insanity defence: he claimed that the so-called witches were in fact weak, hallucinating women who were mad sufferers rather than witches. His attack on witch-hunting and his debunking of spiritual illusions caused consternation among witch-hunters, even though they too believed that witches were predominantly older women. For the witch-hunters, Weyer's claim was a tough challenge, because he made it clear that witches were mad women, and therefore not responsible for their acts. Persecutors simply could not accept his contention, for it would have meant that the so-called witches were not witches at all. Weyer in turn pointed out that claims about all the damages done by witches were utter nonsense – if the devil wanted to harm people, he surely did not need the support or encouragement of witches. According to Roman law, a mere *intention* to do mischief was not punishable; what was needed was a punishable *act*. But this was exactly what the alleged witches were unable to do, because their attempt at doing mischief by entering a pact with the devil was nothing but an 'impossible intention'. It was a futile attempt, because witches were mentally disturbed. Their bad intentions and 'malicious' thoughts were actually hallucinations and harmful only to themselves. Witches did not do damage to others; they suffered from their

52 From Antiquity to the Enlightenment

own intentions. In short, Weyer tried to prove on legal grounds that the crime of witchcraft was impossible (Midelfort 1999, 201–11).

Weyer was nothing short of ingenious in applying Roman and canon law, as well as theological and philosophical arguments, to the elucidation of the human mind and the psychology of hatred. At the same time, he justified on religious grounds a merciful treatment of 'witches'. In this line of reasoning, he followed Erasmus of Rotterdam, the great Renaissance humanist who had argued that heresy did not merit the death penalty. True, witches and other heretics deviated from the Catholic faith, but such deviations were not capital crimes. Weyer was not, however, a forerunner of modern scepticism, because in principle he did not deny the devil's interventions in human affairs – the devil could, for example, blind the eyes, ruin crops, obsess and possess people, transport their bodies through the air, stop the milk of cows and cause incurable seizures and spasms. But Weyer was fearless in his claim that many of the so-called devil's deeds were in fact fabrications conjured up by Catholic priests. Most importantly, jurists could not ignore Weyer's empirical claim that individuals accused of witchcraft were not witches at all; they were mad. Weyer's learned arguments influenced reluctant jurists, who from then on felt that they had to take medical testimony more or less seriously (Midelfort 1999, 112–14, 206; Lederer 2006, 316–20). To honour Weyer as the creator of the modern insanity defence may be an anachronistic exaggeration (Lederer 2006, 316–18), but what is safe to say is that essential parts of his reasoning do represent an early form of medical testimony and an attempt to bring the principle *non compos mentis* ('not of sound mind') to the courtrooms.

How do we explain the witch-craze? A thorny question, indeed. Obviously, there are several factors that contributed to this sad chapter in European history. Theological, political, judicial, economic and social upheavals, developments and crises became intertwined in this phenomenon. According to the judicial view, the empowering of central government in the late Middle Ages made the judicial system more efficient and criminal law more stringent, as a result of which conflicts within communities were brought to court more easily. Simultaneously, the authorities and especially the clergy were more capable of monitoring doctrinaire purity in society. Witch-hunting represented a new, more merciless way of handling local conflicts. On the other hand, sixteenth-century Europe experienced a thoroughgoing demonization. The pious and the learned as well as ordinary people perceived material and spiritual reality in the absolute terms of good and evil, fire and brimstone, chaos and serenity. In the mid-sixteenth century, a specific literary genre, devil-books (*Teufelsbücher*), emerged especially in the Lutheran theology and ethics. The basic idea of the devil-books was that every vice has its source in, or is directed by, a specialized devil. In his satirical book *Praise of Folly* (1509), Erasmus of Rotterdam (1466–1536), no friend of religious fanaticism or hypocrisy, said to himself,

> I don't know why I'm wading through this sea of superstition: Had I a hundred tongues, a hundred mouths, a voice of iron, I could not count the types

of fool, nor yet enumerate the names of every kind of folly. The ordinary life of Christians everywhere abounds in these varieties of silliness, and they are readily permitted and encouraged by priests who are not unaware of the profit to be made thereby.

(Erasmus 1971, 130)

Witch-hunting involved the judicial system, the Church, savants (including physicians) and local communities. Interpretations of this complex phenomenon are partly contradictory, but it is exceedingly difficult to give an all-embracing explanation of something that had many different national, religious and local contexts. But one thing is beyond doubt: witch-hunting is a perfect example of human folly.

Folly

The fourth representative of late medieval and early modern madness are the court fools, holy fools and jesters. The tradition of court fools has its origins in earlier times, but especially during the Renaissance fools formed a distinct subgroup among the motley crew of madmen, simpletons and lunatics. In German-speaking Europe, even physicians who specialized in the treatment of madness began to be called 'fool-doctors' (*Narrenarzt*). Folly and madness were nearly synonymous words, but while both behaved irrationally, fools were regarded as simple and mirthful people, but not as mad. Furthermore, fools suffered from a congenital mental defect, while madness could seize upon its victims at any time. Therefore, while madmen were treated by constraints, isolation, religious rites or – sometimes – just making them feel safe and comfortable, fools were considered unchangeable and not in need of any kind of treatment (Korhonen 1999, 135–6). As for the court fools, the majority of them were treated as talking pets, whose jokes and jests entertained the king's and the prince's entourage but who could also be subjected to brutality and cruelty. German Europe abounded in court fools, who were entertainers above all, witty and fun to watch perhaps, but not 'daring fools' who were licensed to proclaim inconvenient truths that nobody else dared to say out loud.

In the sixteenth century, folly referred to human weakness and to the inability to act adequately in one's interest. Cultural infatuation with folly found its most popular literary expression in Sebastian Brant's satire *Ship of Fools* (*Narrenschiff*, 1494). Brant was a jurist and Strasbourg chancellor whose disillusionment with the Church, secular authorities and the human condition in general prompted him to write a book that touched a raw nerve among contemporary Europeans. Many new editions of the book appeared in the late fifteenth and early sixteenth centuries, and it was translated into other languages, which was quite unprecedented at that time. A new printing technique, invented by Johannes Gutenberg in around 1439, enabled a wide dissemination of the book, as did the language in which it was written: Brant chose to write in the language of the common people (dialect

54 From Antiquity to the Enlightenment

of Swabia), not in Latin, which was the lingua franca of learned Europeans at that time. Brant used the word *Narr* (fool) as a blanket term to describe all sorts of weaknesses and sins, and apparently his readers were amused by his quips about priests and monks. Brant condemned monks as 'inept monkeys' who choose the monastic life only in order to 'gorge themselves on food'. Brant did not spare the students either:

> Students should likewise not be skipped,
> With fool's caps they are well equipped,
> When these are pulled about the ear
> The tassel flaps and laps the rear,
> For when of books they should be thinking
> They go carousing, roistering, drinking.
> A youth puts learning on the shelf,
> He'd rather study for himself,
> What's useless, vain – an empty bubble;
> And teachers too endure this trouble [. . .]
> Thus money spent to train and school,
> Has often gone to rear a fool.
> (Brant 1962, 124–5)

Brant's book was entertaining, but its main point was serious: in the last analysis, we are all fools, and we are sailing on a ship that is bound for a total shipwreck – Hell.

For modern readers, a more well-known treatise on folly is Erasmus of Rotterdam's *Praise of Folly* (*Stultitiae Laus*, 1511), a more sophisticated and forgiving satire than Brant's straightforward attack on human weaknesses. Erasmus elevates two forms of folly above others: one is Dame Folly (*Stultitia*), which refers to folly of love, sexual desire, family ties and simple bodily pleasures. Another form of folly is Pauline folly, 'the irrational, ecstatic madness that carries a Christian beyond his everyday, commonplace rational and empirical bearings and into a mystical relation to Christ that no pagan wise man could have imagined' (Midelfort 1999, 234). Erasmus saw folly in a more positive light than Brant did, but he did agree with Brant in the latter's condemnation of its selfish and sinful forms. The ship of fools metaphor was also used by Hieronymus Bosch in his famous painting *The Ship of Fools* (painted ca. 1490–1500).

For some reason, both Brant and Erasmus ignored the popular meaning of folly, which referred, first, to the 'natural fools' or the 'retarded' and, second, to the 'professional fools' or jesters, pranksters and tricksters who imitated madness and joked about folly. Natural fools were typically outsiders, laughable creatures who were at the bottom of social hierarchy together with children and the crippled. Indeed, the physical incapacity of cripples and dwarfs corresponded with the mental incapacity of the natural fools. Princes, lords and courtiers may have treated fools humanely out of pity or 'for the sake of God', but they certainly did not have any respect for the putatively deeper or secret wisdom of the fools. To keep pitiful outsiders in courts was a form of entertainment and a sort of status symbol, but the presence of fools was also a reminder to courtiers that common humanity included defect and deprivation. Yet, princes and courtiers could simultaneously sadistically abuse fools and treat them as pets or freaks (Midelfort 1999, 275–6).

Historical sources do not give a reliable answer to the question of whether some fools were seen as having special abilities, such as clairvoyance, verbal courage or wit. In addition to their roles as entertainers, pets and specimens of distorted humanity, they probably had another important function: they defied the increasingly formal and rigid courtly behaviour and etiquette as well as the delicate standards for courtesy. At any rate, fools could talk and act in a way that was not permitted to the members of the court, and such social transgressions were amusing and funny to those who were painfully aware of the rules of proper conduct. One such master of social transgression was the famous Claus Narr, who lived in Saxon courts during the latter half of the fifteenth and early part of the sixteenth century. Claus gained a wide reputation for his childishly witty remarks, but also for his uncanny ability to foresee the future. An example of *Narrenfreiheit* was an occasion when Claus was visiting a castle with his master, the elector of Saxony. Claus became so annoyed at not getting any wine to drink that he attacked his host by saying to him: 'Lord Captain von Hilberg, you have a pious wife, and yet [you have] many whores in the city'. Claus' outburst provoked a roar of laughter around him. The very ability of fools to break the boundaries of convention and to blur social roles signified their inability to attain the status of an honourable man. They were inferior, ridiculed specimens of a distorted humanity. Hence they shared the fate of cripples, dwarfs, hunchbacks and the 'retarded' (Midelfort 1999, 261–70). Court fools, including the beloved Claus Narr, did not escape beatings and other forms of abuse. I will end this section with a reminder of the total imbalance of power in court:

> As late as 1660, the prince bishop of Bamberg kept a fat, stammering fool at his table, to whom on one occasion he gave hazelnuts and commanded that he crack them by smashing them on the table with his forehead. He let the sadistic joke go on until blood was streaming down the fool's face.
>
> (Midelfort 1999, 265)

* * *

In the next chapter, I will first go back one more time to the devil and to the European demonomania of the early modern age before I move to the dawn of the new era, the culmination of which was the eighteenth-century Age of the Enlightenment.

Bibliography

Bailey, M.D. (2001) 'From sorcery to witchcraft: clerical conceptions of magic in the later Middle Ages', *Speculum*, 76: 960–90.

Bailey, M.D. (2003) *Battling Demons: Witchcraft, Heresy, and Reform in the Late Middle Ages*, University Park, PA: Penn State University Press.

Bartholomew, R.E. (2001) *Little Green Men, Meowing Nuns and Head-hunting Panics: A Study of Mass Psychogenic Illnesses and Social Delusion*, Jefferson, NC: McFarland & Company.

Brant, S. (1962) *The Ship of Fools*, trans. E.H. Zeydel, orig. German edn 1494, New York: Dover Publications.

Briggs, R. (2002) *Witches & Neighbours: The Social and Cultural Context of European Witchcraft*, Oxford: Wiley-Blackwell.

Caciola, N. (2003) *Discerning Spirits. Divine and Demonic Possession in the Middle Ages*, Ithaca, NY: Cornell University Press.

Erasmus (1971) *Praise of Folly and Letter to Martin Dorp*, trans. B. Radice, orig. Latin edn 1511, Harmondsworth: Penguin Books.

Goldthwaite, R.A. (2008) *The Economy of Renaissance Florence*, Baltimore, MD: Johns Hopkins University Press.

Huizinga, J. (1972) *The Warning of the Middle Ages*, trans. F. Hopman, orig. Dutch edn 1924, Harmondsworth, Middlesex: Penguin Books.

Kanerva, K. (2014) 'Disturbances of the mind and body. Effects of the living dead in medieval Iceland', in S. Katajala-Peltomaa and S. Niiranen (eds) *Mental (Dis)Order in Later Medieval Europe*, Leiden: Brill.

Katajala-Peltomaa, S. (2014) 'Demonic possession as physical and mental disturbance in the later medieval canonization processes', in S. Katajala-Peltomaa and S. Niiranen (eds) *Mental (Dis)Order in Later Medieval Europe*, Leiden: Brill.

Katajala-Peltomaa, S. and Niiranen, S. (2014) 'Perspectives to mental (dis)order in later medieval Europe', in S. Katajala-Peltomaa and S. Niiranen (eds) *Mental (Dis)Order in Later Medieval Europe*, Leiden: Brill.

Korhonen, A. (1999) *Fellows of Infinite Jest. The Fool in Renaissance England*, Turku, Finland: University of Turku.

Kramer, H. and Sprenger, J. (2011) *Malleus maleficarum*, trans. M. Summers, Windhaven Network (e-book).

Lederer, D. (2006) *Madness, Religion and the State in Early Modern Europe*, Cambridge: Cambridge University Press.

Lovejoy, A. (1936) *The Great Chain of Being*. Cambridge, MA: Harvard University Press.

MacDonald, M. (2008) *Mystical Bedlam: Madness, Anxiety and Healing in Seventeenth-century England*, Cambridge: Cambridge University Press.

Midelfort, E. (1999) *A History of Madness in Sixteenth-century Germany*, Stanford, CA: Stanford University Press.

Nenonen, M. and Kervinen, T. (1994) *Synnin palkka on kuolema. Suomalaiset noidat ja noitavainot 1500–1700-luvulla*, ed. A.-R. Isohella, Helsinki: Otava.

Rankin, A.M. and Philip, P.J. (1963) 'An epidemic of laughing in the Bukoba district of Tanganyika', *Central African Journal of Medicine*, 9: 167–70.

Rider, C. (2014) 'Demons and mental disorder in late medieval medicine', in S. Katajala-Peltomaa and S. Niiranen (eds) *Mental (Dis)Order in Later Medieval Europe*, Leiden: Brill.

Schott, H. and Tölle, R. (2006) *Geschichte der Psychiatrie*, Munich: C.H. Beck.

Waller, J. (2008) *A Time to Dance, A Time to Die*, London: Icon Books.

Weyer, J. (1991) *Witches, Devils, and Doctors in the Renaissance*, eds G. Mora and B. Kohl, trans. J. Shea, original Latin edn 1563, Binghamton, NY: Medieval & Renaissance Texts & Studies.

4

FROM THE DEVIL'S TEMPTATION TO WRONG THINKING

Madness in the seventeenth and eighteenth centuries

This chapter focuses on madness during the transitional period between the Thirty Years' War (1618–48) and the Age of the Enlightenment (ca. 1690–1800). As I will show in this chapter, there were fashionable illnesses or 'contagious diagnoses' even before the last centuries of the millennium: Europe experienced an Age of Melancholy in the late sixteenth and early seventeenth centuries. To think of melancholy, mania and other forms of madness purely in terms of medicine and science was still very rare in those days – madness was too strange and mysterious to be confined in a medical, psychological or physiological framework; it seemed to require a moral, religious or magical language to make it comprehensible. Although Europe was becoming modern and 'enlightened', it was not that easy for the learned men to expel the devil from the world of madness. That is not to say that there were no attempts to change the supernatural way common Europeans perceived reality: it was during this period that intellectual culture was changed as the first secular philosophers (Descartes, Spinoza, Hobbes, etc.) created ideas that were not only intrinsically rational, but also empiricist, materialistic and at least implicitly anti-religious if not atheist. I will examine this intellectual turn towards the veneration of reason, scepticism and secularism, which had profound effects on the way madness was understood and explained.

What this chapter underlines is that in the early modern age there were still no distinct boundaries between philosophy, natural philosophy (i.e. science) and medicine. Therefore, the theories and practices of both scientists and physicians were heavily influenced by the systematic reasoning of thinkers such as Descartes, Hobbes and Locke. These thinkers shaped the intellectual articulations of madness and contributed to the naturalization of mental disorders, especially after the Thirty Years' War when European elites were weary of religious strife,

58 From Antiquity to the Enlightenment

persecution of 'witches' and general social and cultural instability. The intellectual and socio-cultural transformation of Europe was simultaneously a transformation of madness.

Dawn of a new era

Despite all the confusion, discord and disintegration, early modern Europe experienced a cultural renewal that found expression in all forms of creative activity, including painting, poetry, architecture, music, science and political thinking. The so-called scientific revolution was inaugurated by the great astronomers (Copernicus, Kepler, Tycho Brahe and Galileo) and culminated in the mathematically ordered universe of Isaac Newton (1642–1727). Concurrently, physicians began to have a more sceptical attitude towards religious fanaticism. During and after the Thirty Years' War, witch-hunting was very common, but gradually physicians in western Europe and especially in England, the most liberal (or, least illiberal) country in Europe, started to question witchcraft. They noticed the connection between religiosity and madness, as both phenomena were characterized by speaking in tongues (*glossolalia*), convulsions, weeping, hallucinations and moaning. Thomas Willis (1621–75), an English pioneer of neurology, excluded the devil from the list of the possible causes of madness and explained possession as a lesion or defect of the nerves and the brain. Another English doctor, an eager advocate of Isaac Newton's scientific theories, interpreted the religious visions of Quakers as madness caused by 'stronger impulses of the warm-up brain'. Yet another saw possession and other afflictions putatively caused by demonic intervention as 'vulgar errors . . . the bugbears of children and women' (Porter 2002, 29–30). In these statements we can see the rise of a materialistic 'neuroparadigm' and the revival of the naturalistic medicine of antiquity.

The medical profession's naturalistic accounts of witchcraft and madness found a receptive audience in the learned elites of western Europe. From the mid-seventeenth century onwards, they ushered in a new social order based on a secular and independent judicial system, the natural rights of man (yes, women were first largely excluded from this emancipation process) and even democracy, or at least constitutional or parliamentary monarchy such as existed in England after the 'glorious revolution' of 1688. Parallel to this gradual 'enlightening' of western Europe, ideas of madness began to assume a more naturalistic form, albeit slowly. David Lederer has demonstrated how beliefs in demons as well as 'spiritual physick' practised especially by the Catholic clergy, persisted in western Europe until the eighteenth century. As late as 1756, a 14-year-old Bavarian girl accused of witchcraft was burned to death (Lederer 2006, 298).

Next, I will give an account of a seventeenth-century German painter who claimed to have made a fateful pact with the Prince of Darkness. The painter's story illustrates how the experiences of past peoples need to be seen in the context of their own belief systems and the prevailing world views.

A deal with the devil

When Europeans looked for the causes of madness in the early modern age, the usual suspects were still the devil and demons. In 1677, the German painter Christoph Haizmann (ca. 1650–1700) confessed to the prefect of Pottenbrunn that, several years previously, he had met the devil in the forest, disguised as a venerable old man and accompanied by a black dog. The devil persuaded him to sign a pact with him; the pact dictated that the devil would help Haizmann in his life, and as a reward the painter would give the devil power over his soul when nine years have passed. Hesitant at first, Haizmann finally agreed to sign a pact, first in ink, and then in blood: 'I Christoph Haizman assign myself to this Lord to be his own bodily son in the ninth year' (MacAlpine & Hunter 1956, 57). Now, said the terrified Haizmann to the prefect, nine years have passed and, next month, it will be time to give the devil his due.

Suffering from seizures, Haizmann begged to be sent to a shrine in Mariazell (in today's Austria) to be exorcised. In Mariazell, an exorcist performed rituals continually for three days and nights, ordering the devil to appear at the altar, return the pact and save Haizmann. Finally, at 12 o'clock midnight, Haizmann saw the devil, who was holding the written pact, written in blood, at the altar. Haizmann rushed to the devil and managed to tear the scrap of paper out of his hand. Immediately after this dramatic encounter, Haizmann's seizures stopped. He stayed at Mariazell to paint this dramatic incident, and then he moved to Vienna. The story did not end there, however, because seizures and possession returned after a month:

> Haizmann had several frightening visions of the Devil in Vienna, which he recorded in a diary. And at last, in early May 1678, he returned to Mariazell, asking once again for the rite of exorcism. On May 9, after much priestly invocation, the Devil gave up the [first] pact, the one written [in ink]. Thereafter, according to clerical accounts, Haizmann was fully free from demonic bondage. For the rest of his life he was tempted by the Devil to sign another pact, but he never again yielded. In 1700 Haizmann died peacefully.
> (Peterson 1982, 20)

The story we have is derived from Haizmann's diary, his two pacts, his nine paintings as well as eye-witness accounts, which were all preserved by the churchmen at Mariazell as proof of a successful exorcism and miracle. In the hands of modern psychomedical interpreters, such as Sigmund Freud, Haizmann's 'case' has been diagnosed as a 'neurosis of demoniacal possession' and as schizophrenia, both of which are questionable diagnoses when applied to an early modern era visionary artist. In his diary, written after his first exorcism, Haizmann gives a colourful description of his terrifying visions and unusual tactile sensations – for him, they were not hallucinations but very real and very disturbing encounters with the personal embodiment of evil. One winter day at his home in Vienna, for example,

60 From Antiquity to the Enlightenment

a 'feverish shivering' came over him. His sister asked him to sit by the fire, which he did. This is what happened next:

> I had hardly sat down when six evil spirits came and wanted to charge at me and pull me to pieces. I shouted out Jesus, Mary and Joseph! stand by me; so they drew back, but soon moved forward again. The struggle between us lasted for one whole hour. Then the priests came, and as soon as they had come, so they [evil spirits] vanished one after the other. Afterwards I got up from the floor.
>
> (MacAlpine & Hunter 1956, 81)

A few days later, after the midday meal,

> four evil spirits came and started to torture me terribly. Throughout the whole afternoon and the whole night until the next morning they went for me; one of them sat on my tongue, so I took my hand and tore out the evil spirit. During this time several people watched over me, who were also so horror-stricken that they became seriously ill and saw visions.
>
> (MacAlpine & Hunter 1956, 81)

To himself and his contemporaries, Haizmann was not mad but plagued by the devil.

Haizmann's experiences were very similar to the legend of Faust, a scholar who sold his soul to the devil for power and knowledge. In a written form, the Faust legend has its beginnings in a book called *Historia von D. Johann Fausten*. This cheap 'chapbook' of stories concerning the life of Johann Georg Faust was written by an anonymous German author and published in 1587 in Frankfurt. Apparently, plays and puppet theatre loosely based on the Faust legend were popular in sixteenth-century Germany, where Faust and Mephistopheles (demon in German folklore) were commonly portrayed in a coarse, comic light. Scholars have speculated whether the story was influenced by a real-life figure of Dr Johann Faust (1480–1540), a German maverick scholar who appeared to have many roles during his life: he was a magician, alchemist, astrologer and physician. The Catholic Church denounced him as a blasphemer and he was often accused of being a fraudster. No wonder there were numerous tales circulating in Germany about the real Dr Johann Faust, a 'smooth operator' if ever there was one. Quite fittingly, he is said to have died in an explosion while making alchemical experiments (Baron 1978).

As an English translation (*The Historie of the Damnable Life, and Deserved Death of Doctor Iohn Faustus*, 1592), the Faust book became a main source for Christopher Marlowe's famous play *The Tragical History of Doctor Faust*, which was published in 1604. The legend obviously struck a chord in Europe, for now there are hundreds of versions of Faust or *Faustus*, ranging from operas, musicals and paintings to films, novels and plays, the most famous of them being Johann Wolfgang von

Goethe's tragic play *Faust* (1806, 1831), the German movie director F.W. Murnau's *Faust* (1926) and the German writer Thomas Mann's novel *Dr Faustus* (1947). It is a distinct possibility that the Faust legend stimulated the imagination of Christoph Haizmann and many other 'crazy' Europeans who, over the past 400 years, have believed they have struck a deal with the devil. And as fans of blues music know very well, the popularity of this legend is not confined to Europe: the American blues singer and musician Robert Johnson's (1911–38) short life and magical music have given rise to the Faustian myth that in order to become a great musician he sold his soul to the devil, who appeared in the form of a large black man at a crossroads in Mississippi. Johnson achieved his goal (although he remained unknown during his lifetime), but whether or not the devil did the same cannot be verified (Wald 2004).

Anatomy of melancholy

Together with the Netherlands, England was at the forefront of social and political development in early modern Europe. This did not mean that the English abandoned traditional conceptions of health and illness (see MacDonald 2008); rather, traditional assumptions and practices persisted among the common people, whereas the learned men and members of the growing middle class in urban centres became more and more disdainful of folk healing, traditional wisdom and what they regarded as religious fanaticism. The most well-known treatise dealing with madness in this period is the Oxford don Robert Burton's (1577–1640) *magnum opus Anatomy of Melancholy* (1621), a work on which Burton spent most of the last 20 or 30 years of his life. In its more than 1,000 pages, the author overwhelms the reader with the parade of all possible forms, colours and scents of melancholy. In Burton's time, melancholy had become a fashionable illness in Europe. Its popularity was boosted by the widely used Galenic humoral doctrines and the common assumption that a large number of European princes had a melancholic temperament. Renaissance artists and savants typically believed that creativity was linked with melancholic madness (Midelfort 1999, 23).

There were many European authors who wrote about melancholy, but it was Burton who became the most famous anatomist of melancholy. His book was an instant 'best-seller', and for the later scholars it remains a valuable document of the early seventeenth-century world view and ideas of self. The book is much more than a treatise on melancholy; it is a plunge into the world of an erudite man in early modern Europe. This world was populated by demons *and* natural philosophers (i.e. scientists), superstition *and* reason, magic *and* naturalism. *Anatomy of Melancholy* conveys the picture of an obsessive 'melancholy mania', for Burton does not leave a stone unturned in his relentless search for causes and symptoms of melancholy and in his prescriptions for treatment. It was as if Burton had decided to outsmart melancholy by compiling all possible knowledge and assumptions of this formidable plight: 'I write of melancholy, by being busy to avoid melancholy' (Burton 2001, 20). Far from being a clinical researcher in today's sense of the word, he was a veritable bookworm whose 'data' did not consist of patient records or clinical interviews, but of learned treatises that filled his desk in Oxford.

Anatomy of Melancholy is a bridge between medieval and modern thought, a blend of scholasticism, humoral doctrines and deductive reasoning, which proceeds from one or more general statements (premises) to reach a logically certain conclusion. When Burton describes a melancholy caused by witches and wizards, he is sceptical of 'our religious madness' and 'absurd and religious traditions and ceremonies'. He differentiates melancholy from madness, which is 'a vehement dotage, or raving without a fever, far more violent than melancholy, full of anger and clamour, horrible looks, actions, gestures, troubling the patients with far greater vehemency both of body and mind' (Burton 2001, 54, Part I, 140). Melancholy is agony and pain, but it is not madness. Those 'most subject to melancholy' include:

> [s]uch as have the Moon, Saturn, Mercury misaffected in their genitures; such as live in over-cold or over-hot climes; such as are born of melancholy parents; as offend in those six non-natural things [i.e., things not innate: air, diet, sleep and waking, motion and rest, excretions and retentions, and passions of the mind], are black, or of a high sanguine complexion, that have little heads, that have a hot heart, moist brain, hot liver and cold stomach, have been long sick; such as are solitary by nature, great students, given to much contemplation, lead a life out of action.
>
> (Burton 2001, Part I, 172)

Men are melancholic more often than women, but melancholic women are 'far more violent, and grievously troubled'. Autumn is the most melancholy season of the year. As for the stages of life, melancholy is almost inseparable from old age, 'but this artificial malady is more frequent in such as are of a middle age' (Burton 2001, Part I, 172).

When Burton meticulously catalogues various causes of melancholy, we can see that he is a man of two worlds; one part of him lingers in medieval times, while another part lives in the modern age. For Burton, causes include supernatural agents, such as God and His angels, the devil and his ministers, witches and magicians, and fiery spirits. Of natural causes, he proposes 'primary and universal' causes and 'secondary and more particular' causes. The former category refers to heavens, planets and stars, while the latter includes poverty and want, bad education, loss of liberty, old age, parents (by propagation), bad diet, retention, bad air, immoderate exercise, solitariness, idleness and, in some cases, sleep. Regarding the more psychological causes, he describes, among other things, 'passions and perturbations of the mind', force of imagination, sorrow, fear, shame and disgrace as well as superfluous industry, such as that of an alchemist who 'spends his fortune to find out the philosopher's stone'. In short, almost anything from starry skies to seven deadly sins (wrath, greed, sloth, pride, lust, envy and gluttony) can make

From devil's temptation to wrong thinking **63**

a person melancholic, at least when he (and, sometimes, she) has a melancholic temperament to start with.

Burton is especially interested in love melancholy and religious melancholy. He sees the latter form of melancholy as a particularly serious condition that can lead the afflicted to the throes of death and damnation. The whole of humanity is stained by original sin, and melancholy is a visible manifestation of mortality and the wretchedness of the human condition. This is how Burton poetizes melancholy in the 'author's abstract':

> I'll change my state with any wretch,
> Thou canst from gaol or dunghill fetch;
> My pain's past cure, another hell, I may not in this torment dwell!
> Now desperate I hate my life, Lend me a halter or a knife;
> All my griefs to this are jolly, Naught so damn'd as melancholy.
>
> (Burton 2001, 13)

'Naught so damn'd as melancholy.' Burton was still living in a world where original sin, fall from grace and diabolic possession were very real and passionately felt fears and threats. Weak and sinful people could not easily resist the devil's temptations, the most diabolic of which was religious melancholy. At the end of his exhaustive and bewildering book, Burton exhorts the reader to 'observe this short precept', the ultimate prevention and cure for melancholy: 'Be not solitary, be not idle' (Burton 2001, Part III, 432). For Burton, the devil finds work for idle hands, and a solitary person is vulnerable to his allure. The idea that melancholics should not be left inactive and brooding was derived from Greek medicine, which also proscribed sexual intercourse to melancholic victims of passionate love (that is, intercourse with someone other than the beloved).

Melancholics were doomed to mental pain, but they did not suffer from the insanity of the lunatic or the frenzy of the maniac. In melancholy, madness in fact verged on genius, just as, in art, genius was seen to approach madness. The idea of the mad poet was invented by the ancient Greek tragedians, and Renaissance humanists revived it almost 2,000 years later by envisioning a tragedy in which a poet, inspired by divine insight or transcendental fire, goes off the rails and loses his mind. In *Symposium*, Plato described the poet as a man driven by divine breath or fury, and in England during the Renaissance this idea was adopted by Shakespeare, for whom, in *A Midnight Summer's Dream* (1590), 'the lunatic, the lover and the poet, are of imagination all compact' (Shakespeare 1966, Act 5, Scene 1, lines 7–8). To call a poet a madman was not an insult but a compliment. The question of the connection between madness and genius was revived again by the early nineteenth-century Romantic thinkers, and since then the images of the mad genius and the ingenious madman have been part and parcel of the western cultural landscape (think of Lord Byron, Edgar Allan Poe, Nietzsche, van Gogh, Fritz Lang's *Dr Mabuse* movies and, more recently, mathematician John Nash and musician Brian Wilson).

64 From Antiquity to the Enlightenment

Fragile glass people

The history of melancholy includes a peculiar delusion that a person is made of glass, or some part of the person is made of glass (Speak 1990). These 'glass people' thought they were fragile, and they were afraid that they would break. They usually did not like to expose themselves to the sun. Some of them believed they were oil lamps, chamber pots or some other object made of glass, while others were imprisoned in a glass bottle. One of the first cases of glass delusion was Charles VI (1368–1422), king of France, who became insane in his mid-twenties. In order to protect himself from being touched during his psychotic episodes, he wore reinforced clothing. He was first called Beloved, and then Mad (*Le Fol*) (Famiglietti 1986).

Glass delusion was more common among noblemen, savants and lovers, and for this reason it has been associated with a more well-known affliction called 'scholar's melancholy'. 'Glass people' may have read about this delusion in the older medical treatises or in the contemporary, still rather scant literary descriptions of this affliction. The author of *Don Quixote* (1605, second book 1615), Miguel de Cervantes, describes in his short story 'The Glass Graduate' (El licenciado Vidriera, 1613) a man who goes mad, thinking that he is made of glass. He is terrified of physical contact, eats only fruit served in a chamber pot and drinks out of his hands. In the mid-sixteenth century, the Dutch physician Levinus Lemnius (1505–68) had a patient who refused to sit down, because he was afraid that his glass bottom would break. So he had to stay in an upright position when defecating. There are also depictions of glass hearts, glass chests, broken glass heads as well as bones and hands made of glass. Many glass people appeared to believe that they were chamber pots or piss-pots. This preoccupation with urine may have derived from the classic Hippocratic humoral theory, which associated the dark colour of urine with melancholy. In those days (the sixteenth and seventeenth centuries), so-called 'piss-pot prophets' appeared on the medical scene; they were physicians and quacks who specialized in treating syphilis and urethritis. Such association between melancholy and urine can also be seen in Burton's *Anatomy of Melancholy*, where he makes a few short references to glass delusion (Burton 2001, Part I, 403, 410, 421). A little later, the philosopher Thomas Hobbes referred to the same delusion when he discussed various forms of madness in his *Elements of Law, Natural and Politic* (1650):

> There [are] other examples of madness, and the degrees thereof, proceeding from too much vain fear and dejection: as in those melancholy men that have imagined themselves brittle as glass, or have had some other like imagination; and degrees hereof are all those exorbitant and causeless fears, which we commonly observe in melancholy persons.
>
> (Hobbes 2013, Part I, 52–3)

In glass delusions and similar obsessions we can see how contemporary Europeans were preoccupied with the nature of body and soul. Moreover, their assumptions

From devil's temptation to wrong thinking **65**

were shaped by the doctrine that health and longevity required that 'vital life force' had to be contained in a fragile and transparent vessel. At the same time, sinfulness was occasionally associated with a broken vessel while glass was associated with purity and chastity. Glass people often seemed to believe in the vulnerability of their selves, which was symbolized by fragile glass. Glass delusion is an example of how beliefs, values and customs governed the ways in which one's own mental and physical states were experienced and how they were explained. After the early modern age, glass delusion more or less disappeared, although there are a few records of odd cases in the last century or two. In recent decades, the two most famous people who have exhibited symptoms of glass delusion are legendary pianists Vladimir Horowitz and Glenn Gould, both of whom were afraid that their fragile fingers would be damaged. Horowitz even felt as if he was transforming into glass, and Gould would go nowhere without his gloves – even a light pat on the shoulder horrified him, because it caused pain and numbness in different parts of his body (Johannisson 2012, 30).

Age of Reason, sort of

Robert Burton, the author of *Anatomy of Melancholy*, died in 1640, in the middle of a restless and violent century. The Thirty Years' War ravaged the Continent, and in England there was a constant state of tension between the king, the nobility and the bourgeoisie, the new, middle-class segment of society which was becoming politically and economically more powerful as England was changing from an agricultural to a commercial society. The great majority of people lived in poverty and deprivation, without political rights, even in the most developed parts of Europe. Serfdom was still in practice in Russia, Scotland and in some parts of the Habsburg Empire, and elite groups of society did not care much about the well-being of ordinary people; rather, they were wary of any signs of rebellious spirit among commoners. At the same time, European colonies and footholds in America, Africa and Asia brought fortunes to chartered companies (such as the British East India Company and the French Company of One Hundred Associates), merchants, bankers, the developing administration and, of course, the nobility. All these actors were also enriched by the African slave trade. It is not too much of an exaggeration to say that European affluence was created at the expense of slaves, serfs and poor peasants. Simultaneously, Europe was tormented by religious fanaticism, witch-hunts and social unrest.

Gradually, a new Europe began to emerge out of this chaos. After the mid-1650s, the modern idea of citizenship took shape, implying that people were no longer considered to be mere subjects of the sovereign. When western Europeans became citizens, they began to possess political rights, such as the right to life, property and equal protection under the law. The new, post-Thirty Years' War Europe was also slowly becoming more secular, more tolerant and less ferocious than the old Europe. Western European elites and especially the (still small) educated class were tired of religious conflicts, superstition, fanaticism and senseless

66 From Antiquity to the Enlightenment

persecutions of witches, Jews and other religious minorities. To this rather rosy historical picture of increasing enlightenment we need to add some darker colours, because religious intolerance did not disappear until the mid-eighteenth century or later. The Catholic Church continued its assaults on heretics, but the Protestants were hardly more tolerant towards other denominations. Well into the nineteenth century, the Ottoman Empire, centred in today's Turkey, had a more tolerant policy towards religious minorities than Christian Europe, where religious freedom diminished in the seventeenth century. All through the era of the Enlightenment (from the late seventeenth to the late eighteenth century) religious intolerance had a damaging impact on European societies, albeit to a lesser extent in the Netherlands, France and England (Kaplan 2007). In Germany, the whole of the seventeenth century was a golden age of witch-hunts, diabolic possessions and religious strife. In Scotland, a 19-year-old medical student was accused of blasphemy and executed by hanging in 1697. In Sweden, the last victim of witch-hunting was burned to death in 1704. Thirty years later (1734), a new law in Sweden decreed that witchcraft was to be punished by the death penalty, and in the middle of the century some Swedish women were convicted of witchcraft. Their conviction was, however, cancelled when some enlightened opponents of witch-hunts intervened on behalf of the condemned women. The law became less draconian in 1779 when it was amended. This happened in the heyday of the Enlightenment.

I am not keen on debunking the Enlightenment. There is no doubt whatsoever that the lives of ordinary citizens were improved politically, socially and economically during the eighteenth century. The bourgeois class especially became an increasingly powerful political group, but budding industrialization and growing commerce benefited the common people as well. European societies became less violent, economies more dynamic, people more healthy and robust. Intellectually, the era from the mid-seventeenth century to the French Revolution of 1789 was innovative and exciting, to say the least. In France, René Descartes (1596–1650) was developing a new kind of rational and mostly secular philosophy, and the one-man think tank Gottfried Wilhelm Leibniz (1646–1716) was doing much the same a few decades later in German lands. One of the most radical thinkers of the Enlightenment was the Dutch Jewish philosopher Baruch Spinoza (1632–77), whose great and dangerous innovation was to reject Cartesian dualism and suggest that reality was of one substance, which conflated body and mind into one, reduced God and nature to the same thing and jettisoned tradition and spiritualism by invoking reason as the sole guide. Spinoza was radical in his argument that faith and reason are in irreconcilable opposition to each other, and that any dualistic and theistic attempts to solve the question by differentiating between body and soul, matter and spirit, are intellectually unsatisfactory (Israel 2006, 39–40). Compared to Spinoza and his followers, a much more moderate, and much more influential, philosopher was the Englishman John Locke (1632–1704), who developed philosophical arguments to justify the natural rights of man, the 'sacred and inviolable right to private property' and market economic relationships.

The Enlightenment philosophy was certainly political, but it was also anti-clerical, even anti-religious, at least that was the case with the radical enlightenment of 'spinozists' and the French encyclopaedists, such as Denis Diderot and Baron d'Holbach. It was during the Enlightenment that the influence of the superlunar sphere started to decrease: angels and demons no longer intervened in the lives of (educated) people, and in the deistic hands of moderate Enlightenment thinkers God became the universal watchmaker, intelligent designer who had retreated from the world after the Creation and did not intervene in the affairs of mortals. Isaac Newton opened a new chapter in the annals of science with his mathematical language and mechanistic physics, and the founding of scientific societies, such as the Royal Society in London in 1660, signified an institutional strengthening of scientific culture in western Europe. In this sense, the Enlightenment was a true light-bringer – a rational world view, the natural rights of Man, the emergence of political citizenship, tolerance, secularism, materialism and equality (to some degree) were at one and the same time magnificent goals, values and accomplishments that fundamentally changed Europe for good. As can be imagined, the Enlightenment also changed the perception of madness.

Madness on the threshold of the modern age

The modern conception of madness as a mental illness was born in the seventeenth century, more on a philosophical than a medical basis. Cartesian dualism, which gained popularity among educated elites in Europe, divided humans into bodily (material) and mental (spiritual) parts so that the (self-conscious) soul is free, whereas the body is like a machine that follows the laws of mechanics. This doctrine meant, among other things, that animals, which are soulless, are no different from machines. Indeed, the material world as a whole is mechanical, like a huge clockwork. In the Cartesian rationalist logic, movements of the material world can be explained by mathematical calculations and laws. Descartes also argued that even though the soul is non-material, it has a physiological matrix in the pineal gland located in the centre of the brain. To locate the soul in a tiny organ in the brain seemed plausible in Descartes' time, because the pineal gland is the only unpaired organ in the brain – just like the soul, it is one and indivisible. Descartes adhered to an outdated (even in his own time) view that the pineal gland is the seat of animal spirits, brought to it by small arteries surrounding it. These spirits supposedly had a subtle influence on the pineal gland (matter), or, alternatively, they (the soul or the mind) were influenced by the pineal gland, which resulted, for example, in perception and bodily movements. The soul is thus joined to the whole body. But as Galen had already discovered, the pineal gland is surrounded by veins rather than arteries. Moreover, Descartes believed that animal spirits inflate the ventricles just as the sails of a ship are inflated by the wind. Yet a full century earlier an Italian anatomist, Niccolò Massa, had discovered that the ventricles are not filled with some air-like or vaporous spirit but with fluid or liquid. More generally, the Cartesian dualistic theory of the self could not satisfactorily

68 From Antiquity to the Enlightenment

explain interaction between mind and body, or illustrate mental functioning and its causes (on Descartes' dualism, see Baker & Morris 2002).

However, Cartesian philosophy challenged the prevailing spiritualist conceptions of madness by arguing that humans are essentially rational beings. If this was the case, what, then, could explain madness, which by definition meant a condition in which a person is *devoid* of reason? Could madness be caused by anything else but physiology, that is, body or *soma*? Is madness caused by delicate defects or lesions in the brain? These were difficult and disturbing questions, not only to the educated elites but also to the Church, because Cartesian philosophy and science removed in one fell swoop gods, demons and possession from explanations of madness. Cartesianism also provided an important foundation for the rationalist view that madness is a physical and somatic illness, or at least that the *cause* of madness is physical. For the first time since Greek and Roman medicine of late antiquity, madness was again naturalized. Still, in medical and especially religious practices, beliefs about diabolic possession and the healing effects of exorcism continued in Europe long after the era of the Enlightenment. In some Catholic countries, possession is considered a real phenomenon even today, and exorcism has not been totally discredited. The most famous recent case is that of a Catholic West-German woman, Anneliese Michel, a young student who had a strict religious upbringing. Anneliese began to see her epileptic seizures, depression and psychotic symptoms as signs of possession, and her parents concurred in her interpretation. Hesitating at first, the local bishop finally gave permission to two priests to perform exorcist rites to cast out demons plaguing her in 1975. About ten months after the first rite of exorcism, Anneliese died as a result of emaciation. Upon her death she weighed only 30 kilograms (66 pounds). The ensuing court case received wide media attention, and a public discussion of the Catholic tradition of exorcism and the legitimation of its medical use flared up in German-speaking Europe (Goodman 1981; Schott & Tölle 2006, 32).

Descartes made the controversial assumption that the human mind contained innate ideas, the purpose of which was to organize empirical information as a sort of pre-programmed mental machine or operating system. This theory was opposed by later British empiricists, who refuted the theory of innate ideas. Radical materialists, such as Diderot, d'Holbach (Paul-Henry Thiry) and Julien Offray La Mettrie, in turn, rejected Descartes' contention about the immortality of the soul (which he may have proclaimed in order to avoid being branded an atheist) as well his dualism. These French materialists were also philosophical monists who argued that matter is the substance of everything, and that the task of (natural) philosophers is to explicate the properties and laws of matter. A famous early modern materialist was the English political philosopher Thomas Hobbes (1588–1679), who did not have any rosy illusions about human nature: to Hobbes, humans are driven by self-interest and self-preservation, and in the state of nature they are engaging in a continuous 'war of all against all' (*bellum omnium contra omne*). In his theoretical thought-experiment, Hobbes described a pre-social condition of humanity, and his point was that humans are prepared to renounce their rights in order to live under protection and security provided by the sovereign. Hobbes' main work *Leviathan* (1651) deals with this sort of social contract between the people and the sovereign, and with the ensuing emergence of a (authoritarian) political community. The purpose of the Hobbesian commonwealth is the promotion and maintenance of peace and secular order, not the furthering of political rights of citizens or, even less, the religious power of the Church – to Hobbes, the civil power rules over the religious authorities.

Hobbes became a famous philosopher in England maimed by the Civil War (1642–51). His explicit materialism and implicit atheism shaped the emerging conception of human nature, according to which all knowledge is derived from sensual perceptions, and human functioning follows the causal laws of matter in motion. The then prevailing views on the spiritual world, demons and witches were nothing but mental illusions to Hobbes. As a materialist, he saw madness as a 'principal defect of the mind', which results from extraordinarily strong and vehement passions:

> Dejection, subjects a man to causeless fears; which is a madness commonly called MELANCHOLY, apparent also in divers manners; as in haunting of solitudes, and graves; in superstitious behaviour; and in fearing some one, some particular thing. In sum, all passions that produce strange and unusual behaviour, are called by the general name of madness. But of the several kinds of madness, he that would take the pains, might enrol a legion. And if the excesses be madness, there is no doubt but the passions themselves, when they tend to evil, are degrees of the same.
>
> (Hobbes 2008, 49 (I, 8, 20))

Hobbes pointed out that although there were different kinds of madness, such as spiritual madness, learned madness and 'rage and madness of love', the common features in all of them were obsessiveness and extremity. Hobbes and other materialist thinkers discarded and ridiculed medieval spiritualist beliefs about madness. Religious madness was transformed into a naturalistic mental condition and medical affliction devoid of any divine dimension. The learned elites of western Europe began to have an increasingly suspicious and condescending attitude towards those who tried to prove the existence of the superlunar world populated by God, angels, demons and other supernatural beings. Holy fools turned into plain fools and insane persons who were in need of confinement and care rather than a credulous audience taking their mad visions and preaching seriously. Little by little, people tormented by spiritual crisis were taken to the doctor, and the clergy started to lose their prestige in the management of madness. In short, the 'Hobbesian' turn in the history of madness meant that madness became a mental illness, a medical condition to be explained and treated materialistically and naturalistically.

'To think wrongly is madness': John Locke and madness as fallacy

Before we proceed to the rise of 'modern' mental illnesses, let us continue our philosophical journey with a short discussion of Hobbes' compatriot John Locke, called the 'father of classical liberalism'. Locke had a degree in medicine and he became a personal physician to Lord Anthony Ashley Cooper, better known as the 1st Earl of Shaftesbury (whose grandson, the 3rd Earl of Shaftesbury, became a famous moral philosopher who opposed Hobbes' 'egoistic' doctrines). Locke's political philosophy has had a tremendous influence on western political thought and epistemology (the branch of philosophy concerned with the nature and scope of knowledge). In his *Essay Concerning Human Understanding* (1690), Locke rejected Cartesian innate ideas and introduced the basic argument of empiricist epistemology, according to which the origin of all thoughts is in sense perception. He famously argued that the human mind is at birth a blank slate (*tabula rasa*), without any mental inborn predispositions, principles or content. This means that what is called the 'self' is a product of learning and other modes of sense experiences. To Locke, humans are the sum total of their experiences. Therefore, upbringing and education are of the utmost importance in the shaping of the mind and the development of the self. In the Lockean empiricist theory, knowledge is the result of the association of ideas, and ideas originate in sense perception. Correspondingly, false knowledge is the result of the wrong association of ideas. The popularity of this associationist view had significant consequences for the explanations of madness in the Anglo-American world: according to the Lockeans, madness was a form of erroneous association of ideas, which resulted in confused thinking. Locke compared madness and 'idiotism' as follows:

> Madmen [. . .] seem to suffer by the other extreme [than idiots]. For they do not appear to me to have lost the faculty of reasoning, but having joined together some ideas very wrongly, they mistake them for truths; and they err as men do that argue right from wrong principles. For, by the violence of their imaginations, having taken their fancies for realities, they make right deductions from them. Thus you shall find a distracted man fancying himself a king, with a right inference require suitable attendance, respect, and obedience: others who have thought themselves made of glass, have used the caution necessary to preserve such brittle bodies [. . .] In short, herein seems to lie the difference between idiots and madmen: that madmen put wrong ideas together, and so make wrong propositions, but argue and reason right from them; but idiots make very few or no propositions, and reason scarce at all.
>
> (Locke 1979, Book II, Ch. XI, Sec. 13)

Locke's empiristic epistemology, like his political philosophy, had a profound effect on the European Enlightenment. Likewise, his idea of madness as 'false consciousness' influenced the ways in which mental illness was understood, especially in Britain and North America. The Lockean take on mental illness was both rationalistic and optimistic: if mental illness denotes a wrong kind of thinking, the afflicted can be cured by teaching them to think *right*. Thus it is possible to change false consciousness into a right kind of consciousness.

Yet Lockean associationism has a more sinister dimension: it could be used to renounce all sorts of wrong thinking ('to think wrongly is madness'). Thus if madness is fallacy, then fallacy is madness (Porter 2006, 241). In the following decades and centuries, Locke provided ammunition for those who wanted to attack 'wrong' ideas and beliefs, such as socialism, feminism or sexual libertinism. This Lockean medicalization of 'false consciousness' became more pronounced in the 'psychopolitical' debates during the latter half of the nineteenth century, when the political and social ideas of opponents were discredited by labelling them pathological symptoms of madness. The political reasoning of many British suffragettes, for example, was denounced as 'hysterical' – the wrong ideas of suffragettes were evidence of their unsound mind. Winston Churchill, for example, referred to suffragette activists of the early twentieth century as 'a band of silly, neurotic, hysterical women' (Leneman 1995, 87).

In the early modern age, madness was discussed by the philosophers, but it was also treated or managed in a handful of hospitals across Europe. I will discuss the history of mental asylums in the later chapters; suffice it to say here that, in England, the first institution for the confinement of the mad was the Bethlem hospital in London. Founded in the mid-thirteenth century, Bethlem became an asylum exclusively for the mad in 1377. Operating continuously for over 600 years, today it is Europe's oldest extant psychiatric hospital. It has also given birth to the popular designation 'bedlam', which has been synonymous with madness since the seventeenth century. If someone was 'stark Bedlam mad', it was a sure sign that the person was more than slightly deranged (on Bethlem and other mental hospitals of the medieval and early modern era, see Chapter 5).

Modern illnesses for modern people

During the Age of the Enlightenment, the European conception of human nature changed as the political institution called the 'individual' was born. As western Europeans became individual citizens with inalienable rights and relative autonomy, their language became more psychological and secular (Taylor 1989, 143–76). The age-old, cultural archetype of the immovable 'great chain of being' faded out as the more dynamic, progressive conception of society and the self became prevalent among the educated class, which was simultaneously becoming a larger and more hetereogeneous group. The Enlightenment also gave science and universities a much more prominent place in society. Inevitably, the 'scientification' of intellectual and material culture changed medical science as well. The long-revered tradition of Galenic and Hippocratic medicine gave way to a more empirically oriented medicine that aimed to replace text-based medical wisdom

72 From Antiquity to the Enlightenment

with the experimental methods of anatomy and physiology. Nature and human nature became objects of a new kind of laboratory science based on systematic observation.

Together with the breakthrough (of sorts) of the rational and secular conception of human nature, madness became a more humane and 'flat' phenomenon, at least compared to the colourful ancient and medieval images of divine madness and holy fools. To simplify, among the enlightened physicians and scholars of the eighteenth century, madness became mental illness, and mental illness began to be seen as erroneous thinking, irrationality or disturbance in the mental machinery. The new materialistic understanding of mental illness did not, however, provide a reliable new key for solving its riddles or for curing it. Little by little, rites of exorcism, prayers, flogging, cupping and the prescription of various emetics and laxatives were no longer considered respectable methods of treatment, but attempts to restore sanity to the senseless mind were not very promising.

Even diagnostic classification was still very rudimentary in the eighteenth century, and in colloquial language the mentally ill continued to be called madmen, fools, deranged, maniacs and lunatics (the full moon was associated with madness). William Battie, the chief physician at St Luke's Hospital for Lunatics in London, noted in his *A Treatise on Madness* (1758) that there are several names given to madness, including 'Lunacy, Spleen, Melancholy [and] Hurry of the Spirits' (Battie 1758, 1). As physicians did not yet have a hegemonic position in the management of madness, a medical framework for explaining, naming and treating mental illness existed side by side with the religious and popular frameworks that centred on the expertise and 'social capital' of the clergy, folk healers and wise men and women, especially in the countryside.

* * *

To a large extent, changing moral, political and cultural values and assumptions have determined how madness has been seen at different times in the history of Europe. It was only during the nineteenth century that the medical idea of mental illness became firmly established in western Europe and Scandinavia, as we shall see in the following chapters. So far, the pace has been rather fast – we have covered more than 2,000 years in three chapters. Henceforth, the pace slows down and the focus becomes sharper. In the chapters that follow we will concentrate on the history of madness since the end of the eighteenth century.

Bibliography

Baker, G. and Morris, K. (2002) *Descartes' Dualism*, London: Routledge.
Baron, F. (1978) *Dr. Faustus: From History to Legend*, Munich: Fink.
Battie, W. (1758) *A Treatise on Madness*, London: J. Whiston & B. White.
Burton, R. (2001) *The Anatomy of Melancholy*, 1st edn 1621, New York: New York Review of Books.
Cervantes, Miguel de (1998) 'The glass graduate', orig. Spanish edn 1613, in *Exemplary Stories*, Oxford: Oxford University Press.

Famiglietti, R.C. (1986) *Royal Intrigue: Crisis at the Court of Charles VI, 1392–1420*, New York: AMS Press.

Goodman, F.D. (1981) *The Exorcism of Anneliese Michel*, Eugene, OR: Resource Publications.

Hobbes, T. (2008) *Leviathan*, 1st edn 1651, Oxford: Oxford University Press.

Hobbes, T. (2013) *Elements of Law, Natural and Political*, 1st edn 1650, ed. F. Tönnies, Abingdon: Routledge.

Israel, J. (2006) *Enlightenment Contested*, Oxford: Oxford University Press.

Johannisson, K. (2012) *Melankolian huoneet*, trans. U. Lempinen, orig. Swedish edn 2009, Jyväskylä, Finland: Atena.

Kaplan, B.J. (2007) *Divided by Faith: Religious Conflict and the Practice of Toleration in Early Modern Europe*, Cambridge, MA: Belknap Press.

Lederer, D. (2006) *Madness, Religion and the State in Early Modern Europe*, Cambridge: Cambridge University Press.

Leneman, L. (1995) *A Guid Cause: The Women's Suffrage Movement in Scotland*, Edinburgh: Mercat Press.

Locke, J. (1979) *An Essay Concerning Human Understanding*, ed. P.H. Nidditch, 1st edn 1690, Oxford: Oxford University Press.

MacAlpine, I. and Hunter, R. (1956) *Schizophrenia, 1677: A Psychiatric Study of an Illustrated Autobiographical Record of Demoniacal Possession*, London: W. Dawson.

MacDonald, M. (2008) *Mystical Bedlam: Madness, Anxiety and Healing in Seventeenth-century England*, 1st edn 1981, Cambridge: Cambridge University Press.

Midelfort, E. (1999) *A History of Madness in Sixteenth-century Germany*, Stanford, CA: Stanford University Press.

Peterson, D. (ed.) (1982) *A Mad People's History of Madness*, Pittsburgh, PA: University of Pittsburgh Press.

Porter, R. (2002) *Madness. A Brief History*, Oxford: Oxford University Press.

Porter, R. (2006) *Madmen. A Social History of Madhouses, Mad-Doctors and Lunatics*, Stroud: Tempus.

Schott, H. and Tölle, R. (2006) *Geschichte der Psychiatrie*, Munich: C.H. Beck.

Shakespeare, W. (1966) *A Midsummer-Night's Dream*, in *Complete Works*, ed. W.J. Craig, London: Oxford University Press.

Speak, G. (1990) 'An odd kind of melancholy: reflections on the glass delusion in Europe (1440–1680)', *History of Psychiatry*, 1: 191–206.

Taylor, C. (1989) *Sources of the Self*, Cambridge: Cambridge University Press.

Wald, E. (2004) *Escaping the Delta: Robert Johnson and the Invention of the Blues*, New York: Amistad.

PART II

The great transformation: medicalization of madness in the long nineteenth century

5

THE AGE OF THE ASYLUM

The insane asylum is always a prison.
(Peter Kropotkin in 'Prisons and their Moral Influence on Prisoners', 1877)

This chapter will focus on the history of mental hospitals in the western world. It is a long and winding story encompassing the nineteenth and twentieth centuries, and we can only explore some of the main developments and give room to the experiences of mental patients who were incarcerated in asylums. 'Asylum' was the common term for mental hospitals in the nineteenth and early twentieth centuries, and at first it suggested a 'refuge from the maddening world' (Gamwell & Tomes 1995, 9). Later, when an institutional care was reduced to a custodial function, 'insane asylum' became a negatively conceived term, which prompted the medical authorities to introduce less stigmatizing terms, such as 'nerve sanatorium' or 'mental hospital'. As a prologue to the story of asylums I will introduce a controversial key idea that has shaped our understanding of the history of mental hospitals since the 1960s: 'the great confinement'.

Question of 'the great confinement'

In his classic work *History of Madness* (*Folie et Déraison. Histoire de la folie à l'âge classique*, 1961), the French historian and philosopher Michel Foucault (1926–84) claimed that the period from the mid-seventeenth century to 1800 was the era of 'the great confinement' (*le grand renfermement*). His influential thesis has found many supporters among the so-called 'critical' historians, including the German psychiatrist and scholar Klaus Dörner (Dörner 1981).

Stripped to its bare essentials, this is what Foucault's thought-provoking thesis says: when the state apparatus started to develop after the devastating Thirty Years' War (1618–48), first in France, then elsewhere in Europe, the deviant groups

78 The great transformation

began to be incarcerated in prisons, hospitals and mental asylums. And when leprosy ceased to be a European-wide epidemic, hospitals ('leprosaria') could be used for other purposes. Simultaneously, the attitude of western European elites towards madness began to change. In Foucault's view, in the early modern era madness was still engaged in a creative dialogue with reason, but at the onset of the great confinement madness began to be considered a sheer negation of reason; it changed into 'unreason' or irrationality that called for isolation, disciplining and taming. Until the seventeenth century, madness had its own dimension of freedom and truth, and it occupied its own socio-cultural and intellectual niche. This all changed with the great confinement, when madness was 'amputated' – madness became a sheer nuisance and a potential threat to the social order. According to Foucault, the authorities wanted to suppress the voice of unreason and exclude the mad from the sphere of reason and order. The Age of Reason reduced madness to silence (Foucault 2006, 44).

Throughout Europe, and especially in the most developed regions – the Netherlands, England, France and German-speaking Europe – hospitals, workhouses and penitentiaries began to be established. In these new types of penal societies, the insane, paupers, beggars, vagabonds and criminals were confined in 'modern' disciplinary institutions:

> The world of confinement was home to a strange parade. In the second half of the seventeenth century the venereal, the debauched, the dissolute, blasphemers, homosexuals, alchemists and libertines found themselves on the wrong side of the dividing line, and were thrown together as recluses in asylums destined, in a century or two, to become the exclusive preserve of madness. Suddenly a new social space was opened and defined. It was not exactly a place of poverty, although it was born out of great concern about indigence, nor was it exactly a place of illness, although the day would come when sickness would take it over. It was rather the result of a singular sensibility, unique to the classical age.
>
> (Foucault 2006, 101)

The main reason for this governmental persecution of suspected deviants was that these social groups were unwilling to work. Intrinsic to the emerging ideas of political community and citizenship was the supreme bourgeois virtue of social utility. If, for some reason or another, men and women did not work, they easily became suspect in the eyes of elite groups. 'Work-shy' citizens set a bad moral example for others, and for this reason they had to be controlled and adjusted to the demands of the increasingly work-oriented society (Foucault 2006, 69–72). The proper treatment for these worthless flotsam and jetsam was forced labour. The socio-political marginalization of people who were unwilling or unable to work meant the loss of their honour and human dignity. The insane became irrational animals, whose needs were extremely simple. They could manage very well without clothing and shelter and with a very meagre amount of food. Being animal-like, the insane could be chained, flogged and locked up behind bars in order to discipline them and tame their wild unreason. There was no longer any need to enter into a dialogue with madness. At the same time, the insane were an important reminder to the sane about proper standards of conduct and the bourgeois virtue of self-control and sound religiosity (Stevenson 1988, 31).

Historian Roy Porter has summarized Foucault's assessment of the great confinement and divided it into three related claims (Porter 2006, 19–22; see also Bowers 1998, 102–4). First, madness was silenced and annulled. Second, the insane were locked up in institutions on a large scale. Third, the rough confinement of the insane together with other marginal groups was motivated by the need to control social anarchy and disorder. These claims are all sweeping, provocative and suggestive, but to what extent are they historically accurate? Porter admits that, during the Age of the Enlightenment, deviant individuals – different, difficult and dangerous – were increasingly incarcerated while the Enlightenment philosophers encouraged people to think for themselves. The authorities' stance towards the insane was, to a large extent, as harsh as it was towards the lawbreakers. For example, the English Vagrancy Act of 1714 linked lunatics with vagrants, beggars and rogues, and it empowered the Justices of the Peace to confine the 'furiously mad, and dangerous' in houses of correction, workhouses and other 'secure places' where they kept company with a motley crew of troublemakers. The emerging state certainly had a repressive approach to social questions (Porter 2006, 19–20).

While acknowledging that Foucault's thesis is insightful, Porter admonishes it for portraying a distorted picture of madness in the 'classical age' (ca. 1650–1789). Most importantly, Foucault's sweeping claim about the scope of the confinement is not valid except in France, and even there the confinement was hardly 'great'. In the history of England during the seventeenth and eighteenth centuries, which Porter himself has studied, 'there was no coordinated drive by government, central or local, to sequester the mad poor' (Porter 2006, 20). During the whole of the eighteenth century, the number of confined lunatics was small. When official figures were compiled in the early nineteenth century, fewer than 5,000 people were detained in British madhouses or in houses of correction. A century later (1900), there were 3,000 inmates in one single asylum (Colney Hatch) alone. This means that, in Britain, as in France or Germany, the Age of the Asylum began in the nineteenth century. Corresponding figures of the number of mental patients all over Europe confirm the view that the great confinement only gained momentum in the nineteenth century. But to Foucault, the great confinement had already come to an end by 1800.

Second, Foucault's claim about work as a moral obligation is unsupported by developments in Britain. Eye-witness reports suggest that, until the early twentieth century, the British asylum life was characterized by *idleness* instead of industry and toil. Third, contrary to what Foucault contends, patients were *not* regarded as 'animals', and their treatment was not particularly cruel or degrading. As Porter points out, Foucault's claim that 'inmates were regarded as brutes and treated with exemplary cruelty [. . .] seems positively perverse, since that is precisely the image

80 The great transformation

of madness which leading Enlightenment writers on insanity were repudiating' (Porter 2006, 21). Certainly, there were examples of brutal treatment, but in general mental patients were treated more humanely during the Enlightenment than at any other time in the Christian era. Fourth, the great confinement was hardly driven by the elites to police the poor and downtrodden. Although the great majority of patients, as well as the whole population in western Europe, were from the lower orders, there were representatives of the bourgeoisie, gentry and nobility among the inmates. As a matter of fact, it was the affluent clientele that in Britain enabled the eighteenth-century entrepreneurial 'trade in lunacy' (Parry-Jones 1972). When the asylum system expanded in nineteenth-century Britain, most patients confined in public hospitals were ordinary people, but not exclusively so. By paying a little extra, patients could lead more comfortable lives in asylums. Their food was better and the equipment was of a better quality, the staff treated them in a more friendly manner and they might have had a private room.

If very little resembling Foucault's great confinement took place in Britain, in other European countries the confinement was, if anything, opposite to 'great'. The authorities across Europe had no intention of chaining 'unreason' between the mid-seventeenth and the beginning of the nineteenth century. It did not really happen even in Foucault's home country, France, where the number of incarcerated lunatics remained small; French hospitals mostly housed relatively few insane patients. In the Hôtel-Dieu in Paris, for example, there were fewer than two dozen mad patients at any one time throughout the eighteenth century. Instead of taking active measures to confine lunatics in the name of law and order, the public authorities in most European countries – Scandinavia, Spain, Ireland, Poland, Russia, etc. – did next to nothing to them. In Catholic Europe, the majority of confined patients were tended by religious orders and charities, and in the more clearly capitalist regions of north-west Europe (Britain, Germany, the Netherlands), private entrepreneurs ran small madhouses for profit. Nor does the Islamic hospital in general fit in well with Foucault's thesis; hospitals in Islamic regions were not intended for the incarceration of paupers and other disadvantaged people who were not ill. Also, the number confined was anything but great: even the largest institutions, such as the famous Mansūri Hospital in Cairo, 'probably contained only a few dozen insane patients at one time – a very small number in relation to the entire population of Cairo' (Dols 1992, 129). Furthermore, the idea that the insane were insensible to cold, pain and injury was not the cruel invention of Foucault's 'classical age'; it was proclaimed in canon law in the Middle Ages. In short, throughout Europe, the mental medicine of the Enlightenment era was in the main not to treat the mad brutally, and the authorities were not particularly keen on controlling the rabble on the basis of some overarching ideology.

Does this mean that the grand thesis of the great confinement should be rejected once and for all? Yes and no. 'Yes' because the thesis gives an inaccurate picture of the history of madness between 1650 and 1800 – there simply was no *great* confinement in Europe at that time. Moreover, Foucault's thesis may govern the historian's empirical observations and thereby advance a historically doubtful or even false understanding of the history of early modern madness. On the other hand, when one removes the wrong timing, over-generalizing universalism and highly exaggerated claims from Foucault's explanatory framework, something essential remains, namely *challenge*. Foucault's thought-provoking thesis challenges experts in 'madness studies' to find out whether it is valid in regard to their own research: 'Do I see in my source material ideas, practices and beliefs that give evidence for or against Foucault's arguments?' When the great confinement is seen to encompass the period from the early nineteenth to the mid-twentieth century, it does not seem inaccurate at all. And when Foucault's more provocative arguments regarding the 'dialogue with unreason', social control of madness and the importance of the bourgeois work ethic are specified and particularized in different national and regional contexts, they may suddenly turn out to be quite insightful. During the great confinement of the nineteenth and twentieth centuries, the insane, the feeble-minded, the demented as well as epileptics and alcoholics were incarcerated in large numbers throughout Europe and North America. At the same time, criminals were put in prisons and the disabled in institutions for the disabled, while young men were called up for military service.

What is also correct in Foucault's modified thesis is that the ability and willingness to work became the supreme civic virtue in many parts of Europe, including in Nordic countries. Increasingly, citizens were valuable to society to the extent they could earn a living, which meant that (occupational) health became an essential aspect of governmental policy. From this utilitarian perspective, the insane were often regarded as useless members of society – they were not dutiful taxpayers or workhorses who contributed to the total national wealth. What is also true, unfortunately, is that the attitude of the authorities and the medical community towards the mentally ill was sometimes contemptuous, as if the insane were inferior or even subhuman. The racial hygiene ideologies and practices of the early twentieth century in particular are fitting 'Foucauldian' examples of the modern control-political management of deviance (see Chapters 6 and 11).

Foucault was not silent about the later developments in the history of madness. He did not deviate from the critical path when he turned his attention to the emergence of the asylum system, which he described as a 'gigantic moral imprisonment' (Foucault 2006, 511). Following Foucault's verdict, critical historians of the 1960s and 1970s tended to view mental hospitals as institutes of human misery, anti-therapeutic black holes that sucked the patients inside and turned them into human wrecks. Asylums had soft cells, hard attendants and staggering patients whose identity was stolen and whose minds were confused by the merciless machinery of the 'system'. We have read and heard about abuses in the 'loony bin', 'bughouse', 'nuthouse', 'booby hatch' (etc.), including mental and physical violence, mechanical and biochemical restraints, poor diet, dirt, noise, negligence and an overall ambience of brutality and inhumanity. As the recent scholarship has demonstrated, to portray the asylum as some sort of snake pit is a gross over-statement, but in the public imagination asylums are still seen as colossal human warehouses, the dreadfulness of which stems from institutional insanity rather than from the mental derangement of patients.

82 The great transformation

Such a picture is not altogether truthful. In 1878, Anna Agnew was certified lunatic in Indiana and committed to an asylum. This followed repeated attempts to commit suicide, and an attempt to kill one of her children. When the asylum engulfed her, she experienced a strong sense of relief. Her madness was acknowledged. Her family was safe. As she later wrote, 'my unhappy condition of mind was understood, and I was treated accordingly'. In this case, she received humane treatment (King 2002; Sacks 2009). One instance does not prove the rule, but not all patients experienced confinement negatively. At least some, such as Anna, welcomed being institutionalized.

The prevailing negative view on mental asylums is one-sided and, at its worst, distorting. The fate of institutionalized patients might very well have been sad and bleak, but in recent decades historians have devised a multidimensional picture of asylums and asylum life. Within this picture, Anna Agnew is almost as good an example of the Therapeutic Machine called the asylum as is an anonymous chronic who languished years or even decades in the back wards of the mental institutions and unlearned all the social skills needed in the 'outside' world.

Establishment of mental hospitals

During the High and Late Middle Ages, hospitals in Europe were shelters, almshouses and asylums rather than institutions of medical treatment in the modern sense of the term. They provided food, bed and prayer for the sick, but also for the indigent, aged and pilgrims (Siraisi 1990, 39). When epidemics of leprosy ravaged late medieval Europe, hospitals were established for the confinement of the lepers (leprosy is an infectious disease that causes disfiguring skin sores and nerve damage in the arms and legs). These leper hospitals or leprosaria signalled the modest beginnings of what we now call a 'hospital'. Unlike the lepers, the mentally ill mostly lived in their own communities before the founding of asylums for the mad, and they were taken care of by their families. This had been the case also in classical antiquity, and Roman law had imposed severe penalties on offspring who neglected their mentally ill parents. The same held true in Islamic society, where the responsibility for the insane lay with the family. If families did not fulfil their obligations, or the insane did not have families, they might have been left to their own devices if they were harmless. In this case, they probably survived on the charity of their communities. But if they were agitated or violent, they might have been thrown into a dungeon, prison or worse. Sometimes the insane were taken to numerous shrines, temples and churches in the hope of a supernatural cure (see Chapter 2). The Bethlem hospital in London, established in the thirteenth century, specialized in the care of lunatics in 1377, and in the town of Uppsala in Sweden, lunatics were treated in a madhouse established by the Church in the early fourteenth century. In Valencia, Spain, a madhouse (Casa de Orates) was established in 1409 (Schott & Tölle 2006, 234). Monks, nuns and priests who were in charge of the well-being of the lunatics were not always interested in their physical or mental condition; rather, they may have focused on the 'fact' that the patients were possessed by the devil. Consequently, their 'treatment' of the mad could include whipping and other harsh methods. Rules and practices in these proto-hospitals revolved around diurnal rhythm, diet and various duties rather than any guiding principles of medicine.

All over Europe, the insane were taken to a hospital, church, monastery or shrine only after the family's or local community's resources, options and nerves were exhausted. The moral imperatives of kinship and Christian charity required family and community members to treat the insane humanely or at least not brutally. Raving lunatics were often chained or confined in their cells, but it is an open question whether this was done out of cruelty or rather because there was no other way to prevent the mad from hurting themselves or people around them. At the same time, there is slim evidence on the veneration of some madmen and -women as holy fools or mystical prophets uttering words of wisdom. The great majority of the mad and the feebleminded were neither venerated nor abused; lunatics usually lived and died among their family and community members (Midelfort 1999, 362).

Occasionally, Christian charity and patience were nowhere to be seen. In late seventeenth-century Sweden, for example, the king enforced canon law by putting parishes in charge of the insane. In practice, the village elders were responsible for taking care of the poor, the ill and the mad within their administrative territory. What happened was that, if families did not take care of their insane family members, they were moved from one house to another as if they were cattle. The idea behind this practice was that all households in the village and its surroundings should contribute to the care of the local insane. The lot of such indigent mad was truly pitiable. In Sweden, they were often kept in chains, and they suffered from chronic malnourishment, cold and neglect. Even the seriously ill insane or feebleminded were mercilessly moved from house to house. Sometimes they died en route to a new master (Sarvilinna 1938, 572–3).

Before the advent of moral treatment in the early nineteenth century, madhouses were not usually expected to cure their patients or clients. They functioned mostly as shelters that provided physical security, often coupled with religious instruction, not as institutes of medical treatment. For centuries, clergy had provided 'spiritual physick' to Christians, and they were only gradually replaced by professional mad-doctors, psychiatrists or alienists. Especially in Britain, there were all sorts of private entrepreneurs who sought profit as owners of madhouses, prisons and poorhouses. Common people also turned to folk healers, astrologers, charlatans, wise men and women as well as to village elders.

I will now turn to the early history of mental asylums in four western nations, France, Britain, the United States and Germany.

Managing madness in France during 'the great confinement'

In 1676, King Louis XIV – the Sun King – decreed that a *hôpital général* (general hospital) was to be established in every city of the kingdom. If we are to believe Foucault, this decree signified the true beginning of the 'great confinement', as

84 The great transformation

marginal groups of society began to be confined in these general hospitals (an *hôpital général* had already been set up by a royal decree in Paris in 1656). Despite its name, an *hôpital général* was not so much a hospital as a workhouse storing vagabonds, beggars, criminals, the elderly, the crippled, prostitutes and the indigent insane. As Foucault notes, this 'general hospital'

> bore no resemblance to any medical idea in either its purpose or functioning. It was rather an instrument of order, of the new bourgeois and monarchical order that was beginning to take shape in the France of that time. It was directly connected to the power of the king, who had placed it under the authority of the civil government.
>
> (Foucault 2006, 49)

In 1764, another institution for the confinement of the insane was created. The *dépots de mendicité* were workhouses intended for the detention of able-bodied beggars. This particular group could not be adequately dealt with by general hospitals, but soon these workhouses began to resemble general hospitals in that they 'catered' for other marginal groups as well. In particular, women with venereal diseases and lunatics abandoned by their families were confined in the workhouses. In the whole city of Paris there was only one public hospital, Hôtel-Dieu, for the curable insane. It was an age-old, ramshackle storehouse for fewer than 100 patients. By the end of the eighteenth century, the authorities had acknowledged that the mere confinement of lunatics might not be a satisfactory solution to the social problem of madness. In the optimistic spirit of the Enlightenment, the purely disciplinary approach favoured by the state was challenged by the therapeutic approach – maybe, after all, madness was curable, and the insane could re-enter society if they were treated in a 'real' hospital? On the eve of the revolution of 1789, a new health-political approach to insanity was created in France (Goldstein 1987, 41–2).

An official directive on the management of madness was published some years before the Revolution. Written in the spirit of enlightened absolutism, the Instruction was a concise, medico-political handbook for the administrators. Its two authors were members of the Royal Society of Medicine, and its purpose was to introduce uniformity and enlightened attitudes into an area of policy particularly relevant to the *dépots* or workhouses. The Instruction described the insane, together with children, as the weakest members of society. Both groups inspired pity, but they differed fundamentally in that whereas children aroused *hope* and the natural sympathies of people, the insane aroused *horror* which incited people 'to flee them'. For this reason, lunatics 'require especially the attention and the surveillance of the government'. The official policy towards them had two related goals:

> First, in order to 'prevent [lunatics] from troubling society' and to assuage 'public fear' of them, they must be incarcerated. This was the practice already adopted in all of the civilized (*policé*) countries of Europe, and especially in

France. But 'pity' demanded more and stipulated a second goal: a concerted attempt to cure them, or at least to diminish their suffering, or at the very least to refrain from exacerbating it.

(Goldstein 1987, 45)

We can see here the typically ambivalent attitude towards the insane, an attitude that has dominated both the governmental and private approaches to madness since antiquity. On the one hand, the insane needed to be disciplined and incarcerated or segregated from the rest of the populace. On the other hand, the insane inspired compassion and humanitarian willingness to help them. During the era of the Enlightenment, the latter attitude became more pronounced. This could clearly be seen in France, where madness became a problem that could be solved with the help of science and a rational health policy. One French physician used a very apt term to describe his understanding of the hospital: it was a 'healing machine' (*machine à guérir*). This term symbolized the emerging ideal of scientific medical care that represented rationality, efficiency and humanity.

As we will see in the next section, the development of the asylum system in Britain differed in some fundamental respects from that of France (or the Nordic countries).

Private and public management of madness in Britain

In England, the history of mental hospitals started in 1377, when the Bethlem hospital, founded in the mid-thirteenth century, became exclusively an asylum for the mad. In 1547, Bethlem was officially turned into a mental asylum, and its ownership was transferred to the City of London. For a long time, the number of patients at Bethlem remained low: at the beginning of the fifteenth century, the asylum housed six patients, and by the end of the sixteenth century the number had grown only to about 20. Small and squalid, it remained the only mental asylum in England until the mid-seventeenth century. When the asylum was burned down by fire, it was relocated and rebuilt in 1677, and then it was a much bigger, almost palace-like building that housed 100 patients. Bethlem continued as a mental hospital in the City of London until 1948. From the seventeenth century onwards, the asylum was known as 'Bedlam', which became a widely used slang term for utter madness. When diagnosing one of his patients the seventeenth-century clergyman and healer Richard Napier wrote down the words 'stark Bedlam mad' (MacDonald 2008, 122). Bedlam was both a mental asylum and a national symbol of madness, and it was open to visitors who out of curiosity or malice paid admission fees to gape at the inmates (Chambers 2009).

The treatment of mental patients became a public affair, if not a scandal, in 1818. That was when Urbane Metcalf, a former patient at Bethlem, wrote a book in which he reported on the abuses he witnessed in the asylum (*The Interior of Bethlehem Hospital Displayed*). His eye-witness report was trustworthy, because Metcalf

FIGURE 5.1 Bethlem (Bedlam) depicted in William Hogarth's *A Rake's Progress* (1732–5), a series of eight paintings showing the decline and fall of Tom Rakewell, wayward son of a rich merchant. The original paintings are in the collection of Sir John Soane's Museum in London.

Source: © Heritage Image Partnership Ltd / Alamy

did not deny being insane and in need of confinement and care (he suffered from the delusion that he was heir apparent to the throne of Denmark). Metcalf described Bethlem as a morally corrupt institution where patients were routinely abused and brutalized:

> It would extend far beyond the limits of this little work to pourtray the villainies practiced by the Jacks in the office, bribery is common to them all; cruelty is common to them all; villainy is common to them all; in short everything is common but virtue, which is so uncommon they take care to lock it up as a rarity.
>
> (Peterson 1982, 90)

Metcalf's revealing book, which he sold all over London for three cents a copy, confirmed the 1815 report of the government committee, which was the first

The Age of the Asylum **87**

systematic survey of the conditions in mental asylums in Britain (Higgins et al. 1982). In the report, Bethlem was described in rather unflattering terms:

> Patients were often chained to the walls as well as manacled and [. . .] one of the female patients had been chained without release for eight years. They also reported the case of a patient named Norris who had been chained for twelve years. Artist's prints, depicting Norris' confinement, were exhibited before the House [of Commons]. An iron collar, attached by a chain to a pole at the foot of his bed, restrained him by the neck. His ankles were chained to the foot of his bed, and an iron frame enclosed his torso. The governors of Bethlehem, however, defended his treatment insisting that his confinement appeared 'to have been, upon the whole, rather a merciful and humane, than a rigorous and severe imposition'.
>
> (Peterson 1982, 74)

This was not all. It was discovered that the recently deceased surgeon to Bethlem had himself been mad, 'so insane as to have a strait-waistcoat'. The medical staff of Bethlem incriminated each other, but the greatest blame for therapeutic failures was directed at the chief physician Thomas Monro, for it was Monro who had accepted, even encouraged, the deployment of physical restraints, such as irons and chains. Monro admitted that the main point of such 'treatments' was not to cure but secure, and that their use was motivated not by medical needs but by the rank and wealth of the patients. While lunatics at Bethlem were manacled to reduce staff costs, in Monro's private asylum no physical restraints were used, being 'fit only for pauper lunatics: if a gentleman were put in irons, he would not like it' (Porter 2006, 160). Yet, Bethlem did not differ that much from the mental asylums in Continental Europe. True, irons, chains, straitjackets and obsolete treatment methods – indiscriminate bloodletting, purges, antiquated drug treatments – were in use, but at least the patients were not chained up in dark cellars on damp and filthy ground, which was not untypical across the Continent. Besides, patients at Bethlem were not sentenced to life: an average length of confinement was one year. If the patients did not get better within a year, they were usually discharged uncured.

The 1815 government report on mental asylums aroused strong feelings and led to a reform campaign initiated by the authorities and some enlightened members of the middle class. But it took decades before true reforms were achieved in Bethlem and elsewhere in Britain. An early landmark in the legislative regulation of madhouses was the 1774 Act for Regulating Private Madhouses, which stipulated that private madhouses should be licensed. The first attempt to develop publicly provided mental health care was an Act of Parliament of 1808. This law was weak in the sense that it *allowed* counties to provide asylums through local property taxes, but it 'did not actually require them to do *anything*, though, and most of them did nothing, in some cases claiming that there were "no lunatics" within their boundaries' (Freeman 2006, 118). But at least the law was a step forward in

88 The great transformation

that it established the important principle according to which institutional mental health care could be provided by public funds. The 1808 Act stipulated that the maximum number of patients per hospital was 300, and that there must be medical staff in every asylum. It also gave instructions about the location of asylums as well as their architecture. Two decades later the Mad House Act (1828) attempted to improve conditions in the hospitals and the treatment of the patients through licensing, regulating and monitoring mental health care in Britain.

What characterized mental health care in eighteenth- and nineteenth-century Britain was that care was provided by both public and private asylums and madhouses. In the eighteenth century, there were only two charitable hospitals exclusively for the mentally ill in Britain – Bethlem and St Luke's in London. There was also one mental hospital – St Patrick's – in Dublin. As for the entrepreneurial 'trade in lunacy', it became a small-scale industry from the mid-eighteenth century onwards (Parry-Jones 1972). In 1815, there were already 72 private madhouses, some of them very small, others housing several hundred patients. They were often family businesses and therefore rather informal and non-bureaucratic establishments. Patient records were kept in the head rather than on paper, and keepers were reluctant to give any information about their clients, who typically shunned publicity when they placed their family members in madhouses. What was not a secret was that one could make a decent profit in this economy of insanity. The rise of private madhouses was largely due to the fact that there was clearly a market for such a business. And because there were no legal regulations of the 'madness business' before 1774, it was relatively easy to establish and maintain a private madhouse. Until 1828, madhouses could be run without medical staff, which meant that there were establishments that were never visited by doctors. Furthermore, there were no nurses in the modern sense of the term; lunatics were taken care of by various sorts of attendants, assistants and wardens. Parliament tried to prevent the exploitation of the mentally ill by passing several acts, but such laws were rather inefficient, because there were not enough administrators to enforce them on the shop floor level (Freeman 2006, 117).

In addition to the few charitable mental asylums and a large number of private madhouses, lunatics began to be confined in *workhouses*, which were established to reduce the costs of poor relief. The economic purpose of workhouses was simple: conditions there should be so unattractive that poorly paid labourers and 'sturdy beggars' would prefer to find any kind of work rather than take refuge in workhouses. But an unintended consequence of the opening of the national network of workhouses was that they attracted people who had no place in the labour market. Quite unexpectedly, orphaned children, frail old people, abandoned mothers, the sick and the disabled flooded into the workhouses (Freeman 2006, 118). The last group included the mentally ill, who could be kept tied to the bed or in a straitjacket all day long. To the workhouse keepers they were difficult cases, because threats and punishments failed to discipline the mad and make them follow the rules of the house. An important step towards the hospitalization of the mentally ill was taken in 1845, when the County Asylums Act and the Lunacy Act were introduced by Parliament in England and Wales. These acts stipulated that every county or group of counties *had* to establish an asylum from its locally raised funds. Furthermore, every asylum *had* to hire a medical officer, and a national Lunacy Commission was set up to monitor the operation of both private and public asylums. In Britain, this Act signified the beginning of the Age of the Asylum as well as the emergence of the psychiatric profession. Mental asylums were mostly intended for pauper lunatics, and as such they followed both a medical and humanitarian agenda, while the rationale behind the workhouses was predominantly utilitarian and economic (Freeman 2006, 119).

Britain did not experience the 'great confinement' in the early decades of the nineteenth century. In 1826, only a small proportion of the mentally ill (less than 5,000) was confined in a hospital, and almost a third of all patients were committed to private establishments. This was a small number in a kingdom of 10 million people. After mid-century, the publicly funded asylum system began to grow, while the number of private proprietors began to decline. An important step was taken in 1874, when the British government decided to use taxation to support asylums: the state began to pay counties a small regular subsidy for pauper patients confined in their asylums. As the psychiatrist and historian Hugh Freeman notes, 'this was the first time that any payment had been made from central taxation for any health or welfare purpose' in Britain (Freeman 2006, 120). The Age of the Asylum was truly established in Britain during the last third of the nineteenth century.

Moral treatment

By far the most well-known private asylum in early nineteenth-century Britain was York Retreat near the town of York. It was founded in 1796 by the tea merchant William Tuke (1732–1822) and his Quaker brothers, who decided to create the Retreat after one Quaker woman had unexpectedly died in suspicious circumstances in York Asylum, the local charitable hospital. In a way, York Retreat was conceived of as a non-medical and religious counterpart to York Asylum. The Retreat became famous for the so-called moral treatment, which is still regarded as an exemplary humane method of treatment, even if Foucault and his kindred spirits disagreed: for them, Tuke's – and the French alienist Pinel's – moral treatment was tantamount to a gigantic moral *imprisonment* (Digby 1985; Foucault 2006, 511).

York Retreat was certainly not representative of early nineteenth-century mental health care, simply because it only accepted Quakers as patients, and Quakers constituted a relatively small and ideologically uniform minority in Britain. The sort of moral treatment the Tuke family championed was directed at the volitional and social side of the patients' personality. The therapeutic goal was to strengthen the power of self-control and to help patients adjust to the demands of everyday life so that they could return to their communities with their souls reawakened. As a rule, patients were to be treated with kindness and humanity, even if there were also punishments for recalcitrant and disobedient patients. Compared to

90 The great transformation

most other establishments, mechanical restraints were used less, and all drugs were prohibited at least during the early years of the Retreat. What surely had positive effects on the mental health of the patients was that they were offered different kinds of activities, such as reading, writing, painting, various games, warm baths, walking tours outdoors as well as light domestic work that benefited the whole community. Last but not least, both the patients and the staff ate the same nutritious and abundant meals. The Retreat became widely known when Samuel Tuke (1784–1857), grandson of the founder, depicted it in very favourable terms in his book *Description of the Retreat* (1813). Tuke's book inspired the reformist members of Parliament and elevated the Retreat to the status of a model institution. At last, the British could be proud of a madhouse that was truly therapeutic. Soon the Retreat and moral treatment received international acclaim. Asylums modelled on the Retreat began to be established in the early decades of the nineteenth century in the United States.

This is how Samuel Tuke described one case:

> Some years ago a man, about thirty-four years of age, of almost Herculean size and figure, was brought to the house. He had been afflicted several times before; and so constantly, during the present attack, he had been kept chained; that his clothes were contrived to be taken off and put on by means of strings, without removing his manacles. They were however taken off, when he entered the Retreat.
>
> (Tuke 1964, 146)

The staff at the Retreat did not treat the patient like a frightening maniac; instead the superintendent conversed with him as if he was sound in mind. The superintendent told him:

> [t]hat it was his anxious wish to make every inhabitant in the house, as comfortable as possible; and that he sincerely hoped the patient's conduct would render it unnecessary for him to have recourse to coercion. The maniac was sensible of the kindness of his treatment. He promised to restrain himself, and he so completely succeeded, that, during his stay, no coercive means were ever employed towards him. This case affords a striking example of the efficacy of mild treatment.
>
> (Tuke 1964, 146–7)

In the surviving letters written by former patients, one can see how they were often thankful for the humane care they received at the Retreat. Yet, according to Britain's hospital statistics, its treatment results did not differ much from those of other establishments of similar size. It seems they very much depended on the financial resources of the private proprietors and on their willingness to invest in the infrastructure and staff. The Retreat was a rather luxurious madhouse in that it was purpose-built in a well-laid-out estate of 11 acres. There were no window bars, no forbidding walls, no chains and restraints. And its staff–patient ratio was at about one to ten – very generous in those days, and even today. As Roy Porter has pointed out, 'the trade in lunacy produced palaces as well as pigsties' (Porter 2006, 187).

What truly distinguished York Retreat from other asylums and madhouses was its religiosity. Bible-reading was one of the treatment methods, and patients participated in the religious meetings of fellow Quakers. Central to the Quaker ethos was the idea that a true Christian was his brother's keeper, and this sort of group solidarity was very visible at the Retreat. Its activities were directed at the religious restoration of the moral self, and for this reason its therapeutic programme was difficult to implement in mental asylums, which were not functioning on religious but on medical principles and which did not have such a homogeneous patient population. Most asylums in Britain and the Continent did not have much in common with York Retreat, which in a way continued the early modern tradition of 'spiritual physick' (Lederer 2006, 21). The non-medical and spiritual therapeutic ethos of the Retreat challenged the newly established mental medicine revolving around drug treatments, restraints and discipline.

York Retreat was not the only asylum in Europe that provided moral therapy. In Paris, Philippe Pinel developed liberal treatment ideology based on the humane and rational principles reflecting the core values of post-revolutionary France: liberty, equality, fraternity. In Pinel's asylum, there was not to be 'the stillness of the grave, and the silence of death' (Pinel 2009, 59). Even before Pinel, enlightened humanitarian regulations for the mental asylum were introduced in Florence by the Italian pioneer psychiatrist Vincenzio Chiarugi (1759–1820). In 1788, Chiarugi was appointed chief physician of the medieval Bonifacio Hospital, which was rebuilt and restructured along Chiarugi's plans to fulfil the medical and human needs of mental patients and invalids, who were typically homeless, unemployed and poor (Bonifacio also accepted patients with skin conditions). Chiarugi, who also specialized in dermatology, published an important three-volume work *On Insanity and Its Classification* (*Della Pazzìa in Genere e in Specie*) in 1793–4. In this work, he introduced his therapeutic principle, which was clear, simple and innovative at that time: in addition to providing shelter for patients, mental asylums had another, more essential obligation – they needed to provide medical care for the mentally ill. Chiarugi has the honour of being the first psychiatrist to create humanitarian regulations concerning the treatment of mental patients (Gerard 1997).

Establishment of asylums in the United States

Pennsylvania Hospital, the first hospital in the colonies, was founded in 1752 in Philadelphia, the largest town in what was to become the United States. The founding of the hospital reflected the widespread fear of the violent insane, as can be seen in the petition written by the civic leaders of Philadelphia, one of whom was Benjamin Franklin. Referring to the increasing number of lunatics in the colony, Franklin stated how 'going at large [the lunatics] are a terror to their

92   The great transformation

neighbors, who are daily apprehensive of the violences they may commit' (Gamwell & Tomes 1995, 20). In addition to the lunatics, the Pennsylvania Hospital admitted patients with somatic ailments. The insane patients were put in cells in the basement, where they received all the cutting-edge treatments available at the time: their heads were first shaved and then blistered; their blood was drawn until they fainted; they were given such powerful purgatives that their rectums emitted nothing but mucus. Between treatments that were supposed to restore their reason, the patients were chained to the wall (Deutsch 1949, 60). Benjamin Rush (1746–1813), one of the founding fathers of American psychiatry, worked at the Pennsylvania Hospital from 1783 to 1813, and his ambition was to control and conquer insanity by a 'therapeutic' combination of patriarchal discipline and mental stimulation. It would appear Rush and his staff looked upon themselves as animal tamers who ascribed bestial nature to the mentally ill (Gamwell & Tomes 1995, 32–5).

Like Bethlem in London, the Pennsylvania Hospital admitted visitors – free initially, then against payment – to the wards to gawk at the patients. Sometimes the visitors provoked raging fury among the patients, which was apparently considered great fun. This human zoo was a popular attraction in Philadelphia until the custom of public visits was discontinued in the 1830s. Following the logic that the loss of reason was equal to the loss of humanity, the insane were typically seen as subhuman species, and the first mental hospitals were designed to protect people from the threat of social disorder posed by manic lunatics. Still, eighteenth-century colonists appeared to be rather tolerant of the madmen and -women in their communities. As the historians Lynn Gamwell and Nancy Tomes point out, 'colonial records are filled with examples of people who behaved in bizarre and disruptive ways yet were allowed to move about freely, and even to retain important positions of responsibility' (Gamwell & Tomes 1995, 20).

Medicalization of madness did not altogether replace the shameful custom of selling the mentally ill at auctions, often at local markets. At these auctions, paupers, orphans, the disabled, the feebleminded and the insane mingled with horses and pigs, and they were auctioned off to the *lowest* bidder. After the sale was complete, they would join their purchasers' households as some sort of talking animal. Usually, the contracts were made for a relatively short period of time – between a week and a year – and this meant that many mentally disordered individuals were sold at auctions time and time again. For the magistrates and the town fathers, auctions were a cost-efficient way of getting rid of their mad and disabled dependents. And to many crafty farmers, the mentally disordered and other social outcasts constituted a cheap and relatively useful labour force – they had strong backs and weak minds (Deutsch 1949, 117–18). Occasionally, the new owners were required to give a written guarantee that they would treat these vulnerable individuals humanely, but such a guarantee was pure formality, as there were no administrative structures for monitoring how farmers exploited the slave labour. Masters could pretty much do as they pleased. This practice was the predominant form of poor relief in the countryside from the Declaration of Independence (1776) to the early decades of the nineteenth century. In some southern states this practice continued well into the twentieth century.

The first hospital to confine exclusively the insane was the Eastern Lunatic Asylum of Virginia, founded in 1773 in Williamsburg. This was followed by the acceptance of lunatic patients to New York Hospital in 1791 and to Maryland Hospital in 1798. In 1817, the Asylum for the Relief of Friends Deprived of Their Reason, established near Philadelphia, helped to introduce moral treatment to America. In the same year, the Connecticut Retreat for the Insane (known as the Hartford Retreat) was opened in Hartford, and in 1818 the McLean Asylum for the Insane was founded in Boston. The state hospital system began to be established in the 1830s when the Massachusetts State Lunatic Hospital was opened at Worcester in 1833. The expansion of public institutions was partly propelled by asylum reformers who actively persuaded legislators to establish state hospitals. The most well-known asylum reformer of the antebellum period was Dorothea Dix (1802–87), a deeply religious woman who found her life mission in improving the care of the indigent insane. The first federally funded mental hospital, established in 1855, was the Government Hospital for the Insane in Washington, DC (it was also called St Elizabeth's Hospital). In 1844, when the Association of Medical Superintendents of American Institutions for the Insane (later renamed the American Psychiatric Association) was founded, there were more than 20 mental hospitals in the United States (Gamwell & Tomes 1995, 55–6).

Unlike in Britain, there was very little trade in lunacy in the promised land of private entrepreneurship. Although many American hospitals were privately owned, they were funded by corporations and charitable donations from members of the upper and middle classes. Being partly charitable, non-profit establishments, hospitals accepted a number of pauper patients. American asylums adopted the optimistic principles of moral treatment with its promise of a cure against insanity. Private hospitals in particular tended to stress humane care, amusement and various programmes of patient activities, but the few state hospitals also tried to adopt a daily course of therapeutic exercise, work and amusement with books, games, sporting events and so forth. In the United States, moral treatment developed into a much more medicalized treatment than in the former mother country. American medical doctors typically saw medical and moral therapies as complementary rather than conflicting methods of treatment.

European and American asylums had similar class and gender distinctions, and in the latter there was also a racial divide between white and black patients. In the northern states of America, the number of free blacks was relatively small, and it was typical for private asylums in the North not to admit blacks at all, while state mental hospitals placed them in separate buildings or segregated wards. It was most common for insane blacks to be confined in jails and almshouses instead of hospitals, which was a more expensive form of confinement. In the antebellum South, the question of race and treatment was much more concrete and visible than in the North. If southern asylums accepted black patients at all, they tended to put them in segregated and inferior wards. A rare exception was the Eastern Lunatic

94 The great transformation

Asylum of Virginia, which admitted free blacks from its opening in 1773 and integrated some of its wards in the mid-nineteenth century. Even the 'pro-black' asylum doctors, such as John M. Galt in Virginia, tended to share the widespread prejudice that slavery was beneficial to the mental health of the blacks, who were supposed to be ill-equipped to live in freedom. This assumption reflected a more general belief that 'primitive' peoples would be struck with insanity if they were granted political freedom. Associating civilization with higher intellect, many asylum doctors maintained that 'savages' were incapable of independent living in a democracy. Hence, they had to be 'protected' from the dangers of freedom by the institution of slavery and, in the case of Native Americans, by confinement to reservations. There was even a diagnosis created exclusively for the slaves who obsessively yearned for freedom: *drapetomania*, or 'flight-from-home madness'. This diagnosis was invented in 1851 by Samuel E. Cartwright, a professor of medicine specializing in 'diseases of the Negro' at the University of Louisiana. Cartwright claimed that slaves who tried to run away from the masters more than twice were insane (Gamwell & Tomes 1995, 56–9, 100–3).

Whereas the blacks were seen to suffer from the consequences of political freedom, the abolitionists were also pathologized by segregationists. John Brown, a radical, white abolitionist sentenced to death for instigating an armed slave insurrection in Virginia in 1859, was called a monomaniac by his attorney as well as by a New England philanthropist who wanted to help Brown – in their view, Brown must be a monomaniac because his derangement centred exclusively on the subject of slavery. However, Brown refused to plead insanity to save his life, and other radical abolitionists rejected the suggestion that Brown was a madman on the grounds that champions of justice and equality were easily judged insane by the complacent and corrupt defenders of the status quo. Even Abraham Lincoln's credentials were questioned by some commentators in the popular press who described his opposition to slavery as a symptom of insanity. Some white immigrant groups were also singled out as 'inferior' and 'primitive'. This was especially the case with the Irish, who met with hostility from native-born, overwhelmingly Protestant Americans, who in times of economic recession regarded the Catholic Irish immigrants as a burden and a threat. Due to the fact that the families of the Irish were either back in Ireland or on the lowest rung of the society ladder, immigrants who became jobless, sick or disabled were often admitted to public welfare institutions, such as state mental hospitals (Gamwell & Tomes 1995, 59, 80–2).

By the late nineteenth century, the care of the mentally ill was decisively divided into private institutions and state mental hospitals. McLean Hospital in Boston (the 'alumni' of which later included the poet Sylvia Plath, the mathematician John Forbes Nash and musicians Ray Charles and James Taylor) and other elite mental institutions continued to provide a gracious and humane therapeutic environment for their affluent patient-clients, while state mental hospitals, suffering from overcrowding, lack of resources and an increasing number of chronic and demented patients, 'specialized' in providing custodial care for members of the lower classes. The situation was, if anything, even worse in public asylums run by cities and counties, where chronically ill patients often received no medical treatment and spent their days in squalid and depression-inducing circumstances. By the mid-twentieth century, half of all hospital beds in the United States were occupied by mental patients, and only a small portion of them were offered the 'country club' type of environment à la McLean in Boston (Beam 2001). In this sense, American mental asylums did not differ that much from those in Europe, where mental health care was based on public hospitals. There was one European country where the alternative to the system of public asylums was not so much private care as clinic- and research-based care of the mentally ill: Germany.

Clinics and the rise of psychiatric research in Germany

As in Britain and France, the more systematic and publicly funded institutionalization of the mentally ill began in Germany during the first half of the nineteenth century. The enlightened German state bureaucrats were keen on turning traditional madhouses into modern mental asylums based on both medical and administrative principles. The founding and functioning of the asylum were linked to the consolidation of state power, which entailed extensive administrative reforms in local government, the penal system, education, religion and medicine. To some extent, the German asylum system developed as a consequence of the secularization of Church properties. Monasteries, castles and other ecclesiastic institutions were transformed into public mental hospitals. They were designed to be therapeutic establishments (*Heilanstalten*) in contrast to the purely custodial institutions that functioned as human warehouses, workhouses or penitentiaries (*Arbeits- und Zuchthäuser*) (Schott & Tölle 2006, 236–9). However, by mid-century the early therapeutic optimism had dwindled away, and alienists were gripped by a sense of disappointment and dissatisfaction. Responding to the crisis, the authorities decided to complement the existing system with large institutions for the confinement and detention of chronically ill patients. As a result, separate institutions for curable and incurable patients began to be replaced by institutions combining medical and custodial responsibilities (*Heil- und Pflegeanstalten*). With these mid-century reforms, the Age of the Asylum was truly launched in Germany: there were soon almost 80 public asylums in German lands, and more were established every year. Unlike in highly centralized and statist France, there was no unified and uniform mental health care system in Germany. Due to its patchy and fragmented past as a nation, Germany was characterized by a wide variety of institutions, systems and regulations devoid of coherence and unified health care policy (Engstrom 2004, 18).

When the German Empire was founded in 1871, mental health care entered a new phase with the introduction of the academic system of university clinics. These psychiatric clinics were designed to be elite institutions, where the most up-to-date medical methods and techniques would be developed and applied to solve the persistent problem of madness. Unlike asylums, university clinics were not predicated on the demand for strictly regulated social and moral principles.

Asylums were designed to maximize normality, and they maintained therapeutic and patriarchal power that was legitimized by the asylum doctors' benevolent control of the patient's body and mind. By contrast, physicians at university clinics were preoccupied with the scientific analysis of 'clinical material' – namely patients – and they paid more attention to the diagnostic tools, classifications and laboratory equipment than to the social milieu of the clinic. Clinical psychiatrists and neurologists analysed the patient's body and mind in the hope of finding keys to solve the puzzle of mental illness. As top-notch medical institutions, clinics served scientific, pedagogic and educational purposes, providing medical students with practical opportunities to observe the mentally ill. This project of turning alienists into medical scientists required a systematic and rigorous attempt at naming and classifying disease entities. To achieve this goal, psychiatrists began to look at the life of their patients through the narrow window provided by the diagnosis. By the early twentieth century, psychiatric explanations of insanity in Germany were governed by the demands of diagnostic classification.

In practice, clinical observations were not always easy to make. Even if the necessary infrastructure, such as lecture halls, textbooks and medical instruments, were available, and even if both students and 'clinical material' were organized, there remained some didactic pitfalls. A major problem was the unpredictability of patients when their symptoms were demonstrated in lecture halls. Under the gaze of medical students, a patient's cardinal symptoms might just evaporate. The temporary disappearance of desired symptoms threatened to sabotage the whole clinical setting:

> One clinician was frustrated by melancholic patients who had been chosen to illustrate symptoms of anxiety: as soon as many of the patients glimpsed the students in the lecture hall, their anxiety disappeared entirely. Another influential clinician warned that when manic patients were confronted with a room full of students, they often became reserved and shy and thus useless for demonstrative purposes. In fact, it was often impossible to predict the success or failure of the demonstration: 'maniacs often quieted down, delirious patients became lucid, and paranoic patients often feigned mental health'.
>
> (Engstrom 2004, 162–3)

How to demonstrate an illness that is suddenly invisible?

German psychiatrists strived to incorporate their own specialty into medical education. Their goal was to make every medical student adept at quickly recognizing insanity outside the asylum. This required that all medical students have psychiatric training. Psychiatrists had an ambition to make interventions in the lives of the increasingly *less* disordered individuals in Imperial Germany – psychopaths, neurotics, alcoholics, prostitutes, vagabonds, the feebleminded and other maladjusted and deviant individuals had to be subjected to diagnosis and therapy. An implementation of such an expansion of mental health expertise required that the medical community as a whole should monitor the population and search for signs of potential mental deviance in general practice. This would amount to the relative psychiatrization of the whole of German society. In late nineteenth-century Imperial Germany, as in the Nordic countries some decades later, psychiatrists aspired to become guardians of national mental health. At the same time, the asylum system in western Europe expanded rapidly – the great confinement was in full swing.

The significance of clinics and hospitals for continuous and systematic research on mental disorders is difficult to overestimate. It was only after the large-scale establishment of institutional medical care that physicians had an adequate number of patients and forms of mental illness at their disposal to classify different mental illnesses. Increasingly, they began to notice that not all lunatics suffered from the same three or four mental illnesses (mania, melancholia, idiotia or dementia). Getting to grips with this basic fact prompted alienists to classify different types of mania (e.g. monomanias). The first step to the classification of mental disorders was possible only because asylums and clinics were established. But, as we will see in the following chapters, there was much more in asylums than just much-needed 'clinical material' for the more ambitious alienists.

Asylums in the colonies and in Argentina

The Age of the Asylum was simultaneous to the Age of Imperialism and Colonialism. European powers annexed much of Africa, parts of the Middle East and Asia, and established colonies in Australia and New Zealand. In these colonies, the management of madness followed the rules and logic of the host country, but to some extent colonial psychiatry also adapted to local culture. In what follows, I will briefly describe the asylum system in three distinct non-European areas that were all Europeanized either through colonization or, as in the case of the sovereign Argentina, through an influx of European immigrants and settlers. What was 'colonial madness' like in these areas?

Colonial asylum system in the Australasian world

In the Australasian colonies (Australia and New Zealand), the asylum system and mental medicine were largely based on British practices and directly related to developments in the Anglo-American world. Asylums, such as Gladesville Hospital for the Insane in Sydney (operating from 1838) and Auckland Mental Hospital in New Zealand (established in 1853), were public institutions, and a large cross-section of society was housed in these institutions. There were a few very small private asylums in these colonies. Until 1901, Australia and New Zealand were not independent nations, but even after joining a federation and becoming states, intrinsic to their systems of managing the insane was the governance of colonial populations. Obviously, there were various inter-colonial and intra-colonial meanings of the asylum that were circulated among representatives of mental medicine from the mid-nineteenth century to 1914 (Coleborne 2010, 21–39).

98 The great transformation

The picture that evolves from descriptions of colonial life suggests that mental suffering was often related to social dislocation, loneliness and isolation. This was true of both wealthy settlers and poor immigrants. A word that was frequently used in letters and diaries of the era was 'anxiety'. Among men, loneliness and isolation often triggered the use and abuse of alcohol, while women, especially if they lived in out-of-the-way places, might suffer from 'terrible isolation' and worry about real and imagined dangers surrounding them. In medical and advice books, the terms 'homesickness' and 'nostalgia' were used to denote a condition experienced by a number of people in the colonies. Feelings of dislocation and displacement appeared to be quite common among the settlers (Coleborne 2010, 32–47).

As the historian Catharine Coleborne has noted, asylum doctors took into account descriptions of mental breakdown offered by the patient's relatives and community members. In the colonies, families seemed to be strongly involved in the admittance and discharge of mental patients, and even during the patients' stays in the institutions families were often engaged with the asylum both practically and emotionally. Towards the end of the nineteenth century, the question of heredity – does insanity run in the family? – became more pronounced. An increasing preoccupation with heredity and 'mental hygiene' in the colonies derived from the widespread acceptance of the European doctrine of degeneration as well as from the overall attempt to transform psychiatry into a 'brain science' or at least to make it look like a respectable branch of clinical medicine. At the same time, as Coleborne points out, a medical interest in heredity 'had some basis in the empirical observations of the insane and their families' (Coleborne 2010, 43, 106, 152).

The composition of the patient population in the colonies varied and changed over time. In 1887, the number of registered insane persons in the Australian colonies was around 8,500 (1 in every 349 persons); in New Zealand, the ratio was slightly lower. Compared to statistics in Britain and Ireland, there was a smaller number of insane per head of population. According to official documents, there were only 21 Maori (the 'native' or first peoples of New Zealand) patients admitted to asylums in New Zealand in 1900. Ten years later, the number of Maori patients had increased significantly, and it is quite probable that, in all colonies, more indigenous people were incarcerated than official documents claim. Coleborne has examined patient records and they show that, in 1900, 'there were more Maori patients than reported in the annual reports' (Coleborne 2010, 39).

In Australia, indigenous patients are rarely noticeable in the records, and this may have been due to the colonial policies of segregation and the indigenous people's removal and dispersal throughout Australia. However, indigenous inmates were not separated from European patients in the asylums, perhaps because as a distinct minority they were not considered a threat to the 'white' identity of the institutionalized settlers. What was less fortunate was that 'very few Maori patients were discharged from Auckland when compared to European patients'; more than half of the Maori inmates died in the asylum (Coleborne 2010, 36–42, 111, 134). If the white settlers sometimes felt uprooted in the colonies, there is hardly any doubt that indigenous people felt insecure and disempowered in an

Colonial madness in French North Africa

Scholars have written much about the ways in which colonial medicine was used to promote scientific racism and to serve the purposes of the colonialist elites. But as the historian Richard C. Keller points out, French psychiatrists were also inspired by what they regarded as the Pinelian legacy: psychiatrists needed to renew and reform mental health care on foreign soil. From the late nineteenth century onwards, French alienists made study trips and practised in the North African colonies in Algeria, Tunisia and Morocco (so-called Maghreb countries). Until the mid-twentieth century, new mental hospitals were established in these French colonies, and psychiatrists aspired to modernize the management of madness in North Africa. At that time, a minority of mentally ill Muslims were confined in the traditional *maristans*, hospices for the mentally ill, where they were treated by *marabouts* (spiritual healers). *Maristans* were generally in a dilapidated condition, and the French psychiatrists saw it as their duty to demolish them, cast out superstitions and turn the treatment of insanity into progressive clinical science. To the local people, the problem with this sort of emancipation was that it was predicated on the submission to a French order (Keller 2007, 14–15, 45–6).

The main architect of North Africa's mental health system was Antoine Porot, who was also instrumental in the development of the Algiers School of French psychiatry from the mid-1920s onwards. Due to their close contact with indigenous inmates in colonial hospitals, members of this school became the French Empire's leading experts in the intersection of race and psychopathology. The flagship institution that was designed to implement the medical and humanitarian principles of French psychiatry was the Hôpital Psychiatrique de Blida in Algiers, established in 1927. Blida was a modern therapeutic facility where, in the spirit of Pinel, 'madman was elevated to the dignity of the patient'. Blida and other hospitals in the Maghreb appeared to raise the management of madness in North Africa to a whole new level (Keller 2007, 3, 80–1).

Between the two world wars, colonial psychiatrists examined almost exclusively the normal and pathological mind of the indigenous population. They devised theories about the 'primitive mentality' and 'criminal impulsiveness' of North Africans. As if this were not degrading enough, even the 'normal' consciousness of a Muslim was described as containing 'a mixture of insanities in varying doses', as one French psychopathologist put it in 1908. If the more 'docile' Tunisians were 'dreamy' and prone to mysticism, the mind of the 'aggressive' Algerians was presented as a threat to public safety. In addition, more invasive treatments, such as psychosurgery and shock methods, were first tested on Muslim patients (Keller 2007, 7–16, 108, 138).

Colonial psychiatry had its critics. The sharpest 'internal' critic was the psychiatrist Frantz Fanon (1925–61). Born in Martinique and educated in France,

100 The great transformation

Fanon moved to Algiers in 1953 and worked in the Blida Hospital. When the Algerian War erupted in 1954, he sided with the insurgency and described his own discipline as an insidious tool of imperial domination. He painted a dismal picture of Blida, which was handicapped by overcrowding, medical racism and a systematic neglect of patients. An advocate of political violence himself, Fanon saw his patients as subjects of the unbearable brutalities of colonial rule (Keller 2007, 3–4). In *The Wretched of the Earth* (1961) Fanon described the way the French colonists treated the Algerian people as 'born slackers, born liars, born robbers and born criminals', and how the colonists routinely referred to the North African's 'predatory instinct' and 'intense aggressivity' (Fanon 2001, 239, 241). Fanon's critique is harsh and probably exaggerated, but there is no doubt about the validity of his observations. Indeed, it is documented that many indigenous patients and their families protested against incarceration and regarded the European healing system as inadequate to their needs. Their discontent was aggravated by the language barrier (few staff members spoke Arabic), invasive treatments and the absence of spiritual healing provided in *maristans* (Keller 2007, 116–17).

Sadly, Blida as well as other mental hospitals in the Maghreb lacked the continuous support and necessary resources to ensure their smooth functioning. Over the years they degenerated into psychiatric warehouses, decrepit custodial institutions that ended up being very much like the detested *maristans*, devoid even of the spiritual and cultural dimension that had characterized these traditional healing sites. The atrocious Algerian War (1954–62) gave a mortal blow to the progressivism of French colonial psychiatry. Colonial psychiatrists were quick to diagnose members of the nationalist liberation movement the FLN (Front de Libération Nationale) as 'deviant fanatics' (Keller 2007, 152; on the Algerian War of Independence, see Horne 2006).

After independence, mental health care deteriorated in the Maghreb countries, all of which have remained underdeveloped and conflict-ridden to this day (this is especially true of Algeria). The Blida Hospital, later renamed Centre Hospitalier Universitaire Frantz Fanon, was once the therapeutic jewel of colonial psychiatry; today it is 'in a state of near ruin [. . .] The hospital is overcrowded with chronic patients, some of whom have been confined there since Fanon's day [i.e. the 1950s]' (Keller 2007, 225). It is a cruel irony that Blida became a warehouse of madness and as such the reverse of what its founders and caretakers, including Fanon, had envisioned and hoped. The therapeutic promises of psychiatric social engineering in French North Africa vanished into thin air.

Madness in the pampas

The history of madness in Argentina is an excellent illustration of the ways in which social, political and cultural changes affect mental health care. 'Madness in the pampas' makes historical sense only in the context of often dramatic fluctuations in Argentine society. Indeed, the very identity of Argentina as a nation seems to be discontinuous and fragmented rather than cohesive and clearly demarcated.

Since the late nineteenth century, Argentina has fluctuated between authoritarian and liberal and democratic regimes. Since mental health care has been the responsibility of the state, these political tumults have perforce impacted asylums, clinics and the mental health profession. Unfortunately, there has been one relatively continuous current underlying these changes: many psychiatrists have tended to see their patients as potential criminals who should be involuntarily confined for the good of social order. This negative professional view, which persisted until the 1960s and beyond, probably derived from the late nineteenth-century convergence of the fields of criminology, penology and psychiatry. An unintended long-range consequence of this convergence was that the neglect and abuse of mental patients should not be seen as an aberration but rather as an integral part of the development of mental health care in a nation where social control of deviance was intrinsic to modernization and nation building. From the military coup of 1943 to the end of the last dictatorship in 1983, the military's upper echelons defeated attempts at formal democracy (Ablard 2008, 3–5, 184).

For a few decades in the early twentieth century, Argentina was a representative democracy and one of the most affluent nations in the world. It was also a nation of immigrants: in proportion to the native-born population, more immigrants entered Argentina than the United States. In 1914, over a third of Argentina's population was foreign born, and immigrants were over-represented in the asylums. A massive influx of mostly European immigrants worried the elites. They made demands that the state should focus on the control of a population in which there were unpredictable and potentially dangerous elements, such as criminals, radical socialists and anarchists. Not surprisingly, immigration and its social consequences were interpreted through the lens of degeneracy theory, which continued to influence mental medicine until the 1940s (Plotkin 2001, 6, 15).

The asylum system began to be built in the mid-nineteenth century when two asylums were established in the capital city of Buenos Aires: Convalecencia for women and Casa de Dementes for male patients (Ablard 2008, 24–5). For decades, mental health care was very centralized, which meant that patients from the provinces were brought to the asylums in Buenos Aires. Argentina's urban elite followed the western model of social reformism in envisioning mental asylums as sites of medical healing and benevolent social control. The medical community regarded the developing mental health care system as an important sign of the republic's maturation into a modern nation, a nation just like France or England that had functioned as models to educated Argentinians. Very little resembling a 'great confinement' occurred in Argentina: in 1930, there were 14,000 inmates at mental hospitals, 1.26 in every 1,000 persons – only a small minority of Argentina's mentally ill were confined in asylums. Nevertheless, it was during this period that mental health care advanced and an atmosphere of therapeutic optimism was created in asylums and among the psychiatric community.

The 'golden age' came to an end with the military coup of 1930, after which Argentina was sucked into the spiral of political instability and economic underdevelopment. For the next 50 years or so, there were periods of optimism and

102 The great transformation

progress mixed with more troubled and violent times. During Colonel Juan Perón's presidency (1946–55), there were attempts to reform and reorganize Argentina's outdated public health care. By the mid-1950s, Argentina had one of the largest mental health systems in Latin America, but Peron's government failed to create a more solid foundation for public health (Ablard 2008, 7, 180). Then, between 1955 and 1983, military regimes alternated with civilian ones, and the general political climate was deeply affected by social polarization and violence.

From the start, asylums were hampered by two chronic problems: overcrowding and understaffing. Moreover, hospital buildings, laboratories, recreational facilities, in a word, infrastructure, remained chronically inadequate. True, these same problems haunted mental health care throughout the world, but in Argentina they have endured to this day. A serious obstacle to progress has been the reluctance of Argentine governments to systematically develop social programmes and structures of public welfare. According to the historian Jonathan Ablard, the state's parsimony was

> in large part fuelled by suspicion towards the growing population of foreign-born people whose arrival was seen as an engine of economic development but also source of political unrest and social decay and the primary cause of the overcrowding of the country's hospitals.
>
> (Ablard 2008, 6, 88, 116)

After mid-century, both progressive and conservative members of the Argentine psychiatric community began to embrace psychoanalysis. To some, psychoanalysis represented a viable alternative to the traditional biological psychiatry that was often associated with the Argentine military or, more recently, with the economic, scientific and ideological domination of the United States. To others, psychoanalysis was attractive because it was 'modern', intellectually exciting and in tune with the more permissive cultural climate of Argentina in general and Buenos Aires in particular. The Freudian boom was not restricted to mental medicine: psychoanalysis became an integral element of urban culture, attaining extraordinary levels of popularity in the media and affecting the daily lives of people as well as politics and even the Catholic Church. In the early 2000s, as psychoanalytic writings gather dust in the libraries of medical schools in Europe and North America, Freud's works 'are still gospel', psychoanalysts 'host political and cultural TV shows' and 'psychoanalytic jargon permeates Argentines' everyday speech' (Plotkin 2001, x).

While psychoanalysis flourished, the political situation changed from bad to worse when Argentina was ruled by a murderous military junta between 1976 and 1983. The new regime persecuted leftist activists, Jews (the regime was virulently anti-Semitic) and intellectuals, torturing and murdering up to 30,000 people during a seven-year political nightmare. To the generals, both Marx and Freud were mortal enemies. Still, psychoanalysis survived, partly because, like the Church, it was already too deeply entrenched in Argentine culture to be annihilated. The

1976 coup destroyed a decades-old but tenuous alliance between progressive psychiatry and the state. While many leftist psychiatrists suffered during these years and at least 13 psychiatrists 'disappeared', other psychiatrists participated in the repression. This volatile political climate had detrimental effects on mental hospitals in terms of resources, personnel and long-term planning (Ablard 2008, 163–4).

The military junta was forced to step down in 1983. Since then, Argentina has been a democracy, but the 'perennial' problems of mental health care are still there: overcrowding, lack of funding and the neglect of mental hospitals and their patients. As Jonathan Ablard wrote in 2008,

> Argentina's large psychiatric institutions remain plagued by horrific conditions. The renewed decay of these hospitals is a product not just of the military's political legacy, but also of more recent neo-liberal reforms, which have compelled the state to reduce outlays in social services and public health.
>
> (Ablard 2008, 7)

It may very well be that a walk through any Argentine mental hospital today is a rather depressing experience. Still, the way the mentally ill are managed and treated in all developed countries is dependent on social structures, political power and cultural dynamics. In this sense, Argentina is anything but an anomaly. A study of the history of madness in Argentina is inseparable from the study of the history of the conditions under which Argentinians have lived – and suffered.

* * *

From the early nineteenth to the late twentieth centuries, madness was 'institutionalized' in two fundamental ways. First, madness was increasingly managed and explained in the context of the mental asylum. Second, a medical specialty called psychiatry or alienism was developed to manage and explain insanity. What these two developments added up to was a massive medicalization of madness that took place in the nineteenth century. In this chapter I have given an outline of the origins and development of the Age of the Asylum in different national settings. Next, I will examine the development towards the medical explanation and management of madness in the nineteenth century.

Bibliography

Ablard, J.D. (2008) *Madness in Buenos Aires. Patients, Psychiatrists and the Argentine State, 1880–1983*, Calgary, Canada: University of Calgary Press.

Beam, A. (2001) *Gracefully Insane. Life and Death Inside America's Premier Mental Hospital*, New York: Public Affairs.

Bowers, L. (1998) *The Social Nature of Mental Illness*, London: Routledge.

Chambers, P. (2009) *Bedlam: London's Hospital for the Mad*, Sittingbourne, Kent: Ian Allan.

Coleborne, C. (2010) *Madness in the Family: Insanity and Institutions in the Australasian Colonial World, 1860–1914*, Basingstoke: Palgrave Macmillan.

104 The great transformation

Deutsch, A. (1949) *The Mentally Ill in America*, New York: Columbia University Press.

Digby, A. (1985) *Madness, Morality and Medicine: A Study of the York Retreat 1796–1914*, Cambridge: Cambridge University Press.

Dols, M.W. (1992) *Majnun: The Madman in Medieval Islamic Society*, ed. D.E. Immisch, Oxford: The Clarendon Press.

Dörner, K. (1981) *Madmen and the Bourgeoisie*, orig. German edn 1969, Oxford: Basil Blackwell.

Engstrom, E.J. (2004) *Clinical Psychiatry in Imperial Germany: A History of Psychiatric Practice*, Ithaca, NY: Cornell University Press.

Fanon, F. (2001) *The Wretched of the Earth*, orig. French edn 1961, London: Penguin Books.

Foucault, M. (2006) *History of Madness*, ed. J. Khalfa, trans. J. Murphy and J. Khalfa, orig. French edn 1961, London: Routledge.

Freeman, H. (2006) 'Psychiatry and the state in Britain', in M. Gijswijt-Hofstra and H. Oosterhuis (eds) *Psyhiatric Cultures Compared: Psychiatry and Mental Health Care in the Twentieth Century*, Amsterdam: Amsterdam University Press.

Gamwell, L. and Tomes, N. (1995) *Madness in America. Cultural and Medical Perceptions of Mental Illness before 1914*, New York: Cornell University Press.

Gerard, D.L. (1997) 'Chiarugi and Pinel considered: soul's brain/person's mind', *Journal of the History of the Behavioral Sciences*, 33: 381–403.

Goldstein, J. (1987) *Console and Classify. The French Psychiatric Profession in the Nineteenth Century*, Cambridge: Cambridge University Press.

Higgins, G. et al. (1982) 'Parliamentary inquiry into madhouses', in R. Hunter and I. MacAlpine (eds), *Three Hundred Years of Psychiatry, 1535–1860*, 1st edn 1963, Hartsdale, NY: Carlisle Publishing.

Horne, A. (2006) *A Savage War of Peace: Algeria 1954–1962*, 1st edn 1977, New York: New York Review of Books Classic.

Keller, R.C. (2007) *Colonial Madness. Psychiatry in French North Africa*, Chicago: University of Chicago Press.

King, L.J. (2002) *From Under the Cloud at Seven Steeples, 1878–1885: The Peculiarly Saddened Life of Anna Agnew at the Indiana Hospital for the Insane*, Zionsville, IN: Guild Press/Emmis.

Kropotkin, P. (2002) 'Prisons and their moral influence on prisoners' (1877), in *Anarchism. A Collection of Revolutionary Writings*, Mineola, NY: Dover Publications.

Lederer, D. (2006) *Madness, Religion and the State in Early Modern Europe*, Cambridge: Cambridge University Press.

MacDonald, M. (2008) *Mystical Bedlam: Madness, Anxiety and Healing in Seventeenth-Century England*, 1st edn 1981, Cambridge: Cambridge University Press.

Midelfort, E. (1999) *A History of Madness in Sixteenth-Century Germany*, Stanford, CA: Stanford University Press.

Parry-Jones, W. (1972) *The Trade in Lunacy*, London: Routledge & Kegan Paul.

Peterson, D. (ed.) (1982) *A Mad People's History of Madness*, Pittsburgh, PA: University of Pittsburgh Press.

Pinel, P. (2009) *A Treatise on Insanity*, orig. French edn 1801, Milton Keynes: General Books.

Plotkin, M.B. (2001) *Freud in the Pampas. The Emergence and Development of a Psychoanalytic Culture in Argentina*, Stanford, CA: Stanford University Press.

Porter, R. (2006) *Madmen. A Social History of Madhouses, Mad-Doctors and Lunatics*, Stroud: Tempus.

Sacks, O. (2009) 'The lost virtues of the asylum', *The New York Review of Books*, 24 September.

Sarvilinna, A. (1938) *Mielisairaanhoidon kehityksestä Suomessa vuoteen 1919: lääketieteellis-historiallinen tutkielma*, Uusikaupunki, Finland: Helsingin yliopisto.

Schott, H. and Tölle, R. (2006) *Geschichte der Psychiatrie*, Munich: C.H. Beck.

Siraisi, N.G. (1990) *Medieval & Early Renaissance Medicine*, Chicago, IL: University of Chicago Press.

Stevenson, C. (1988) 'Madness and the picturesque in the Kingdom of Denmark', in W.F. Bynum and R. Porter (eds) *The Anatomy of Madness: Essays in the History of Psychiatry*, Vol. III: *The Asylum and its Psychiatry*, London: Routledge.

Tuke, S. (1964) *Description of the Retreat, an Institution near York, for Insane Persons of the Society of Friends*, 1st edn 1813, London: Dawsons of Pall Mall.

6

THE MEDICAL MANAGEMENT OF MADNESS

This chapter examines how madness was changed into mental illness, a medical or psychomedical disorder that belonged to the purview of medical experts called 'psychiatrists' or 'alienists'. This change amounted to a massive medicalization of madness, which brought with it new explanations and methods of treatment from the early nineteenth century onwards. As a new group of medical specialists, psychiatrists started to name and classify mental disorders, provide medical treatment in mental hospitals and explain the causes of mental illness. The birth of psychiatry was part of a larger medical movement towards empirical science and reductionist analysis of phenomena. Physicians started to make dissections and autopsies of the human body on a large scale, while mechanistic physiology and materialistic psychology became the epistemological and methodological starting points for scientists. Gradually, the materialistic world view, with its monistic emphasis on the corporeality and concreteness of reality, decisively pushed spiritualism and idealism to the margins of science. This triumph of materialism can be seen in the early history of psychiatry too. As this chapter shows, within the scope of one century (1800–1900), the picture of madness changed from being heterogeneous and varying to becoming rather homogeneous and stable. By 1900, psychiatrists had more or less attained a monopoly in the management of madness.

The origin myth of psychiatry

The origin myth of psychiatry has its heroes. The most important hero is the French physician Philippe Pinel (1745–1826), who liberated the insane from their chains at La Bicêtre Hospital in Paris in 1793. Two years later he did the same in La Salpêtrière, which was probably the largest hospital in the world at the time, with a capacity of 10,000 patients. Pinel's act became a symbol of the dawn of a new era for mental health care. The Enlightenment ideals of humanity, rationality and secular progress were now embodied by psychiatrists, the fearless and dispassionate pioneers of mental medicine (Weiner 2000; Vandermeersch 1994).

Like myths in general, the power of this psychiatric myth is not undermined by its historical inaccuracies or pedantic remarks about Pinel not being the first physician to free mental patients from chains. Certainly, Pinel did not only unlock chains – or give orders to his staff to do so – he laid the foundation of scientific psychiatry by educating the first generation of French psychiatrists and by writing the text book *A Treatise on Insanity* (*Traité médico-philosophique sur l'aliénation mentale*, 1801; English translation 1806). Pinel's book on 'mental alienation' had a tremendous influence on French and Anglo-American medicine and it has deservedly attained the status of a classic in psychiatric literature. To the modern reader, the term 'alienation' may seem odd, but during the nineteenth century mental illness was commonly understood as the insane persons' alienation from themselves (their true identity) as well as from their social environment. Psychiatrists working in mental asylums were typically called 'alienists' until the early twentieth century (*aliéniste* in French). They were experts in the medical treatment of 'mental alienation' or estrangement. The German physician Johann Reil introduced the term 'psychiatry' (*Psychiaterie*) in 1808, but it was not a widely used term in nineteenth-century mental medicine.

Psychiatry first became an independent medical specialty in France. The French medical community was at the forefront of medical science, and France was a pioneer country in the development of governmental science policy. In fact, France was the first country in modern Europe to build a modern nation with its administration, national agencies and body of civil servants.

Pinel as the 'founding father' of psychiatry

Philippe Pinel arrived in Paris full of enthusiasm and ambition in 1778 (on Pinel's life and work, see Goldstein 1987). To his dismay, he soon found out that finding a position in the extremely hierarchical and rigid medical community of pre-revolutionary France was difficult. Disillusioned with medicine, he even began to toy with the idea of emigrating to the United States when a medical journal hired him the post of editor in 1784. It was during this time that insanity began to attract his attention on a personal and professional level. He had a young friend who had become afflicted with 'nervous melancholy', which then developed into full-blown mania. Pinel watched helplessly as his friend's mental health deteriorated. Pinel had to take him to the age-old, decayed mental hospital Hôtel-Dieu, where the friend's condition improved. Then his worried parents demanded he return to his home village. Soon after going home, the young man escaped to the woods, where he was found dead a few days later, holding Plato's dialogue about the immortality of the soul in his hands. The tragic fate of his friend haunted Pinel, who began to wonder whether better treatment could have saved his life. He applied for a job in a private sanatorium that specialized in the treatment of the mentally ill. He had a rather low regard for the sanatorium's chief physician,

108 The great transformation

who seemed to be happy when his wealthy patients did *not* get well. Despite his misgivings, Pinel worked at the sanatorium until the year of the Revolution 1789, gaining experience in the study and treatment of madness (Goldstein 1987, 68–9).

The Revolution and its aftermath were beneficial to Pinel, a dedicated republican. When the republican physicians took over the medical establishment, the hospital committee of Paris decided to appoint 'citizen Pinel' as the chief physician of La Bicêtre Hospital. In his own words, Pinel found 'chaos and confusion' at Bicêtre (Pinel 2009, 21). Soon after his promotion, he was appointed Professor of Hygiene in the newly founded medical faculty. By 'hygiene' Pinel meant the sort of 'internal medicine' of both body and mind in which patients were treated as whole personalities and not only as carriers of mental illness or bodily ailments. In 1795, Pinel moved from La Bicêtre to its counterpart La Salpêtrière, which had become a huge general hospital for lower-class women. He saw the traditional 'asylums for maniacs' as nothing but warehouses for people regarded as a menace to society. In his own words, 'the managers of these institutions, who are frequently men of little knowledge and less humanity, have been permitted to exercise towards their innocent prisoners a most arbitrary system of cruelty and violence' (Pinel 2009, 22). By contrast, at the Bicêtre the staff followed the 'maxims of enlightened humanity'. This meant that the 'domestics and keepers are not allowed, on any pretext whatever, to strike a madman; and that straight waistcoats, superior force, and seclusion for a limited time, are the only punishments inflicted' (Pinel 2009, 51).

Pinel's book on 'mental alienation' (*Traité médico-philosophique sur l'aliénation mentale*, 1801) showed the way for the future generations of psychiatrists in France and many other countries. One of its lasting legacies was the introduction of moral treatment (*traitement moral*). By moral treatment Pinel referred to a therapy that aimed directly to influence the patient's reason and emotions in contrast to the traditional interventions directed at the patient's body, such as cupping, emetics and purgatives. Pinel was not urging a total abandonment of traditional methods, but he obviously considered them inefficient, even cruel: 'I cannot speak without horror of the barbarous methods for the repression of maniacs, which are still employed at some hospitals, and which I know to be in too many instances the cause of premature death' (Pinel 2009, 61). Pinel freely admitted that he was not the first physician to employ the methods of moral treatment; in Greek and Roman antiquity, Aulus Cornelius Celsus and Caelius Aurelanius (fifth century) were early pioneers of a 'psychological' approach to mental maladies, and in recent times some British healers had introduced moral treatment in Britain (especially the Tuke family, to whom I referred in Chapter 5). He also acknowledged his debt to folk healers, who were often skilful therapists despite their lack of medical education. His experiences at the Bicêtre had convinced him that the unofficial art of healing commanded respect, and that progress in the study of mental illness required an understanding of healing traditions. The kind of respect for folklore and folk healing that Pinel expressed was very common in late eighteenth-century medical discourse animated by egalitarian republican ideology on both sides of the

The medical management of madness **109**

Atlantic (Goldstein 1987, 75–6). Nevertheless, Pinel pointed out that folk healers lacked the medical knowledge and proper language in which to express observations and instructions systematically and precisely.

Pinel defined mental illness broadly as 'lesions of the functions of the understanding', and he endorsed the Enlightenment philosopher Condillac's Lockean conception of madness as the arbitrary power of unorganized imagination (Pinel 2009, 33; Williams 1994, 81–2). In his moral treatment, he stressed the role of passions in the aetiology of mental illness, and he wanted to cure his patients by appealing to their passions in a controlled manner. This focus on the therapeutic 'manipulation' of passions was at the heart of his moral treatment. In Pinel's time, passions were conceptually close to the concept of 'desire', but they also denoted a more fundamental power that moved people's minds and emotions: passions drove men to seek power and glory. In the European intellectual tradition, passions were commonly seen as potentially negative forces, suppressing reason and leading to improper acts and deeds (e.g. when a person was animated by hatred, jealousy, greed or burning love). In the Enlightenment thinking of the latter half of the eighteenth century, passions began to be interpreted more positively as a necessary companion to reason, if not as a power *ruling* reason, as the Scottish philosopher David Hume argued. At the same time, passions became an object of medical inquiry, as can be seen in Pinel's and other early psychiatrists' ardent interest in the relationship between madness and passions (Huneman 2008).

Pinel had a positive approach to passions in his medical conviction that 'sick' passions should not be destroyed or suppressed. Instead, more powerful and constructive passions should be set against the sick passions that drive people crazy. To Pinel, passions were part and parcel of human nature, as Jean-Jacques Rousseau (1712–78), another Swiss-French philosopher whom Pinel admired, passionately argued in his writings. Also very Rousseauean in Pinel's thinking was his idea that the insane were estranged from their authentic selves. Pinel identified curing as a method of overcoming alienation, as the patients' return to their own selves. This sort of thinking had a political dimension as well. A year after the revolution of 1789, Pinel suggested that a revolutionary renewal of society had therapeutic effects on people, because revolution increases the vitality of the human soul. Ten years later, his and his republican colleagues' medical Rousseaueanism was not so radical anymore: now Pinel himself represented the medical establishment, and he saw political unrest leading to an *increase* in mental illness, because it gave enormous stimuli to all human passions (Goldstein 1987, 94–101). Pinel was a pioneer in the medicalization of passions, which paved the way for the massive medicalization of emotional life in the twentieth and twenty-first centuries.

Pinel's clinical work

The starting point of Pinel's moral treatment was simply the alleviation of mental suffering. He combined this humanitarian attitude with an attempt at scientific rigour. He was one of the first medical scientists to use statistics to quantify the

110 The great transformation

effects and efficiency of treatment as well as to compile data on diagnoses, age, sex, occupation and possible hereditary illnesses running in families. His 'Newtonian' ambition was to turn an expertise in mental alienation to an exact science, which would be characterized by mathematical precision and statistical probabilities.

In his clinical work, Pinel laid great stress on the power of case histories to reveal crucial aspects of mental illness, and on his exceptional ability to find a proper cure for insanity. One of his patients was a watchmaker, who thought that his head was not his own. The patient was also obsessed with the idea of building a perpetual motion machine, which had first vexed him, then made him lose his sleep and finally drove him mad. His mental confusion reached a climax during the tumultuous aftermath of the revolution, when he was struck by the delusion that he had lost his head on the scaffold. He believed his head was thrown in a big pile of other victims' heads, but then the judges repented of their sentence and ordered that all heads must be placed upon the shoulders of their respective owners. Unfortunately, the poor watchmaker did not get his own head back. This accidental exchange of heads occupied the man's mind day and night, as a result of which his relatives decided to send him to the Hôtel-Dieu, from where he was transferred to the Bicêtre. There, Pinel and his assistants marvelled at the thoughts and acts produced by the patient's 'heated brain'. When his mind was not preoccupied with the exchange of heads, the man was busy designing a perpetual motion machine.

Pinel decided to fulfil the watchmaker's wish. So the watchmaker's friends sent him tools with which to construct the machine. For a month the man built his machine with great zeal until he lost his nerve and broke the machinery into a thousand pieces: he had made a false start. He took it upon himself to build a new machine. This time he was happy with the result – he had invented a perpetual motion machine! The man rushed to break the exciting news to other patients and the staff. But then his joy turned sour: the wheels of his machine stopped. To avoid public humiliation, he declared that the problem could be easily fixed, but as he was now tired of this sort of labour, he would return to the device later. Now he turned his maniacal attention again to the exchange of heads. This prompted Pinel to hire a recently recovered patient to play the role of a trickster. In the presence of other patients, the convalescent made a pun that was aimed at relieving the patient of his obsession. The confederate referred to the famous Saint Denis, who was decapitated in Paris in the year 257, and whose statue can be found in Notre Dame Cathedral; the statue depicts Saint Denis holding his head in his hands. According to the legend, Denis got up after his execution, picked his head up, kissed it and walked 10 kilometres, preaching a sermon the entire way. Then he gave his head to a Christian woman and collapsed on the ground. The watchmaker insisted that this incident was a fact, as was the loss of his own head. Ridiculing this belief, the confederate

replied with a tone of keenest ridicule: 'Madman as thou art, how could Saint Denis kiss his own head? Was it with his heels?' This equally unexpected and unanswerable retort forcibly struck the maniac. He retired confused amid peals of laughter, which were provoked at his expense, and never afterwards mentioned the exchange of his head.

(Pinel 2009, 53)

A few months later, the watchmaker's mental health was restored and he was sent back to his family.

Apparently, Pinel could follow the overexcited train of thought of his patients and attune to their mental wavelengths. Then he tried to achieve a therapeutic turn which would be in accordance with the extraordinary logic of his patients, but which would also channel their streams of consciousness away from the pathological obsessions and delusions. Instead of branding the thoughts of his patients as senseless ravings, he tried to find in them a therapeutic key that would open the locked mind and prepare the way for recovery. At least, this is the way he wanted to present his cases. As was usual in the history of psychiatry, he did not refer to any therapeutic failings. Obviously, an essential element in Pinel's moral treatment was the therapeutic principle that doctors are not allowed to dismiss patients and their experiences. In *A Treatise on Insanity*, he notes that clinical observation of maniacs made him realize that 'insanity was curable in many instances by mildness of treatment and attention to the state of the mind exclusively, and when coercion was indispensable, that it might be very effectually applied without corporal indignity' (Pinel 2009, 66).

In the French political climate of moderate liberalism, the authorities favoured Pinel's method of moral treatment, because it acknowledged the value and dignity of all patients regardless of their rank or status. Unfortunately, Pinel's humane principle was trampled underfoot during the nineteenth century as mental asylums became bigger, patients' illnesses more chronic and the therapeutic ethos changed into a custodial one.

Pinel's legacy in France

Pinel's most important pupil was Jean-Étienne Dominique Esquirol (1772–1840), who very skilfully institutionalized Pinelian psychiatry in France. At the Salpêtrière, Esquirol launched clinical courses in which different cases were presented to crowded audiences. Esquirol also had his own private hospital, the staff of which consisted of his pupils. Located near Paris, his hospital provided medical services to the mentally ill of the privileged classes.

Esquirol made study trips to mental hospitals in the 1810s to create an overall picture of French mental health care. He continued the Pinelian project of medicalizing the management of madness, which included the 'purification' of medical language from colloquial words. For example, the vulgar term *folie* (madness) used by common people had to be replaced by the psychiatric term *alienation*, and mental hospitals were to be called *asylums* (*asile* in French), not madhouses. Esquirol was also an innovative 'namegiver' to various mental disorders. In his view, each

112 The great transformation

form of alienation had its own dominant passion (*passion dominante*). He coined these varying forms 'monomanias' (Huneman 2008). Following his philosophically oriented teacher Pinel, Esquirol had a firm belief in the power of words: the language we use influences the way we think. His own writings and administrative skills inspired his colleagues in France and other parts of Europe, for example in Germany and Switzerland (Schott & Tölle 2006, 64).

Esquirol's pupils attained positions in the provincial mental hospitals and disseminated 'Parisian-Esquirolian' expertise across France. Esquirolians considered themselves progressive light-bringers in the gloomy wards of provincial hospitals, but local doctors often resented the hegemony of Esquirol's Parisian school. Moreover, Esquirol had rivals, whose own pupils competed with the young physicians of the Esquirol school for positions and reputation. The career of Antoine-Laurent Bayle (1799–1858), the 'anti-Pinelian' discoverer of general paresis (see Chapter 8) and a promising young psychiatrist, was sabotaged by the Esquirol circle, because he was regarded as an opponent of Esquirolian theories and Esquirol's diagnostic innovation, the group of monomanias (Brown 1994).

Esquirol's favourite pupil Étienne-Jean Georget (1795–1828) took the next step in the professional expansion of psychiatry. In the 1820s, Georget suggested that monomania, a new diagnostic category developed by Esquirol, would provide a foundation for the judicial *non compos mentis* ('not of sound mind'), which in the legal setting means that the defendant was considered not responsible for his criminal act. Monomania referred to a mania that manifested itself only in specific instances, such as in the person's irresistible urge to set things on fire (pyromania), steal (kleptomania), to fall madly in love (erotomania) or, in the case of women, to have promiscuous sex (nymphomania). There was one specific monomania, 'homicidal monomania' (*monomanie homicide*), which urged the mentally ill to commit violent acts (Goldstein 1987, 165). Homicidal monomania was caused by a 'lesion of the will', and its main symptom was the maniac's inability to resist the violent urge. In other words, those suffering from monomania could not be held guilty of deliberate homicide because the necessary criminal intent was lacking. In 1826, Parisian physicians were asked to give a medical statement in a murder case involving a young servant girl, who had suddenly and without any reason killed her host family's small child. A respected physician stated that the servant suffered from homicidal monomania, which made her legally irresponsible. This was the first court case in which this new diagnosis was used in the mental examination. The servant was found guilty of murder, so in this sense the psychiatric advocates of monomania lost the case. Still, the diagnosis became widely known in France, because the press and general public had followed the case with great interest.

If monomania could be considered a valid criterion in the legal assessment of the defendant's guilt, then it might open the doors of courtrooms to psychiatrists on a massive scale. The idea of irresponsibility due to mental illness was not new in the early nineteenth century. Roman law had taken into account the possibility of mental illness in court proceedings, as had the recent Napoleonic penal code. Both judicial systems, however, assumed that laymen could easily recognize mental illness and give testimony of the defendant's state of mind. What Georget had in mind was quite different: he was trying to create a demand for forensic psychiatry by his claim that even if murderers showed no signs of mental disturbance, they were insane, because they had been propelled to act by an urge they could not resist. For the representatives of the penal system, this claim was difficult to swallow, because the idea that *medical* expertise is required in the assessment of the defendant's mental condition was alien to the early nineteenth-century French courts. Many jurists pointed out that monomania was nothing but a new and fancy name for traditional and very common crimes of passion, which were discussed daily in French courts. Critics argued that a 'monomania craze' was at bottom a questionable reduction of all passions to one sweeping medical explanation. The civil servants and conservative supporters of the severe Napoleonic penal code with its stress on capital punishment, in particular, criticized monomania for being hypocritical and unsuitable for court cases. They tried to demonstrate that the doctrine of monomania was damaging to society and its morals in its apparent rejection of the concept of criminal responsibility altogether.

Even physicians themselves did not always deem it necessary to make statements in court. One surgeon remarked that neighbours and other laypeople who knew the defendant were much more reliable sources of information than medical doctors. As a consequence of the psychiatric invasion of courts, the distinction between madness and badness became blurred (Harris 1991, 8–9; Goldstein 1987, 162–3). On the other hand, the liberal press supported monomania for its scientific aura and moral optimism – the moral message of monomania was that, far from being an intrinsic part of human nature, evil was a pathological deviance from the intrinsic goodness of humanity. Besides, said the liberals, to give a death sentence to sick individuals was both barbarian and pointless (Goldstein 1987, 165–84).

The popularity of monomania began to decline rapidly in the mid-nineteenth century, but it did not entail the disappearance of psychiatry from courtrooms. On the contrary, during the latter half of the nineteenth and in the twentieth century, psychiatrists who had first gained access to court with the help of monomania continued to give medical statements for defendants who may have been 'not of sound mind' during the criminal act. The psychiatric diagnoses have just changed from monomania to ones that are still in use, such as paranoia, paranoid schizophrenia and psychopathy (personality disorder).

French psychiatrists had a red letter day in 1838 when the law governing compulsory hospital admission of persons with mental illness was passed. The 1838 law mandated the establishment of asylums across the country for all mentally ill people, which was a realization of Esquirol's fundamental goal. The law is still in force today. It was a great triumph for psychiatrists, because it was a governmental acknowledgement of the status of psychiatry and its professional monopoly over

114 The great transformation

public asylums. The law made French psychiatrists representatives of state power, and as such they were officially assigned to study and treat mental illness (Goldstein 1987, 195). Still, the governmental 'ointment' of psychiatry did not mean that its position as a respectable medical specialty was now secured. On the contrary, around mid-century it had become painfully clear to both psychiatrists and administrators that patients did not often recover from their illness in asylums. The great therapeutic expectations raised by alienists were not being fulfilled. This meant that alienists had to prove their usefulness to the state and society in order to retain their medical credibility and professional privileges. The insecure status of French psychiatry played into the hands of the Catholic priests, who retained remarkable authority in the treatment of mental disturbances, particularly in provincial towns and the countryside.

From Romanticism to materialism: the rise of German psychiatry

Unlike France and Britain, Germany was not unified until 1871. Until then, Germany consisted of a number of independent kingdoms (such as Bavaria and Prussia), duchies and principalities. Even after the unification, the newly founded German Empire consisted of 27 constituent territories, the most important of which was Prussia. The German Empire (1871–1918) was an industrial, technological and scientific giant that played a leading role in medicine and psychiatry. By contrast, in the early decades of the nineteenth century, German science and medicine lagged behind France, even though German kingdoms and grand duchies were increasingly supporting science to show the outside world how progressive they were, and also because the German elites acknowledged the importance of science and research as engines of social, economic and cultural progress. Numerous universities were established and academic medicine was boosted by a new kind of research-oriented clinics that were affiliated to medical faculties. These clinics offered possibilities for studying acute cases and for medical students to see patients in a setting that simulated reality in a hospital.

While early German psychiatry did not a have central figure comparable to Pinel in France, there were two important physicians who shaped mental medicine in Germany from different perspectives. One was Johann Reil (1759–1813), who became a professor in medicine in Berlin in 1810. In 1803, when he was working as a hospital doctor in Halle, he published 'Rhapsodies about Applying the Methods of Treatment to Disorganized Spirits' (*Rhapsodieen über die Anwendung der psychischen Kurmethode auf Geisteszerrüttungen*). In this book, Reil related madness both to loss of reason and to social conditions, and introduced the influential idea that advances in civilization created more 'disorganized spirits'. Reil was a tireless writer, medical reformer and an ardent German nationalist. He wanted to bring the miseries of mental hospitals to public attention and find support for establishing modern asylums. In his own words, madhouses (*Irrenhäuser*) were neither hospitals nor asylums giving shelter to the incurably insane. Rather, they were poky holes where society threw individuals regarded as public nuisances, namely the insane, criminals and other 'antisocial' elements (Schott & Tölle 2006, 270). Reil advocated the idea that psychiatric treatment should be directed to the education of the insane, and he defined psychiatric expertise as an ability to treat the patient's mind. Yet, he opposed the purely psychic treatment and stressed the holistic healing process, in which different mental, physical and chemical elements are in balance.

Reil's younger colleague Johann Heinroth (1773–1843) differed from Reil in his conviction that mental illnesses had no physiological foundation or counterpart – they were essentially psychic disturbances. Heinroth became the first professor of 'psychological therapy' in Germany (at the University of Leipzig) in 1827. He saw mental illness resulting from an aberration of the developmental process of consciousness. The reason for such an aberration in turn resulted from the individual's errors, sins and vices, which had their origins in the increasingly immoderate abandonment of reason and the excessive rule of passions. To Heinroth, mental illness was at least partly induced by the free but aberrant will of the individual. This meant that the mentally ill themselves were responsible for their affliction. At the root of all psychiatric suffering lay the weak will, which led individuals to yield to the power of corrupting passions, such as greed, envy, imprudence and hatred. Enslaved to these passions, an individual's mental life became diseased (pathological), and this mental and spiritual corruption resulted in both mental and physical deterioration. As a firm believer in free will, Heinroth saw the loss or corruption of will leading to the worst possible mental decay. For a man of science, these were rather unusual opinions, and his medical colleagues criticized him for his extreme commitment to the moral and psychological explanatory framework as well as for his sanctimonious mysticism. When Heinroth's former student tried to explain his psychiatric ideas to Esquirol, who disdained unenlightened doctrines, Monsieur Esquirol apparently shook his head and exclaimed, 'Ah, this German obscurantism!' (Marx 1990, 377–8).

Heinroth's 'sin psychiatry' was disparaged, but many German physicians believed in his doctrine about the connection between insanity and sin. He was not openly challenged for his assertion that Christianity was the only religion that could get individuals out of the clutches of insanity. One who most certainly did not agree with sin psychiatry was Wilhelm Griesinger (1817–68), an innovator who more than anyone else contributed to a paradigm change in German psychiatry. In 1845, at the age of 28, Griesinger published a ground-breaking book *Pathology and Therapy of Mental Illnesses* (*Die Pathologie und Therapie der psychischen Krankheiten*). The book and its later, enlarged edition was a cornerstone of international scientific psychiatry. Griesinger made a clean break with a science and medical epistemology that embraced religion, an idealistic 'inner perception' and synthetic 'wholeness'. In their place, Griesinger offered empirical natural science, rationalism and rigorous analysis. In his early career, he moved from university to university and worked in an asylum until he was appointed professor of internal medicine. In 1865, he moved to Berlin, where he became the first professor of psychiatry and neurology in Germany. In Berlin, he also worked as the chief physician at the Charité clinic. The years in Berlin were the most productive period in his career, but at the age of 51 his life was cut short by diphtheria (a bacterial infection that affects the membranes of the throat and nose) (Schott & Tölle 2006, 66–78).

Griesinger's main argument was that the mentally ill suffer from brain disease. From this axiom follows quite naturally the suggestion that psychiatry is just like any other branch of medicine, therefore the psychiatric approach to illness and health should be natural-scientific and naturalistic. In Griesinger's view, many diseases and disorders were localized in different parts of the brain so that a disorder of the speech centre, for example, resulted in aphasia (disturbance of the comprehension and formulation of language). An empirical proof for aphasia was provided in 1861 by the French neurologist Paul Broca. Griesinger is also known for his ardent advocacy of urban psychiatric clinics, which would function as clinical research and teaching centres. He infuriated many traditional alienists by arguing that the scientific progress of psychiatry required an abandonment of rural asylums and the guild-like isolation of alienists from the medical community. His wish was partly fulfilled when psychiatrists began to work in clinics affiliated to medical faculties in urban centres. Yet, rural asylums were definitely not abandoned in Germany or anywhere else. Instead, more and more asylums were built all over Europe from the mid-nineteenth to the mid-twentieth century.

Readers may be inclined to classify Griesinger as a zealous devotee to 'brain psychiatry' who snubbed psychological and social issues. In fact, the opposite is true: he was one of the first academic psychiatrists to be seriously interested in psychology. He understood the significance of subjective psychic processes to mental health and of the medical attempts to come to grips with the *mind* of the mentally ill. For him, the subject of psychiatric treatment was not the illness but the person who was ill. In his clinical work, Griesinger combined somatic and psychological methods, and he strove to avoid all mechanical restraints, such as straitjackets (Schott & Tölle 2006, 70–6). In this sense, he was a pioneer of both biological and psychodynamic psychiatry. Sadly, the psychological part of Griesinger's work was neglected and forgotten as the 'brain paradigm' became dominant in late nineteenth-century European psychiatry. In his multidimensional approach to mental illness he was markedly ahead of his time.

At the time of Griesinger's death in 1868, Germany was becoming the centre of medical and also psychiatric research. In 1880, there were no fewer than 21 chairs in psychiatry in the German Empire – more than anywhere else in the world. German academic psychology was also developing rapidly. Due to his untimely death, Griesinger did not participate in the shaping of experimental and physiological psychology, but the following generations of psychiatrists were familiar with nascent psychological research in general and Wilhelm Wundt's psychology in particular. Wundt, who had a medical degree, had established a psychological laboratory at the University of Leipzig in 1879, and the research he and his colleagues conducted there attracted some of the leading lights of German psychiatry (on Wundt as the founder of experimental psychology, see Rieber and Robinson 2001).

By the end of the nineteenth century, psychiatry had attained a relatively secure status in most western countries. The rise of psychiatric clinics, a partial integration of psychiatry into other branches of medicine and a widening of the scope of expertise from severe mental illnesses to the neuroses and other milder disorders were important milestones in the professionalization of psychiatry. Indications of psychiatric independence were the founding of scientific journals and societies, the establishment of new chairs, the publication of textbooks and the organization of conferences. Instead of being mere alienists looking after inmates in isolated asylums, psychiatrists were assuming the role of guardians of the mental health of nations. Around 1900, psychiatry came of age.

Bodily signs of madness

In nineteenth-century medicine, it was technically impossible to go under the skin of live patients and do research on the brain, nervous system and internal organs – there were no PET scans or other modern machines for brain imaging. What other option was there for those who had to make do with what we might call 'stone age technology'? The option was to look for signs of illness, temperament or intelligence in the skin, smell and facial features of patients, in the size and formation of the skull and in the structure of the body.

Nineteenth-century Europeans were attracted to a doctrine called *physiognomy*, which revolved around the assumption that outer appearance and especially facial traits of individuals disclosed aspects of their personality (Pearl 2010). The art of 'face reading' is ancient, but in the modern era it was revived and popularized by the Swiss pastor and poet Johann Kasper Lavater. His nicely illustrated book on 'physiognomic fragmentations' (1775–8) gained great popularity in central Europe and Britain, and it caught the attention of the medical community. Lavater's book also fascinated members of the urban middle class, who began to make physiognomic interpretations of other town dwellers. Laypeople's interest in physiognomy was partly motivated by their willingness to learn a method that would help them to recognize potentially harmful individuals, such as criminals, madmen and bullies. Physiognomy was also used for 'racial profiling', for example in Britain, where the Jews, the Irish and other 'alien' groups were singled out by their appearance (Pearl 2010, 106–47). Physiognomy also inspired artists and writers, such as Honoré Balzac in France, Edgar Allan Poe in the United States and, most famously, Oscar Wilde in Britain; his novel *The Picture of Dorian Gray* (1890) is almost a textbook example of the cultural impact of physiognomy.

In Paris, Pinel measured the dimensions of his patients' skulls and noticed some deformations, particularly when patients suffered from 'idiotism' or feeblemindedness. Yet, he admitted that the anatomy and pathology of the brain was shrouded in mystery (Pinel 2009, 71, 75). Pinel's pupil Esquirol was more convinced that a study of the physical traits of the lunatics makes it easier for alienists to make

FIGURE 6.1 Théodore Géricault's 'Portrait of a Woman Suffering from Obsessive Envy' (*Monomane de l'envie*), 1822.
Source: © Lyon MBA – Photo Alain Basset

the right diagnosis. Esquirol invited artists to visit asylums in Paris to draw the inmates' features, which he believed revealed something about the nature of their illness. These drawings portray, for example, a 'fanatical priest', a 'melancholic banker' and a 'military man who calls himself the King of Sweden'. The most famous artistic portrayals of madness of that era are Théodore Géricault's (1791–1824) paintings of monomania from the early 1820s.

In the second half of the nineteenth century, physicians became interested in the photography of mental illness. Photography brought new life to physiognomy, which had received scathing criticism from sceptical scientists. The British psychiatrist and physiognomist Hugh Welch Diamond (1809–86) and his colleagues wanted to illustrate different forms of mental illness with the help of a camera, but they also believed in the therapeutic effects of photographs: when mental patients were shown pictures of themselves, they might recognize their

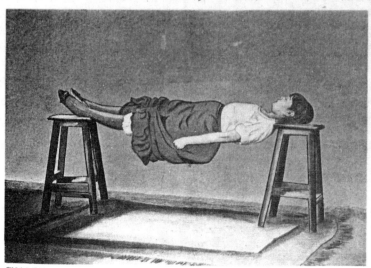

FIGURE 6.2 Experiences relating to spasms provoked in hysterical patients at the Salpêtrière in Paris. From *Leçons Cliniques sur L'Hysterie et L'Hypnotisme* (1891).

Source: © Wellcome Library, London

120 The great transformation

insanity in them, which then might push them towards the path of recovery (Diamond 2014, 23; Pearl 2010, 150). Physiognomic photography was used for various kinds of research purposes. Francis Galton (1822–1911), Charles Darwin's half-cousin, polymath and founder of eugenics, used the method of composite photography to detect physiognomic characteristics of health, beauty, race and personality (notably criminality). Galton's method was to photographically superimpose two or more faces by multiple exposures and then define physiognomic characters of, for example, violent criminals or the mentally ill (Pearl 2010, 202–3).

In Paris, neurologist Jean-Martin Charcot (1825–93) had a small photographic laboratory at the Salpêtrière, which he used for photographing his hysterical and epileptic female patients in the 1870s and 1880s. Charcot was fascinated by the gestures, postures and facial expressions of the hysterics, even if they appeared to be faked or simulated by the lower-class women patients to please Monsieur Professor. Charcot's enthusiasm was shared by the father of modern evolutionary theory: Charles Darwin (1809–82) wanted to capture photographically facial features and emotional expressions of the insane, because 'they are liable to the strongest passions, and give uncontrolled vent to them' (Darwin 1993, 366). Darwin pioneered the use of photography as an essential part of scientific argument in *The Expressions of Emotions in Man and Animals* (1872), which contains several photographs of emotional expressions of humans and animals (Darwin 1993). Darwin was assisted by James Crichton-Browne (1840–1938), the young chief physician of the large West Riding Asylum in Wakefield, who had set up an asylum laboratory that included photographic equipment. Darwin questioned Crichton-Browne about blushing, facial muscles and expressions of bereavement and grief. Crichton-Browne sent Darwin about 40 photographs of patients, providing interesting evidence of the proximity of the expression of emotions in humans and other animals. Most famously, one photograph of a female patient whose hair was occasionally erect 'just like wire' indicated that the hair of humans, just like that of other mammals, can become erect due to fright or anger (this was the only photograph sent by Crichton-Browne that Darwin used in his book). Crichton-Browne could also prove that blushing, which occurs most often with public interactions, 'may occur in solitude and in the dark' (Crichton-Browne 1930, 64). Darwin dedicated one chapter of his book to the description of the expressions of 'low spirits, anxiety, grief, dejection and despair'.

The challenge of phrenology

In addition to physiognomy, two related doctrines, *phrenology* and *craniology*, gained popularity in nineteenth-century Europe. The founder of phrenology was the Austrian physician and neuroanatomist Frans Joseph Gall (1758–1828), who performed a series of technically innovative brain operations in late eighteenth- and early nineteenth-century Vienna. On the basis of these operations, Gall claimed to have demonstrated the anatomical and functional versatility of the brain. In particular, Gall argued that different mental activities have their own locations in the brain. He then developed a specific method to assess the character of mental and moral faculties: based on his investigations of the external shape of the skull, he inferred that each faculty and emotion had a corresponding organ in the brain. Contrary to the accusations directed at his 'pseudo-scientific' doctrine by the later generations of scientists and scholars, Gall did not even try to find 'precise "organs" within the brain corresponding to the 27 "faculties" of his psychological theory' (Williams 1994, 109). These faculties included 'impulse to propagation', 'parental love' and 'sense of locality', and Gall predicted that future research would reveal the location and characteristics of the various sections of the brain where the mental faculties were situated. Gall called his doctrine 'organology' or 'doctrine of the skull' (*Schädellehre*), and he never accepted the more pompous term 'phrenology', which means 'study of the mind' and which was taken into use by a British doctor in 1815. Gall's ardent follower, the German physician Johann Spurzheim (1776–1832), with whom he had a falling-out in 1812, popularized 'phrenology' in his extensive travels across Europe and called himself the other creator of this doctrine (Tomlinson 2005, 50–76).

Gall's theory of the localization of mental functions in the brain stimulated neurological brain research and contributed to the naturalistic and materialistic approach to human psychology. But Gall went further than his colleagues in his claim that a study of the formation of the skull and its bumps disclosed information about the mental faculties. Bumps in the skull were important indications of mental activity, because the skull conformed to the size and shape of the brain and its organs. Thus an investigation of the size of the different organs of the brain would yield valuable information about the relative power of these organs (Harrington 1987, 8). In the English-speaking world, an energetic advocate of phrenology was the Scottish lawyer George Combe (1788–1858), founder of the Edinburgh Phrenological Society (1820) and the author of the popular book *Constitution of Man* (1828). Combe was a late representative of the Scottish Enlightenment, an advocate of naturalism and secularism whose rational and progressive mindset tallied well with the radical political reputation of phrenology. Indeed, Gall himself had to leave Vienna and move to Paris in 1807 when the authorities of the Habsburg Empire harassed him on account of the dangerous implications of his theory to morality and religion. The conservative guardians of public morality had good reason to be suspicious of Gall. His doctrine of the 'Parliament of Little Men' was radical, because the idea of the relative autonomy of the different parts and layers of the brain was impossible to harmonize with the theological conception of the soul as the unifying ruler of mental activities. As one medical opponent of Gall's theory put it in 1804,

> if each modification of the heart and spirit [*esprit*] were regarded as a distinct faculty, dependent on a particular organ, there would no longer exist any morality in the actions of men. The unfaithful and adulterous women, the swindler, the thief, even the murderer [. . .] would justify themselves by accusing nature [itself].

(Williams 1994, 110)

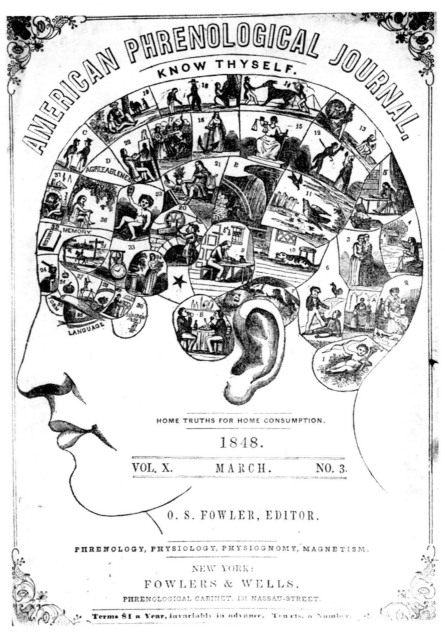

FIGURE 6.3 Cover of *American Phrenological Journal*, 1848.

Many of Gall's supporters held that the human mind was a biological phenomenon and as such a part of nature, and they had a political agenda that was directed against mysticism, theology, aristocracy and the holy scriptures. Phrenology appealed to the younger generation of French psychiatrists, who preferred a purely materialistic and naturalistic conception of mental illness. Gall argued that mental illness was causally related to an abnormal growth of a particular organ in the brain, or to an inflammation or other strong irritant, which could trigger the onset of illness. This was a plausible theory especially because the rival explanations were no more convincing.

Phrenology influenced a more technical doctrine called *craniology*, which was preoccupied with measuring the skull and its proportions and drawing psychological, moral and racial conclusions based on these measurements. Craniometric methods were occasionally used for measuring the skulls of the mentally ill, even though the more enlightened psychiatrists were suspicious of the scientific value of such investigations. The Italian psychiatrist Enrico Morselli (1852–1929) probably represented the views of many of his medical colleagues in his comments on craniology: 'Whoever tries to convince you that alienists measure the skulls of the mad to deduce whether or not they are disturbed in the mind shows that he has learned to tell tales' (Guarnieri 1988, 107). Craniology and phrenology were parts of a larger anthropometric research on the external appearance of humans, which lasted from the late eighteenth to the mid-twentieth century. After World War II, anthropometry – 'the measurement of Man' – was tainted and discredited by the racialist, racist and scientifically unsound tenets and methods exemplified in the more extreme forms of physical anthropology, criminology, eugenics and intelligence testing, in which intellectual capacity was judged by cranial capacity. In this quasi-scientific game, 'negroes', Indians, Sami people and other 'inferior races' were usually at the receiving end of vicious prejudices and white-supremacist statements dressed in quantitative scientific jargon. Today, anthropometry is no longer used for racist or political purposes.[1]

The dream of exact science

In the early 1820s, the Parisian psychiatrist Antoine-Laurent Bayle dissected the brains of some deceased, seriously ill mental patients, and he noticed some lesions that he could not find in the brains of other mental patients. As he could not know that the brains had been damaged by syphilis, he called the disease 'general paresis' (*paralysie générale;* on neurosyphilis, see Chapter 8). And in the case of such neurological diseases as dementia, pathological-anatomical research could demonstrate its connections with atherosclerosis (clogging or hardening of blood vessels caused by plaques). When the French neurologist Paul Broca (1824–80)

---

1 Nowadays anthropometry is understood as a technique of measuring the human body in terms of dimensions, proportions and ratios such as those provided by the cephalic index (ratio of the breadth of the head to its length).

124 The great transformation

succeeded in discovering the speech centre in the frontal lobe in 1861, the theory of the localization of mental faculties entered the medical limelight. Localization theory represented the new positivist science, which triumphantly challenged the metaphysical-idealistic approach to nature and human nature.

Positivism denotes a set of beliefs about the certainty of scientific knowledge. It relies heavily on the ideal view of the natural sciences as empirical, exact, experimental and value-free. During the latter half of the nineteenth century, positivism exerted a strong influence on medicine and the emerging sciences of mind and society (psychology, sociology and anthropology). Auguste Comte (1798–1857), the pioneer of French sociology, was a sort of high priest of positivism, a savant who wanted to replace religion by his technocratic Religion of Humanity. Following Comte's lead, the French positivists stressed empirical analysis, compilation of facts and 'evidence-based' generalizations. The positivist programme was ambitious and in tune with the increasingly widespread scientific world view. Nevertheless, the impact of the positivist mindset on mental medicine was rather weak or contradictory. Many alienists did not even regard themselves as medical scientists but rather as professional caretakers and moral educators of the insane, whose expertise was a result of craftsmanship: they had refined their skills over years as 'apprentices' to master craftsmen (superintendents of asylums and other senior alienists) (Watson 1998). Furthermore, asylum alienists tended to have a cool if not suspicious attitude towards medical and scientific novelties and 'fads' that promised much but delivered little. Even the 'hard-nosed' neuropsychiatrists had to admit that the positivist conception of science did not help much in the empirical search for undisputed knowledge about the anatomy and physiology of brain diseases. More psychologically oriented psychiatrists in turn stressed that mental illness is just what it says: an illness of the mind (*maladie mentale* in French; *Geisteskrankheit* in German; *disturbo mentale* in Italian). What this implied was that it was unnecessary to try to turn mental illness into a brain disease.

During the latter half of the nineteenth century, positivism functioned as the ideal model and not so much as a concrete research methodology. By and large, the development of medicine followed the positivist – and phrenological – ideal in its adherence to the materialist and empiricist conception of knowledge. For example, the German physician, biologist and anthropologist Rudolf Virchow (1821–1902) developed cellular pathology on the basis of nascent cell biology to which he himself made significant contributions (among other things, he is considered to have been the first to recognize leukaemia cells). The work of Virchow and other cell biologists definitively discredited humoral theory and convinced the majority of scientists of the necessity to search for causal mechanisms and relations between entities, and also between smaller and larger entities, such as cells and tissues (Mayr 1982, 652–80).

Evolution and heredity

The pre-psychiatric mad-doctors as well as the first-generation psychiatrists believed in the heritability of mental illness. In his *A Treatise on Madness* (1758), the British physician William Battie (1703–76), chief physician at St Luke's Hospital for Lunatics in London, refers to 'the striking oddities that characterize whole families derived from Lunatic ancestors' and to 'the frequent breaking forth of real Madness in the offspring of such illconcerted alliances' (Battie 1758, 59–60). John Haslam (1764–1844), the chief physician at the Bethlem mental hospital, observed that if one of the parents has suffered from mental illness, it is very probable that some signs of madness can be detected in the descendants too. In France, Pinel and Esquirol were keenly interested in the heritability of mental illness. According to Esquirol, 110 out of 482 melancholic patients at the Salpêtrière had inherited their illness from their relatives. He calculated that in 150 out of his 264 wealthy private patients the cause of illness was heredity. No wonder Esquirol saw heredity as the most common cause of mental illness, or, to use more modern language, he saw heredity as an important risk factor. This view is very common even in today's psychiatry. In the early nineteenth century, Johann Reil referred to a 'disposition' (*Anlage*) to mental illness, which quickly became part of psychiatric vocabulary. The founding fathers of psychiatry agreed that if there is mental illness in the family, it increases the risk of insanity in the offspring (Shorter 1997, 28–9).

The problem for the scientifically oriented physicians was that the meagre results of brain research threatened the hard-won prestige of academic medicine in general and psychiatry in particular. If psychiatrists could not convince the authorities, policy makers, privileged classes and ordinary people of the materialist origin of mental illness, there was a risk of mental medicine losing its monopoly over the management of madness. Physicians had to be wary of the clergy in particular, because the Church remained a powerful rival to secular medicine until the twentieth century. No wonder psychiatrists looked to other sciences to find a more solid foundation for their research on mental illness. One potential disciplinary ally to psychiatry was evolutionary biology.

Darwin's theory of natural selection, as well as other evolutionary ideas and theories, shaped European psychiatry from the mid-nineteenth century onwards. The psychiatric community adopted the biological assumption that when hereditary predisposition was combined with specific environmental determinants (such as poverty, poor nutrition and hygiene, or nervousness of urban life), such a combination could result in mental illness. This was believed to be true especially in the case of the so-called *endogenic* illnesses, which were seen to be caused by some internal factor in the human organism in contradistinction to the so-called *exogenic* illnesses, which allegedly originated in 'external' pathogens, such as somatic diseases (e.g. influenza or encephalitis), syphilis infection, alcoholism or ageing. In the discussions of the Darwinian 'struggle for existence', pathogenic environmental factors were seen to affect the hereditary disposition to afflictions such as melancholy or nervousness. It was widely believed by late nineteenth-century psychiatrists and neurologists that a co-determination of behaviour by heredity and environment might result in various mental disturbances. Consequently, mental disorders became emphatically hereditary illnesses caused by bad 'germ plasm', a pre-genetic term employed to designate the biological unit of heredity (Faber 1997). In short, the representatives of mental medicine widely considered heredity the principal determinant of mental illness, whereas the environment played a secondary role.

126 The great transformation

In Germany, these 'Darwinian' or, rather, 'pseudo-Darwinian' ideas became widespread at the end of the nineteenth century, when many psychiatrists started to talk about 'hereditary psychopathic disturbances' and 'inferiority' and about the threat these hereditary taints posed to the social order. When this concern was combined with the theory of degeneration, it initiated a creation of a massive medical and cultural panorama of hereditary evils, in which the destiny of the whole nation was at stake. To ward off this impending threat, the authorities needed to take measures and, in cooperation with physicians, save the nation from psychophysical decay. To understand the evolution of this socio-cultural mentality of fear, we need to go to mid-nineteenth century Paris, home town of degenerationism.

The Doomsday doctrine of degeneration

In France, the plausible idea of the heritability of mental illness was connected with the moralistic doctrine of degeneration. This doctrine was related to the hardened attitudes towards the deviant during the last decades of the nineteenth century. In the public discussions, the disabled, the feebleminded and the insane were often portrayed as inferior specimens of humanity. They were described as useless or even harmful 'parasites' partly because they were not considered productive citizens in industrializing western nation states that were in need of capable workers and dutiful citizens. They were deemed inferior also because they damaged the racial quality of the nation simply by breeding: their offspring inherited the harmful 'germ plasm' or 'genes', as the units of inheritance began to be called in the early twentieth century. Furthermore, the very presence of criminals, prostitutes, work-shy vagrants, sexual perverts and other inferior groups lowered the moral quality of the nation and threatened the fabric of society.

The French psychiatrist Bénédict Augustin Morel (1809–73) introduced the idea of human degeneration in a book published in 1857 (*Traité des dégénérescences physiques, intellectuelles et morales de l'espèce humaine et des causes qui produisent ces variétés maladives*). Morel's main thesis was that, in some families, harmful personality traits and lifestyles produce a cumulative process of worsening mental, physical and moral health, which continues from one generation to another until the whole family might become extinct. Four generations of cumulative degeneration could be enough to sink a family in the abyss of irreversible decay. At first, family members might show symptoms of nervousness, then of mental alienation until finally they suffer from severe mental disturbances, idiocy and sterility. Predisposing and precipitating factors include alcoholism, immorality, poor nutrition and unhealthy living conditions (e.g. cramped housing, dirt and bad air) (Huertas & Winston 1992).

Morel was not an armchair theorist. He had worked among urban industrial workers in Rouen as well as among families living in remote areas in the countryside, so he had first-hand experience of people living in poverty (Dowbiggin 1991, 118). On the basis of Lamarck's theory of evolution, Morel argued that degeneration was both hereditary and cumulative. Individuals may inherit an organic predisposition to a certain illness or deficit from their parents, and such pathological signs of Cain may become pronounced over the years, particularly if the vulnerable individuals are exposed to harmful environmental pathogens, such as alcohol, poor nutrition or bad company. Such pathogens exert a harmful effect on the already 'neuropathic' or damaged nervous system of these people. The following generation would then inherit the same predispositions, but in a more pathological and defective form. For Morel, such organic diseases as *paralysis agitans* (Parkinson's disease), chorea (involuntary neurological movement disorder), migraine and asthma were hereditary, as also were diverse psychopathological disorders, such as hysteria, epilepsy, 'suicidal mania' and alcoholism.

Morel and his colleague Jacques-Joseph Moreau (1804–84), who had similar ideas about degeneration, found a receptive audience to their medical alarmism. If organic diseases and 'neuropathic' predispositions were both hereditary and cumulative, the French had good reason to be worried about the future of their glorious nation. How many degenerate, neuropathic families were there in France? Could anything be done to prevent this 'biological deterioration'? Morel did not know for sure, although he paid some attention to the environmental factors, such as alcohol and drug abuse. The temperance movement, which Morel supported, was the only practical attempt to get rid of one particular cause of degeneration. Familiar with animal and plant breeding, Morel warned against sibling marriage, which he regarded as the greatest threat to the health and longevity of races. In the decades following the publication of Morel's book, the list of so-called stigmata of degeneration became longer and longer, as all sorts of mental and physical abnormalities were added to it. Unusual ears or rows of teeth, hairy hands, harelips, drooping mouths, unsymmetrical forms of skull, weak chin and conspicuous feminine traits in men, as well as masculine traits in women were all potential signs of degeneration. In short, degenerationism compiled a catalogue of all the possible negative and undesirable characteristics and explained them in medical and psychological language.

Degenerationism spread from France to other parts of Europe, gaining popularity in German-speaking Europe, Italy, the Nordic countries and Britain. It became a helpful, scientific-sounding explanation of mental illness, feeblemindedness and social problems, such as prostitution, criminality and the growing menace of socialism. It was also used in military arenas. When the German Army defeated the French in the Franco-Prussian War of 1870–1, many degenerationists saw it as an indication of the physical and moral inferiority of the French in comparison to the Germans (Dowbiggin 1991, 155–6). In Germany, an evangelist for degenerationism was the neurologist Paul Julius Möbius (1853–1907), who is (in)famous for his misogynistic pamphlet on the 'physiological feeblemindedness of women' (*Über den physiologischen Schwachsinn des Weibes*, 1900).

For degenerationists, madness was in the blood, and the effects of heredity were cumulative: the milder form of madness or neurosis of one generation became full-blown insanity in the next generation. This misleading evolutionary framework gave late nineteenth-century mental medicine its emphatically pessimistic if not fatalistic character. Degenerationists did not derive their hereditarian ideas from

128 The great transformation

Darwin's theory but from the French naturalist Jean-Baptiste Lamarck's (1744–1829) theory of the inheritance of acquired characteristics. After mid-century, Lamarck's theory of evolution was revived as neo-Lamarckism, which confused inherited and acquired traits in its basic tenet that characteristics, customs and the external appearance of a person were passed on to the next generation. As some Darwinians and especially the German biologist August Weismann (1834–1914) pointed out, Lamarckism went astray in its assertion that new or acquired traits were heritable. If this were true, then a blacksmith or a boxer with well-developed muscles would carry in his sex cells 'muscularity', a trait which could be passed from parent to offspring. Likewise, a hopeless drunkard would pass his overwhelming desire for liquor on to the next generation via inheritance, ditto a stutterer. Weismann undermined the Lamarckian theory with his own theory of germ plasm, which argued that acquired characteristics, such as muscularity or the ability to dance, could not be transmitted to offspring, because germ cells in the ovaries and testes that produce egg and sperm cannot be modified by cellular changes in the other body cells. As a Lamarckian science, degenerationism was biologically flawed from the start, but ultimately very influential in Europe, North America and South America (Pick 1989).

To the alienists, degenerationism provided a convenient explanation for therapeutic inefficiency: since madness was in the blood, the institutionalized insane were almost or wholly incurable. If patients did not get better, it was due either to the seriousness and chronicity of their disease or their inherent neuropathies. In both cases, doctors could only confine them, control their environment and regulate their behaviour. Even though the clinical criteria for degeneration were very vague and haphazard, degenerationism was a flexible and adjustable doctrine that could be used for many different purposes. Small wonder, then, that the late nineteenth-century French alienists often began the patient record with the words 'mental degeneration, with . . .' ('dégénérescence mentale, avec . . .') (Ellenberger 1994, 281).

Social and cultural commentators in France and other western countries used degenerationism to explain the increasingly unpredictable behaviour of radical individuals and the anonymous masses swelling in the streets of ever-growing European cities. Dirty proletarians, idle loafers, petty thieves, debauched hookers, smelly drunkards in beer joints and the insane confined in asylums had all fallen into the swamp of decay and corruption that extinguished reason, morals and free will. The word 'atavism' was used to describe a particular kind of degeneration in which individuals in a large group regressed to older, more primitive behavioural tendencies, governed by blind instincts and archaic memories of their ancestors. Such atavistic tendencies made the degenerate individuals more impulsive, unpredictable and violent, particularly when they gathered together (Pick 1989, 4). Degeneration was seen as an exclusively western scourge, because insanity, alcoholism, neurosyphilis and other 'diseases of civilization' appeared to be rare among the 'primitive' peoples in Africa and elsewhere (Kraepelin 2007). In the heyday of European imperialism and colonialism, this seemingly positive observation did not exactly reduce the disrespectful and abusive treatment of ethnic peoples.

Degenerationists resembled vulgar Marxists and fundamentalist psychoanalysts in their cunning ability to dismiss all possible objections and empirical evidence simply by referring to the infallible formula of their closed conceptual system. Hence if the stigmata of degeneration were clearly visible in the family history, it was a sure sign of degeneration. If there were *no* such stigmata or they were vague, one only had to look a bit closer at the family members; surely some of them were eccentrics, neurotics, drunkards or various sorts of immoderate enthusiasts. Inevitably, some psychiatrists grew impatient with degeneration fanaticism, which was useless in clinical work (Schott & Tölle 2006, 101). In the early twentieth century, degenerationism began to lose scientific credibility as well as cultural authority. Statistical research failed adequately to support the theory of the inheritance of neuropathies, while neurology and the new science of genetics contributed to a research model that took a Darwinian turn after World War I, leaving no room for Lamarckian speculations of inheritance. French psychiatrists had to admit that their understanding of the mechanisms of inheritance was rather vague – conjectures and speculations did not meet the criteria for scientific theory (Dowbiggin 1991, 124). When, in 1905, the spirochete bacterium causing syphilis was found, it made the medical community more critical of degenerationism, which considered neurosyphilis an inherited disease caused by degeneration.

By the early twentieth century, psychoanalysis and other forms of 'dynamic psychiatry' had taken up unconscious conflicts and psychic processes for psycho-medical discussion, and in this emphatically psychological framework there was no place for the doctrine of degeneration. Concurrently, mental disorders began to be divided into the two basic categories of psychoses and neuroses, which meant that neurosis was no longer regarded as a potential precursor of insanity but as an independent mental disorder. And when medicine and psychiatry became more socially oriented, ill health began to be seen in the context of social conditions, including poverty, malnutrition, urban squalor and poor hygiene. An emphasis on environmental factors directed medical attention to the prevention of diseases and delegitimized the pessimistic biology-as-destiny doctrine of degeneration. The war neuroses of World War I, which showed that in adverse circumstances even 'normal', healthy men may exhibit signs of 'neuropathy', further undermined the claims of degenerationists. For decades, degenerationism had moved uneasily between medical diagnosis and racial prophecy before it sank into medical and cultural oblivion. Before this happened, however, degenerationism-influenced racial hygienic ideology and practice which became a veritable scourge for the mentally ill and the feebleminded during the first half of the twentieth century.

Racial hygiene as an ideology and social policy

The pessimistic and fatalistic doctrine of degeneration prompted many doctors and members of the governing elites to wonder if there was anything to be done to forestall the threat of racial degeneration. Such a concern paved the way for twentieth-century racial hygiene or eugenics, as it was called in the

130 The great transformation

English-speaking world. Eugenics was the invention of the British polymath Francis Galton, Charles Darwin's half-cousin, who in his new doctrine combined evolutionary theory, statistics and his extraordinary enthusiasm for the genealogies of eminent families, such as those of his famous half-cousin (Keynes 1993; Fancher 1998). Galton was worried about the dominance of inferior hereditary characteristics. He believed that such traits could result in the fatal decay of the whole family. He suggested that the authorities should prevent the breeding of inferior families that were most likely to produce degenerate individuals. To achieve this goal, marriages should be controlled and regulated so that the nation would be filled with families of 'good stock'. This required that, in the case of humans, the blind evolution of nature should be transformed into planned and controlled human engineering.

By the early twentieth century, eugenics was no longer confined to Britain and Galton's aspirations. As 'racial hygiene', the idea of creating a superior race gained ground in German-speaking Europe and began to influence social policy. The same happened in the United States and later in the Nordic countries, where racial hygiene became a movement that affected legislation and led to the compulsory sterilization and castration of the feebleminded, the mentally ill and other 'inferior' groups in society. In all these countries, the goal of eugenic policy was to eliminate families of low hereditary quality by preventing them from reproducing. This was called 'negative eugenics'. 'Positive eugenics' in turn referred to the ways in which marriages, reproduction and family lives of 'superior' individuals could be encouraged and supported by the authorities. In the early twentieth century, eugenic enthusiasts saw in the rise of Mendelian genetics a much-needed, hard biological science that would constitute the basis of the 'applied science' of eugenics. One could say that, in eugenics or racial hygiene, science functioned as a social transformer in translating the fears and hopes of the white, educated middle class into concepts, theories and social-political activism (Bashford & Levine 2010).

Switzerland was the first European country to pass a sterilization law in 1928 (in the Canton de Vaud). In northern Europe, Denmark was the first country to do the same in 1929. By 1935, the law had come into force in three other Nordic countries: Norway, Sweden and Finland. In ethnically rather homogeneous Nordic countries, sterilizations became a sort of social contraception that saved the state from taking care of children conceived by unfit parents. Sterilization also enabled the release of institutionalized persons from asylums, homes for the feebleminded and epileptics and other public institutes (Runcis 1998, 200; on the Swedish sterilization laws, see Tydén 2010).

The eugenic logic of eliminating the 'unfit' was taken to its extreme in National Socialistic Germany. Germany was the only country in the world where racial hygiene culminated in a systematic killing of those judged to be 'unworthy to live' (see Chapter 11). By the time of the Weimar Republic (1919–33), racial hygiene had a firm foothold in German medicine and health policy. In this troubled period, close ties were established between German and American eugenics, and both the Rockefeller Foundation and the Carnegie Institute generously financed German race biological and medical research. German psychiatry was held in high esteem at the Rockefeller Foundation, which did not have a political but rather scientific motivation to support German science until World War II, although it must be said that the American administrators at Rockefeller must have been either extremely naïve or relatively well-disposed towards the political and social implications of the research they were supporting in Hitler's Germany. The American journal *Eugenical News* praised Germany's new race laws and published articles written by German racialist researchers, whom the American eugenicists relied on to scientifically legitimize their own activities. A few years after the birth of the Third Reich, one American eugenicist complained that 'the Germans are beating us at our own game' (Black 2003, 277). At the same time, Americans were proud of the fact that they had exerted significant influence on Nazi eugenics.

Racial hygienic terror in Germany or eugenic fanaticism with sterilization laws should not prompt us to think that eugenics was an unfortunate aberration in western cultural evolution towards liberal democracy. On the contrary, eugenics was an intrinsic part of modernization especially in the western hemisphere (Turda 2010, 8). The fact that eugenics played a major role in Nordic welfare states proves that the key to understanding eugenics is 'social engineering' or science-based social planning rather than any totalitarian ethos that saw individual citizens as nothing but expendable parts of an organic whole, such as the state, race or nation (*Volk*) (Brückweh et al. 2012). In Sweden, for example, many social-democratic, progressive politicians and intellectuals saw eugenics as an essential part of social organization in the developing welfare state, while in Britain Fabian socialists and other leftist intellectuals found support for their rationalistic vision of an ordered and well-functioning society in eugenic social and health policy.

It was only during the second half of the twentieth century that eugenics gradually ceased to be modern, scientific and respectable. Still, in many countries sterilization laws remained in force until the 1970s (including the Nordic countries). In the decades after World War II, favourite targets of eugenic sterilization in the United States were slum dwellers, Puerto Rican women and Native Americans living on reservations. So-called racial integrity laws with their 'interracial' marriage prohibitions were gradually repealed, Alabama being the last state to end legally sanctioned eugenic racism. This happened in 2000 (Black 2003, 400–1).

Bibliography

Bashford, A. and Levine, P. (eds) (2010) *The Oxford Handbook of the History of Eugenics*, Oxford: Oxford University Press.

Battie, W. (1758) *A Treatise on Madness*, London: J. Whiston & B. White.

Black, E. (2003) *War Against the Weak. Eugenics and America's Campaign to Create a Master Race*, New York: Four Walls Eight Windows.

Brown, E.M. (1994) 'French psychiatry's initial reception of Bayle's discovery of general paresis of the insane', *Bulletin of the History of Medicine*, 68: 235–53.

132 The great transformation

Brückweh, K., Schumann, D., Wetzell, R.F. and Ziemann, B. (eds) (2012) *Engineering Society. The Role of the Human and Social Sciences in Modern Societies,1880–1980*, Basingstoke: Palgrave Macmillan.

Crichton-Browne, J. (1930) *What the Doctor Thought*, London: Ernest Benn Limited.

Darwin, C. (1993) *The Expression of the Emotions in Man and Animals* [an excerpt], in D.M. Porter and P.W. Graham (eds) *The Portable Darwin*, London: Penguin Books.

Diamond, H.W. (2014) 'On the application of photography to the physiognomic and mental phenomena of insanity', in S.L. Gilman (ed.) *The Face of Madness: Hugh W. Diamond and the Origin of Psychiatric Photography*, 1st edn 1976, Brattleboro, VT: Echo Point Books & Media.

Dowbiggin, I. (1991) *Inheriting Madness: Professionalization and Psychiatric Knowledge in Nineteenth-century France*, Berkeley: University of California Press.

Ellenberger, H.F. (1994) *The Discovery of the Unconscious*, 1st edn 1970, London: Fontana Press.

Faber, D.P. (1997) 'Theodule Ribot and the reception of evolutionary ideas in France', *History of Psychiatry*, 8: 445–58.

Fancher, R. (1998) 'Biography and psychodynamic theory: some lessons from the life of Francis Galton', *History of Psychology*, 1: 99–115.

Goldstein, J. (1987) *Console and Classify. The French Psychiatric Profession in the Nineteenth Century*, Cambridge: Cambridge University Press.

Guarnieri, P. (1988) 'Between soma and psyche: Morselli and psychiatry in late-nineteenth-century Italy', in W.F. Bynum and R. Porter (eds) *The Anatomy of Madness: Essays in the History of Psychiatry*, Vol. III: *The Asylum and Its Psychiatry*, London: Routledge.

Harrington, A. (1987) *Medicine, Mind and the Double Brain*, Princeton, NJ: Princeton University Press.

Harris, R. (1991) *Murders and Madness. Medicine, Law and Society in the Fin de Siècle*, Oxford: Oxford University Press.

Huertas, R. and Winston, C.M. (1992) 'Madness and degeneration, I: From "fallen angel" to mentally ill', *History of Psychiatry*, 3: 391–411.

Huneman, P. (2008) 'Montpellier vitalism and the emergence of alienism in France (1750–1800): the case of the passions', *Science in Context* 21: 615–47.

Keynes, M. (ed.) (1993) *Sir Francis Galton, FRS: The Legacy of His Ideas*, Basingstoke: Macmillan.

Kraepelin, E. (2007) 'On the question of degeneration' (1908), *History of Psychiatry*, 18: 399–404.

Marx, O.M. (1990) 'German Romantic psychiatry, Part 1', *History of Psychiatry*, 1: 351–81.

Mayr, E. (1982) *The Growth of Biological Thought*, Cambridge, MA: Harvard University Press.

Morel, B.A. (1857) *Traité des dégénérescences physiques, intellectuelles, et morales de l'espèce humaine*, Paris: Baillière.

Pearl, S. (2010) *About Faces: Physiognomy in Nineteenth-Century Britain*, Cambridge, MA: Harvard University Press.

Pick, D. (1989) *Faces of Degeneration: A European Disorder, c. 1848–c. 1918*, Cambridge: Cambridge University Press.

Pinel, P. (2009) *A Treatise on Insanity*, orig. French edn 1801, Milton Keynes: General Books.

Rieber, W.R. and Robinson, D.K. (eds) (2001) *Wilhelm Wundt in History. The Making of a Scientific Psychology*, New York: Springer.

Runcis, M. (1998) *Steriliseringar i folkhemmet*, Stockholm: Ordfront.

Schott, H. and Tölle, R. (2006) *Geschichte der Psychiatrie*, Munich: C.H. Beck.

Shorter, E. (1997) *A History of Psychiatry*, New York: John Wiley & Sons.

Tomlinson, S. (2005) *Head Masters: Phrenology, Secular Education and Nineteenth-century Social Thought*, Tuscaloosa: University of Alabama Press.

Turda, M. (2010) *Modernism and Eugenics*, New York: Palgrave Macmillan.

Tydén, M. (2010) 'The Scandinavian states: reformed eugenics applied', in A. Bashford and P. Levine (eds) *The Oxford Handbook of the History of Eugenics*, Oxford: Oxford University Press.

Vandermeersch, P. (1994) '"Les Mythes des origines" in the history of psychiatry', in M.S Micale and R. Porter (eds) *Discovering the History of Psychiatry*, Oxford: Oxford University Press.

Watson, W. (1998) 'Psychiatry as craft', *History of Psychiatry*, 9: 355–81.

Weiner, D.B. (2000) 'A provincial doctor faces the Paris establishment – Philippe Pinel 1778–93', in M.S. Micale (ed.) *Enlightenment, Passion, Modernity: Historical Essays in European Thought and Culture*, Stanford, CA: Stanford University Press.

Williams, E.A. (1994) *The Physical and the Moral. Anthropology, Physiology, and Philosophical Medicine in France, 1750–1850*, Cambridge: Cambridge University Press.

7

LIVING AND DYING IN ASYLUMLAND

The Age of the Asylum was launched with great therapeutic expectations in the early decades of the nineteenth century. Unfortunately, after 100 years the optimism had vanished, leaving doubt and pessimism. During this era there was considerable progress in medicine. Society enjoyed better hygiene, better surgical techniques and a better understanding of the role of cells and germs. But similar progress eluded mental medicine; in truth, it appeared to decline. Even if most psychiatrists were reluctant to admit it, even to themselves, by the early twentieth century it was apparent that the asylum system was metaphorically in a straitjacket, as were some of its patients. In their general assessment of the golden age of asylums (ca. 1870–1970), the German historians Heinz Schott and Rainer Tölle exclaimed, 'looked at from today's perspective, there is surprisingly little that can be described as positive in the asylum system' (Schott & Tölle 2006, 298; my translation). This chapter will describe life in the mental asylum and conclude with an interpretation of the asylum in terms of its fate as an institution. (For the history of twentieth-century psychiatry in different national contexts, see Gijswijt-Hofstra & Oosterhuis 2006.)

The era of therapeutic optimism

During the first decades of the nineteenth century, modern mental asylums were established in western Europe. The prevailing therapeutic principle in these asylums was the importance of serenity and calm. For this reason, asylums were typically built in the countryside away from the 'nerve-wracking' hustle and bustle of towns. Sometimes there were purely practical reasons determining the location. For example, in Germany many isolated monasteries were turned into asylums. It was also considered therapeutic to remove the insane from their families and local communities and replace the potentially harmful and chaotic social environment of the patient with the medical and strictly regulated environment of the asylum.

Alienists naturally promoted the curative aspects of the countryside and the rural asylums. At the same time, they painted a dark picture of the circumstances surrounding the insane in their local communities, where these pitiful individuals were neglected, mistreated and indoctrinated with false beliefs and superstitions. For alienists, it was self-evident that the insane could not recover until they were taken into a mental asylum to receive medical treatment as well as humane care. Establishing asylums in the countryside ensured that Mother Nature would also participate in the treatment of the insane, who were alienated from themselves and their social environment. The ultimate goal of the psychiatric cure was to integrate the recovered patient into the order of society (Engstrom 2004, 19). By the early twentieth century the therapeutic goal began to be formulated in terms of social adjustment, particularly in the United States, the most rapidly changing western nation from the late nineteenth century onwards.

At first, the Age of the Asylum was a period of therapeutic optimism. There were sound reasons for being in a hopeful mood: moral treatment appeared to be a useful therapy. Both the doctors and the authorities had faith in the efficiency of institutional mental health care. The early nineteenth-century optimism was contagious. When one asylum published its excellent recovery rates, other asylums followed suit and began to proclaim the same message: institutional care works. It was easy to present flattering figures about cures at a time when statistics were unreliable and almost any contention could be supported by ambiguous numbers. Superintendents often claimed striking successes in curing insanity. For example, the Ohio Lunatic Asylum reported that 80 per cent of recently admitted patients had recovered. At Worcester Hospital the figures were similar. Comparable figures for the more chronic cases were very different: at Ohio, patients who had been ill for between five and ten years had recovery rates of only 9 per cent; at Worcester the figures for older cases varied between 15.5 and 22.5 per cent (Grob 1994, 99). These figures indicated that the sooner the suffering individual was admitted to an asylum, the better the chance of a full recovery. Conversely, the admission of chronic patients had a negative impact on asylums, where their unchanging or worsening condition created a more pessimistic therapeutic atmosphere.

One important reason for the apparently high ratio of cures in asylums was the ambiguous way the word 'recovered' was used. As was often the case, the same patient was discharged 'recovered' from the same asylum several times within a time span of a few years or even one year. At Bloomingdale Asylum, one woman was discharged six times in one year – always 'recovered'. Another woman was discharged 'recovered' no fewer than 16 times in three years at Worcester Hospital. Because the records only took account of discharges, not admissions, the recovery rates became unrealistically high. Sceptical doctors began to notice that the hospital statistics were unreliable, and this contributed to the weakening of the myth of curability. After mid-century, the pendulum began to swing back to the 'pre-asylum' era view as medical attitudes towards curability became much more negative. One doctor who had previously stated his belief in a 90 per cent curability rate, expressed a radically different opinion in 1857: 'I have come to the

136 The great transformation

conclusion that when a man once becomes insane, he is about used up for this world' (Deutsch 1949, 155).

Yet, as historian Gerald Grob has pointed out, 'the claims of therapeutic successes were not simply imaginary' (Grob 1994, 100). He referred to an early longitudinal study undertaken by the superintendent at Worcester (Dr Park), who gathered data on 984 former patients in the 1880s and early 1890s. He found out that almost '58 percent of those discharged as recovered [at Worcester] never again were institutionalized. Data from other asylums, including Utica, Williamsburg, and Pennsylvania, suggest much the same state of affairs' (Grob 1994, 101). This meant that, for one reason or another, many discharged patients were able to live in their own communities.

By the end of the nineteenth century, the therapeutic optimism of the early part of the century had faded. It had become painfully clear that asylums could not live up to the unrealistic ideals of their supporters, be they patients, their families, alienists, administrators or politicians. Recovery rates declined, the number of chronic elderly patients increased, there were unresolvable tensions among the patients and between the staff and patients and problems related to financing large asylums became acute. These negative developments were further fuelled by the pessimistic doctrine of degeneration and more severe attitudes of the authorities towards the plight of the mentally ill and the feebleminded. Optimism and hope gave way to hopelessness and therapeutic nihilism.

Nevertheless, Gerald Grob makes an important point in his reflections on the pros and cons of asylum care:

> For many patients hospitalization came at crucial moments in their lives. Substantial numbers were discharged after stays that ranged in duration from three to nine months, and then never again were hospitalized. Moreover, the asylum for many severely and persistently mentally ill patients provided access to food, clothing, and shelter. The alternatives at least within the context of nineteenth-century society were hardly attractive. They included confinement in a welfare or penal institution or wandering aimlessly in the community and relying on others for the necessities required for survival.
>
> (Grob 1994, 102)

Even if the asylum system did not live up to its early expectations, it would be an exaggeration to compare it in a Foucauldian fashion to that of prisons. Yet, I have to say that, after reading numerous accounts of asylum life from the perspectives of both the patients and the staff, I cannot fully disagree with the 'anti-psychiatric' critics such as Foucault. There may have been one fundamental problem with mental asylums that remained unresolvable: for the most part, patients did not feel comfortable there. And because they felt uncomfortable, there was a risk of their mental and physical condition deteriorating. In short, the longer one stayed in an asylum, the greater the chances of becoming institutionalized and being forever incapable of coping with the demands of everyday life.

Authority and power in the asylum

The social structure of the mental asylum resembled the prevailing patriarchal European family. The superintendent was the venerated patriarch, whose relationship with the patients was very much like that between father and child. Together with his assistant physicians, nurses and attendants, the patriarch-doctor offered protection, support, security and consolation to his patients. Reciprocally, he expected his patients to submit to his authority and to the rules he had devised for the benefit of the whole hospital community. In the subordinate role, the patient was provided with the basic comfort of home, albeit without freedom, idleness or luxury. If the patients defied the authority of the patriarch, it was his duty to punish them, for example by constraining and confining unruly patients with the help of isolation rooms, straitjackets and other restraints, or by reducing their food or tobacco rations. Recalcitrant patients were treated very much like disobedient children, and their defiance became a symptom of their illness.

A strictly observed hierarchy prevailed in the asylum. Life in the wards was regulated, repetitious and uniform, and it was governed by rigid administrative and normative rules. One day in the asylum was very much like any other – changes and surprises were in principle unwelcome. Throughout the nineteenth century, most mental patients spent their days doing next to nothing, excluding daily rituals such as washing and eating. Later, in the early twentieth century, work became a more important aspect of asylum life. By that time, the ideas of utility and cost-effectiveness had become part and parcel of the social ethos in the western world. Citizens were expected to be useful members of society as taxpayers, workers and family members. Mental asylums conformed to this utilitarian ethos and put patients to work when possible. A gender-based division of labour was the norm in the asylum as it was in society as a whole. Thus, women worked mostly indoors doing cleaning, sewing and kitchen work, while men worked outdoors in the fields, stables and workshops.

A guiding principle in the life of the asylum was regimentation. The 'law and order' approach was justified by the assumption that the patients' path to recovery required becoming conscious of the need to be in *control* of themselves. The main therapeutic idea was to strengthen the inmates' self-control and to reward responsible conduct. To achieve these goals, it was essential that life in the wards was structured and regulated. The conduct of the staff and the patients followed moral and religious principles. Rewards and punishments were meted out. The rules of the mental hospital in Jena, Germany, were simple: 'He who does not work, shall not eat' (Engstrom 2004, 21). In the Schleswig Asylum, at that time part of Denmark, the chief physician emphasized the therapeutic aspects of 'work, activity and order' (Stevenson 1988, 37). If the inmates had at least primary education, they were permitted to read picture books, while 'non-educated' or illiterate inmates worked in the garden. Through rigid structure and the administration of rewards and punishment, the medical management of madness resembled a carrot and stick approach.

138 The great transformation

In the early asylum, the rules and practices of confinement and release were often ambiguous. There were rumours and stories about innocent people being incarcerated and certified as insane without a valid medical reason. It is true that families could place their relatives in private hospitals without anyone interfering. Occasionally the confined family member took the matter to court by pleading *habeas corpus*, a common law principle that requires a person under arrest to be brought before a judge or into court.[1] But it could be exceedingly difficult to prove sanity from the inside of an asylum. If one tried too hard and passionately to convince the staff that 'I'm sane, can't you see!', one's behaviour could easily be regarded as the delusion of a disorganized mind. It was a tricky situation for the patient.

Instead of trying to convince the staff with words, it was better to maintain composure and consistently behave in an organized and rational manner, a criterion which even 'normal' people in the outside world found difficult to fulfil. Another option was to have close relatives or a spouse take you away from the asylum. This happened quite frequently to patients who had relatives who were willing to take responsibility for their care. This was not always the case, and if the patient was restless, bad-tempered or otherwise 'difficult', it was more unlikely that relatives would want to have the patient return home. Of course, the chief physician's word also counted: if he did not recommend releasing the patient, it was more probable that the patient would stay in the asylum. Quite often patients were more or less abandoned by their families, or they did not even have a family to care for them. If these patients did not get better within a reasonable amount of time, approximately one year, they sometimes became chronic cases and remained incarcerated for years or decades.

The use of restraints

At the beginning of the nineteenth century, asylums used a wide variety of mechanical restraints. Chains, straps and manacles were also employed as preventive measures, because the medical staff and attendants believed that they were useful in constraining and controlling the patients' fits of rage. Patients were also pacified by limb restraints or a 'cage bed', which was invented by a French medical doctor in 1845, and which also became known as an 'enclosure bed' or a 'veil bed'. A cage bed was a bed with either metal bars or netting designed to restrain a patient within the boundaries of the bed. It inspired the first superintendent of the Utica State Hospital in the state of New York to design a similar device that became known across the United States as a 'Utica crib'. These beds were used on patients who

---

1 The principle of *habeas corpus* is designed to ensure that a prisoner or an inmate can be released from detention, if it is unlawful in the sense of lacking sufficient cause or evidence. *Habeas corpus* originated in the English legal system, and has been incorporated into the legislation in many countries. Since medieval times, especially in Britain, it has been an important legal instrument safeguarding individual freedom against arbitrary state action.

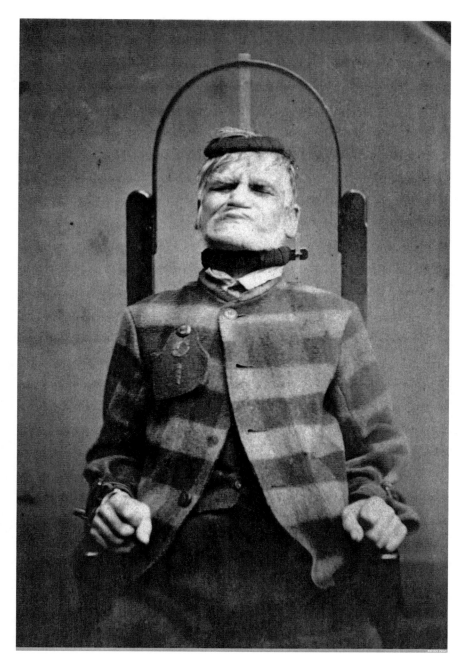

FIGURE 7.1 A patient in a restraint chair at the West Riding Lunatic Asylum, Wakefield, Yorkshire, ca. 1869.

Source: © Wellcome Library, London

140 The great transformation

were likely to get out of bed without warning. As can be imagined, some patients did not sleep very well in these beds, and overcome by anxiety, they might expend an enormous amount of energy trying to get out of them. Physical restraints were also used to reduce the risk of patient violence, which became more common in the increasingly overcrowded and uncomfortable asylums.

Around mid-century, a new attitude towards restraining patients emerged. A non-restraint movement began to influence hospital practices and change the therapeutic atmosphere in British public asylums (Scull 1985). The British alienist John Conolly (1794–1866) regarded the widespread use of restraints as barbarous. In 1839, after his appointment as resident physician to the Middlesex County Asylum at Hanwell, he introduced the principle of non-restraint. Prior to assuming the Hanwell position, he visited a number of asylums and noticed the frequent use of 'various coarse devices of leather and iron' (Tomes 1988, 194). The non-restraint principle had already been put into practice at small asylums (in York Retreat and the Lincoln Asylum). Conolly abandoned restraints in the Middlesex County Asylum, a large asylum, in the face of opposition, and it was largely due to his persistence that the movement spread. British alienists began to reconsider whether or not the patients could be controlled without restraints. In 1856, Conolly presented his therapeutic principles in *The Treatment of the Insane Without Mechanical Restraints*. In his book, Conolly was able to show that it was therapeutic to abandon restraints. His argument gradually gained favour with his colleagues in county asylums, and it gained him international fame as the practice spread to Continental Europe and North America. Conolly did not advocate a complete abandonment of restraints. He admitted that surgical operations required the use of restraints, and that in some cases force-feeding was necessary to prevent the patient's death by self-starvation. American superintendents initially opposed the idea of the total abolition of restraints. They believed that restraint was an important part of asylum treatment. In part their belief was that American freedom-loving patients were more likely to challenge authority and therefore would be more difficult to control and subdue than the more docile Europeans.

Unfortunately, as more and more patients began to flood into the ever-growing public asylums, the humane principles of moral treatment were trampled underfoot. Custodial care, therapeutic pessimism and the use of restraints gained ascendance. During the last decades of the nineteenth century, restraint became a practical issue of patient management in an asylum system devoid of ample resources, professional attendants or a therapeutic atmosphere. Commitment to non-restraint ideals waned in the increasingly bleak world of late nineteenth-century asylum psychiatry (Tomes 1988, 208–17).

Scared to health, or 'get in the swing'

Since ancient times, various kinds of shock treatment had been popular among physicians, the clergy and mad-doctors. Flogging, purgation and emetics were used to expel diabolic spirits or to cleanse morbid humours and toxins from the body. Sudden shock was considered a potentially efficient way to restore order to the disordered mind of the insane. One popular treatment was the Bath of Surprise:

> Suddenly surprising the patient with a plunge into cold water was practiced in several eras from ancient times to the nineteenth century. Boats were constructed which would break up and force patients to swim to the shore in the cold water and there were bridges which would collapse when patients were crossing them. The 'douche ascendante' at the Salpêtrière was a stream of cold water directed on the anus of the naked, seated, unsuspecting patient.
>
> (Jones 1983, 9)

Sometimes the patient was temporarily drowned as a remedy. The Belgian alienist Joseph Guislain (1797–1860) constructed the so-called Chinese Temple for drowning the patient. In this extreme form of 'water therapy', the patient was locked into an iron cage that was mechanically lowered under the water. As Guislain explained, when the desired effect – namely near-drowning – had been produced, the machine was raised from the water (Whitaker 2003, 12). Drowning therapy was also used in the United States. Dr Willard, who ran a private madhouse in a small town in New England, found this treatment useful for breaking the patient's will. Willard's prominent colleague, psychiatrist Isaac Ray, described this method as follows:

> The idea was [. . .] that if the patient was nearly drowned and then brought to life, he would take a fresh start, leaving his disease behind. Dr. Willard had a tank prepared on the premises, into which the patient, enclosed in a coffin-like box with holes, was lowered by means of well-sweep. He was kept there until bubbles of air cease to rise, then was taken out, rubbed and revived.
>
> (Whitaker 2003, 17)

From the point of view of our sensibilities today, many respected alienists renowned for humane therapy used treatments that seem cruel. Guislain, for example, saw 'drowning therapy' as a valid and justifiable treatment, which was designed to heal patients by giving them a mind-shattering shock. The assumption was that a shock or a series of shocks would put in order the disordered associations in the patient's mind. Guislain also wrote a new internal regulation for the mental asylums of Ghent, which stipulated how to treat patients in a decent and therapeutically justified way.

In western Europe, the nineteenth century was the age of industrialization, which was reflected in the new technology-oriented management of madness. Innovative doctors constructed various kinds of mechanical devices that put the patient under great stress. Patients were rotated and swung at high speed in chairs

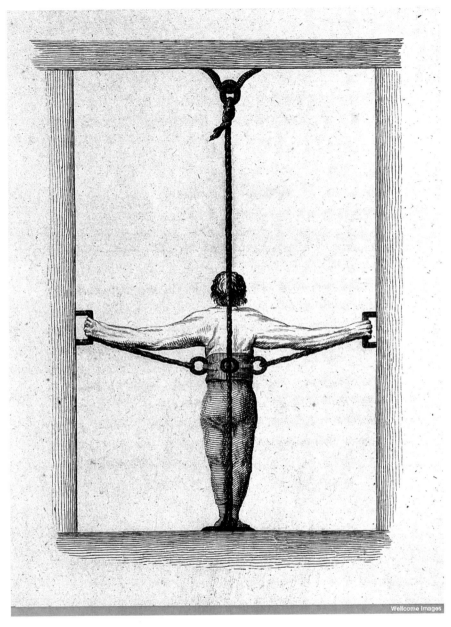

FIGURE 7.2 Method of coercion for violent lunatics, particularly used in Germany. Published in Joseph Guislain's *Traité sur l'alienation mentale et sur les hospices des alienes* (1826).

Source: © Wellcome Library, London

and discs, which produced nausea, dizziness, vomiting, bowel evacuation and even unconsciousness. The most popular mechanical device for such a treatment was invented by the British mad-doctor Joseph Mason Cox (1763–1818), a member of the Mason-Cox-Bompas family who owned a large provincial madhouse near Bristol. His swinging chair, 'hung from a wooden frame, would be rotated rapidly by an operator to induce in the patient "fatigue, exhaustion, pallor, horripilation [goose bumps], vertigo, etc.", thereby producing "new associations and trains of thoughts"' (Whitaker 2003, 12). Cox, who called his swing a 'Herculean remedy', boasted that 'I have witnessed its soothing lulling effects, tranquillizing the mind and rendering the body quiescent; a degree of vertigo has often followed, which has been succeeded by the most refreshing slumbers' (Cox 1982, 597). Inspired by Cox's invention, asylum doctors were keen on applying and modifying his device. In a number of asylums across Europe, spinning beds, boards and stools were introduced to swing the patient.

The American pioneer psychiatrist Benjamin Rush, who wrote the first psychiatric textbook in the United States, employed spinning therapy. But his own particular source of therapeutic pride was the tranquillizer chair. The basic purpose of the chair was to reduce or remove all sensory stimulation; this idea was similar to the mid-twentieth-century psychological experiments in sensory deprivation (see Chapter 13). The patients were strapped into Rush's chair, their limbs were restrained, their head was confined and their vision blocked. The patient could be restrained for a considerable period of time, and therefore a bucket was placed beneath the seat for defecation. Restrained, the patient was an easy target for medical interventions, such as bloodletting (Rush's favourite treatment), or administration of purgatives. Rush believed the chair facilitated blood circulation, which he considered essential to the successful treatment of insanity. Rush was quite delighted with his chair: 'It acts as a sedative to the tongue and temper as well as to the blood vessels' (Whitaker 2003, 16). In principle, Rush was decidedly a 'Pinelian' doctor in his emphasis on the humane treatment of the insane, but he did not shy away from administering more violent cures if his patients behaved, as he described, like the 'tyger, the mad bull, and the enraged dog' (Rush 1835, 173). For such patients, wrote Rush, 'terror acts powerfully upon the body, through the medium of the mind, and should be employed in the cure of madness' (Rush 1835, 209).

The most infamous among the arsenal of patient restraints was certainly the straitjacket. It has become a symbol of repressive psychiatry, and for patients it was probably the most hated piece of clothing. The straitjacket was in continuous use from the eighteenth to the twentieth century. It was easy to use and cheap to make, and it was an effective way of restraining patients without resorting to more brutal restraints, such as chains or manacles. We should devote a few words to try and understand why asylum patients detested it so much. When your hands and arms are confined in a straitjacket, you are nearly helpless to all those small uncomfortable itches and irritations that you can easily find relief to when your hands are free to scratch an itch, or blow your nose or to shoo flies away. One patient who described what it felt like to be tied in a straitjacket is Clifford Beers, the founder of

144 The great transformation

the so-called mental hygiene movement in the United States. He was committed to a mental asylum in the early twentieth century. After one hour in a straitjacket, Beers began to feel pain that increased during the evening and into the following night:

> My right hand was so held that the tip of one of my fingers was all but cut by the nail of another, and soon knifelike pains began to shoot through my right arm as far as the shoulder. After four or five hours the excess of pain rendered me partially insensible to it. But for fifteen consecutive hours I remained in that instrument of torture; and not until the twelfth hour, about breakfast time the next morning, did an attendant so much as loosen the cord. During the first seven or eight hours, excruciating pains racked not only my arms, but half of my body. Though I cried and moaned, in fact, screamed so loudly that the attendants must have heard me, little attention was paid to me.
>
> (Beers 2007, 123–4)

As the great Polish satirist and poet Stanislaw Jerzy Lec put it, a straitjacket should be made to fit madness.

Another widely used restraint was wet packs. They were wet sheets that were wrapped around the naked patient for the purpose of immobilizing the body and tranquillizing the mind. At times, this method calmed the patient within a relatively short time. One patient felt comfortable as if he were a baby inside his mother's womb (Porter 1991, 291–3). At other times, patients became anxious in their state of immobile helplessness. If wet sheets were wrapped too tightly around the patient, they could be extremely uncomfortable, even suffocating, when they dried and shrunk. The patient could have had trouble breathing, and sometimes even the outer layer of skin was scaled or peeled, causing severe pain. The Russian poet Joseph Brodsky suffered the agony of being tightly wrapped in wet sheets in the 1960s, when he underwent political psychiatry in the Soviet Union. In Finland, one 'psychopathic inmate' died in a penitentiary when he was treated with wet packs in 1927.

The therapeutic justification for the use of shock methods and restraints, such as the straitjacket and wet packs, was threefold. First, shocks were considered an efficient way to reorganize the disordered mind of the insane – 'to destroy the links of morbid association', as Cox put it in a Lockean fashion in his *Practical Observations on Insanity* (1806) (Cox 1982). Second, controlled shocks and restraints pacified the maniacs and made them more obedient and thereby manageable. Third, shock treatment and restraints were employed as a punishment for bad, disturbing and violent behaviour. Obviously, this was a sort of justification that was never openly explicated in medical regulations or instructions, or in patient records. In addition to shocks and restraints, isolation was commonly used both to calm down agitated patients and to punish unruly and resistant patients. A century later, new somatic treatments, such as electroshocks and lobotomy, became popular partly for the same reason: they were useful for the pacification of maniacs (see Chapter 12).

Institutionalized humanity

> Where was the sense in having treatment for a depressive illness, when all around things were done to distress and depress?
>
> (An English patient describes her experiences
> of mental hospital in the 1940s,
> *The Plea for the Silent*, 121)

Perhaps the most unfortunate legacy of the Age of the Asylum was the silencing of the patient. As the asylum system developed and hospitals became bigger and less home-like, the dialogue between the patients and the staff was minimized. What replaced the older, more informal and less systematized modes of communication was the antiseptic clinical model, in which the patient was the passive object of medical evaluation and various treatments. Physicians took all the initiatives, while the insane – 'mental patients' in the new professional language – became carriers of symptoms, and their utterances signified nothing. From the larger perspective of madness and its history, we can say that as long as there was madness, the mad had a voice, an agonized and confused voice perhaps, but nevertheless a voice. Madness could not be totally tamed. But during the nineteenth century madness was transformed into mental illness or disorder, and mental patients were clinically silenced. In short, while madness spoke, mental illness was mute.

Even the principles of moral treatment did not necessarily guarantee that the patients were treated with kindness. Former army officer John Perceval (1803–76) described his treatment in two private madhouses in a book published in 1838 (*A Narrative of the Treatment Experienced by a Gentleman*). Both madhouses, one in Sussex, the other near Bristol, were known for their humane approach to insanity. Yet, Perceval felt as if he were reduced to an inanimate object, 'as if I were a piece of furniture, an image of wood, incapable of desire or will as well as judgment' (Peterson 1982, 94). Perceval gives an account of a strange clinical situation that turned into *folie à deux*, 'a madness shared by two'. Both the doctor and the patient refused to communicate by means of ordinary language. The patient believed that whatever he said would only be heard as a verbal sign of mental illness, and the doctor believed that rational discussion with the patient was impossible. In his *Narrative*, Perceval wonders why

> I was never told, such and such things we are going to do; we think it advisable to administer such and such medicine, in this or that manner; I was never asked, Do you want any thing! Do you wish for, prefer any thing? Have you any objection to this or to that? I was fastened down in bed; a meagre diet was ordered for me; this and medicine forced down my throat, or in the contrary direction; my will, my wishes, my repugnances, my habits, my delicacy, my inclinations, my necessities, were not once consulted, I may say, thought of. I did not find the respect paid usually even to a child.
>
> (Peterson 1982, 106–7)

146 The great transformation

A century later, there was still no dialogue between the staff and the patients. In her semi-autobiographical novel *The Snake Pit* (1946), the American writer Mary Jane Ward (1905–81) describes asylum life in a state psychiatric hospital in New York. Her novel, which was turned into a popular Hollywood movie, portrays a world characterized by near-broken or one-sided lines of communication between the patients and the staff. This world was poisoned by dishonesty and severe discipline. Patients were bullied and lied to, and spoken to as if they were on the other side of a thick wall (Ward 1946).

Nineteenth-century psychiatric doctrines taught that illusory ideas and beliefs – delusions – were contagious, and that it made no sense to reason with the insane. In 1810, the Bethlem apothecary John Haslam published the first book to include the voice of a patient (Porter 2006, 322). Historically, the *Lebenswelt* (life-world) of patients has mostly been mediated to readers by psychiatrists or other medical experts. As a result, we are relatively well-versed in the history of mental institutions, in the activities of physicians and in treatment methods, but we know much less about the lives of mental patients. How did they experience their madness? What did they think about life in the asylum? How did they feel about various therapies, daily routines and modes of communication with the staff? Historians need to confront the challenge of seeing the 'cases' described in patient records and medical literature as real individuals with minds of their own. Admittedly, in most cases, our understanding of the individual *Lebenswelt* of mental patients remains fragmentary, no matter how often psychiatrists and nurses have referred to their mental states and modes of behaviour in patient records. We are even more ignorant of all those mentally disordered or deviant individuals who were never confined to mental hospitals. Their life-worlds remain largely *terra incognita* to us.

'A gigantic asylum is a gigantic evil'

Fortunately, and increasingly so the closer we get to our own time, there are published and non-published first-person accounts of what it was like to be an institutionalized mental patient. Judging by these patient narratives, life in an asylum was neither very comfortable nor therapeutic. To many patients, confinement was a shocking and frightening experience. This was especially true of patients who were taken to the asylum against their will, or who were too confused or frightened to understand where they were, and why. It seems that, upon admission, many patients experienced at least a temporary worsening of their symptoms; they became depressed, anxious, fearful and non-responsive. This is how one British patient experienced her confinement in the 1950s:

> More weeks went by and I regained my strength, but I still could not remember who I was, nor how I came to be there, locked up in this vast strange building; sometimes sleeping in a long dormitory, sometimes in a small side room off a long corridor, at others in a padded cell on the floor. Always the

doors were locked. One could tell when nurses passed by the jingle of keys at their waists. Never had I felt so frightened, lost, lonely or desolate.

(*The Plea for the Silent* 1957, 71)

Upon admission, many patients were uncertain about their whereabouts – Where am I? Why am I here? Who are these strange people who give me orders and push me around? Why doesn't anybody listen to me? As Roy Porter notes,

> hallucinations persecuting the sick person often 'came true' in the asylum, full of strange, disorderly people, terrifying authority figures, and, not least [. . .] manacles and chains which brought to mind the torture engines so prominent in the imaginations of the demented.
>
> (Porter 1991, 198–9)

John Thomas Arlidge, a compassionate, mid-nineteenth-century British alienist, disapproved of the move towards larger and larger asylums, because in such 'lunatic colonies' proper medical and moral care as well as supervision became impossible. In his book *On the State of Lunacy* (1859), Arlidge did not mince words about the state of institutional mental health care in England:

> In a colossal refuge for the insane, a patient may be said to lose his individuality, and to become a member of a machine so put together as to move with precise regularity and invariable routine; – a triumph of skill adapted to show how such unpromising materials as crazy men and women may be drilled into order and guided by rule, but not an apparatus calculated to restore their pristine condition and their independent self-governing existence [. . .] A gigantic asylum is a gigantic evil, and, figuratively speaking, a manufactory of chronic insanity.
>
> (Arlidge 1859, 104)

It may have been Arlidge's disaffection with the development of asylum psychiatry that prompted him to leave mental medicine and specialize in occupational medicine (Holdsworth 1998, 461).

An Englishman, who was institutionalized in the 1930s, described how he and his fellow patients were treated like children. The hospital was saturated with the patronizing 'mamma knows best' and 'teacher knows best' ethos. Such an ethos was often protective and sometimes gentle, but it was compromised by a more threatening 'mamma will spank' approach when the patient-children could no longer be controlled and they had to be dragged to bed without supper. The author points out that these 'children' were all grown men who in the outside world were often accustomed to authority. But now the roles had been reversed, and this gave life in the ward a 'crazy-dream quality' (Porter 1991, 247). In the early 1950s, similar observations were made by the future civil rights activist William Moore, who was hospitalized on account of schizophrenia. I will return to

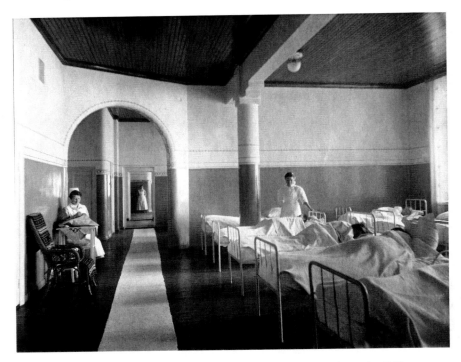

FIGURE 7.3 Hatanpää Mental Hospital in Tampere, Finland, in the early 1920s.
Siurce: © Helsinki University Museum

Moore and his activism later; here I will only refer to his remark about patients being treated as if they were helpless children. As a result of this treatment, many patients became so dependent on their attendant-guardians that upon discharge they could no longer function in the outside world. Unable to cope with the everyday challenges, they sought protection and shelter in well-ordered institutional life. At the same time, patients who struggled to get out of the hospital faced insurmountable difficulties. As Moore writes in his book *The Mind in Chains* (1955), 'no one blames the doctor if the patient is not released, except possibly the patient, who is no one; but many blame the doctor if the patient is released and then gets into trouble' (Moore 1955, 301).

Failure to communicate was the key to many of the problems in mental asylums. It was not easy for the medical staff and attendants to communicate with people whose thoughts and behaviour were often radically different from normal conduct. Understandably, when two different life-worlds collide, it may very well result in confusion and misunderstanding. This is what happened when 'rational' alienists and the 'irrational' insane tried to get their respective messages across the gulf of mental illness. In addition to the chronic problems with communication, both the patients and the staff had to face threatening situations, verbal abuse and physical violence. In closed wards, it was not uncommon for agitated patients to attack each other or attendants, who in turn learned to use brute force to calm patients or to punish transgressors. The frustrations and discontentment of both the patients and the attendants could lead to violent outbursts, and violence in turn created an atmosphere of fear and insecurity.

Before the introduction of modern psychiatric drugs in the 1950s, aggression and violence were commonplace in most mental asylums in Europe and North America. This was the case also in the Oulu District Mental Hospital in northern Finland. Patient records of the Oulu Hospital from the 1920s and 1930s routinely report how the severely ill patients hit each other or attendants; how patients smashed utensils, tore bed sheets or their own clothes; how they masturbated and smeared themselves with faeces; how they tried to commit suicide; and how they shouted, screamed and gesticulated wildly. When the staff members became nervous and restless, so did the patients. And when the nervous patients became agitated and aggressive, the staff members became even more nervous and restless. Such a vicious circle was poisonous to the therapeutic atmosphere. In acute and closed wards at night, when there were no night attendants, or when they were in another room, there was no escaping fear. And fear is not exactly conducive to sleep. Acute wards were also used as a place of punishment for recalcitrant patients (see e.g. *The Plea for the Silent* 1957, 36–7). In an American textbook for psychiatric nurses, published in the mid-1950s, significant space was devoted to mastering fear. This was an important instruction, because the manifest anxiety and fear of the nurses directly correlated with the increased rates of patient violence (Schwartz & Shockley 1956). After World War II, efforts to break the vicious cycle of violence became more concerted as the idea of 'therapeutic community' gained popularity, hospitals invested in non-invasive therapies and recreation and new psychiatric medication succeeded in calming many agitated patients.

Mental asylums were also places where people died. In overcrowded wards, infectious diseases spread easily, and as many patients were malnourished or in a weak condition already, they easily contracted viral and bacterial diseases, such as meningitis, typhoid fever, pneumonia and hepatitis. Consumption and typhoid fever were especially widespread and deadly diseases in mental hospitals. If hygiene was poor and the therapeutic atmosphere pessimistic, transmission of infection was even more common. Particularly in times of social crisis, hospitals often had to make do with a very sparse diet. It has been estimated that during World War I as many as 70,000 mental patients died of malnourishment in Germany alone (Schott & Tölle 2006, 174). At the Nikkilä Mental Hospital near Helsinki, Finland, during the severe winter of 1941–2, patients were so starved that, when the spring came and they were taken to the hospital yard, some patients ate grass as a last resort. Mental hospitals were very unhealthy environments well into the mid-twentieth century (Pressman 1998, 204).

An intrinsic problem with (public) asylums was that they suffered from a chronic lack of resources. In practice, this meant that the patients usually did not receive any treatment at all. Also, patients had very little to do because there were no recreational activities. Smoking, eating and (for some) reading were highlights of the day. Many patients spent their time just sitting or standing or looking outside through barred windows. It was not rare for the uneducated and poorly paid attendants to harass patients or beat them, if the 'loonies' became agitated or refused to follow orders. The custodial function of asylums was further strengthened by the late nineteenth-century therapeutic belief that mental patients should be put to bed like patients in general hospitals. Such passive 'bed therapy' was detrimental to the physical and mental health of the inmates, and it was outright harmful to the patients who suffered from the catatonic forms of what came to be called schizophrenia. Daily life of sustained inactivity could further isolate these already non-communicating patients from the realities of the outside world. During the 1920s and the 1930s in Europe, the therapeutic ideology changed and the 'bed-oriented' care was abandoned in favour of 'work-oriented' care. This in turn meant that many asylums started to resemble labour camps.

Another major problem with asylums was the lack of public monitoring. Governments failed to pass legislation to regulate and control mental hospitals, and if such laws existed, there were not enough dutiful administrators who would have systematically monitored whether hospitals actually followed the official regulations. Within asylums, supervision was lax also. The hospital boards were reluctant to interfere in the activities of the superintendent and his medical staff, and medical staff did not intervene in the activities of nurses and attendants. The lack of efficient supervision and control gave leeway to all sorts of violations. Violence and arbitrary discipline were often concealed and hushed up rather than brought out into the open. The board and the superintendent were predisposed to protect the reputation of the hospital at all costs rather than to enter into public discussion of problems, such as the abuse of patients. Therefore, social control and consistent surveillance should not be considered a purely negative exercise of power, as Foucauldians seem to think. Deep inside the wards of asylums, the problem was often the *lack* of surveillance – at least from the point of view of powerless patients.

What happened to the great expectations?

Faith in the healing power of asylums had already started to wane in the mid-nineteenth century. Recovery rates did not meet expectations, asylums began to be filled with patients with more chronic conditions and the mysteries of mental illness remained unsolved. Frustration and pessimism began to haunt the psychiatric community, one outlet of which was the fatalistic doctrine of degeneration. As the nineteenth century drew to a close, the noble dream of turning madhouses into therapeutic hospitals began to vanish.

Perhaps the most serious problem facing asylum doctors was overcrowding – asylums began to resemble not so much hospitals as custodial institutions. In Britain, there were almost 100,000 asylum patients at the turn of the twentieth century, and *Lunacy Commissioners* estimated that only 7 per cent of the mentally ill could be cured. In mid-nineteenth century Prussia, 1 in 5,300 persons was confined in an asylum; by 1911 the number had increased tenfold to 1 in 500. In

Switzerland, the number of patients admitted doubled between 1890 and 1911. The trend was similar all over western Europe. The growth of the patient population was not restricted to public asylums; private hospitals and sanatoria also received an increasing number of patients. Asylums became more accessible during the second half of the nineteenth century when railway lines were built across Europe, which contributed to the overcrowding.

What could have been the root cause of such a tremendous increase in the number of mental patients? Many contemporaries saw the increase as merely a by-product of population growth – more people equals more mentally ill people. Other commentators pointed to the detrimental psychophysical consequences of social evolution, asserting that modern urban civilization was unnatural or even 'pathogenic'. This suggested that western civilization caused degeneration which manifested itself in madness and other forms of mental and physical decay. Those who paid close attention to statistics could speculate that there was an increasing number of certified lunatics simply because there was an increasing number of administrators and medical doctors who were preoccupied with the question of mental health in the general population. Others claimed that medical progress itself, including better hygiene and improved diagnostic tools, contributed to a greater number of patients who survived in hospitals, where mortality had traditionally been high.

Undoubtedly, one reason for the growth of the patient population was the heavy medical and administrative emphasis on the importance of institutional care. At the same time, psychiatrists created new diagnoses and classifications, expanding their scope of expertise from severe mental illnesses to neuroses and other milder disorders. Due to the development of social organization, medical education was expanded and more medical faculties were established. Medical professionals became more specialized in their expertise, and those who specialized in psychiatry were trained to find mental abnormalities in their patients as well as in the general population. This medicalization of madness brought with it increased care demands by families and communities. As early as 1850, the American alienist Edward Jarvis (1803–84) examined mental asylums and their relationships to local communities. He noticed that populations near asylums tended to become sensitized to the idea of mental illness and its institutional care. The mere existence of a mental asylum in the region popularized the belief that the insane should be treated at public institutions (Grob 1994, 50). The phenomenon of overcrowding was also due to the belief that potentially curable patients should be admitted to a hospital as soon as possible. If admission was delayed, acute patients were easily transformed into chronic, incurable cases (Engstrom 2004, 32–3). Finally, what certainly increased patient population was that there were more elderly people in the asylums. To some extent, asylums began to function as nursing homes for demented and abandoned elderly people (Grob 1994, 120).

Historians have provided explanations to account for long-term changes in social structures. One institution heavily affected by societal changes was the family. Due to industrialization, urbanization, the division of labour, geographic and social mobility as well as the development of public social policies, traditional,

152 The great transformation

rather static and 'earth-bound' lifestyles disintegrated as rural populations moved to towns and communities close to industrial centres. For example, in 1801, Manchester had 75,000 inhabitants; by 1850, the number had grown to 300,000 – a fourfold population increase in just two generations. In Birmingham, another industrial town, the respective numbers were 71,000 in 1801 and 233,000 in 1850. This transformation of western Europe created a large-scale social 'dislocation', which for many people signified a better life in the hustle and bustle of towns and cities teeming with people, jobs and nervous energy. For others, dislocation meant a painful separation from family and community. Some of those who felt uprooted, lonely and lost in a strange and perhaps unwelcoming environment lived under mental strain, which could cause unmanageable confusion. This in turn could lead to poverty, sickness and deprivation. From the larger historical perspective, the great social transformation caused by the Industrial Revolution was undoubtedly a blessing, but when this transformation is studied at street level, as it were, it may also look like a curse. Research on the rise of neuroses confirms the suggestion that societal changes, notably industrialization and its consequences, had an impact on the 'phenotypes' or outward appearances of mental suffering. These historical changes may even have been pathogenic factors in the sense that, for some people, they created or at least intensified mental distress and aggravated symptoms (Pietikainen 2007).

Governmental health policies played a leading role in the development of asylums in most European countries. The emergence of the notion of *public health* contributed to the construction of a national mental health care system, which relied on large-scale institutions and a sort of mass-production of mental health services. Without doubt, around the turn of the twentieth century, new asylums were established on a monthly if not weekly basis in different parts of Europe. Still, this 'great confinement' did not necessarily mean that governments were eager to incarcerate and silence 'misfits'. As a matter of fact, psychiatrists complained, and not without reason, that public authorities were inefficient in organizing mental health care. Administrators needed financial resources for the implementation of health care policy, but politicians were in most cases reluctant to 'waste' taxpayers' money on the medical management of madness, because the insane were stigmatized in comparison with the somatically ill. In many cases, the latter group could be restored to health and become productive citizens again. By contrast, the mentally ill were typically considered to be unproductive because they were incapable of sustained work, or of doing anything 'useful'. As mental patients were perceived to be a debit to the social balance sheet, policy makers were not particularly sympathetic to their plight. Politicians and administrators were more inclined to invest in general hospitals and in the treatment of the physically ill. Still, the authorities and leading physicians had to face the fact that all the beds in mental hospitals were filled as soon as they became vacant, and new hospitals had to be built to meet the growing demand for institutional care. After all, there were no viable alternatives – the insane could not be left to their own devices, for then they would become a burden to poor relief, the prison administration and local communities.

Asylums – total institutions?

Are mental hospitals total institutions? Are they comparable to prisons? Do individuals lose their sense of self when they are committed to a hospital? One who gave affirmative answers to these questions was the Canadian-American sociologist Erving Goffman (1922–82). Goffman's *Asylums*, published in 1961, was a landmark study on institutional life in mental hospitals. The book was partly based on his own experiences as a temporary field worker at St Elizabeths, a large, federally funded mental hospital in Washington, DC, in the mid-1950s. According to Goffman's influential definition,

> a total institution may be defined as a place of residence and work where a large number of like-situated individuals, cut off from the wider society for an appreciable period of time, together lead an enclosed, formally administered round of life.
>
> (Goffman 1961, xiii)

Mental hospitals, prisons, boarding schools and the military are 'forcing houses for changing persons', and as such they shape the inmates' identity and create for them a specific role that facilitates their adjustment to a regimented life. Total institutions tend to rob individuals of their autonomy and sense of self. The institutional arrangement of such places 'does not so much support the self as constitute it' (Goffman 1961, 168).

Goffman made acute observations of the ways in which the 'ill person' is socialized into the role of a mental patient. After the onset of the illness and the ensuing 'pre-patient phase', the patients are taken into the hospital, where they are subjected to an 'institutional ceremony'. In this ceremony, individuals become patients whose case history is constructed in a way that justifies incarceration and the harsh treatment of the hospital staff. The consequence of the institutional ceremony is the shrinkage of the patient's personality and the objectification of his or her life history. The case history gives the impression of demonstrating that all along they were getting sick, that they finally became sick and that if they 'had not been hospitalized much worse things would have happened' (Goffman 1961, 145).

Once the individuals are inmates, their behaviour is controlled and sanctioned so that 'good' behaviour is rewarded while 'bad' behaviour is punished. The self of the patient becomes a cluster of symptoms, which is named, monitored and manipulated. Goffman was especially interested in the patients' 'moral career' in mental hospitals. By 'moral career' he referred to a process in which the self is constructed in total institutions. Predictably, a central feature of such a career is the loss of civil rights and autonomy. Simultaneously, the patient's image of self underwent changes. What usually happened was that patients began to look at themselves as failures; their sense of self was damaged. They were told by the staff that their attitude towards life was wrong and that they needed to change their way of dealing with people and their way of understanding themselves. The

154 The great transformation

mental universe of the patients began to be characterized by self-loathing and, as its counterweight, self-delusion, as the patients thought that the illness had struck other people rather than themselves.

Goffman wrote his book at a time when many hospitals in the United States and elsewhere had for a long time functioned as custodial institutions. As human warehouses, they were symbols of anti-utopian medicine, devoid of therapeutic optimism and inspiration. By the time *Asylums* was published in 1961, the Age of the Asylum had lasted for more than 150 years. A few decades later, the era of institutional mental health care came to an end. In the United States, the number of institutionalized patients was highest in the mid-1950s (more than 500,000 patients), but in many European countries the zenith of the 'great confinement' was reached in the 1960s or, in some cases (in Finland, for example), not until the 1970s. Goffman's concept of the total institution had a direct impact in that it influenced mental health professionals and social critics across the western world. In West Germany, Goffman's ideas contributed to reforms in mental health care during the 1960s and the 1970s (Schott & Tölle 2006, 208–9, 312). Goffman may have exaggerated the damaging aspects of life in total institutions, but his 'one-sided' approach to asylums served the important purpose of provoking debates and promoting reforms.

Concluding remarks on the history of mental asylums

The last few decades have witnessed intense historical research on mental hospi-tals. An important conclusion to be drawn from these studies is that the asylum system was simultaneously many things. It was subject to constant negotiations involving different parties, such as families, poor relief administrators, police, superintendents of hospitals and the patients themselves (Porter & Wright 2003, 4–5). Historians have begun to emphasize the active role of the family and local community in the management of madness. This is an important corrective to the earlier, 'control-oriented' approach that focused on a 'top-down' history and on the power of psychiatrists and the authorities. Historians have observed how, upon the admission of new patients, asylum doctors often just officially confirmed the certificate of madness already made by the families, local poor relief administrators or other non-medical community members. Thus there is a scholarly need to study not only mental hospitals themselves but also the role of families and local communities – even in the Age of the Asylum, many mentally ill family members lived in their own homes or in the local homes for the elderly and disabled.

Recent studies have refuted the popular assumption that nineteenth-century asylums functioned primarily as dumping grounds or warehouses for misfits and undesirables. Obviously, families and local communities used confinement as a convenient way to get rid of difficult or unwanted individuals, but this was not the rule. Indeed, my own study of the patient records of the Oulu District Mental Hospital between 1925 and 1975 suggests that patients admitted to the hospital were often seriously ill persons whose families could no longer take care of them (if they had families).

For the sake of illustration, let us take the example of Ireland, which was one of the first nations to establish a national asylum system. In proportion to its population, Ireland had more asylum inmates than any other nation in the world in the late 1950s, when there were more than 21,000 mental hospital patients in the Irish Republic. This was a staggering 0.5 per cent of the population. In most cases, patients were committed to an asylum at the initiative of local people, who often complained to the local police about the violent behaviour of a family member, neighbour or some other community member. In the nineteenth century, economic and social deprivation as well as famine – or, the threat of famine – encouraged relatives to commit their lunatic family members to institutional care simply because living conditions were so harsh, especially in rural Ireland. What differentiated the Irish mental health care system from that of other western countries was the strong connection between lunacy and criminality. Due to the legislation focusing on 'Dangerous Lunatics' (the Acts of 1828 and 1867), a large proportion of asylum inmates were committed as criminals during the nineteenth century. Moreover, many Irish who were mentally ill were locked up in prisons. Compared to other western European countries, which were not exactly safe havens for the mentally ill either, Ireland's asylum system was particularly stigmatizing and cruel to those declared insane. This is how the historian Elizabeth Malcom summarizes the plight of the Irish sufferers:

> They were generally taken into custody by the police after a complaint from relatives; they were certified by one doctor normally untrained in mental health matters; they appeared in court before the local landowners and businessmen acting as magistrates, where an indefinite sentence of committal was passed; and they were transported by the police to the asylum. There they had no right to have their diagnosis or committal reviewed. If and when they were released depended upon the decision of a lay board of governors, advised by a medical officer who might have no training in the treatment of mental illness. All in all the Irish committal process gave enormous powers to the ignorant and the potentially malicious. It criminalized the mentally ill and allowed them few if any avenues of redress. It was a formula for abuse that operated from the 1830s into the 1940s.
>
> (Malcolm 2003, 325)

It has been suggested that Ireland's dismal history of mental health care was at least partly a result of the cruel excesses of Britain's colonial rule. It is true that the interventionist British government was inclined to test out social policies in Ireland. This suggestion is, however, undermined by the incontestable fact that 'committals were in the main instigated by families, not by government officials or even by doctors' (Malcom 2003, 330). The situation was further aggravated by the Catholic Church's suspicious attitude towards psychiatric medicine. Irish

156 The great transformation

universities in turn were not very keen on establishing chairs in psychiatry, and the Irish medical profession appeared to have very little interest in the problem of insanity. So the impact of British colonialism on Irish mental health care is not as strong as one might imagine, at least if one has read Foucault and other critics of governmental, imperialist and capitalist power structures. Sometimes the 'culprits' can be found very close, among relatives, neighbours and other community members rather than among the corridors of administrative power. Obviously, one important explanation for the gloomy history of Irish mental health care was the draconic legislation regulating the asylum system for more than a century. It made committal too easy, gave too much power to ignorant laypeople and, worst of all, branded all the mentally ill as dangerous.

From a comparative perspective, we can say that, regarding the management of madness, every nation has its own unique path. Still, mental hospitals had both distinct differences and similarities across the western world. I will briefly return to the more recent history of asylum in Part IV, where I explore the developments before and after World War II.

* * *

Finally, was Erving Goffman right in naming the mental asylum a 'total institution'? I think he was, but I want to elaborate my agreement with him by reminding readers that there was no evil intention or malicious power-mongering involved in the creation of the asylum system. The American philosopher and psychologist William James (1842–1910) pointed out the intrinsic problem with 'total institutions' cogently and eloquently in a lecture he delivered in 1908 at Oxford University: 'Most human institutions, by the purely technical and professional manner in which they come to be administered, end by becoming obstacles to the very purposes which their founders had in view' (James 1909, 96). Following James, we can say that it was not so much that mental asylums developed in the wrong direction and lost their essential therapeutic purpose; rather, the problem was in the very design of the asylum system. But as nobody could foresee this when the first 'modern' mental hospitals were established in the early nineteenth century, it is better not to blame the founding fathers of the mental asylum for going astray. As another deep thinker, the Scotsman Adam Ferguson, pointed out in the late eighteenth century, human history is largely a history of unintended consequences – we often cannot foresee, let alone control, the consequences of our actions. For this reason, we should not judge the so-called errors of the previous generations too harshly: they based their decisions on what was then considered solid knowledge and reliable assumption about the proper treatment of madness.

Bibliography

Arlidge, J.T. (1859) *On the State of Lunacy and the Legal Provision for the Insane; with Observations in the Construction and Organisation of Asylums*, London: John Churchill.

Beers, C. (2007) *A Mind that Found Itself*, 1st edn 1907, Milton Keynes: Filiquarian Publishing.

Conolly, J. (1856) *The Treatment of the Insane without Mechanical Restraints*, London: Smith, Elder & Co.

Cox, J.M. (1982) "'A Herculean remedy": the swing', in R. Hunter and I. MacAlpine (eds) *Three Hundred Years of Psychiatry, 1535–1860*, Hartsdale, NY: Carlisle Publishing.

Deutsch, A. (1949) *The Mentally Ill in America*, New York: Columbia University Press.

Engstrom, E.J. (2004) *Clinical Psychiatry in Imperial Germany: A History of Psychiatric Practice*, Ithaca, NY: Cornell University Press.

Gijswijt-Hofstra, M. and Oosterhuis, H. (eds) (2006) *Psychiatric Cultures Compared: Psychiatry and Mental Health Care in the Twentieth Century*, Amsterdam: Amsterdam University Press.

Goffman, E. (1961) *Asylums*, Garden City, NY: Anchor Books.

Grob, G.N. (1994) *The Mad Among Us*, New York: The Free Press.

Holdsworth, C. (1998) 'Dr John Thomas Arlidge and Victorian occupational medicine', *Medical History* 42: 458–75.

James, W. (1909) *A Pluralistic Universe*, New York: Longmans, Green & Co.

Jones, W.L. (1983) *Ministering to Minds Diseased*, London: William Heinemann Medical Books.

Malcolm, E. (2003) '"Ireland's crowded madhouses": the institutional confinement of the insane in nineteenth- and twentieth-century Ireland', in R. Porter and D. Wright (eds) *The Confinement of the Insane. International Perspectives 1800–1965*, Cambridge: Cambridge University Press.

Moore, W.L. (1955) *The Mind in Chains: The Autobiography of a Schizophrenic*, New York: Exposition Press.

Peterson, D. (ed.) (1982) *A Mad People's History of Madness*, Pittsburgh, PA: University of Pittsburgh Press.

Pietikainen, P. (2007) *Neurosis and Modernity. The Age of Nervousness in Sweden*, Leiden: Brill.

Porter, R. (2006) *Madmen. A Social History of Madhouses, Mad-Doctors and Lunatics*, Stroud: Tempus.

Porter, R. (ed.) (1991) *The Faber Book of Madness*, London: Faber & Faber.

Porter, R. and Wright, D. (eds) (2003) *The Confinement of the Insane. International Perspectives 1800–1965*, Cambridge: Cambridge University Press.

Pressman, J.D. (1998) *Last Resort: Psychosurgery and the Limits of Medicine*, Cambridge: Cambridge University Press.

Rush, B. (1835) *Medical Inquiries and Observations Upon the Diseases of the Mind*, Philadelphia, PA: Grigg and Elliott.

Schott, H. and Tölle, R. (2006) *Geschichte der Psychiatrie*, Munich: C.H. Beck.

Schwartz, M.S. and Shockley, E.L. (1956) *The Nurse and the Mental Patient. A Study in Interpersonal Relations*, New York: Russell Sage Foundation.

Scull, A. (1985) 'A Victorian alienist: John Conolly, FRCP, DCL (1794–1866)', in W.F. Bynum, R. Porter and M. Shepherd (eds) *The Anatomy of Madness: Essays in the History of Psychiatry*, Vol I: *People and Ideas*, London: Tavistock Publications.

Stevenson, C. (1988) 'Madness and the picturesque in the kingdom of Denmark', in W.F. Bynum, R. Porter and M. Shepherd (eds) *The Anatomy of Madness*, Vol. III: *The Asylum and Its Psychiatry*, London: Routledge.

The Plea for the Silent (1957), London: Christopher Johnson.

Tomes, N. (1988) 'The great restraint controversy: a comparative perspective on Anglo-American psychiatry in the nineteenth century', in W.F. Bynum and R. Porter (eds) *The Anatomy of Madness: Essays in the History of Psychiatry*, Vol. III: *The Asylum and Its Psychiatry*, London: Routledge.

Ward, M.J. (1946) *The Snake Pit*, New York: Random House.

Whitaker, R. (2003) *Mad in America*, New York: Basic Books.

8

NAMING THE MAD MIND

To say that it has been difficult to have a scientific grip on madness is an understatement. Unlike many somatic diseases, mental illness cannot be detected by blood test, cytopathological study of cells or neuroimaging scans. For this reason, psychiatry has been very dependent on the classification of mental disorders, which has brought some structure and apparent scientific order to the study of mental disorganization. However, the psychiatric naming and classifying of various forms of madness is different from the naming and classifying of flora and fauna. Plants are 'natural entities', and as such their characteristics are 'objective' and unchangeable, or subject to very slow evolutionary modifications. Hence what is said about nettles, for example, is not in principle dependent on the subjective state of the observer, because nettles exist independently of the observer. The same is not the case with madness. An observer of various forms of madness resembles a sculptor who creates forms out of formless material (Berrios 1996, 11).

Unlike the nettle, madness is not a part of objective reality, but it is not a merely contractual thing either. Instead, madness is more like a historically changing hybrid that has characteristics of nature and culture, the latter denoting the totality of human social activity. Madness in the sense of the breakdown of normal behaviour is known all over the world, and in some cases madness is a natural entity more than a cultural illness, neurosyphilis and pellagra (caused by vitamin B deficiency) being obvious examples. At the same time, madness assumes different forms and elicits different interpretations depending on its cultural climate. Schizophrenia is not exactly alike in Zambia and New Zealand, and such milder disorders as the neuroses are very different in different cultures.

For modern westerners, the diagnosis of mental disorders is primarily based on what people tell experts about their inner states, ideas, emotions and moods. There are no visible signs of mental pathology, and we cannot be sure if mental illness is caused, for example, by a hereditary predisposition or social stress, or both, or if the illness is serious or not. We live in a world where mental disorders are often the result of negotiations between different parties, such as physicians, patients and their families, patient organizations, insurance companies, the public sector, drug companies and other private enterprises. This chapter explores how nineteenth-century mental medicine named and explained various forms of madness from severe insanity to milder maladies.

Classifications of madness

How to explain something as protean as madness? At times it manifests itself in the raging fury of a maniac, at other times in the complete autism of a catatonic, the wandering sensations of pain of a hypochondriac, the ceaseless howling of a lunatic, the trembling of a hysteric or the self-destruction of a melancholic (Porter 2006, 233). The philosopher Thomas Hobbes noted in his classic work *Leviathan* (1651) that 'of the several kinds of madness, he that would take the pains, might enrol a legion' (Hobbes 2008, 49). In addition to its bewildering variety of mani-festations, madness is an extraordinary phenomenon in other ways as well. For example, sometimes its symptoms appear and disappear in a peculiarly regular fashion. In his book on mental alienation (1801), Pinel wrote about a maniac at the Bicêtre, whose seizures appeared regularly every spring, lasted for three months and disappeared in mid-summer. Another patient became a raging maniac annually for 15 days while remaining sane and calm for the rest of the year. For three others, episodes of mania returned every 18 months and lasted for exactly 3 months. What sort of illness can possibly appear and disappear so regularly and be absent the rest of the time?

Until the nineteenth century, madness had many faces but only a couple of names. From Greek antiquity, madness was typically divided into three main diagnostic categories: mania, melancholy and phrenitis. *Mania* denoted a state of confusion and over-activity, in which hallucinations, delusions and delirium were common. The counterpart to mania was not so much melancholy as stupor, a condition of greatly dulled or completely suspended sense or sensibility. According to humoral theory, stupor was caused by an excessive cooling of phlegma in the brain. Such a cooling made behaviour muted and produced a state of mental iner-tia (Healy 2008, 7). Attempts to explain the states of confusion in stupor were . . . confusing. For lack of a better explanation for the twilight state of consciousness, the medically credible term 'disorientation' was taken into use. During the second half of the nineteenth century, psychiatric efforts to find an adequate explanation for the states of confusion led to the introduction of the term 'psychosis'. Thus, the terms 'mania' and 'attacks of mania' were replaced by 'psychosis' and 'psychotic states' or 'episodes'. Regarding the two other main illnesses, *melancholy*, of which I will speak a little later, was not the same as today's depression, while *phrenitis* is no longer in medical use. Phrenitis was defined in Hippocratic medicine as an inflammatory disease of the brain, and its main symptoms were fever and mental confusion or delirium. Pinel was the last eminent physician who used phrenitis in

160 The great transformation

his classification. Today, such diagnoses as meningitis and encephalitis are used to name similar disorders.

In the history of classification, a place of honour has been reserved for Carl (von Linné) Linnaeus (1707–78), the Swedish naturalist and the grand classifier of flora and fauna. Linnaeus also placed humans in his system of biological classification, but his name is not usually associated with madness, even though he was one of the first taxonomists or nosologists of mental illness. In the 1740s, he gave lectures on the taxonomy of diseases at the University of Uppsala, and a student attending the lectures carefully wrote down extensive notes that are now stored in the collections of the Swedish Medical Society. These notes reveal that, in addition to somatic diseases, Linnaeus also lectured on mental diseases (*morbi mentales*). Linnaeus was an empiricist for whom knowledge was only true if it was quantifiable and measurable. Small wonder, then, that he concentrated on external signs and symptoms of diseases in his classification. He divided *morbi mentales* into three 'orders', namely diseases of reason, the imagination and the will. Diseases of reason (*morbi judicales*) included dementia, which denoted a weakness of mind without accompanying fever, and mania, which denoted fury and delirium (confusion). Diseases of the imagination (*morbi imaginarii*) included, among other things, disturbances of the senses (such as buzzing in the ears), optical delusions and hypochondriac symptoms, such as heart trouble and stomach pain as well as such emotional maladies as dejection and anxiety. The third order – the diseases of the will (*morbi voluntarii*) – were comprised of afflictions characterized by diminished capacity or desire. According to Linnaeus, such diseases included 'love madnesses' such as female *nymphomania* and male *satyriasis*. Common to both of them was the inability to restrain the passion of (sexual) love. Diseases of the will also included morbid longing for home, or *nostalgia*, immoderate desire to drink (*dipsia*) and dance (*tarantismus*) as well as various phobias and feelings of disgust (Uddenberg 2012).

Linnaeus' classification of mental diseases was never published, unlike his ground-breaking taxonomy of flora and fauna (*Systema naturae*, 1735), which he expanded all through his life and which made him world famous (the first edition had 11 pages, the twelfth edition published 1766–8 no fewer than 2,400 pages). For this reason, his admirably systematic approach to mental illness never became the foundation for psychiatric classifications. It was only in the latter half of the twentieth century that a more systematic classification of mental disorders emerged. This fact speaks volumes about the difficulties involved in the scientific efforts to systematize various forms of madness.

When Philippe Pinel was carving a special niche for psychiatry at the turn of the nineteenth century, his simple diagnostic classification was far from Linnaeus' elaborate systematic approach. Pinel still had faith in the two traditional diagnoses of mania and melancholy; he only added two other diagnoses in his system: *dementia* and *idiocy*. According to Pinel, those suffering from dementia have lost their faculty of judgement, and their 'ideas appear to be insulated, and to rise one after the other without connection, the faculty of association being destroyed'. Idiotism in turn is a 'partial or total abolition of the intellectual and active faculties' (Pinel 2009, 86–7). In Germany, the pioneer psychiatrist Johann Christian Reil (1759–1813) also used four diagnostic categories, which were fixed delusions (*fixer Wahn*), mania (*Wuth*), folly (*Narrheit*) and feeblemindedness (*Blödsinn*). Reil estimated that about a quarter of the inmates confined in asylums were feebleminded persons who had formerly been mentally ill (Marx 1990, 366). Reil assumed that mental illness can lead to full-blown idiocy, and this belief was shared by the later French degenerationists. Pinel in turn noted that 'the most numerous class of patients at lunatic hospitals is undoubtedly that of ideots [sic]; who, when viewed collectively, exhibit every degree and form of stupidity' (Pinel 2009, 88). So it seems that, right from the start a considerable number of asylum patients were feebleminded rather than mentally ill. Medical and social attention to the 'problem of feeblemindedness' increased during the last decades of the nineteenth century, and with the rise of racial hygiene or eugenics in the early twentieth century the feebleminded were singled out as the most serious threat to public health and racial purity.

There have been hundreds of classificatory systems of insanity in the course of history, but most of them have been devised in the last 150 years. An important reason for the increased interest in psychiatric taxonomy was the establishment of asylum-based mental health care. When patients were under medical scrutiny for longer periods of time – maybe two or even ten or twenty years – alienists noticed the importance of *temporality*: different illnesses developed in different ways so that the phases of illness X followed a certain pattern while the phases of illness Y followed a different course. For this reason, time became an essential element of mental illness. An understanding of the temporal dimension of illness was a big step forward for psychiatry. Before the Age of the Asylum, changes in the symptoms, illness behaviour and the whole mental configuration of the mad had gone largely unnoticed, or such changes were not explicated in any systematic fashion. Certainly, since antiquity doctors had made observations of the outbreak of illness, its different phases and variations as well as the whole life situation of the mad. But they had not looked at mental illnesses as temporally structured phenomena. Neither had they based their knowledge on observations of the relationship between changing symptoms and the essence or basic characteristics of illness. Hence they had only a vague understanding of the outbreak of an illness, the course it takes and the factors involved in recovery. The temporal dimension of mental illness started to influence the formation of diagnoses only in the nineteenth century. Moreover, in Pinel's and Reil's time mental patients often suffered from various somatic symptoms and maladies, such as infectious diseases, which are rare today. Pinel and other founding fathers of psychiatry were acutely aware of the fact that in most cases the mentally ill were plagued by various bodily ailments.

In the mid-nineteenth century, psychiatry was still lacking a system of diagnostic classification and a generally accepted theory that would have guided clinical observations in asylums. Even within individual countries there were differences in theory and practice, mostly due to the relative geographic and scientific isolation of asylums. One solution to the lack of a common classificatory system was

162 The great transformation

to abandon the whole endeavour and to deny that different forms or 'families' of mental illness even existed. In this view, what were considered different illnesses were in fact different phases of a single disease process (Schott & Tölle 2006, 331–3; Engstrom 2004, 27).

Even if there were not anything like a universally accepted classificatory system, some diagnoses were more popular than others. In what follows, I will give an account of the major mental disorders classified and discussed in nineteenth-century psychiatry. I will start with the disease entity that has had staying power since antiquity: melancholy.

Melancholy

The first-century Cappadocian physician Arataeus described melancholy as a condition in which the spirit is low because of a single fantasy which differed from patient to patient. Above all, the afflicted mind is overwhelmed by sadness and despair, and those with melancholic dispositions are sorrowful. Melancholics differ from each other, but all of them are either wary of poisoning, fleeing to desert in a state of misanthropy, superstitious or end up hating life. Roman doctors believed that melancholy could lead to a more serious form of madness or mania. To the Romans, melancholy was an earlier or milder form of mania (Healy 2008, 10–11).

Melancholy remained a major illness throughout the Middle Ages, and in the late sixteenth century it became a fashionable malady among European elites, both men and women. One reason for the popularity of melancholy was the academic physicians' ability to place their patients' symptoms in different diagnostic classes, melancholy of course being one of them (Midelfort 1999, 319–78, 386). Moreover, Robert Burton's *Anatomy of Melancholy* (1621), the most well-known book on melancholy in early modern Europe, was published in the middle of this melancholy boom (see Chapter 4).

During the second half of the eighteenth century, melancholy was transformed into a nervous illness in Britain. It was then considered to be a typically British illness, a belief which appeared to be confirmed by numerous suicides in Britain. The luxurious lifestyle of the higher orders of society and the advanced level of civilization were thought to sensitize the nervous system and predispose the British to melancholy. Together with some other nervous illnesses, melancholy began to be called the English malady, which was also the title of a popular book by the physician George Cheyne (1671–1743), published in 1733. Conditions resembling melancholy were labelled vapours, spleen or hypochondriasis. *Vapours* was used to name women's melancholy in particular, while *hypochondriasis* was more common among men. They were all classified as *nervous disorders* until 1769, when the Scottish physician William Cullen (1710–90) invented a new diagnostic category, *neuroses* (Berrios 1996, 299).

In the early nineteenth century, Pinel described melancholy in a familiar manner: the illness was characterized by reticence, ruminative and reflective contemplation, dark forebodings and a longing for solitude. Pinel noted that one can find such characteristics also in people who are otherwise healthy, even successful in life. Yet, he wrote that he could not find a more horrible condition than melancholy, and because a more serious form of melancholy was often followed by a real loss of reason, the melancholic sentiments of sadness and loss could be a source of mental alienation. Thus Pinel followed the ancient Romans in his contention that melancholy could develop into mania or other serious illnesses. One distinctive characteristic of melancholics was their obsessive interest in a single idea at the expense of all others. Later, Esquirol began to call this mental obsession 'monomania' (Pinel 2009, 77–8).

Modern medicalized depression was born in the mid-nineteenth century, when a medical discussion of a specific type of 'emotional illness' emerged. Such an illness was considered a form of partial insanity that denoted losses, inhibitions, dejection and mental regression. This partial insanity started to be called mental or psychological depression, a term derived from Latin *depressionem* (nominative *depressio*), a noun of action from the past participle stem of *deprimere*, 'to press down, depress', which was used in the context of cardiovascular diseases to denote heart failure. To the younger generation of physicians, the term 'depression' was preferable to 'melancholy' (or Esquirol's 'lypemania'), because depression was easier to explicate physiologically, that is, in terms of modern scientific medicine. At first, 'mental depression' was a near-equivalent to dejection, but during the last decades of the nineteenth century a number of other symptoms, such as stupor and gloomy delusions, were included in it. The German psychiatrist Emil Kraepelin (1856–1926), the grand classifier of mental disorders, started to write about 'depressive states', in which he included stupor, melancholic confusion as well as 'simple', 'serious' and 'fantastic' melancholy. Modern depression was assembled from a rather wide variety of clinical symptoms that were partly related to traditional melancholy and partly to the modern psychomedical language of mood disorders.

Psychiatrist David Healy argues that many melancholic conditions of the late nineteenth and early twentieth century would be diagnosed today as schizophrenia or dementia (Healy 2008, 83–4). His colleague German Berrios agrees with him, pointing out that until the early nineteenth century, melancholy was a sort of hotchpotch of different mental pathologies. What was common to all these conditions was that melancholics suffered from delusions that did not, however, dominate their minds. For this reason, Berrios holds that melancholy included milder forms of schizophrenia, which only became an independent diagnostic category at the end of the nineteenth century (with Emil Kraepelin's *dementia praecox*, see below) (Berrios 1996, 299). Other scholars have gone beyond the somewhat restricted and unimaginative clinical approach exemplified by Healy and Berrios. To the Swedish medical historian Karin Johannisson, melancholy is much more than a one-dimensional or even multidimensional illness. To her, melancholy denotes a wide range of emotions, thoughts, musings and other mental states that have a complex relationship with changing cultural values, norms and beliefs. Melancholy signified existential suffering, sorrow and low spirits, but also creative solitude or exuberant manic activity. Johannisson puts it aptly: 'Melancholy speaks, depression keeps silent' (Johannisson 2012, 32; my translation). It is true that, while today's depression is a strictly clinical condition confined by medical discourse, traditional melancholy was a much wider, wilder and 'deeper' condition of the mind and body, sometimes an illness but sometimes a natural condition of humans, derived from birth or occurring because of ageing (Joutsivuo 2014, 45).

Melancholy is not synonymous with twenty-first-century depression, even though sadness and dejection are some of the symptoms characterizing both depression and melancholy. Today's milder form of depression would have been called melancholy only in the nineteenth century.

Wolf-madness, a strange kind of melancholy

In the history of madness, there are a number of illnesses that have come and gone. One of the oldest diagnoses that is now forgotten is *lycantrophy*, or wolf-madness. It was known from late antiquity to the early modern age as one type of melancholia, and its basic symptom was a delusion that one has been turned into a wolf, as a result of which the afflicted person tended to behave accordingly. This is how Oribasius of Pergamon (325–403) describes lycantrophy:

> Such persons went out at night, imitating wolves in every way and staying around tombs until daytime. The signs were paleness, languid expression, eyes dry and without tears; the eyes were hollow, the tongue was extremely dry, and no saliva escaped the mouth; the sufferers were dry and had incurable ulcers on their legs from frequently running into things.
>
> (Jackson 1986, 345)

Oribasius subsumed this condition under the category of melancholy, but he did not explain how lycantrophy is aetiologically related to melancholy. In another treatise, probably written by Aetius of Amida in the sixth century, the symptoms of lycantrophy are similar to Oribasius' description. In his influential medical handbook *Qānūn*, the Arabic philosopher and physician Ibn Sīnā (died 1037) also sees wolf-madness as a kind of melancholia. This illness often appears in the month of February and turns an ordinary man into a fugitive:

> He likes the cemeteries and tombs and has evil intent toward whoever surprises him. He appears at night and conceals himself during the day [. . .] He is extremely quiet, gloomy, and sad; he has a yellow complexion, a dry tongue and a mouth, and sores on his legs that do not heal. The cause of the sores is the corruption of the black bile [which causes melancholia] and much movement of his legs.
>
> (Dols 1992, 84)

Wolf-madness as a diagnosis was different from the popular European folklore concerning werewolves, a sort of man-beast who assumed the form and traits of a wolf and who then attacked humans and animals in search of raw flesh. A belief in werewolves became a more serious superstition during witch-hunts, when alleged werewolves were killed because they were thought to have been meddling in witchcraft or black magic. In France, an amazing number of 30,000 cases of lycantrophy were recorded between 1520 and 1630, at a time when France and all of Europe was in turmoil (Blom 2014, 93). Robert Burton, the author of *Anatomy of Melancholy*, categorized lycantrophy as madness (mania) and added that 'some make a doubt of it whether there be any such disease' (Burton 2001, Part I, 141). Indeed, after the Thirty Years' War (1618–48) there were fewer and fewer references to lycantrophy, and they became shorter and shorter. In the eighteenth-century medical treatises, it was commonly regarded as a delusion of bodily metamorphosis and a type of melancholia. By the nineteenth century, lycantrophy had all but lost its diagnostic status, and in the few instances it was referred to it was listed under some other diagnostic heading, such as 'sensitive insanity' (Thomas Arnold), 'melancholia metamorphosis' (Heinroth) and 'zoanthropy', a form of lypemania (Esquirol). In the twentieth century, it was typically seen as a delusion indicating schizophrenia or manic-depression, or it was conceptualized as a form of depersonalization. According to the systematic review conducted by the Dutch psychiatrist Jan Dirk Blom, there have been only 56 case descriptions of metamorphosis into an animal since 1850, and only 13 of these cases fulfilled the criteria of clinical lycantrophy proper (Blom 2014). While the condition is extremely rare, in its popular version – werewolvism – it has continued to haunt cultural imagination. Werewolves are now rare except in Hollywood studios.

Neurosyphilis

Neurosyphilis, also known as *dementia paralytica, paralysia* and *general paralysis of the insane*, became one of the most common mental illnesses of the nineteenth century. The syphilitic bacterium spirochete (*Treponema pallidum*) itself has a history going back to end of the fifteenth century, when Columbus returned to Europe from his first voyage the New World. For some reason syphilis did not affect the brain and the nervous system for 300 years. It was only in the nineteenth century when the spirochete bacterium became an essential part of modern madness. The first to recognize neurosyphilis as a separate disease was the French psychiatrist Antoine-Laurent Bayle (1799–1858), who was working at the Charenton Asylum near Paris in the 1820s. In the brains of certain deceased patients, Bayle detected clear anatomical changes that he could not find in the brains of other patients. Not knowing that the lesions in the brain were caused by syphilis, he called this new disease 'general paralysis of the insane' (*paralysie générale*) (Brown 1994). Its connection to syphilis was ascertained only in 1905, when two German researchers of parasites found the spiral-shaped spirochete under the microscope. As the symptoms of this disease varied a great deal, it was exceedingly difficult to determine its clinical characteristics. The disease was often called the 'great imitator'.

166 The great transformation

Patients suffering from general paralysis could be exuberantly happy, megalomaniac or raging, only to fall into the deep abyss of depression, delusions and, in the final stages of the disease, dementia. No wonder patients with neurosyphilis were easily misdiagnosed as manic-depressives. Before the final fall into mental darkness, the patient could experience a short episode of unbounded enthusiasm and euphoria. In this so-called tertiary phase of the disease, the spirochete bacterium, which spread throughout the body via the blood and the lymph, was wreaking havoc in the brain and the nervous system. The disease often destroyed the patient's personality, rapidly changing normal, intelligent people into psychotics. No wonder the Swiss psychiatrist C.G. Jung, who treated many neurosyphilitic patients at the Burghölzli Mental Hospital in the early twentieth century, called the disease 'poison of the darkness' (Hayden 2004, xviii).

After Bayle had discovered general paralysis, physicians began to follow the development of all mental illnesses more carefully. The wide variety of symptoms of general paralysis taught psychiatrists the important lesson that specific symptoms, no matter how dramatic and dominant they are, are not illnesses in themselves. What was also extraordinary about general paralysis was that the disease process took years or even decades from the original syphilitic infection to the last and most dangerous phase. If a young man in his early twenties visited a brothel and caught the disease, the spirochete might hit the brain only 10, 20 or even 30 years later. For this reason, the majority of the afflicted were middle-aged men (around 45 years of age) who had had sexual intercourse with prostitutes (Hayden 2004, 53–9).

It is not clear why there is no evidence of neurosyphilis before the end of the eighteenth century. One reason could be biological: perhaps spirochete bacterium underwent a mutation that enabled it to invade the brain and the central nervous system. According to the mutation theory, neurosyphilis was spread throughout Europe by Napoleon's armies. This is a plausible explanation for the disease becoming so common so rapidly. While it is very difficult to make diagnoses of dead people whose afflictions were not (clearly) diagnosed during their lifetimes, we know for sure that the French writer Guy de Maupassant spent his last years in an asylum because of neurosyphilis. Decades later, the notorious gangster Al Capone was diagnosed with neurosyphilis. There has also been speculation about the German philosopher Friedrich Nietzsche contracting syphilis as a young man, which is indeed possible, because the symptoms and the disease process of his later mental breakdown resemble neurosyphilis. Also, such well-known individuals as Ludvig van Beethoven, Abraham Lincoln, Oscar Wilde, Vincent van Gogh, James Joyce and Adolf Hitler have been listed as possible victims of neurosyphilis. It would not be surprising if some of them had indeed suffered from neurosyphilis, because it was one of the most common mental disorders from mid-nineteenth to mid-twentieth century. Less than two decades after Bayle had made the initial diagnosis, between 12 and 16 per cent of all patients in Parisian asylums received the diagnosis *paralysie générale*. In 1874, more than 14 per cent of new patients in Parisian asylums suffered from this disease. Almost every fifth patient treated in a private clinic in Vienna between 1879 and 1891 had general paralysis; they were all middle-aged, middle-class men. According to the Austrian writer Stefan Zweig, at the turn of the twentieth century, one or two out of every ten young men in Vienna suffered from syphilitic disease, usually after having had sexual intercourse with prostitutes (Hayden 2004, xv). Between 1911 and 1920, about 20 per cent of new patients in the New York State mental hospitals were diagnosed with neurosyphilis (Grob 1994, 125). In the 1930s, as many as 30 per cent of the middle-aged Finnish men who were taken to a mental hospital due to their acute mental illness probably suffered from neurosyphilis (Kaila 1966, 111).

It took some decades before general paralysis was connected to syphilis. Danish physicians suggested syphilis as the possible cause of the disease in 1857, and this causal connection was repeated in a Danish doctoral thesis in 1873. These suggestions were challenged in France, but, in the late 1870s, Jean Alfred Fournier, French dermatologist and specialist in venereal diseases, posited the syphilitic origin of general paralysis (Kragh 2010, 473–5). In the following decades, there was more and more medical support for the view that general paralysis was a syphilitic disease, but there were also many psychiatrists who were reluctant to accept this conjecture, usually because they thought that the brain was impenetrable to syphilis. It was only in 1905 that the spirochete bacterium was found. A few years later, the first blood test for detecting syphilis was developed (the Wasserman test). Finding the bacterium revived hopes among psychiatrists that, in the long run, other organic or chemical causes of mental disorders would also be discovered, be they bacteria, viruses or toxic substances. Such discoveries would have been a great victory for medicine and the ultimate scientific breakthrough of psychiatry. Alas, these psychiatric hopes remained unfulfilled.

The first half of the twentieth century witnessed an ultimately successful search for the effective treatment of syphilis. The German physician and biochemist Paul Ehrlich (1854–1915) developed an intravenous drug based on an organic arsenic compound. The drug was called *Salvarsan*, and it killed the syphilis bacterium in its early stages, which meant that it had no curative effect on neurosyphilis (tertiary syphilis). Moreover, *Salvarsan* was difficult to administer and it had serious side effects, such as rashes and liver damage. Still, it became the most widely prescribed drug in the world, and Ehrlich could insist that he (and his Japanese assistant Sahachiro Hata) had developed the first 'magic bullet' (*magische Kugel*), a drug that selectively exterminates pathogenic microbes without damaging the whole organism. Ehrlich, who received the Nobel Prize in Medicine in 1908, called such treatment *chemotherapy* (today, chemotherapy is used in the treatment of cancer).

In 1917, the Austrian psychiatrist Julius Wagner-Jauregg (1857–1940) invented an unorthodox method for treating neurosyphilis at the Psychiatric University Clinic in Vienna. He had experimented with fever-producing bacteria already in the 1880s and 1890s, but had then given up the idea. He returned to the method decades later when World War I was raging. In June 1917, he decided to inoculate syphilitic patients at his clinic with malaria, hoping that the ensuing high fever would kill the bacterium. Indeed, this happened occasionally, although not as

168 The great transformation

often as Wagner-Jauregg claimed (he reported that two-thirds of his paralytics had improved). The prolonged high fevers produced by malaria parasites had one serious side effect: some patients died of malaria. Despite its risks, Wagner-Jauregg's therapeutic innovation was so highly regarded that, ten years after his invention, he was awarded with the Nobel Prize in Medicine (in 1927). It took more than 70 years before the prize was given to a psychiatrist again (this happened in 2002 when the neuropsychiatrist Eric Kandel received the prize). Today, Wagner-Jauregg is not much celebrated in the psychiatric community, and for obvious reasons: he was a notorious anti-Semite, Nazi sympathizer and zealous advocate of racial hygiene, including the forced sterilization of mental patients. From the early 1920s to the late 1940s, malaria fever therapy was widely used in mental hospitals across the western world. When penicillin was taken into therapeutic use in the 1940s, malaria fever therapy became redundant; the first syphilis patient was successfully treated with penicillin in 1943. Yet, in some hospitals, malaria fever therapy continued to be used to pacify unruly and agitated patients in the latter half of the 1940s and the early 1950s. With the introduction of penicillin and other antibiotics on a mass scale, neurosyphilis was virtually wiped out, at least in the western world.

Syphilis is still a cryptic disease – why, for example, are human beings the only hosts of *Treponema pallidum*? And why does it persist in spite of the fact that the bacterium has *not* become resistant to penicillin? Even today, little is known about its life cycle and 'behaviour' in comparison with other bacterial pathogens. What we do know is that neurosyphilis was the first psychiatric illness that was positively demonstrated to be a somatic affliction – it was a *brain disease* without any doubt. Unfortunately, it is also the only major mental disorder that has revealed its secrets; all other illnesses are still unsolved mysteries.

Pellagra

Pellagra is the other well-known example of a somatic disease that seriously affects the mental condition of the afflicted. In the early twentieth century, the causes of both neurosyphilis and pellagra were discovered, and, in the case of pellagra, a simple but effective cure was also found.

Pellagra was (primarily) caused by malnutrition due to a vitamin B3 (niacin) deficiency in the diet. Pellagra was characterized by 'the four D's': diarrhoea, dermatitis (inflammation of the skin), dementia and death. The afflicted often became mentally confused, apathetic and, eventually, demented – they collapsed mentally, probably because lack of niacin can damage brain cells. Pellagra was a potentially lethal disease that struck poor people whose diet was deficient in vitamin B. Just like rickets, another widespread disease of the nineteenth and twentieth centuries, the incidence of pellagra was clearly correlated with the general welfare of people living in the more peripheral and underdeveloped areas. In the late nineteenth century, the relationship between niacin deficiency, pellagra and insanity was observed by British doctors in Egypt, where it was considered an endemic disease (Egyptian peasants attributed it to sorcery or fright) (Dols 1992, 111). In the early twentieth century, pellagra ravaged the southern states of the United States, such as Mississippi and Alabama, where corn (maize) was the principal or even sole source of nutrition. Between 1906 and 1940, more than 3 million Americans were affected by pellagra with more than 100,000 deaths (Bollet 1992). As late as 1934, 0.5 per cent of all psychotic patients admitted to the state mental hospitals suffered from pellagra (Deutsch 1949, 503). In the United States, pellagra was called the 'sharecropper's scourge' or 'scourge of the South', and it was seen as a contagious disease caused by poor hygiene and afflicted the black population in the South particularly. In the 1930s, there were also many cases of pellagra psychosis in the rural areas of Italy and Spain. Pellagra was a disease of the poor and downtrodden.

Doctors who believed in the doctrine of degeneration typically regarded pellagra as the product of cumulative degeneration. A pioneer in the medical *and* social research of pellagra was the Hungarian-born American physician and epidemiologist Joseph Goldberger (1874–1929), who argued that pellagra was associated with poor diet. His theory was based on his experiments with prisoners who received mostly corn-based diets over several years. Goldberger was able to demonstrate that these individuals were at a greatly increased risk of contracting pellagra. In 1926, he stated that the key to the prevention of pellagra was a balanced diet, including fruit and vegetables, or a small amount of brewer's yeast. His theory contradicted the dominant medical opinion that pellagra was an infectious disease. It was also socially and politically unacceptable, because Goldberger made it clear that the best treatment for the disease was the eradication of poverty, which would improve diet and thereby make poor people healthier. Consequently, he failed to gain much support for the dietary treatment of pellagra. Finally, in 1937, eight years after Goldberger's death, the specific mechanism of pellagra (dietary lack of the B vitamin niacin along with reduced levels of the essential amino acid tryptophan) was discovered. Goldberger, who had been nominated five times for the Nobel Prize in Medicine for his work on the aetiology of pellagra, was proved to be right, and in the western world pellagra began to disappear as poor people's diets became more nutritious (Washington 2008, 154; Jones 1983, 54). Today, pellagra is still relatively common in the poorer areas of South America, Asia and Africa. It also affects refugees and other displaced people who are dependent on food aid.

Obsessions and compulsions

The earliest medical term for *obsession* was the German psychiatrist Richard Krafft-Ebing's (1840–1902) *Zwangsvorstellung* from 1867. Krafft-Ebing used the term to describe thoughts that a person was unable to resist or control. He was of course not the first to pay attention to obsessive thoughts; both obsessions and compulsive acts have probably existed since time immemorial, they were just described by religious or colloquial words. During the nineteenth century, obsession was

170 The great transformation

first classified as insanity (monomania), then as neurosis in the neurological sense. Next, obsession was seen as a form of psychosis, after which it became a neurosis again, this time in the psychological sense. This is an early case of obsession documented by Esquirol:

> Mademoiselle F. was a tall, happy-go-lucky 34 year-old female accountant, whose illness started suddenly at age 18 when she began to fear that she might take in 'her pockets objects belonging to her aunt'. She worried lest she got the accounts wrong, and that on touching money something of value might get stuck to her fingers. She accepted that her worries were absurd but could not help it. She started handwashing and fearing that her clothes might touch anything; when this happened she would rub her hands as if to get rid of some invisible substance. The fear began to include food and she had to be fed by her servant, etc.
>
> (Berrios 1996, 153)

In Esquirol's time, obsession (*obsessions pathologiques*) was derived from the parent category 'fixed idea' (*idée fixe*), and compulsion from the term 'impulsion' (*impulsio*). Both were interpreted first as a disorder of volition, then of intellect. Finally, what became the prevailing view was the suggestion that obsessive-compulsive symptoms were the result of *emotional* disturbances. This view won out not so much because of its scientific evidence, but because of the socio-cultural inclination to describe certain abnormal thoughts as indicators or catalysts of emotions. During the second half of the nineteenth century, the fundamental emotion affecting obsessions was identified as anxiety, which in itself was a sort of cultural obsession in France. Frightened by degeneration and humiliated by the Germans in the Franco-Prussian War (1870–1), the French were preoccupied with anxiety, which in turn was deemed to cause obsessions (Berrios 1996, 149–50).

Later, phobias were included in the list of disorders revolving around anxiety. One common phobia was *agoraphobia*, which referred to an intense fear about being in public places where you feel escape might be difficult or embarrassing. The French were also preoccupied with the psychopathological research on emotions. This fascination was seen in the adoption of the diagnoses *neurasthenia* and *psychasthenia* in French psychology and psychiatry. Both of these diagnoses referred to the states of weakness, neurasthenia (of which I will speak later) to the weakness of *nervous* energy and psychasthenia to the lowering of *psychic* energy. The father of the psychasthenia diagnosis was Pierre Janet (1859–1947), a pioneer of psychodynamic psychology. Janet and his colleagues were inspired by the scientific and cultural interest in electricity and energy, which could be seen in the emerging energetic understanding of the self: the human mind was compared to a battery, and the nervous system was described in terms of an electrical circuit (Rabinbach 1992). If the 'human battery' is discharged, it can lead to conditions such as psychasthenia, in which psychic energy is low. When his patients told him that they were unable to complete whatever tasks they had at hand, it prompted Janet to explain their exhaustion and lethargy in the energetic language of 'dynamic psychology', which was then emerging as a new and exciting approach to the subconscious or unconscious psyche. Sigmund Freud, Janet's one-time rival, is obviously an important character in this story. It was on account of Freud's psychoanalytic work that obsessions, phobias and other 'anxiety disorders' were separated from each other at the turn of the twentieth century. They all became different forms of psychological *neurosis*, perhaps the most 'contagious' diagnosis of the twentieth century (Berrios 1985; 1996).

From *hystera* to hysteria

Hysteria was by its very nature a protean illness, a diagnostic *tabula rasa*, the content of which was determined by socio-cultural factors (Micale 1995; Gilman et al. 1993). In the nineteenth century, hysteria, which had been around since antiquity, was the grand dame of the neuroses. Up until the early modern age, hysteria was deemed to be a female malady caused by the restless movements of the womb inside the body – the wandering womb or migratory uterus (the Greek word *hystera* means womb). The main symptom of hysteria was an unpleasant sense of suffocation, or constriction of the throat, caused by the womb pressing on the heart, liver and lungs. Hysterical symptoms were most common among recently widowed women who had suddenly ceased having sexual intercourse. In the Hippocratic writings there are only short lists of symptoms of and cures for hysteria, but no case histories of women suffering from such a malady of the uterus (Midelfort 1999, 5).

It was only in the seventeenth century that the ancient idea of hysteria as the 'suffocation of the mother' (i.e. uterus) began to change. In the 1670s, the British physician Thomas Willis (1621–75) changed the location of hysteria from the generative organs to the brain and the spinal tap. He called hysteria, chronic headaches and other 'female maladies' the 'paralysis of the nerves'. After Willis' reconceptualization, a neurological explanation of hysteria came to the fore, while centuries-long gynaecological and demonological theories faded away (Rousseau 1993, 140–1). Willis' famous colleague and rival Thomas Sydenham (1624–89), 'the Hippocrates of England', is a towering figure in the history of hysteria. First of all, he laid stress on the importance of strong emotions or passions for hysteria. By attributing hysteria to passions such as grief, terror, anger and distrust, Sydenham was a key figure in the psychologization of hysteria. Second, he claimed that men could also become hysterical. In fact, he created the term *hypochondriasis* to refer to hysteria-like symptoms in men. Third, he observed that hysteria mimics other maladies, by which he meant that hysteria is a cultural illness par excellence: historically changing ideas about health, illness, mind and the body shape, the essence of hysteria, which he regarded as the most common ailment in his time ('no chronic disease occurs so frequently as this') (Scull 2009, 32). Fourth, Sydenham set the stage for the eighteenth-century conceptualization of the feminine constitution as 'weak' and 'nervous'. This prejudice about the inferior feminine constitution

172 The great transformation

became one of the medical cornerstones of late nineteenth-century misogynistic language (Rousseau 1993, 138–45).

Before the eighteenth century, hysteria was not clearly associated with mental illness and it was not a particularly popular diagnosis. In Britain, 'hysterical' was synonymous with 'nervous', and nervousness became a popular general term denoting a confusing number of hysterical and hypochondriac symptoms and *syndromes* (groups of symptoms that collectively indicate or characterize a disease, disorder or other abnormal condition). Hysteria made a spectacular comeback as a nervous illness or neurosis in the second half of the nineteenth century, by which time the medical discussion of this protean malady had become more scattered and confused. The medical representation of hysteria was shaped by the discovery of the process of ovulation, the doctrine of animal magnetism as well as the psychopathological idea of the 'hysterical constitution' that laid stress not on the physical symptom profile but on negative character traits, such as eccentricity, impulsiveness and hypersexuality. The fact that these negative traits of the hysterical constitution were usually attributed to women contributed to the revival of the ancient notion that hysteria was a female malady.

As the historian Mark Micale observes,

> the sheer accumulation of meanings of hysteria a hundred years ago is extraordinary. In France during the late nineteenth century, hysteria was employed as a metaphor for: artistic experimentation, collective political violence, radical social reformism, and foreign nationalism. It became shorthand for the irrational, the will-less, the uncontrollable, the convulsive, the erratic, the erotic, the ecstatic, the female, the criminal, and a host of collective 'Others'. It was a synonym for everything that seemed excessive, or extreme, or incomprehensible about the age.
>
> (Micale 2004, 84)

By the end of the 1880s, European middle-class women had been infected by the diagnostic virus of hysteria, the aetiology of which many doctors attributed to the very nature of being female. The popularity of hysteria reflected the misogynistic cultural atmosphere prevalent in late nineteenth-century western Europe, where women were considered essentially inferior creatures, deviations from the universal standard of humanity that was white, middle-class man (Pietikainen 2007, 133–5; Dijkstra 1986).

Charcot, hysteria and hypnosis

The meteoric rise of hysteria during the last decades of the nineteenth century was largely an achievement of the French clinical neurologist Jean-Martin Charcot (1825–93), 'Napoleon of the neuroses' (Goetz, Bonduelle & Gelfand 1995). A chair in nervous diseases at the University of Paris was created in 1882 especially for Charcot; it was the first chair in neurology in the world. Also of paradigmatic importance for the future development of the care of neuroses was the opening of the first outpatient clinic at the Salpêtrière in 1879. The majority of patients in the neurological and psychiatric polyclinics, which started to be established across Europe at the turn of the century, suffered from milder mental afflictions, which made neurosis a very visible illness to physicians. If asylums were swelling with the more severely mentally ill and the demented, psychiatric and neurological polyclinics were usually frequented by people who were neither insane nor in full health; their symptoms were more diffuse and less severe, and, unlike the mentally ill, they could safely remain in the outside world.

Charcot's great contribution to the study of neuroses was his formulation of a neurological model of hysteria. Following his older colleague Pierre Briquet's pioneering work on hysteria (*Traité clinique et thérapeutique de l'hystérie*, 1859), Charcot conceptualized hysteria as a physical dysfunction of the central nervous system, which made the illness comparable to other neurological diseases, such as epilepsy, *paralysis agitans* (Parkinson's disease) and general paresis of the insane. Although he was unable to locate a lesion in the nervous system of hysterics, he was adamant in his conviction that clinicians applying the methods of pathological anatomy would eventually discover a lesion causing hysterical neuropathy in the nervous system. He saw hysteria as constitutional and degenerative, a pathological result of both inheritance and environmental factors, such as physical or emotional shock. He did not pay much attention to cure and potential therapies, but he was famed for the miraculous cures in which the power of his commandment alone repeatedly enabled paralytic individuals (mostly hysterics) to throw off their crutches and walk (Sulloway 1992, 28).

Charcot's reputation spread far and wide partly because he was a master showman. He had an extensive population of hysterical women in the well-stocked wards at the Salpêtrière, an enormous hospital for women, most of whom were near to or at the bottom of the social hierarchy. Charcot took full advantage of these mostly working-class women in the lectures he presented to large audiences as well as in his more informal bedside demonstrations to his pupils. This is how the Swedish nerve doctor Axel Munthe, who studied and worked in Paris in the 1880s, described Charcot's lectures:

> The huge amphitheatre was filled to the last place with a multicoloured audience drawn from tout Paris, authors, journalists, leading actors and actresses, fashionable demi-mondaines, all full of morbid curiosity to witness the startling phenomena of hypnotism [. . .] Sharing the fate of all nerve specialists he [Charcot] was surrounded by a bodyguard of neurotic ladies, hero-worshippers at all cost.
>
> (Munthe 1975, 206, 214)

Charcot's fame did not rest on any ingenious theoretical treatises on hysteria, but on his case studies: he published over 120 richly illustrated case histories that fully revealed the drama that was hysteria, *Grande Hystérie* in particular. His female

FIGURE 8.1 Jean-Martin Charcot giving a clinical demonstration at the Salpêtrière. He is showing his students a woman ('Blanche') in a trance or shock. Painting by André Brouillet, 1887.
Source: © World History Archive/Alamy

hysterics (and 'epileptics') were immortalized in visual representations, notably in the etchings of Paul Richer and the photographs published in the periodical *Iconographie photographique de la Salpêtrière* (1876–9) and its successor, *Nouvelle iconographie de la Salpêtrière*, which were impressive, though largely fabricated, visualizations of hysteria (Didi-Huberman 2003). There was a 'photographic department' attached to Charcot's clinic, showing how important the concrete bodily representation of hysteria was for Charcot and his colleagues.

Charcot's most controversial claim was that hysteria was directly linked to hypnosis. In a presentation given in 1882, he described in detail the three sequential stages of the hypnotic trance: lethargy, catalepsy and somnambulism. His idea created a stir among the French academic community, and, with the help of his considerable scientific authority, he managed to make the study of hypnosis a respectable scientific and medico-clinical activity. His demonstrations of the way he could artificially induce hypnotic fits among his female patients, some of whom became minor celebrities among the public, were spectacular, but not necessarily convincing to the more sceptical physicians. The results of his hypnotic experiments with 'hysterically prone' patients were categorically denied by Hippolyte Bernheim, Professor of Internal Medicine at the University of Nancy. Bernheim and his colleagues, the so-called Nancy School, regarded hysteria as an abnormal psychological reaction that was not 'triggered' by hypnosis. They maintained that, in specific situations, almost anyone could become hysterical, and that the mechanism of hysteria could be accounted for by heightened suggestibility, not by an innate neuropathic disposition or Charcot's auto-suggestion (Pietikainen 2007, 43).

The Nancy School's direct challenge to the Charcotian doctrine made Charcot's explanation of hysteria look implausible and suspicious. When Charcot died in 1893, his reputation as a theorist of hysteria was in decline, and by the turn of the twentieth century, the Charcotian approach to hysteria was largely discredited in academic and medical circles, only to make a comeback in France during World War I, when the phenomenon of shell-shock made the Charcotian understanding of trauma topical again (Micale 2001, 131). Meanwhile, Bernheim and his colleagues in Nancy were instrumental in launching a new, distinctly psychological approach to neuroses and their treatment. This transition from a neurological-physiological model to a psychological one was also advanced by some of Charcot's former pupils, such as Pierre Janet, who, like Bernheim, suggested that hysteria was a *mental* malady.

Neurasthenia and sexual neurasthenia

In 1880, when Charcot was busy studying hysterics at the Salpêtrière, an American physician, George Beard, published a book on a new type of nervous illness that he called 'neurasthenia'; literally 'weakness of the nerves' (Beard 1880; see also Beard 1881). The term 'neurasthenia' was not Beard's invention, for it had been in use at the beginning of the nineteenth century in German Romantic medicine, and the eighteenth-century British physician William Battie had called 'weakness of the nerves' a 'very common phrase' in his *A Treatise on Madness* (Battie 1758, 16, 36).

Beard's book hit the jackpot, as it were, and catapulted the diagnosis of neurasthenia to international stardom. Evidently, Beard was in the right place at the right time when he suggested that neurasthenia was the common origin of a staggering variety of symptoms that signalled profound physical and mental exhaustion. Neurasthenia became a major illness in the larger category of neuroses, which also included hysteria and hypochondriasis. Even before Beard's invention of neurasthenia, physicians had begun to 'find' intermediate and specific neuroses, such as 'spinal irritation' and 'reflex neuroses', which were placed between hysteria and the now obsolete 'minor neuroses' (Shorter 1992). In the late 1860s, Beard had expanded the domain of 'spinal irritation' from the spinal cord to the cerebrum, publishing his first paper on neurasthenia in 1869.

Beard was a nerve doctor and specialist in electrotherapy practising in New York. His specialty was the large and amorphous area of 'functional nervous disorders'. Such disorders differed from organic disorders in that there was no organic or anatomic lesion to be found in the nervous system of the patient. Physicians did not believe that 'functional' meant 'non-organic', but to their frustration they could not detect any anatomic lesion or alteration in the nervous system. Thanks to the germ theory of disease, developed by Louis Pasteur in France and Robert Koch in Germany, late nineteenth-century physicians began to be able to determine the underlying aetiology behind symptoms. The discovery of micro-organisms responsible for major diseases (such as general paralysis) also confirmed the belief that 'functional' denoted 'conditions which had no gross anatomical changes, but were nevertheless thought to have molecular disturbances' (Beer 1996, 241) Neurasthenia became a popular illness for almost half a century in many European countries and in North America. It has been shown that its history in different countries has different characteristics so that, for example, neurasthenia in the United States was not the same as neurasthenia in Germany, or the Netherlands, or Sweden (Gijswijt-Hofstra & Porter 2001; Pietikainen 2007; Schuster 2011).

During the *fin de siècle* (ca. 1890–1914), it was neurasthenia, even more than hysteria, that represented the most widespread and talked-about neurosis. Compared to hysteria, neurasthenia was a more 'heroic' illness, because it initially afflicted the intellectual classes who worked hard and overtaxed their brain day in day out. Initially, neurasthenics were both paragons and victims of modern life; they represented the vanguard of cultural progress, but they were also victims of a modern, increasingly hectic and nerve-wracking urban lifestyle. It was no coincidence that Beard had his office in Manhattan. In the early decades of the twentieth century, neurasthenia shifted from a predominantly somatic to a predominantly psychological disease entity. In Vienna, Sigmund Freud had created the influential 'anxiety neurosis' in the 1890s; in Paris, Freud's rival Pierre Janet developed a sort of psychological version of neurasthenia that he called 'psychasthenia' in 1903; and, in Bern, Switzerland, the nerve pathologist Paul Dubois introduced the term 'psychoneurosis' in 1904. Neurasthenia, psychasthenia and psychoneurosis (as well as 'traumatic neurosis') formed the illness category of 'neurosis', a generic term for milder mental afflictions. During the first half of the twentieth century, neurosis (including its sub-categories) became the most common mental malady in the western world and a major diagnostic category in psychiatry and neurology (Pietikainen 2007).

A significant component of neurosis was sexuality. George Beard devoted a whole book to sexual neurasthenia and claimed that sexual problems, especially impotence, constituted a major factor in nervous illnesses (Beard 1884). His book set the tone for the later conceptualizations of the relationship between 'weak nerves' and disturbances in the sexual sphere. Sexuality was not only a medical, but also a moral problem. Moralistic judgements with regard to sexuality were rampant in western Europe at least until the 1920s and the 1930s. Doctors, clergy and pedagogues formed an unofficial vice squad that monitored and regulated sexuality, condemning, for example, masturbation either as a sin or as a pathology that weakened and eventually damaged both the nervous system and the brain (Laqueur 2003). Likewise, sexual 'deviations', such as homosexuality, were judged negatively both morally and medically (through pathologization). By and large, the European medical community joined forces with the Church in seeing sexuality as a creature from the black lagoon, lying in wait to emerge from the oily water and devour men and women who failed to practise continence or restrict sex to marriage (Pietikainen 2007, 151–9).

Forgotten diagnoses

During the past 200 years, there have been a number of diagnoses that have appeared and then disappeared. Psychosomatic symptoms in particular have been described with different terms at different times. In the nineteenth century, doctors called the strange syndrome of unexplained aches and pains 'spinal irritation', then came the 'hysteria' of functional paralysis, and, towards the end of the century, neurasthenia and psychasthenia (Shorter 1992). All these diagnoses have now disappeared from western medicine, which corroborates the thesis that illness behaviour, (psycho-)medical language and deviant behaviour are a living part of the cultural and intellectual landscape that changes over time. Next, I will describe three illnesses of the modern age that are now either forgotten or unrecognizable as mental maladies.

Today, *nostalgia* is considered to be a harmless longing for home or for the places and times that were once dear to us. But from the late seventeenth century to the end of the nineteenth century, nostalgia was a difficult, sometimes even fatal disease (*algia* means 'pain'). For about 100 years, nostalgia (*Heimweh* or 'homesickness') was known as the 'Swiss illness' (*Schweizerkrankheit*), because it was introduced to the medical community by the Swiss physician Johannes Hofer (1669–1752) with his dissertation on nostalgia (*Dissertatio medica de Nostalgia, oder Heimwehe*, 1688). Hofer believed that the Swiss living in the mountains were especially prone to nostalgia. Carl von Linnaeus included nostalgia in his classification of mental diseases in the mid-eighteenth century, as did the Scottish physician William Cullen some decades later. Nostalgia assumed a more dramatic form in the eighteenth century when some servant girls had such an intense longing for home that they set fire to the houses of their masters or killed the children of their host families. As a consequence of these tragic events, nostalgia became a term used in forensic medicine. In criminal courts, nostalgia could be seen both as the *cause* of the criminal act and as a medical *justification* for the mitigation of sentence, if it could be demonstrated that the defendant was in the state of nostalgia when the crime was committed (Bunke 2009).

Up until the American Civil War (1861–5), physicians took nostalgia seriously. During this period in American history, young men grew up in a very sentimental culture that glorified hearth, home and mother love. Dislocated from familiar surroundings because of the war, young recruits often suffered from severe homesickness, which could make them moody and emotionally unstable, which in turn made them unreliable combatants (Anderson 2010). In the British colonies Australia and New Zealand, it was not uncommon for the settlers to suffer from dislocation, homesickness and nostalgia (Coleborne 2010, 32–47). In general, in times of mass emigration, when more people move around the world and migrate to its different parts, painful longing for home increases.

178 The great transformation

Yet, by the end of the nineteenth century, nostalgia had lost its diagnostic momentum. It was no longer compatible with the emerging illnesses of the nervous system and the psyche, such as neurasthenia, psychasthenia and depression, the latter diagnosis partly occupying the same 'ecological niche' as nostalgia. When Karl Jaspers (1883–1969), German psychiatrist and future theorist of phenomenological psychiatry and philosophy, published his dissertation on 'nostalgia and crime' (*Heimweh und Verbrechen*) in 1909, nostalgia entered the diagnostic scene for the last time and with a minor role. Nostalgia faded away as an illness, but as a term signifying wistful mood it has survived until the present day.

Modern psychiatrists may be surprised to learn how much medical discussion there was about 'diseases of the will' in the nineteenth century. What the physicians usually referred to were functional disturbances in which the will was physically incapable of executing what was intended (motive, desire). The French psychologist Theodore Ribot (1839–1916) was especially interested in the will and its disorders, and his publications disseminated the already existing term *aboulia*, by which he meant a pathological weakness of the will (*aboulia* is Greek and means 'loss of will', cf. 'apathy'). *Aboulia* did not just signify a symptom of laziness or lethargy; it was a more severe condition denoting a paralysis of the will. At the turn of the twentieth century, *aboulia* became a popular term in France, where some experts suggested education of the 'masses' to fight the evil of *aboulia* that was supposedly rampant among the students and the educated classes. During this period, the source of the problem began to be attributed to emotions rather than to the will, particularly by the new professionals who called themselves 'psychotherapists' (Berrios 1996, 362–3).

The third diagnostic specialty of the (late) nineteenth century was *fugue*, a peculiar compulsion that led the afflicted to travel obsessively from place to place. Fugue was a very gender-specific neurosis: only men felt this compulsion to travel. What made it more than a harmless manifestation of *wanderlust* was that its symptoms included memory disturbances and confusion about one's sense of self; men who suffered from this compulsion often did not know who they were or why they travelled. The first compulsive traveller was the Frenchman Albert Dadas, whose mad travelling in the 1880s became known after his physician wrote a thesis on fugue (*Les Aliénés voyageurs*, 1887). 'Fuguers' could travel around Europe, North Africa and the Near East for weeks. The mad traveller's 'unconscious' will seemed to take control of his mind, which as an idea fits in well with the popular psychological conjecture that obsessive urges and compulsions may have their matrix in the mental sphere outside the jurisdiction of consciousness – in the unconscious, the subconscious or the split self. The fuguers represented the urban working class or lower middle class, and, unlike the more prosperous bourgeoisie, they lacked the possibility of tourism or vacationing. Albert Dadas' doctor in fact believed that he suffered from 'pathological tourism'. The epidemic of fugue lasted for a few decades between the 1880s and World War I, and then it faded away. Today, fugue is a very rare disorder known as *dissociative fugue*, which is a diagnostic fossil rather than a 'true' illness. It is explained by the compulsive traveller's unconscious attempt to get rid of a stressful situation or crisis (Hacking 2002).

Fugue was a typical example of a transient mental illness, as the philosopher and historian Ian Hacking has called those disorders that appear at a specific time and in a specific place, and later disappear or fade away (Hacking 2002, 1). This is what happened to all diseases of the will – and to will itself – in the early decades of the twentieth century. Now, a full century later, it is still unclear why will and its disorders disappeared just like that. What is well known is that the will had two enemies, psychoanalysts and behaviourists, the former regarding it as superfluous in the psychodynamic approach to the psyche, and the latter dismissing it outright as a metaphysical and therefore unscientific concept. In academic psychology, 'will' was replaced by the more scientific-sounding concept of 'motivation' (Danziger 1997, 110–16). In the end, there was hardly any crucial empirical 'data' giving evidence to support the suggestion that the will did not exist or that it was a useless concept in the human sciences. Due to the fall of the will and its disorders there is a gaping hole in the psychomedical explanations of the pathology of action. Such pathologies have not disappeared, they have just been reconceptualized (e.g. obsessions) or abandoned (e.g. *aboulia*), while others, such as impulse, remain unexplained. Now there are terms such as lack of 'motivation' and disorders of 'drive' or 'desire', but as the psychiatric historian German Berrios points out, they are 'not more illuminating than the old term disorder of the will' (Berrios 1996, 364). Unsuccessful attempts to redefine and reformulate the concept of will are a bleak reminder of the difficulties involved in psychological and psychopathological research on the human mind and behaviour.

* * *

I will continue my description of the strange world of diagnoses in the next chapter, where I focus on schizophrenia, manic-depression and psychopathy – all disorders that came to dominate twentieth-century psychiatry.

Bibliography

Anderson, D. (2010) 'Dying of nostalgia: homesickness in the Union Army during the Civil War', *Civil War History*, 56: 247–82.

Battie, W. (1758) *A Treatise on Madness*, London: J. Whiston & B. White.

Beard, G.M. (1880) *A Practical Treatise in Nervous Exhaustion (Neurasthenia), Its Symptoms, Nature, Sequences, Treatment*, New York: W. Wood & Company.

Beard, G.M. (1881) *American Nervousness, Its Causes and Consequences*, New York: Putnam's Sons.

Beard, G.M. (1884) *Sexual Neurasthenia (Nervous Exhaustion)*, ed. A.D. Rockwell, New York: E.B. Treat.

Beer, D. (1996) 'The dichotomies: psychosis/neurosis and functional/organic: a historical perspective', *History of Psychiatry*, 7: 231–55.

Berrios, G.E. (1985) 'Obsessional disorders during the nineteenth century: terminological and classificatory issues', in W. F. Bynum, R. Porter and M. Shepherd (eds) *The Anatomy of Madness: Essays in the History of Psychiatry*, Vol. I: *People and Ideas*, London: Tavistock Publications.

Berrios, G.E. (1996) *The History of Mental Symptoms: Descriptive Psychopathology since the Nineteenth Century*, Cambridge: Cambridge University Press.

Blom, J.D. (2014) 'When doctors cry wolf: a systematic review of the literature on clinical lycantrophy', *History of Psychiatry*, 25: 87–102.

Bollet, A.J. (1992) 'Politics and pellagra: the epidemic of pellagra in the U.S. in the early twentieth century', *Yale Journal of Biological Medicine*, 65: 211–21.

Brown, E.M. (1994) 'French psychiatry's initial reception of Bayle's discovery of general paresis of the insane', *Bulletin of the History of Medicine*, 68: 235–53.

Bunke, S. (2009) *Heimweh. Studien zur Kultur – und Literaturgeschichte einer tödlichen Krankheit*, Freiburg: Rombach.

Burton, R. (2001) *The Anatomy of Melancholy*, 1st edn 1621, New York: New York Review of Books.

Coleborne, C. (2010) *Madness in the Family: Insanity and Institutions in the Australasian Colonial World, 1860–1914*, Basingstoke: Palgrave Macmillan.

Danziger, K. (1997) *Naming the Mind: How Psychology Found Its Language*, London: SAGE.

Deutsch, A. (1949) *The Mentally Ill in America*, New York: Columbia University Press.

Didi-Huberman, G. (2003) *Invention of Hysteria: Charcot and the Photographic Iconography of the Salpêtrière*, trans. A. Hartz, orig. French edn 1982, Cambridge, MA: The MIT Press.

Dijkstra, B. (1986) *Idols of Perversity: Fantasies of Femine Evil in Fin-de-siècle Culture*, Oxford: Oxford University Press.

Dols, M.W. (1992) *Majnun: The Madman in Medieval Islamic Society*, ed. by D.E. Immisch, Oxford: The Clarendon Press.

Engstrom, E.J. (2004) *Clinical Psychiatry in Imperial Germany: A History of Psychiatric Practice*, Ithaca, NY: Cornell University Press.

Gijswijt-Hofstra, M. and Porter, R. (eds) (2001) *Cultures of Neurasthenia from Beard to the First World War*, Amsterdam: Rodopi.

Gilman, S.L., King, H., Porter, R., Rousseau, G.S. and Showalter, H. (1993) *Hysteria beyond Freud*, Berkeley: University of California Press.

Goetz, C., Bonduelle, M. and Gelfand, T. (1995) *Charcot: Constructing Neurology*, Oxford: Oxford University Press.

Grob, G.N. (1994) *The Mad Among Us*, New York: The Free Press.

Hacking, I. (2002) *Mad Travelers: Reflections on the Reality of Transient Illnesses*, Cambridge, MA: Harvard University Press.

Hayden, D. (2004) *Pox. Genius, Madness and the Mysteries of Syphilis*, New York: Basic Books.

Healy, D. (2008) *Mania. A Short History of Bipolar Disorder*, Baltimore, MD: Johns Hopkins University Press.

Hobbes, T. (2008) *Leviathan*, 1st edn 1651, Oxford: Oxford University Press.

Jackson, S.W. (1986) *Melancholia and Depression from Hippocratic Times to Modern Times*, New Haven, CT: Yale University Press.

Johannisson, K. (2012) *Melankolian huoneet*, trans. U. Lempinen, orig. Swedish edn 2009, Jyväskylä: Atena.

Jones, W.L. (1983) *Ministering to Minds Diseased*, London: William Heinemann Medical Books.

Joutsivuo, T. (2014) 'How to get a melancholy marquess to sleep?', in S. Katajala-Peltomaa and S. Niiranen (eds), *Mental (Dis)Order in Later Medieval Europe*, Leiden: Brill.

Kaila, M. (1966) *Psykiatrian historia lääketieteen yleiskehityksen ja kulttuurihistorian valossa*, Porvoo, Finland: WSOY.

Kragh, J.V. (2010) 'Malaria fever therapy and general paralysis of the insane in Denmark', *History of Psychiatry*, 21: 471–86.

Laqueur, T.W. (2003) *Solitary Sex: A Cultural History of Masturbation*, New York: Zone Books.

Marx, O.M. (1990) 'German Romantic psychiatry, Part 1', *History of Psychiatry*, 1: 351–81.

Micale, M.S. (1995) *Approaching Hysteria: Disease and Its Interpretations*, Princeton, NJ: Princeton University Press.

Micale, M.S. (2001) 'Jean-Martin Charcot and les névroses traumatiques: from medicine to culture in French trauma theory of the late nineteenth century', in M. Micale and P. Lerner (eds) *Traumatic Pasts*, Cambridge: Cambridge University Press.

Micale, M.S. (2004) 'Discourses of hysteria in fin-de-siècle France', in M.S. Micale (ed.) *The Mind of Modernism: Medicine, Psychology, and the Cultural Arts in Europe and America, 1880–1940*, Stanford, CA: Stanford University Press.

Midelfort, E. (1999) *A History of Madness in Sixteenth-century Germany*, Stanford, CA: Stanford University Press.

Munthe, A. (1975) *The Story of San Michele*, 1st edn 1929, London: John Murray.

Pietikainen, P. (2007) *Neurosis and Modernity. The Age of Nervousness in Sweden*, Leiden: Brill.

Pinel, P. (2009) *A Treatise on Insanity*, orig. French edn 1801, Milton Keynes: General Books.

Porter, R. (2006) *Madmen. A Social History of Madhouses, Mad-Doctors and Lunatics*, Stroud: Tempus.

Rabinbach, A. (1992) *The Human Motor: Energy, Fatigue, and the Origins of Modernity*, Berkeley, CA: University of California Press.

Rousseau, G.S. (1993) '"A strange pathology": hysteria in the early modern world, 1500–1800', in S.L. Gilman et al., *Hysteria Beyond Freud*, Berkeley, CA: University of California Press.

Schott, H. and Tölle, R. (2006) *Geschichte der Psychiatrie*, Munich: C.H. Beck.

Schuster, D.G. (2011) *Neurasthenic Nation: America's Search for Health, Happiness, and Comfort, 1869–1920*, New Brunswick, NJ: Rutgers University Press.

Scull, A. (2009) *Hysteria. The Disturbing History*, Oxford: Oxford University Press.

Shorter, E. (1992) *From Paralysis to Fatigue: A History of Psychosomatic Illness in the Modern Era*, New York: The Free Press.

Sulloway, F.J. (1992) *Freud, Biologist of the Mind*, 1st edn 1979, Cambridge, MA: Cambridge University Press.

Uddenberg, N. (2012) *Linné och mentalsjukdomarna*, Stockholm: Atlantis.

Washington, H.A. (2008) *Medical Apartheid: The Dark History of Medical Experimentation on Black Americans from Colonial Times to the Present*, New York: Anchor Books.

PART III

Naming and managing madness in the Golden Age of Asylums

9

MENTAL MALADIES IN THE TWENTIETH CENTURY

In October 1925, a new patient was admitted to the newly opened Oulu District Mental Hospital in Finland. Leena K. was a 35-year-old primary school teacher who was living in a small village in the north. According to the attendant who brought her to the asylum from another hospital, Leena was a sweet and friendly woman who had led a normal life without misfortunes or bad habits, but may have been under pressure at work. Her symptoms first appeared three years previously when she started to behave oddly. She became hypochondriacal and delusional, and had visual hallucinations. Now she stayed in bed all day and was preoccupied with gloomy thoughts, including the 'fixed idea' that she was doomed to eternal damnation. Her delusions usually related to her being sinful and worthless. Her father, a farmer, was of a nervous disposition, and both her deceased mother and her cousin had been mentally ill.

At the Oulu Hospital, Leena was taken to the ward for restless female patients. There, she appeared totally confused; she was constantly checking her wrist pulse and listening to something very carefully. When she was asked about it, she said she was anticipating future telegraphing that would give her information about another place, even about another world. At times she had sporadic bouts of dyskinesia – she hit her own head and neck with her fists. Occasionally she burst into tears, at other times she cried uncontrollably, or sang and spoke to herself. She also stared intently at some particular spot in the room, pointing at it and shouting 'there it is' without telling anyone what she saw. When she was restless, she had to be wrapped in sheets. Then, one night, having been at the hospital for one and a half years, Leena committed suicide; she tore her bed sheets and made a rope of sorts, and hanged herself in the cantilever of the ventilation window. Unassuming to the end, Leena did it all so quietly that nobody in the ward woke up, and when the night nurse found her, it was too late to save her.

186 The Golden Age of the asylums

Like the great majority of patients at the Oulu Hospital, Leena was diagnosed with schizophrenia. She was a typical case in that her symptoms included delusions, hallucinations, uncontrollable and incoherent behaviour as well as proneness to suicide. In the twentieth century, schizophrenia became by far the most widespread and dreadful mental illness, an archetypal modern form of insanity and the most frightening mental affliction of the industrial nations. Throughout the century, about 1 per cent of the population in the western world suffered from schizophrenia, and, each year, 1 in 10,000 people aged 12 to 60 develops schizophrenia, even today. Schizophrenia became more or less synonymous with *psychosis*, a sign of serious mental disorder referring to a pathological loss of contact with reality. In this chapter, I will examine the origins and development of schizophrenia as well as manic-depression and psychopathy, two other major pathologies of the modern mind.

Dementia praecox: a precursor of schizophrenia or a separate illness?

According to the philosopher and psychiatrist Karl Jaspers, every age has its own characteristic sickness of the soul. In his view, schizophrenia was the characteristic mental malaise of the modern age. But when we look at its history, we find that there have been two or maybe several diagnostic names for the illness, schizophrenia being the last one and the one that became almost a synonym for mental illness. The diagnosis was coined by the Swiss psychiatrist Eugen Bleuler in 1908 and made famous by his 1911 book on schizophrenia. But let us start with its predecessor, *dementia praecox*, which was developed by the German psychiatrist Emil Kraepelin in the 1890s.

With Emil Kraepelin (1856–1926), psychiatry experienced nothing less than a paradigm shift. Especially in Continental Europe, twentieth-century psychiatry was largely Kraepelinian. This was particularly the case in the field of *nosology*, or the systematic classification of diseases, which was based on Kraepelin's diagnostic innovations. With his clinical research programme, Kraepelin's ambitious goal was to describe 'natural disease entities' as precisely and scientifically convincingly as possible (Schott & Tölle 2006, 116–24; Kraepelin 2002). He presented his classificatory system in the nine editions of his *magnum opus Textbook of Psychiatry* (*Lehrbuch der Psychiatrie*, 1883–1927), the rewriting and editing of which was his life-long project. In the fourth edition of the *Textbook* (1893), he introduced dementia praecox, literally 'premature dementia'. In the sixth edition, (1899) he presented the whole classificatory system in a systematic format for the first time. His most significant achievement in the 1899 edition was the division of the so-called *endogeneous* illnesses into two diagnoses, dementia praecox and manic-depressive illness. The term 'endogeneous' refers to the idea that the illness in question is inherent to the patient's physiology, while the term 'exogeneous' denotes afflictions that were precipitated by events in the patient's life history, such as the loss of loved ones, parental abuse or stressful living conditions. In late nineteenth-century psychiatry, the term 'endogeneous' was more or less a cover word for the inconvenient fact that nobody knew the cause of the illness.

Kraepelin did not create dementia praecox merely by observing his patients; his ideas were partly preceded by those of his colleagues in France and Germany. Most importantly, his German predecessors Ewald Hecker and Karl Kahlbaum developed the diagnoses of *hebephrenia* and *catatonia*, which played a crucial role in Kraepelin's construction of dementia praecox. First, in 1871, Ewald Hecker (1843–1909) coined the term 'hebephrenia', by which he meant disorganized speech and behaviour that typically afflicted adolescents, especially boys and young men. The emotions and affects of hebephrenic patients tended to be flat or strange, and they might manifest themselves as inappropriate facial expressions, bellowing or unmotivated laughter. The outlook and prognosis for patients with hebephrenia was poor: 'All cases described by me can be regarded without hesitation as "incurable"' (Hecker 2009, 242). A few years after Hecker's seminal article on hebephrenia, his superior and friend Karl Kahlbaum (1828–99), director of the private mental asylum in Göritz, coined the term 'catatonia'. It denoted a state of motor immobility and a level of consciousness wherein a patient was rigid and mute and more or less unresponsive to stimuli. Kahlbaum called this type of catatonia 'motility psychosis', because he believed that it affects the motor centres of the brain. Catatonic symptoms were first described in the third century by Galen, who called it *catalepsy* (Berrios 1996, 378–96). Catatonic patients typically ignore external stimuli and hold rigid poses for hours or even days, and they may also be trapped in stereotyped, repetitive movements (the Greek word *katatonos* means 'stretching tight') (Goldar, Starkstein & Hodgkiss, 1995). The inner world of catatonic persons was, however, not empty and motionless. On the contrary, after waking up from the catatonic stupor, they were often able to remember even the tiniest details and events around them, as if external happenings were 'registered with photographic exactness' (Freeman & Watts 1950, 402).

Karl Kahlbaum, the great unsung hero of modern psychiatry, also described a condition he named *paranoia*. This was another remarkable diagnostic innovation, for paranoia has become perhaps the most well-known form of mental disorder and a symbol of madness in the public imagination. Paranoid persons seem to behave quite normally in many ways and they do not necessarily display symptoms of insanity until something comes up, be it a topic of discussion, a memory of something or a name of someone. In this very instant paranoia 'conquers' personality and abruptly changes the mode of thinking. In this state of mind, paranoid persons are immune to reasoning that is contrary to their strongly felt beliefs about someone trying to poison them, spies shadowing them, a landlord scheming to kill them, everybody being brainwashed and so forth. Other basic symptoms of paranoia are delusions of grandiosity: individuals with paranoia are kings and queens, prophets and sages, millionaires and generals or they are rulers of the universe or inventors of perpetual motion machines. To Kahlbaum, paranoia was a form of partial insanity manifesting itself in difficult life situations.

In the 1899 edition of *Textbook*, Kraepelin's dementia praecox comprised three forms – hebephrenia, catatonia and paranoia. It was soon clear to the German medical community that Kraepelin had invented an important diagnosis – 'mega disease', if you like – encompassing or covering a great number of symptoms that began to be defined as psychotic. But he also faced direct criticism of his diagnosis. First of all, many colleagues questioned the very name of the illness – why 'dementia'? If Kraepelin's dementia was not identical with the senile dementia of the elderly, then why did he use the same term? Secondly, why 'praecox' ('premature' or 'earlier than expected')? Kraepelin admitted that although the majority of the afflicted were adolescents or young adults, sometimes the illness developed years later, at the age of 40 or 50. Thirdly, many questioned the chronicity and fatality of the diagnosis: Kraepelin's dire prognosis made dementia praecox very much like cancer of the mind – virtually incurable and fatal in the sense that patients typically ended their days in total mental darkness, unable even to feed themselves. Dementia praecox was a fatal sickness of the soul. It was Kraepelin's clinical pessimism that (partly) prompted Eugen Bleuler to develop his own, more optimistic version of the diagnosis in 1908. By the early twentieth century, dementia praecox was so tightly associated with Kraepelin's name that it was suggested that disputes over the name of the illness could be resolved by renaming it Morbus Kraepelini – Kraepelin's Disease (Noll 2011, 88–9).

In the later editions of *Textbook*, Kraepelin continued to subsume more and more sub-categories under dementia praecox. Yet, there was one characteristic feature of the illness that remained the same from one edition to the next, namely the fateful development towards degenerative cognitive impairment and, ultimately, death. Kraepelin did not give much hope to the afflicted and their families, but no-one had the nerve to claim that he lacked clinical experience: for years and years, he observed countless patients first in Dorpat (now the Estonian town of Tartu), then at his clinics in Heidelberg (1892–1903) and Munich (1903–21). He became famous for his close attention to the course of the illness, even after patients were moved from his clinic to local mental asylums. With Kraepelin, *time* became an essential dimension of clinical work: it was all-important not only to record the life course of the patient, including the first appearance of symptoms, but also to make predictions about the future course of the illness (prognosis). Kraepelin's great achievement was to follow the course of the illness for as long as possible. Such a longitudinal, lifetime approach to the study of mental pathology was an innovative method. What probably affected Kraepelin's pessimistic thinking about dementia praecox was his inability to systematically follow the life of discharged patients who never returned to the hospital. This meant that his clinical gaze did not easily capture periodic psychoses and transient forms of illness, which probably would have relativized his dire prognosis for the condition (Baruk 1978, 71–3; Healy 2008, 74). It is probable that Kraepelin's near-fatalistic portrayal of the illness has to some extent functioned as a self-fulfilling prophecy in that patients, their doctors and their families have regarded dementia praecox almost as if it were a death sentence.

Mental maladies in the twentieth century   **189**

What, then, causes dementia praecox? At first, Kraepelin thought that it might be a metabolism disorder, which to some extent resembled a thyroid gland disorder that may cause psychotic symptoms, such as hallucinations, delusions and cognitive impairment. Kraepelin conjectured that when the human organism was in a pathological state of self-poisoning or autointoxication, toxic substances produced in other parts of the body could affect the brain and impair mental functioning. In the fifth edition of *Textbook* (1896), Kraepelin abandoned the theory of autointoxication for lack of evidence, but he retained his belief in the organic, biological foundation of dementia praecox, even if he acknowledged that neuropathology had failed to reveal brain abnormalities unique to dementia praecox. He certainly knew that he was as ignorant as anybody about the cause of this mysterious illness.

After the initial cool reception of his ideas, Kraepelin's influence became more and more pronounced, so much so that much of twentieth-century western psychiatry was Kraepelinian to some extent. Kraepelin's system of classification became a model for subsequent classifications in western psychiatry, and he is famous not only for his invention or discovery of the (predecessor) of schizophrenia, but also for his overall approach to mental illness. He has been vilified as a cold 'brain mythologist', but as a young doctor he had studied psychology in Wilhelm Wundt's psychological research laboratory in Leipzig, and he wanted to connect clinical psychiatry with Wundtian experimental psychophysiological research (Hoff 1992). With his social views, he represented the rather conservative wing of the educated middle class, who detested socialism and were suspicious of the rudimentary forms of the Bismarckian welfare state: 'Our ever-expanding social welfare programmes have the effect of impeding the natural self-purification of our people' (Kraepelin 2007, 400).

After World War I, dementia praecox became a widely used diagnosis especially in German-speaking Europe, Nordic countries and the UK. Together with Sigmund Freud, Kraepelin was then probably the most famous psychiatrist in the world. These two 'scientists of the mind' were not exactly each other's admirers. While Kraepelin had a scornful attitude towards psychoanalytic doctrines, Eugen Bleuler, the inventor of the diagnosis schizophrenia, was the first academic psychiatrist to apply psychoanalytic ideas to the treatment of institutionalized mental patients.

Bleuler's schizophrenia

By the mid-twentieth century, dementia praecox was largely replaced by *schizophrenia*, a diagnosis created by the Swiss psychiatrist Eugen Bleuler (1857–1939) in 1908, when he gave a presentation at a meeting of the German Psychiatric Association in Berlin. Bleuler's theory became widely known three years later when he published his important book *Dementia Praecox or the Group of Schizophrenias* (note the plural form!). Bleuler was Director of the Burghölzli Mental Hospital in Zurich, Switzerland, and Professor of Psychiatry at the University of Zurich (on Bleuler's life and work, see Hell, Scharfetter & Möller 2001). Under

190 The Golden Age of the asylums

his directorship, the Burghölzli became one of the few international centres of psychiatric research, attracting visitors from all over Europe and North America (another centre being Kraepelin's clinic in Munich). Bleuler corresponded with Freud and encouraged his young assistant C.G. Jung to read Freud and to use psychoanalytic ideas in his own work – which Jung of course did, becoming Freud's 'crown prince' in due course. In addition to Jung, a number of future psychoanalysts and psychodynamic psychiatrists were trained at the Burghölzli, including Karl Abraham (psychoanalyst), Ludwig Binswanger (pioneer in existential psychiatry) and Abraham Brill (the first psychoanalyst to practise in the United States).

Bleuler developed his concept as a solution to what he saw as intrinsic problems in dementia praecox. For this reason, and because in the twentieth-century schizophrenia replaced dementia praecox in clinical usage, it has often been assumed that they are more or less identical illnesses. But this is not the case, and some researchers have gone so far as to suggest that far from being identical, schizophrenia and dementia praecox should be seen as separate disease entities (Noll 2011; Berrios, Luque & Villagrán 2003). This is how Bleuler described his diagnostic innovation in his 1908 presentation:

> For the sake of further discussion I wish to emphasize that in Kraepelin's dementia praecox it is neither a question of an essential dementia nor of a necessary precociousness [praecox]. For this reason, and because from the expression dementia praecox one cannot form further adjectives nor substantives, I am taking liberty of employing the word schizophrenia for revising the Kraepelinian concept. In my opinion the breaking up or splitting [*schizein*] of psychic functioning is an excellent symptom of the whole group.
>
> (Kuhn 2004, 362)

In Bleuler's view, dementia praecox was a misleading concept, because the illness, or the group of illnesses, did not develop into (senile) dementia and intellectual (in today's language, 'cognitive') impairment; rather, what happened to the afflicted was that their thought processes were split or broken – this was the reason he decided to call this group of illnesses 'schizophrenia'. What he did *not* mean by this concept was a splitting of the mind in the sense of a multiple personality disorder or double consciousness. To Bleuler, it was a question of the disintegration of thought processes and the loosening of associations, which can result in a serious but not necessarily fatal impairment of mental functioning. Like Kraepelin, he admitted that it was impossible to determine the causal factors operating in the illness, but, again like Kraepelin, he assumed that underlying the manifestations of various mental and motor symptoms there was some unknown brain disease. Bleuler had a high regard for Kraepelin, and he wanted to develop his older colleague's concept of dementia praecox rather than reject it outright.

Whereas Kraepelin's starting point was empirical and his key method painstaking longitudinal observation of the 'natural disease process' from start to finish, the foundation of Bleuler's concept of schizophrenia was theoretical and dynamic. His concept revolves around four As: loosening of associations, disorder of affectivity, ambivalence and autism. *Loosening of associations* was the most fundamental symptom of schizophrenia, and it referred to the loosening or breaking up of the normal patterns of forming and associating thoughts as well as feelings. This key symptom gave rise to three other As (Morgan 2010, 178–9). First, with the disorder of *affectivity*, Bleuler meant the splitting of 'affectively charged complexes', which appear to dominate the mental life of the patient. In this condition, feelings and sentiments are split off and in a state of imbalance: at one time the patient is dominated by specific feelings or moods, only to revert to another emotionally charged or feeling-toned state (of complexes). Loosening of associations and the disorder of affectivity cause *ambivalence*, a condition that makes the patient oscillate between different alternatives and affects. As an illustration of ambivalence, Blauler describes a patient who wants to eat and constantly brings the spoon to his mouth – but then, in his state of ambivalence, he refuses to eat and puts the spoon down. This cycle of will and its negation can go on until the confused patient withdraws from the perplexed external world to the inner world and its subjective fantasies. In this *autistic* condition, the afflicted simply cannot establish connections with other persons, because they are unable to feel a sense of connection or relatedness to themselves, to other persons or to objects in the world. In the mid-twentieth century, 'autism' was adopted by the child psychiatrist Leo Kanner (1896–1981) when he described a syndrome of developmental disturbance affecting small children (Dolnick 1998, 169–80).

In Bleuler's view, the core symptoms of schizophrenia did not include hallucinations, delusions and certain states of confusion, so vividly described by Kraepelin. Rather, Bleuler thought they were primarily psychological *reactions* to the illness, and therefore secondary symptoms related to the life experiences of the sufferers. If Kraepelin was a hard-nosed philosophical realist, Bleuler was more inclined to develop ideas on the basis of their internal cohesion or heuristic power. At the same time, Bleuler was a keen observer of patients and spent many hours every day in clinical work, and Kraepelin was an imaginative thinker in addition to being a 'scientist of the soul'.

Bleuler himself was mystified by schizophrenia. What was the essence of this strange affliction? Like all generations of psychiatrists after him, he was struck by the extraordinary ways of thinking and acting of schizophrenic patients. This is how he described their behaviour:

> In short, they oppose everyone and everything and, consequently, become exceedingly difficult to handle [. . .] They may eat only secretly or at unusual times. [. . .] To 'good day' [such patients] say, 'good-bye'. They do their work all wrong; sew buttons on the wrong side of their clothes. They eat their soup with a fork and their dessert with a soup spoon. They continually sit down in somebody else's place, enter every bed but their own [. . .] A hebephrenic [. . .] is supposed to go down the staircase but resists; then suddenly

192 The Golden Age of the asylums

takes the whole flight in one great leap [. . .] Frequently, a request will be complied with as soon as the proper time for it has gone by.

(Sass 1994, 110)

Bleuler's schizophrenics remained maladjusted, difficult to deal with and unresponsive except when there appeared to be nothing to respond to.

The diagnostic popularity of schizophrenia exceeded Bleuler's expectations. Between 1920 and 1940, schizophrenia replaced dementia praecox in western psychiatry, and it became by far the most common and widespread – and most mysterious – mental illness of the twentieth century. For example, in Britain, the name 'schizophrenia' had replaced that of dementia praecox in the academic journals by 1935 (Dalzell 2010, 329). Bleuler is also known for his humane treatment methods and his empathic attitude towards his patients. Indeed, he has become a sort of Abraham Lincoln or Nelson Mandela of modern psychiatry – it is very rare to find anyone reproaching his views or criticizing his theories. A typical comment is that of the British psychiatrist Henry Devine who in 1927 stated that Bleuler was held in the 'highest respect by psychiatrists in the British Empire' (Devine 1927, 441). It was only in the early 2000s that Bleuler's role in the history of Swiss racial hygiene was revealed and discussed in public. In fact, it was not only Bleuler but also his predecessor (Auguste Forel) and his successor as the Director of the Burghölzli Hospital (who happened to be his son Manfred Bleuler) who were central figures in *Rassenhygiene*, which included compulsory sterilizations, castrations and other radical eugenic interventions directed at the feebleminded and the mentally ill (Huonker 2003). Such an active role in a medically sanctioned campaign against the weakest members of society has inevitably tarnished Bleuler's reputation, even if he was at the same time an exceptional psychiatrist in his personal commitment to his patients.

In Europe, the German psychiatrist Kurt Schneider (1887–1967) contributed to the final breakthrough of schizophrenia with his influential list of 'first-rank' and 'second-rank' symptoms (see *Clinical Psychopathology*, 1959). Following Kraepelin rather than Bleuler, Schneider emphasized auditory hallucinations, so-called broadcasting of thought, delusions of control and delusional perception, and he listed them as first-rank symptoms. It was partly due to Schneider's list of symptoms that delusions and hallucinations began to be considered cardinal features of schizophrenia, especially in Anglo-American psychiatry. Schneider himself believed that 'when first-rank symptoms are present, that always means schizophrenia to us'. Yet, he continued: 'But first-rank symptoms are not always present' (Shorter 2005, 275). In fact, Schneider thought that schizophrenia did not exist as a separate disease; rather, he regarded it as a *type* of mental illness. Clinical psychologist Richard Bentall, who has studied hallucinations and delusions, has wondered whether Kraepelin, Bleuler and Schneider even talked about the same disease, because they all had such different approaches to it (Bentall 2003, 37).

Quite predictably, such a major mental illness as schizophrenia has not been immune to socio-cultural and racial influences. What is quite apparent is that lower-class patients have been diagnosed with schizophrenia and other psychotic illnesses more frequently than middle-class patients (Hollingshead & Redlich 1964, 240–9). And what happened during the civil rights era in the United States was that 'angry black men' began to be diagnosed with schizophrenia, paranoid schizophrenia in particular. Especially in the 1960s and the 1970s, schizophrenia was overwhelmingly applied to African American protesters, for example in Michigan, where the Ionia State Hospital for the Criminally Insane confined black men for political rather than medical reasons. At the end of the 1960s, more than 60 per cent of the inmates were schizophrenic black men, who were 'dangerous' and 'paranoid'. Many of these men hailed from urban Detroit, a city strongly shaped by racial tensions in the 1960s. All over the United States, there were more and more black men diagnosed with paranoid schizophrenia, a mental disorder that appeared to afflict African Americans much more often than the white majority. In short, schizophrenia was transformed into a racialized illness. Even today, psychiatrists are prone to overdiagnose schizophrenia in African American men (Karasic & Drescher 2005, 39; Metzl 2009, xviii). The psychiatrist Jonathan M. Metzl has studied the rise of 'protest psychosis', the increasing diagnostic application of schizophrenia to 'difficult', angry black men, some of whom allegedly suffered from 'delusional anti-whiteness' in the 1960s and the 1970s. Metzl is outspoken in his conclusion: psychiatric diagnoses can 'define, circumscribe, and contain abject populations in ways that harm people in these populations in the guise of helping them' (Metzl 2009, 203). This is a sobering thought for those who like to think that medicine is only peripherally linked to politics and racial bias.

In today's psychiatry, schizophrenia is divided into acute and chronic schizophrenia. In the recently published fifth edition of the *Diagnostic and Statistical Manual of the American Psychiatric Association* (DSM-5), two diagnostic criteria have to be met to be diagnosed with schizophrenia: first, delusions, hallucinations or disorganized speech, and, second, severely disorganized or catatonic behaviour. In today's conceptualization of schizophrenia, there are clear traces of Kraepelin's and Schneider's symptoms. As for Bleuler's influence, there is of course the very name of the disease, but also something else: Bleuler's main symptom, loosening of association, is still the defining feature of the disease. And if we are to believe Bleuler, then we should talk about a *group* of schizophrenias rather than one clear-cut disease. It seems that Bleuler was right in using the plural form: schizophrenia is such a mysterious and multidimensional disease entity that it is better to see it as an umbrella diagnosis that consists of a number of partly contradictory symptoms and syndromes.

To sum up, schizophrenia has an absolutely dominant position among psychiatric diagnoses, and there is no other psychiatric illness that has been studied as much as schizophrenia. Between 1998 and 2007 alone, more than 30,000 articles on schizophrenia were published, and the number of trials relevant to schizophrenia is constantly rising from about 35 per year in the 1950s and 1960s to 650 per year in the 2000s (Miyar & Adams 2012). There is no lack of research, but unfortunately there is neither a scientific nor therapeutic breakthrough in sight. Today,

194 The Golden Age of the asylums

more than a century after the introduction of dementia praecox and schizophrenia, we still do not know what causes this strange and mysterious disorder – or group of disorders.

Patients with schizophrenia

In October 1931, Katri J., a 31-year-old, working-class woman, was admitted to the Oulu District Mental Hospital. She worked at a sweet factory, was single and had a 'nervous' father who had spent some time at a local nerve sanatorium. It was discovered that, a couple of years earlier, she had lived and worked for a while in Toronto, Canada, probably as a domestic servant. There, she had spent a few months at a mental hospital, during which time she suffered from visual and auditory hallucinations. Apparently, she was very fond of the son of the master of the house where she had worked and could not get him out of her mind. Now, back in her home country, she had tried to get back on her feet, but again she became disoriented, hallucinated, talked to herself and laughed without any reason. Frightened by her own condition, she had voluntarily asked to be admitted to the hospital. She said she wanted to die, because the boy in Canada had appeared to her and talked to her, and now she thought the boy had died. In the interview, she told the asylum psychiatrist that the spirit of the boy had entered her and now they thought and spoke together. As she now had two lives inside her, she was no longer deemed to be suicidal. She was diagnosed with schizophrenia.

At first, Katri behaved calmly and refused to take medication, because drugs produced unpleasant thoughts in her head. But then, after a few months in the hospital, she became restless and violent, attacking attendants and other patients. Her condition did not improve, and in summer of 1933 she tried to escape. In late 1934, she was still ill, confused and sometimes aggressive. Probably on the initiative of her family, she was discharged in January 1935. In her patient file there are three unsent letters that she wrote during her stay in the hospital. One of these letters was addressed to her host family in Toronto, and in it she simply wrote: 'I love Mr C–. I like Canada.'

Katri J. was one of a countless number of mental patients whose 'illness narratives' gather dust in the hospital archives, if the patient records are not destroyed. Patients such as Katri are forgotten by all, perhaps with the rare exception of the later generations of their families, and rediscovered only by chance if a historian happens to read their patient file and decides to make the 'patient case' public. Fortunately, there are a number of published writings of schizophrenic patients, and these authentic descriptions of the illness are often terrifying and sad. In the early twentieth century, Ms Thelmar, a journalist, suffered from frightening auditory hallucinations:

> What those [thousands of mad] voices are like defies description. No human being who has not actually experienced it can imagine such hell-torment. The voices seemed to be legion, and each separate voice felt like a charge of

dynamite exploding in my head, rending and shattering the living substance of my brain.

(Peterson 1982, 185)

One paranoid woman, writing in the early 1950s, imagined that she was persecuted not by any single person, devil or group of malicious people, but by the 'System', a world-like entity encompassing all people. At the top of the System,

[there] were those who gave orders, who imposed punishment, who pronounced others guilty. But they were themselves guilty. Since every man was responsible for all other men, each of his acts had a repercussion on other beings. A formidable interdependency bound all men under the scourge of culpability. Everyone was part of the System.

(Porter 1991, 150)

John Custance, who suffered from bouts of manic-depressive episodes from the late 1930s to the early 1950s, experienced a sudden revelation of the unreality of the universe, including his inner world:

There I was, shut in my own private universe, as it were, with no contact with real people at all, only with phantasmagoria who could at any moment turn into devils. I and all around me were utterly unreal. There in the reflection lay proof positive. My soul was finally turned into nothingness – except unending pain.

(Peterson 1982, 270)

When Lisa Wiley described her feelings of disintegration in the middle of the twentieth century, they resembled Eugen Bleuler's definition of schizophrenia as a splitting of the mind:

One evening while mowing the lawn, it seemed that my brain cracked right through the middle and divided into two sections. I could hardly stand it. I thought I was slowly dying.

(Peterson 1982, 279)

Wiley also noticed how 'intense darkness' was setting in at the back of her head:

This darkness enclosed my entire mind very slowly but completely in a period of about two and one-half weeks. The light of life had gone. When this darkness began to creep in, a feeling of deadness came over me, for I found I was losing emotion little by little [. . .] Although I could still think and knew what I was doing, my thoughts were lifeless.

(Peterson 1982, 279)

196 The Golden Age of the asylums

Wiley felt she had committed a 'spiritual suicide'. Yet, she survived her 20-year ordeal. As is well-known, persons with schizophrenia are more suicidal than the general population, and a spiritual suicide can sometimes lead to 'physical' or real suicide. These illness narratives of Ms Wiley, Mr Custance, Ms Thelmar and Katri J. are so painful that, after reading them, you may not be too inclined to agree with the radical 'anti-psychiatrists' of the 1960s, who tended to romanticize madness as an 'authentic mode of being', an escape from the madness of normality or a fascinating journey into one's inner world. When the Norwegian philosopher Arne Naess (1912–2009) reminisced about his short tenure as an assistant at the Vienna Psychiatric Clinic as a young man in the mid-1930s, he wrote that he has never been able fully to recover from what he experienced there. He saw such terror and despair in the mental patients that, decades after this short episode in his life, these unfortunate people still appeared in his dreams during the long nights (Naess 1997, 107).

In stark contrast to the above-mentioned, more or less anonymous patients, our last schizophrenic patient is a legendary figure. The Polish-Russian Vaslav Nijinsky (1890–1950) was a phenomenal ballet dancer and the brightest star of the famous Russian ballet company Ballets Russes during the pre-World War I years. Nijinsky was a virtuoso who combined technical dancing skills with dramatic artistry and enigmatic charisma. After his triumphs as a dancer – including Stravinsky's *Petrouchka* – he became ballet's first innovative choreographer. To his audience in Europe and America, Nijinsky was one of the wonders of the world (Acocella 2006, x). Then, in the midst of his brilliant career, he started to lose hold of reality.

Nijinsky had exhibited some signs of mental instability during World War I, and he gave his last public performance in 1917 in Montevideo, Uruguay. His final collapse occurred in early 1919, by which time he had left Ballets Russes and was living in St Moritz, Switzerland. His worried wife Romola took him to the Burghölzli Mental Hospital, where he was examined by Eugen Bleuler. After a short interview, Bleuler showed Nijinsky out of his office and asked Romola to come in. By that time, Bleuler had had a long clinical experience with psychotic patients, and he quickly gave his grim evaluation of Nijinsky to Romola: her husband was incurably insane. When Romola returned to the waiting room, 'the dancer looked up at her and uttered the words now famous in the Nijinsky legend: "Femmka [little wife], you are bringing me my death warrant"' (Acocella 2006, xxi). A few days later, Nijinsky was transferred from the Burghölzli to the Bellevue Sanatorium nearby. There, his psychosis overwhelmed him; he was now hallucinating, attacking his attendants, tearing his hair out and making bizarre declarations.

Bleuler had advised Romola to divorce Nijinsky and take their children away from him. But Romola did not give up that easily. In the following years she consulted a number of doctors, who gave all sorts of statements and therapeutic suggestions regarding her husband's schizophrenia. After meeting with Manfred

FIGURE 9.1 Vaslav Nijinsky in Stravinsky's ballet *Petrouchka*, ca. 1910.
Source: © Jerome Robbins Dance Division, The New York Public Library for the Performing Arts, Astor, Lenox and Tilden Foundations

Sakel, Romola decided to try insulin coma treatment on her husband. In 1938, Nijinsky was given a series of no fewer than 228 insulin shocks. The treatment had some beneficial effects on him, but only temporarily (Shorter & Healy 2007, 51–2). For most of his adult life, Nijinsky lived in a mental hospital as a chronic schizophrenic.

In early 1919, when he was still at home in St Moritz, Nijinsky kept a diary for about seven weeks. This published diary is an authentic and dramatic document of a progressive disintegration of a creative mind. In his first diary entries, Nijinsky's text is a mixture of nascent confusion and discursive reasoning. As the days go by, his condition deteriorates and his psychosis surfaces more and more disturbingly. He shuts himself in his studio, where he writes in his diary and makes drawings of staring eyes. The red thread that runs through his diary is his conviction that his soul is married to God, as a result of which he has ascended to a higher plane of understanding. God uses him as a messenger to the world, and the message is: people should not think but feel. Nijinsky also strongly identified with Christ and called himself 'infinity' and 'life in infinity'. He knew that people would regard him as mad, and at times he recognized that he was going crazy: 'I am incurable. My soul is sick.' But he did not hurt anyone: 'I am a madman who loves people. My madness is love for people' (Acocella 2006, 32).

The fact that Nijinsky was occasionally aware of his condition brings a tragic dimension to his notes. His diary is a textbook example of Bleuler's cardinal symptom of schizophrenia: loosening of associations. He could start off with sentences that look reasonable enough, but then he makes a random reference to something quite different and starts to follow a new path of associations. Suddenly, his thinking changes direction again, and then again, and then again so that his train of thought totally loses its coherence and becomes word salad or a confused mixture of seemingly random words and phrases. In the last pages of the diary, Nijinsky's text has degenerated into mad, onomatopoetic rhymes: 'Ma fa sol est ton sol. Sol sol sol sol sol sol sol. Je suis sol avec un sol. Je suis sol avec ton sol. Sol est sol sont pas un sol [etc. etc.]' (Acocella 2006, 281).

Apart from his diary, there is not much left of Nijinsky: there is a short film of the ballet *Faun* and some photographs (for an excerpt from Faun, see www. youtube.com/watch?v=Vxs8MrPZUIg). But his legend is alive, not least because it is easy to see him as an archetypal example of the thin line between genius and madness.

Next I will turn to manic-depressive insanity, the other great twentieth-century illness created by Kraepelin and developed by others.

Manic-depressive insanity

In 1899, Emil Kraepelin created the diagnostic category of manic-depressive insanity (*manisch-depressiv Irresein*), which has become the other great 'functional' (non-organic) mental illness in modern psychiatry. Unlike schizophrenia, manic-depression has never become a widespread mental illness, even though its prevalence has varied a lot at different times and in different places. This may be largely due to the fact that it is often difficult to recognize it as distinct from both schizophrenia and depression. Its reputation partly derives from the assumption that exceptionally talented and creative persons are more prone to having mood swings and becoming manic-depressive – it is considered a price these gifted individuals, such as the painter Vincent van Gogh and the composer Robert Schumann, have to pay for their abilities. Among asylum inmates, manic-depressives were clearly in the minority in the twentieth century, and it seems that, compared to schizophrenics, they were more often members of the middle class.

According to Roy Porter, our strong interest in manic-depression may reflect the western cultural fascination with myths of polarity (Porter 1995, 415). Such polar opposites include good and evil, heaven and hell, pure and dirty, light and dark, consciousness and the unconscious and sanity and insanity. Manic-depressive bipolarity can easily be associated with the idea that within all of us there is an 'eternal' struggle of opposites, which creates dynamic psychological tension, which in turn may be channelled into creative work as well as into madness. In other words, we are potentially both Dr Jekyll and Mr Hyde, creative and destructive, male and female, hypomanic and depressed.

Manic-depressive insanity was not, strictly speaking, Kraepelin's diagnostic innovation. In the late eighteenth century, Philippe Pinel had already noticed that, when melancholy was connected with delirium (state of confusion), the illness was manifested in two contrasting ways. On the one hand, melancholics may regard themselves as exceptional individuals having absolute power or inexhaustible riches. On the other hand, melancholia with delirium is sometimes 'characterized by great depression of spirits, pusillanimous apprehensions and even absolute despair. Lunatic asylums afford numerous instances of those opposite extremes' (Pinel 2009, 78–9). Half a century later, Pinel's compatriots Jules Baillarger and Jean-Pierre Falret separately created the diagnostic category of manic-depression, but it was Emil Kraepelin whose 1899 *Textbook* brought the diagnosis to the international medical limelight, as it also did to dementia praecox.

The French psychiatrists had emphasized the repetitive and predictable alterations between mania and depression as the characteristic feature of the illness. Unconvinced, Kraepelin claimed that such cyclic alterations were not intrinsic to manic-depression, because the same sort of circularity or cyclicity can be detected in dementia praecox and neurosyphilis. But if there is an occasional relief from, or a total disappearance of, manic states, then it is a sign of a single disease process. As in the case of dementia praecox, Kraepelin depended on his German colleague Karl Kahlbaum rather than the French alienists when he was constructing manic-depressive insanity. He borrowed the terms 'circular insanity', 'cyklothymia' and 'dysthymia' from Kahlbaum and described them as parts of a single pathological process. As an acute observer of symptoms, Kraepelin noticed that the illness behaviour of patients was not consistent – within a scope of one single day many patients moved between manic and depressive states, or they were at the one and same time both manic and depressed as depression gave way to feverish over-activity and mania was suddenly replaced by stupor or mental numbness. It almost seems as if Kraepelin, who valued order and punctuality, was irritated by the 'irresponsibility' of his patients who appeared to move between the opposite poles of mania and depression quite recklessly.

Kraepelin may not have been interested in manic-depression as a separate disease entity. Rather, what he was looking for was a complementary opposite of dementia praecox, an illness that – unlike dementia praecox – would not lead to a total collapse of the personality. He believed that the long-term prognosis of manic-depression was much better than that of the 'prematurely demented': whereas he considered it possible or even probable that manic-depressive patients recover from their illness, patients with dementia praecox much more likely deteriorated psychically to the point where they either died or became totally and incurably insane. In his later career, Kraepelin admitted that manic-depressive insanity and dementia praecox could not always be distinguished, at least when the manifestations of illness alone were taken into account. Yet, he insisted on the fundamental differences between these two disease processes:

> We cannot help but maintain that the two disease processes themselves are distinct. On the one hand [dementia praecox] we find those patients with irreversible dementia and severe cortical lesions. On the other [manic-depressive insanity] are those patients whose personality remains intact. This distinction is too overwhelming for us to accept much overlap between the two groups, particularly as we can often predict the course of the two from the clinical signs.
>
> (Kraepelin 1992, 505)

Here is a typical case of manic-depressive insanity, with an emphasis on the manic aspects of the illness: Niilo T. was admitted to the Oulu District Mental Hospital in November 1925. He was a 50-year-old foreman with a wife and seven children. His father and brother had been mentally ill but had both recovered. He led a normal life, was very diligent, serene and energetic. The first symptoms appeared in late summer, when he became absent-minded, had flights of fancy and difficulties in sleeping. In the autumn, he hardly slept at all, was busy running errands, selling and buying horses and initiating court cases. The doctor who referred him to the hospital described him as 'manic' and full of whimsical ideas. Upon admittance to the hospital, Niilo was restless, walked around and chatted with other patients. He was treated with long, calming baths. After a few days, he was more composed and said he wanted to help the attendants in cleaning up the wards. He appeared spirited but no longer driven by his compulsions, and his mood was uplifted. He said he knew that he had been ill, and he attributed his affliction to physical exhaustion and insomnia. He understood that such excessive over-activity was pathological, but now his health had been restored. Four months after his admittance, he was discharged from the hospital as cured.

Of all mental disorders, manic-depression is most closely associated with creativity and ingenuity. The fact that this particular illness has become a romanticized mental affliction may be due to the commonplace observation that creative individuals may experience dramatic mood swings at short intervals. Not surprisingly, then, Isaac Newton, Ludwig van Beethoven, Charles Dickens, Edgar Allan Poe, Jack London, Edvard Munch and Marilyn Monroe have all been diagnosed as manic-depressives posthumously, and Vincent van Gogh has been called both schizophrenic and manic-depressive as well as epileptic and neurosyphilitic, to name just a few of the nearly 30 different diagnoses that have been hurled at him (on van Gogh's illnesses, see Blumer 2002). In the last analysis, to psychiatrically diagnose historical figures is a futile and dubious enterprise – who are we to judge whether Michelangelo or Isaac Newton were manic-depressive, schizophrenic, Aspergerian or just eccentric personalities in their own times, which differ so much from our own?

Bipolar disorder

Between the late 1960s and the mid-1970s, manic-depressive insanity was transformed into 'bipolar disorder', which was divided into Type 1 and Type 2 (Healy 2008, 142–51). According to the American psychiatrist David Dunner, bipolar I disorders referred to patients who had been hospitalized for both manic and depressive episodes. By contrast, patients suffering from bipolar II disorders had been hospitalized for depression only, but they had also had hypomanic episodes that had not led to hospitalization. Bipolar I was, by and large, similar to the traditional manic-depressive insanity in that the symptoms and the course of the illness resembled manic-depression. Manic-depression had been a relatively rare illness, afflicting something like 0.1 per cent of the population in Europe and North America, whereas bipolar II was, according to some estimates, a very common disorder. Jules Angst, one of the creators of bipolar disorder, claimed in the late 1990s that as many as 5 per cent of the population suffered from bipolar disorder of one or another type (Healy 2008, 147–9). What this meant was that, all of a sudden, bipolar disorder had become a major mental disorder in terms of its prevalence. And this could only happen because of the introduction of bipolar II, which as 'bipolar *lite*' guaranteed a large pool of potential consumers for the new generation of mood stabilizers from the mid-1990s onwards.

What made bipolar disorder a truly contagious diagnosis was that it started to be applied to people who suffered from both depressive and hypomanic episodes, *neither* of which necessarily required hospitalization. Bipolar II was evolving into a diagnostic category that began to resemble borderline personality disorder, on the one hand, and what was formerly known as depressive neurosis, on the other. Moreover, it began to overlap with substance abuse disorders. The division of mood disorders into unipolar and bipolar disorders was codified in the American Psychiatric Association's influential DSM-III in 1980. The publication of DSM-III contributed to the situation in which more and more Americans have been classified as bipolar patients. This is a remarkable transformation of a relatively rare and serious mental illness, manic-depressive insanity, into a relatively widespread disorder that incorporates both the traditional Kraepelinian version (bipolar I) and the milder and allegedly much more common form of mood disorders (bipolar II). For a sceptic, this is an exemplary case of disease-mongering (Moynihan & Cassels 2005).

The rise of psychopathy

There are very few diagnoses that are as firmly anchored in the public imagination as psychopathy. When one associates psychopathy with figures in fiction or in real life, one might think of someone like Hannibal Lecter, a character memorably played by Anthony Hopkins in the film *Silence of the Lambs* (1991). Lecter is a cold-blooded serial killer, an archetypal mixture of evil intentions and a sick mind, who nevertheless radiates charm and 'sex appeal'. Dexter in the TV-series of the same

202 The Golden Age of the asylums

name is a more moderate version of the same archetype – he is a homicidal, 'blood spatter pattern analyst' who kills mass murderers and other heinous criminals. In real life, the ultimate psychopath of the recent decades is the Norwegian mass murderer Anders Breivik, who is described as an extremely callous and emotionless psychopath. Fictitious as well as 'real' psychopaths titillate our imagination because they represent to us the dark and horrifying side of human nature that we hardly ever see in everyday life but that produces in us vivid images of something evil and monstrous. As a concept, psychopathy is infused with sinfulness, vice and criminality, and its psychopathological mark of Cain is the lack of guilt, remorse and shame.

The history of the concept of psychopathy is complicated. There are some scattered references to psychopathy as early as in the treatise of the Greek philosopher Theophrastus in the fourth century BCE but it was only in the early nineteenth century that something even remotely resembling twentieth-century psychopathy began to take shape. In England, Dr James Cowles Prichard (1786–1848) formulated the concept of moral insanity, by which he denoted a derangement of only some parts of our mental faculties, especially those that govern emotions and the moral sense. To Prichard, who was influenced by the evolving concept of monomania in French psychiatry, moral insanity was a disease of the passions that did not necessarily affect intellect. After the publication of Prichard's *Treatise on Insanity* (1835), moral insanity became an important and much-debated illness both in British and American psychiatry (Augstein 1996). Another pioneer psychiatrist who contributed to the development of the diagnosis was Benjamin Rush, an American doctor who was interested in giving medical explanations for criminal behaviour. Both moral insanity and monomanias – especially homicidal monomania – were useful diagnostic tools in the 'psychiatrization of criminal danger' (Foucault 1978, 3). By the end of the nineteenth century, however, moral insanity had lost its credibility among alienists. This disenchantment with the diagnosis was partly due to its vagueness as a concept, but an even bigger problem was that it was very difficult to use in court. Should criminals not be sentenced if the crimes were apparently committed while in a state of insanity? For example, if one killed one's child, friend or neighbour, one was committing an unnatural and senseless crime, a crime against nature. How could people commit such a horrendous crime unless they were out of their mind? And if they were out of their mind, should they be considered legally irresponsible or not? To jurists, judges and juries, weighing these questions in the light of moral insanity or monomania failed to resolve them. To the psychiatrist, moral insanity became a liability rather than an asset.

The term 'psychopathy' was introduced in 1845 by the German physician Ernst von Feuchtersleben, who in a rather unspecified manner referred with this concept to a psychological lesion or psychosis. Gradually, the term began to be used in a clinical setting. In the English-speaking world, 'psychopathic' at first referred to acute psychopathological conditions in general; for example, Boston Psychopathic Hospital, founded in 1909, did not 'cater' for psychopaths but for all acutely ill mental patients. The current meaning of psychopathy began to take shape in 1888 when the German psychiatrist J.L. Koch (1841–1908) wrote about 'psychopathic inferiorities' (*Die psychopathischen Minderwertigkeiten*) in his psychiatric textbook. Some years later, Koch published a three-volume work on psychopathic inferiorities. He had two reasons for employing the term 'inferiority'. First, he claimed that psychopathies were caused by a congenital or acquired 'inferiority' of the structure of the brain. Second, while psychopathies were abnormal behavioural states, they were not 'mental diseases' in the sense the word was used in German psychiatry – Koch did not talk about psychopathic 'diseases' or 'illnesses'. He divided psychopathies into three classes: psychopathic sensitivity, psychopathic taint (*Belastung*) and degeneration. Many of the twentieth-century types of psychopathies were first described by Koch. For example, one now largely forgotten type was used to refer to persons with an 'abnormal' psychic sensitivity or fragility. These sensitive psychopaths had a weak and vulnerable personality structure (Koch 1891–2).

In the early twentieth century, psychopathy began to be associated with negative evaluations of socially harmful personality types. Henceforth, it functioned as a diagnostic tool that was applied to unsocial, immoral and other deviant individuals and groups, such as homosexuals, criminals, vagabonds, prostitutes and sexually 'irresponsible' lower-class women whose behaviour made them stand out in their social environment. Early twentieth-century psychiatrists became rather infatuated with the concept of the 'psychopathic constitution', which suggested that, in terms of treatment and curability, psychopaths were more or less beyond the pale. The psychiatric inclination to think in terms of hereditary disposition or congenital tendencies was probably strengthened by the nascent genetic research as well as by Cesare Lombroso's psycho-criminological research on 'born criminals'. Consequently, 'wicked' children were among those who began to be called psychopaths. Emil Kraepelin contributed also to the development of psychopathy with his concept of 'psychopathic personalities', which strengthened the social dimension of the diagnosis. Psychopaths became 'public enemies' (*Gesellschaftsfeind*) (Wetzell 2000, 59, 146).

An important contributor to the construction of psychopathy was the German psychiatrist Kurt Schneider, who was also instrumental in the establishment of schizophrenia. Compared to his predecessor Koch, Schneider was more successful in his attempt to describe psychopathy in value-neutral terms. In his *Psychopathic Personalities* (*Die psychopathischen Persönlichkeiten*, 1923), he avoided talking about 'unsociality' and especially 'inferiority'. His starting point was statistical: 'abnormal personalities' were statistical deviations from the estimated mean. This sounds appropriate enough, but the thorny problem here is that Schneider was unable to find a robust definition of 'mean value' – what exactly is the norm, the deviation from which represents abnormality? In other words, what are the properties of the normal distribution? In Schneider's model, abnormality included exceptionally creative and intelligent individuals, who were not *pathologically* abnormal or psychopathic personalities. What distinguished psychopaths from other statistically exceptional individuals was *suffering*: psychopaths were those 'who themselves suffer, or make society suffer, on account of their abnormality' (Berrios 1996, 431). In this category, Schneider placed ten psychopathic groupings: hyperthymic (energetic and enthusiastic), depressive, insecure, fanatical, lacking in self-esteem, labile in affect, explosive, wicked, aboulic (weak-willed) and asthenic (lacking in strength). Most importantly, Schneider, like Koch, did not regard psychopaths as mentally disordered but as pathologically abnormal personalities. Schneider's psychopathy was a very flexible and pragmatic concept, and it was easy to subsume all sorts of dislikable abnormalities under the heading 'psychopathic personalities' (Sass & Herpertz 1995, 639–40).

To some extent, psychopathy may have been a rather useful diagnosis for psychiatrists, because, like the neuroses, it helped psychiatrists to expand their scope of expertise from the disorders of institutionalized patients to those of the jetsam and flotsam of society hanging around on street-corners, in bars and brothels, or confined in jails and other correctional institutions. Notwithstanding these 'usual suspects', there were also ordinary, rather decent or law-abiding people diagnosed with psychopathy, because they were considered deviant (homosexuals, for example) or they had trouble coping with the demands of everyday life. Distressed, nervous soldiers in World War II were often diagnosed with 'constitutional psychopathy' if they ended up in military hospitals; then there were individuals whose lives were in disarray as a result of, for example, alcohol abuse or difficulties holding a job or getting along with other members of the family or the community. We should be on our guard lest we continue the dubious tradition of labelling psychopaths of yesteryear as ruthless exploiters, cold-blooded swindlers or habitual wife-beaters. Certainly, some of them were repulsive characters, while others were good-natured and kind. Psychopathy encompassed many aspects of what has been considered deviant, abnormal and harmful human behaviour.

Psychopathy as maladjustment

What 'psychopathy' signified above all was maladjustment to social norms and rules. Such maladjustment required decidedly antisocial behaviour patterns in order to qualify as a form of pathology. Hervey Cleckley (1903–84), the pioneering American researcher on psychopathy, put it aptly when he wrote that psychopaths wear the 'mask of sanity' in order to give an appearance of full health while keeping their true condition hidden (Cleckley 1964). After World War II, 'psychopathy' (and 'sociopathy') became a fashionable concept in the United States. Its popularity was largely based on the interest of the mass media in criminals and all sorts of rabble rousers. Hollywood films, the newly invented television, pulp fiction and radio exposed Americans to the dangers of psychopaths who kill, steal, lie and cheat without any scruples. They could even attend the same ballroom dances as your daughter and seduce her. When white musicians copied rhythm and blues from African Americans in the mid-1950s and created their own, more palatable version called rock and roll, many white Americans became truly worried, not so much because of the noisy primitive music itself, but because their sons and daughters were attracted to this 'musical travesty' and, most alarmingly, to the sexually

Mental maladies in the twentieth century **205**

and culturally reprehensible lifestyle these musicians (Elvis Presley, Gene Vincent, Jerry Lee Lewis, Eddie Cochran, etc.) seemed to promote and celebrate. If All-American boys and girls become subject to bad influences, such as rock and roll, 'trashy' literature and cartoons, disrespect towards the authorities and social order would increase, which in turn could awaken dormant psychopathic tendencies in the youth. In the classic film of the era, *Rebel without a Cause* (1955), James Dean played an unforgettable role as a 'maladjusted' adolescent who gets into trouble with authority figures, including his father. The film was loosely based on the psychiatrist Robert Lindren's 1944 book of the same name, albeit with a subtitle that was not used in the film: *The Hypnoanalysis of a Criminal Psychopath*. The idea of psychopaths as public enemies fitted well with Cold War anxieties regarding nuclear war with the Soviet Union, the danger posed by the Communists in and outside the United States and massive dislocation as the salaried middle classes moved from the inner cities to the suburbs. One psychiatric book warned that psychopathy is a serious threat to the American way of life and to the security of people.

When the socio-cultural norms and rules began to change, the idea of maladjustment changed with it. This is what happened in the tumultuous decade of the 1960s, when western societies experienced political radicalization and cultural liberalization. In places like Paris, Tokyo, London, Helsinki and campuses across North America, students and the younger generation as a whole began to question the prevailing ideals of adjustment and conformity, which were seen as bourgeois, repressive and outdated if not reactionary. Cultural radicals opposed the Vietnam War, read leftist intellectuals (such as Herbert Marcuse), listened to the Rolling Stones and the Doors and began to promote the idea that if you become too well adjusted to your social environment, it could be a sign of your mental pathology. This was because the capitalist society itself was sick, alienated and inadequate. According to the 'anti-psychiatric' critics of society, individuals were sane when they displayed political alertness, sexual permissiveness and cultural liberalism and were emancipated from the ossified normative system of their parents' generation. At the same time, if you uncritically accepted the norms, values and demands handed down to you by the authorities, your parents and educators, you were in danger of becoming either a mentally alienated sufferer or the Cheerful Robot memorably described by the radical American sociologist C. Wright Mills (Mills 1967, 171–3).

This critical questioning or outright rejection of the prevailing ideology of adjustment inevitably shaped the concept of psychopathy or 'sociopathy', as it was officially called in post-World War II American psychiatry (Cleckley 1964). For many younger psychiatrists, the whole concept was superfluous and redundant, as it only gave social norms and prejudices a psychomedical, pseudo-scientific clothing. An inclusion of homosexuality in the list of psychopathies was a striking example of how diagnostic categories were used as stigmatizing labels. Others began to portray 'deviants' and 'misfits' in positive terms as, for example, archetypal outsiders who dared to challenge the social order and the medical and judicial rules and norms that legitimized the status quo (Ernst 1995, 648).

Some longitudinal studies in the 1960s and the 1970s suggested that the most important single determinant in the development of psychopathic personality was antisociality during childhood and adolescence. As adults, antisocial children were much worse off than normal children ('controls'), and it is well-established that antisocial behaviour, including impulsive aggression, easily leads to social alienation, which in turn increases antisocial behaviour. Such studies have supported the widespread assumption that psychopathic personality traits are relatively stable or even permanent (Robins 1966, 1979). For this reason, it is exceedingly difficult to treat psychopathic personalities. Medication has no effect on them, while psychotherapy could be counter-productive: in psychotherapeutic discussions psychopaths could learn how better to manipulate people.

Here is a very typical case of psychopathy from the Oulu District Mental Hospital in Finland: Ville S., a 34-year-old man of working-class background, was committed to the hospital in 1954 – for the eleventh time. His two brothers had committed suicide, and there were 'nervous' family members on both the father's and the mother's side. He was considered feebleminded, but the real problem with him was that he was a difficult misfit, a scheming liar and a thief. He was constantly making demands and threatening people if he could not get what he wanted. He denied his binge drinking and blamed his near ones, especially his mother, for his misfortunes. According to his medical record, he peppered his speech with veiled threats, roundly lambasted all the doctors and nurses, and explained that he was definitely not drunk when he was taken to the hospital:

> Well these nurses here, they are so timid that they don't dare to speak the truth [. . .] of course the nurses need to curry favour with the doctors and even the professor believes everything Dr. L.– is saying and doesn't bother to find out for himself. [The previous chief physician] was an even bigger scumbag than this one [the present chief physician].

Ville S. received the diagnosis of *constitutio psychopathia asocialis*. He was one of those numerous 'maladjusted' individuals who were not really mentally ill but whose psychopathology was manifest in his grossly deviant behaviour. These people were dwelling at the crossroads of crime, insanity and moral corruption.

Today, psychopathy is no longer an official diagnosis in the International Classification of Diseases or DSM, but in the everyday language the word is still widely used: when you Google 'psychopath', you get 2,770,000 results (January 2014). The diagnosis that is perhaps closest to psychopathy today is 'antisocial personality disorder', and its two distinct features are a proneness to impulsive risk taking and lack of guilt, remorse and empathy. Psychopaths may have a deficient comprehension of social contracts, which means that they do not (adequately) understand rules and obligations regulating human behaviour. They are often described as pathological liars, short-tempered and crafty. If you want to have an exhaustive list of all terms connected with psychopathy, you can check Henry Werlinder's book on the conceptual history of psychopathy. There, Werlinder lists no fewer than 176 terms connected with the 'psychopathy complex', ranging from 'discordant personality' and 'constitutional inferiority' to 'egopathy', 'moral fool' and 'reasoning mania' (Werlinder 1978, 191–2). It may very well be that most of us find terms on this list that seem to characterize some less than flattering aspects of ourselves . . .

Nowadays, much psychiatric research focuses on the genetic aspects of diseases and disorders, and this is the case in psychopathy too. Or rather, psychopathy, like schizophrenia, is typically seen as resulting from both biological and environmental factors, such as neglect and abuse during childhood. This is the standpoint of the eminent criminal psychologist Robert D. Hare, who developed the Hare Psychopathy Checklist (PCL-Revised), which is widely used to evaluate cases of psychopathy (Hare 1999). Another researcher, Ken Kiehl, has estimated that as many as 1 per cent of all males may be psychopaths – and from 15 to 35 per cent of American prisoners. To Kiehl and his collaborator Joshua Buckholtz, the most important research goal is to find an effective treatment for psychopathy, because it would have an immediate effect on violence, crime and incarceration rates (Kiehl & Buckholtz 2010).

These ideas of Kiehl and his colleagues have a history going back at least to early nineteenth-century France, where alienists began to argue that the perpetrators of homicides were often sick individuals who suffered from 'homicidal monomania' (Harris 1991). Debates surrounding the relationship between crime and madness have continued ever since, and there is no end in sight to the medicalization of crime: in addition to psychopathy ('personality disorder'), the so-called 'adult ADHD' is nowadays conjured up to explain criminal behaviour and the psychology of prisoners. A zealous search for psychomedical causes of crime typically produces ungrounded assertions, such as the one reported by the *Guardian* in 2009: 'Research by the UK Adult ADHD Network revealed that almost 20% of prisoners probably suffer from undiagnosed ADHD' (Hill 2009). Such claims remind me of Samuel Butler's satirical depiction of a fictional country called *Erewhon* (1872), where criminals are treated by 'straighteners' as if they were ill, whereas people with illnesses are punished as criminals (Butler 1985).

'All that I could figure out was, "I'm not sane"'

Throughout the twentieth century, schizophrenia remained the most diagnosed severe mental illness, and the majority of institutionalized patients suffered from schizophrenia. At the end of the millennium, new diagnoses were introduced to international psychiatry: in the American Psychiatric Association's DSM-IV (1994), there were almost 300 diagnoses. DSM-5, published in 2013, has approximately the same number of conditions as in DSM-IV. It seems that people affected by western psychiatry now suffer from a large number of personality disorders (including psychopathy), attention deficit disorders, mild and severe depressions and all sorts of pathological addictions which abound in our modern bazaar of madness (see Furedi 2004). Diagnoses, syndromes and countless disorders enter

208 The Golden Age of the asylums

and exit the stage, while both psychomedical experts and the general public alike seem to have lost the thread of their effort to understand the human condition.

Let us give the last word to the mental patient. This is how the late Finnish novelist Harri Sirola described the diagnoses applied to explain his condition in the mid-1990s:

> I am still not able to understand psychiatric slang. At one time I was doomed to neurosis, at other times to depression, then to severe depression, panic disorder, anxiety and anxiety neurosis – separately or simultaneously. All that I could figure out was, 'I'm not sane'.
>
> (Sirola 1996, 70; my translation)

Bibliography

Acocella, J. (ed.) (2006) *The Diary of Vaslav Nijinsky*, trans. K. Fitzlyon, Urbana and Chicago: University of Illinois Press.

Augstein, H.F. (1996) 'J.C. Prichard's concept of moral insanity', *Medical History*, 40: 311–43.

Baruk, H. (1978) *Patients Are People Like Us*, trans. E. Finletter and J. Ayer, orig. French edn 1976, New York: William Morrow and Company.

Bentall, R. (2003) *Madness Explained: Psychosis and Human Nature*, London: Allen Lane.

Berrios, G.E. (1996) *The History of Mental Symptoms: Descriptive Psychopathology since the Nineteenth Century*, Cambridge: Cambridge University Press.

Berrios, G.E., Luque, R. and Villagrán, J.M. (2003) 'Schizophrenia: a conceptual history', *International Journal of Psychology and Psychological Therapy*, 3: 111–40.

Bleuler, E. (1950) *Dementia Praecox; or, The Group of Schizophrenias*, trans. J. Zinkin, orig. German edn 1911, New York: International Universities Press.

Blumer, D. (2002) 'The illness of Vincent van Gogh', *American Journal of Psychiatry*, 159: 519–26.

Butler, S. (1985) *Erewhon*, 1st edn 1872, London: Penguin Books.

Cleckley, H. (1964) *The Mask of Sanity*, St Louis, MO: The C.V. Mosby Company.

Dalzell, T.G. (2010) 'The reception of Eugen Bleuler in British psychiatry, 1892–1954', *History of Psychiatry*, 21: 325–39.

Devine, H. (1927) 'Professor Eugen Bleuler', *Journal of Mental Science*, 73: 439–41.

Dolnick, E. (1998) *Madness on the Couch: Blaming the Victim in the Heyday of Psychoanalysis*, New York: Simon & Schuster.

DSM-5 (2013) *Diagnostic and Statistical Manual of Mental Disorders*, 5th edn, Arlington, VA: American Psychiatric Association.

Ernst, W. (1995) 'Personality disorders – social section', in G.E. Berrios and R. Porter (eds), *A History of Clinical Psychiatry: The Origin and History of Psychiatric Disorders*, London: Athlone.

Foucault, M. (1978) 'About the concept of the "Dangerous Individual" in 19th century legal psychiatry', *International Journal of Law and Psychiatry*, 1: 1–18.

Freeman, W. and Watts, J.M. (1950) *Psychosurgery in the Treatment of Mental Disorders and Intractable Pain*, 1st edn 1942, Springfield, IL: Charles C. Thomas.

Furedi, F. (2004) *Therapy Culture*, London: Routledge.

Goldar, J.C., Starkstein, S.E. and Hodgkiss, A. (1995) 'Karl Ludwig Kahlbaum's concept of catatonia', *History of Psychiatry*, 6: 201–17.

Hare, R.D. (1999) *Without Conscience: The Disturbing World of the Psychopaths among Us*, New York: Guilford Press.

Harris, R. (1991) *Murders and Madness. Medicine, Law and Society in the Fin de Siècle*, Oxford: Oxford University Press.

Healy, D. (2008) *Mania. A Short History of Bipolar Disorder*, Baltimore, MD: Johns Hopkins University Press.

Hecker, E. (2009) 'Hebephrenia. A contribution to clinical psychiatry, I–II' (1871), *History of Psychiatry*, 20: 1–2, 87–106, 233–48.

Hell, D., Scharfetter, C. and Möller, A. (eds) (2001) *Eugen Bleuler – Leben und Werk*, Bern: Verlag Hans Huber.

Hill, A. (2009) 'All prisoners to be tested for ADHD', *Guardian*, 27 December.

Hoff, P. (1992) 'Introductory remarks on the translation of Emil Kraepelin's paper "Die Erscheinungform des Irreseins"' (1920), *History of Psychiatry*, 3: 499–529.

Hollingshead, A.B. and Redlich, F.C. (1964) *Social Class & Mental Illness: A Community Study*, 1st edn 1958, New York: Science Editions.

Huonker, T. (2003) *Diagnose: 'Moralisch defekt'*, Zurich: Orell Füssli.

Karasic, D. and Drescher, J. (eds) (2005) *Sexual and Gender Diagnoses of the Diagnostic and Statistical Manual (DSM): A Reevaluation*, New York: The Haworth Press.

Kiehl, K.A. and Buckholtz, J.W. (2010) 'Inside the mind of a psychopath', *Scientific American Mind*, September/October: 22–9.

Koch, J.L.A. (1891–2) *Die Psychopathischen Minderwertigkeiten* I–II, Ravensburg, Germany: O. Maier.

Kraepelin, E. (1990) *Psychiatry: A Textbook for Students and Physicians*, ed. J. M. Quen, trans. H. Metoul and S. Ayed, orig. German edn 1899, Canton, MA: Science History Publications.

Kraepelin, E. (1992) 'The manifestations of insanity', *History of Psychiatry*, 3: 504–8.

Kraepelin, E. (2002) 'Self-assessment: clinical autograph in historical context' (orig. text in German written between 1920 and 1924), trans. E.J. Engstrom, W. Burgmair and M.M. Weber, *History of Psychiatry*, 13: 89–119.

Kraepelin, E. (2007) 'On the question of degeneration' (1908), *History of Psychiatry*, 18: 399–404.

Kuhn, R. (2004) 'Eugen Bleuler's concepts of psychopathology', *History of Psychiatry*, 15: 361–6.

Metzl, J.M. (2009) *The Protest Psychosis: How Schizophrenia Became a Black Disease*, Boston: Beacon Press.

Mills, C.W. (1967) *The Sociological Imagination*, 1st edn 1959, Oxford: Oxford University Press.

Miyar, J. and Adams, C.E. (2012) 'Content and quality of 10 000 controlled trials in schizophrenia over 60 years', *Schizophrenia Bulletin*, doi: 10.1093/schbul/sbr140.

Morgan, A. (2010) 'Schizophrenia, reification and deadened life', *History of the Human Sciences*, 23: 176–93.

Moynihan, R. and Cassels, A. (2005) *Selling Sickness: How the World's Biggest Pharmaceutical Companies Are Turning Us All into Patients*, New York: Nation Books.

Naess, A. (1997) 'Insulin shock method and the economic crisis in Vienna in 1934', in T. Heiskanen (ed.) *Some Notes on Madness*, Helsinki: The Finnish Association for Mental Health.

Noll, R. (2011) *American Madness*, Cambridge, MA: Harvard University Press.

Peterson, D. (ed.) (1982) *A Mad People's History of Madness*, Pittsburgh, PA: University of Pittsburgh Press.

Pinel, P. (2009) *A Treatise on Insanity*, orig. French edn 1801, Milton Keynes: General Books.

210 The Golden Age of the asylums

Porter, R. (1995) 'Mood disorders – social section', in G.E. Berrios and R. Porter (eds), *A History of Clinical Psychiatry: The Origin and History of Psychiatric Disorders*, London: Athlone.

Porter, R. (ed.) (1991) *The Faber Book of Madness*, London: Faber & Faber.

Prichard, J.C. (1835) *A Treatise on Insanity and Other Disorders Affecting the Mind*, London: Sherwood, Gilbert and Piper.

Robins, L.N. (1966) *Deviant Children Growing Up: A Sociological and Psychiatric Study of Sociopathic Personality*, Baltimore, MD: Williams & Wilkens.

Robins, L.N. (1979) 'Longitudinal methods in the study of normal and pathological development', in K.P. Kisker, J.-E. Meyer, C. Müller and E. Strömgren (eds), *Psychiatrie der Gegenwart*, Vol. 1, Heidelberg, Germany: Springer.

Sass, H. and Herpertz, S. (1995) 'Personality disorders – clinical section', in G.E. Berrios and R. Porter (eds) *A History of Clinical Psychiatry: The Origin and History of Psychiatric Disorders*, London: Athlone.

Sass, L.A. (1994) *Madness and Modernism. Insanity in the Light of Modern Art, Literature and Thought*, Cambridge, MA: Harvard University Press.

Schneider, K. (1958) *Psychopathic Personalities*, trans. M.W. Hamilton, orig. German edn 1923, Springfield, IL: C.C. Thomas.

Schneider, K. (1959) *Clinical Psychopathology*, trans. M.W. Hamilton, orig. German edn 1950, New York: Grune and Stratton.

Schott, H. and Tölle, R. (2006) *Geschichte der Psychiatrie*, Munich: C.H. Beck.

Shorter, E. (2005) *A Historical Dictionary of Psychiatry*, Oxford: Oxford University Press.

Shorter, E. and Healy, D. (2007) *Shock Therapy. A History of Electroconvulsive Treatment in Mental Illness*, New Brunswick, NJ: Rutgers University Press.

Sirola, H. (1996) 'Kaikki mitä muistan kolmen vuoden kuolemasta', *Image* No. 5: 62–78.

Werlinder, H. (1978) *Psychopathy: A History of the Concepts*, Uppsala, Sweden: Acta Universitatis Upsaliensis.

Wetzell, R.F. (2000) *Inventing the Criminal: A History of German Criminology, 1880–1945*, Chapel Hill: University of North Carolina Press.

10

MENTAL TREATMENT FROM MAGNETISM TO PSYCHOANALYSIS

When we look at the ways in which the mentally ill have been treated over time, we also look at the ways in which madness has been explained and diagnosed. The preferred methods of treatment and the preferred modes of explanation have been interconnected since the emergence of the rudimentary forms of mental medicine in ancient Greece. The main reason for this interconnection is that the prevailing medical views on mental pathology and the more general cultural assumptions about madness and human mental functioning have directly influenced the development of therapies.

When we talk about treatments for mental maladies, we need to say something about their curative aspects. What is now commonplace is that the ill person's faith in the efficiency of therapies administered to them has played a crucial role in mental health care. For this reason, the history of (mental) medicine is largely a history of placebo treatment, an example of which is magnetism (see below) (Benedetti 2009). In fact, all methods of treatment, whether they have a placebo effect or not, are contingent on the personality and behaviour of the doctor or healer. When the trustworthy family doctor has sat by the bedside, held the patient's hand and spoken comforting words, it has often had a positive therapeutic effect on the patient. Ted Kaptchuk of Harvard Medical School is an expert in placebo studies, and he has found an early example of placebo treatment in the sixteenth-century rites of exorcism, to which I referred in Chapters 3 and 4 (Kaptchuk 2009). Obviously, the placebo effect can be seen in today's extensive use of antidepressant medication as well (Kirsch 2009). In the history of madness, there is a tendency to regard radically interventionist therapies, such as shock treatments, psychosurgery and heavy medication, as particularly efficient methods of treating mental disorders.

I will begin my account of the history of modern treatments for madness by looking at the most popular form of suggestive therapy that started with a German

212 The Golden Age of the asylums

nerve doctor and magnetic healer, and culminated in the therapeutic innovation of an Austrian nerve doctor and mental healer who asked his patients to lie on a couch and say whatever came into their mind.

From mesmerism to hypnotism

The German physician Franz Anton Mesmer (1734–1815) began to use 'healing metals' in 1774. Mesmer gave one of his female patients a preparation including iron, and then he placed magnets on different parts of her body. The patient informed Mesmer that the procedure caused her severe pain, but after the initial reaction her condition improved for several hours. After continuing his therapeutic experiments with magnets for two years, Mesmer came to the conclusion that mineral magnetism did not in itself have therapeutic effects; rather, he suggested that his own 'animal magnetism' was transmitted to the body of the patient, which then restored the patient's natural harmony. The true healing agent was the physician's body. He then generalized this idea by claiming that some healers have inherent magnetic potency that can be applied to the treatment of such disorders as haemorrhoids, paralysis, convulsions and hysteria. With his term *magnétisme animal* Mesmer conjured up the so-called *fluidum*, an energetic and invisible life force that connected the human body and mind to the whole universe. He refined his technique accordingly, using touches, magnetic conductors, mirrors and music, or simply pointing with his fingers or with an iron rod. Animal magnetism à la Mesmer was a natural producer of harmony, and some physicians had it, others did not (Crabtree 1993, 3–11).

Mesmer contended that animal magnetism could be used in the treatment of nervous diseases, and indirectly also in the treatment of other diseases and disorders. Nervous diseases were particularly amenable to animal magnetism, because magnetism always involved the patients' nervous system, mental processes and the whole universe, which was filled with *fluidum*. Mesmer, however, did not create a specific psychological theory to account for the influence of animal magnetism; he was a healer, not a theorist. When his controversial therapy created a furore in Vienna, members of the Vienna Medical Faculty turned against him and his treatment. In 1778, Mesmer moved to Paris and established a flourishing animal-magnetic practice there. It was in France that the next step in the development of magnetism was taken, but not by Mesmer.

In 1784, Marquis Chastenet de Puységur (1751–1825) decided to use the method of animal magnetism on one of the peasants on his large estate. Puységur, an artillery officer, began to magnetize the peasant, who suffered from a fever and congestion of his lungs. To his great surprise, after less than ten minutes, Victor (the peasant) fell asleep in Puységur's arms, like a baby. This was not all: soon Puységur noticed that Victor was *awake* while asleep:

> He spoke, occupying himself out loud with his affairs. When I [Puységur] realized that his ideas might affect him disagreeably, I stopped them and

tried to inspire more pleasant ones. He then became calm – imagining himself shooting a prize, dancing at a party, etc . . . I nourished these ideas in him and in this way I made him move around a lot in his chair, as if dancing to a tune [. . .].

(Crabtree 1993, 38)

At the end of this episode, Puységur calmed Victor, who was then given something to eat and drink. Victor slept the night through, and the following day, not remembering his master's visit the previous evening, told the marquis how much better he felt. Puzzled, Puységur decided to travel to Paris to meet Mesmer and to learn the basics of animal magnetism from the master. After acquiring the necessary skills, he began to experiment with animal magnetism in the provinces. He realized that an artificially induced sleep state could have curative effects, but at the same time the induced sleep may lead to a trance-like condition, in which the patient-dreamer's personality changes – the somnambulist patient becomes someone else. This extraordinary state of altered consciousness began to fascinate psychological and psychiatric researchers across Europe, particularly in France, where magnetic somnambulism and, later, hypnotism, became an object of intensive psychopathological study. Many researchers were intrigued by Puységur's suggestion that magnetic sleep reveals an area of mental activity which is unknown to the conscious mind, but which nevertheless may affect thinking and behaviour. After Puységur's invention became widely known, animal magnetism split into the physicalist school of Mesmer and the psychological direction of Puységur (Crabtree 1993, 38–53).

Puységur's method of magnetic sleep influenced the development of psychological healing as well as psychic research, which was later known as 'parapsychology' (clairvoyance, mindreading, telepathy). In 1819, a 'professor extraordinarius' was appointed in the field of animal magnetism at the University of Bonn in Germany (Schott & Tölle 2006, 162). Yet, most representatives of academic medicine had a distinctly negative attitude towards a method that smacked of quackery. In 1784, a prestigious scientific commission, appointed by the king of France, had conducted a series of experiments with Mesmer's method in Paris, and their final verdict had been negative: 'The commissioners concluded that magnetism did not produce any noticeable effects on those who were sceptical' (Crabtree 1993, 26) – in other words, if you were a sceptic, then there was no placebo effect. Together with homeopathy, which emerged around the same time, animal magnetism and magnetic sleep were the most recent links in the tradition of folk healing, in which the role of official medicine had always been negligible.[1] Common people

---

1 Homeopathy was developed by the German physician Samuel Hahnemann (1755–1843), who gave his idiosyncratic approach to medicine the name 'homeopathy'. The fundamental doctrine of Hahnemann's version of 'alternative medicine' is 'like cures like', which means that a substance that in large doses causes the symptoms of a disease in healthy people will in small doses cure similar symptoms in sick people.

were accustomed to seeking help from folk healers, who were usually on the same mental and cultural wavelength as their patients. Magnetism is a model example of a placebo treatment that is predicated on the bond of trust between the patient and the magnetist-healer.

Magnetism had its heyday in the late eighteenth and early nineteenth century. It was gradually replaced by a therapeutic innovation introduced by the British doctor James Braid (1795–1860) in the early 1840s. Practising in Manchester, Braid noticed that the trance state and the ensuing curative aspects of magnetism were due to the special kind of somnambulism that was induced psychologically. He coined this somnambulic state 'hypnotism' and distinguished it sharply from the paranormal phenomena reported by magnetists (Braid 1843; Yeates 2013). Hypnotism spread from Britain to Continental Europe, where it became fashionable during the last two decades of the nineteenth century. Hypnosis began to be used in the treatment of milder psychological and psychosomatic afflictions, such as hysteria, neurasthenia, sleep disorders, alcoholism and drug addiction. In the strongly developing therapy market, hypnotherapists promoted their expertise by providing treatment for nervous illnesses, which were also treated by nerve doctors using low-voltage electricity, by homeopaths and by spas and private sanatoria offering a water cure, healthy diet, exercise, massage and pleasant forms of social interaction to mostly upper- and upper-middle-class patient-clients. Hypnotism aroused popular interest across Europe, and the one who contributed most to its medical popularity was the famous French nerve specialist Charcot, who gave flamboyant 'live shows' at the Salpêtrière Hospital in Paris, where he showcased his allegedly masterful skills at hypnosis before large audiences (see Chapter 8). European newspapers published sensational reports on extreme hypnotic phenomena, especially on various criminal acts rumoured to have been committed in the state of somnambulism (this theme was later used to a great effect by the German film director Robert Wiene in his classic film *Dr. Caligari's Cabinet*, 1919). Moreover, across Europe one could find a number of travelling hypnotists, who made their living by giving public demonstrations and hypnotizing members of the audience for money (Gauld 1992).

Apparently, many people wanted to be hypnotized out of sheer curiosity, and when they had tried it once, they had no appetite for more. The popular demand for hypnosis and hypnotherapy declined towards the end of the century, at a time when hypnotism began to be associated with spiritualism. Such a coupling of medical hypnosis with the somewhat controversial method of hypnosis used in spiritism, clairvoyance, telepathy and other supernatural phenomena damaged the medical and scientific reputation of hypnotism. Moreover, when hypnotherapists published positive results of their treatment, they managed to irritate neurologists and other representatives of academic medicine, who had a very meagre therapeutic arsenal at their disposal (Pietikainen 2007, 178–80). On top of this, Charcot's and the Salpêtrière School's fall from grace in the 1890s did not go unnoticed in Europe, where many physicians, including Sigmund Freud, had learned about hypnotism through Charcot's writings and teaching. With the collapse of the whole Charcotian construction of hysteria and hypnosis, the shadow of doubt fell on all hypnotherapists, regardless of whether they adhered to the Salpêtrière School or the Nancy School headed by Charcot's archrival Hippolyte Bernheim, who in his later professional life rejected the 'special state' of hypnosis.

In the early twentieth century, new, non-hypnotic forms of psychotherapy emerged, and the medical and therapeutic interest in hypnotism waned. A rise in psychological, neurological and psychoanalytic research removed hypnotism from the centre to the margins of psychological healing, and neurasthenics and hysterics began to be treated with a wide variety of both psychological and physical therapies. In this process, waking suggestion or 'psychotherapy' was differentiated from hypnotism and considered to be an effective method of treatment in itself. Hypnotism declined partly because of the emergence of rival, less authoritarian therapies, but also because there were many doctors who were not that good as hypnotists (Freud among them). Furthermore, as Henri Ellenberger has pointed out, 'it became obvious that many patients pretended to be hypnotized when they were not' (Ellenberger 1994, 171). Hypnotism has now persisted for more than a century as a marginal phenomenon, and there are no indications that another golden age of hypnosis, comparable to the period between 1880 and 1900, is about to emerge. To some extent, hypnotism may continue to haunt the public imagination, but we will probably encounter it much more often on TV than at the doctor's surgery or medical clinic.

From hypnotism to psychotherapy

Charcot's medical nemesis, Hippolyte Bernheim, Professor of Internal Medicine at the University of Nancy, played a significant role in the transition from hypnotism to psychotherapy. Together with his like-minded colleagues (who formed the so-called Nancy School), Bernheim maintained that, in specific situations, almost anyone could become hysterical, and that the mechanism of hysteria could be accounted for by heightened suggestibility, not by an innate neuropathic disposition or Charcot's auto-suggestion. Bernheim and his colleagues at Nancy were instrumental in launching a new, distinctly psychological approach to the neuroses and their treatment. Bernheim began to refer to 'psychotherapeutic action' (*l'action psycho-thérapeutique*), by which he meant the curative influence of the therapist's personality and his/her focus on the mental state of the patient. Due to Bernheim's own influence, hypnotherapy began to change into suggestive therapy and then into psychotherapy. In the latter half of the 1880s, 'suggestive therapy' began to be offered at a clinic in Amsterdam. A few years later, the name of the therapy was changed into 'suggestive psychotherapy'. The term 'psychotherapy' was introduced into the English language in the 1870s (Shamdasani 2005, 4). Such a transition from a neurological-physiological model to a psychological one was also advanced by some of Charcot's former pupils, such as the clinical psychologist Pierre Janet, who, like Bernheim, suggested that hysteria was a mental malady.

216 The Golden Age of the asylums

Another major figure in the early history of psychotherapy was the Swiss nerve doctor Paul Dubois (1848–1918), who coined a new diagnosis, *psychoneurosis*, which was tailor-made for the psychotherapeutic treatment. According to Dubois, the goal of psychotherapy was to educate the psychoneurotic patients through 'persuasion', by which he meant that the psychotherapist had to rationally demonstrate to patients that their problems and the responses they made to them were irrational and illness-inducing. Dubois was one of the most well-known nerve doctors in Europe, but he enjoyed his greatest influence in the United States, where his book on the psychoneuroses was published as an English translation in 1905 (*The Psychic Treatment of Nervous Disorders*). While hypnotism and suggestive therapy were in decline in the early twentieth century, Dubois and some other experts in 'nervous disorders' succeeded in bringing psychotherapy into the medical and cultural limelight (Shamdasani 2005, 1–10).

As is very well known, the Viennese nerve doctor Sigmund Freud (1856–1939) created his own, astonishingly successful form of psychotherapy, which he termed 'psychoanalysis' in the late nineteenth century. Freudian psychoanalysis became virtually synonymous with psychotherapy in the twentieth century, while his French colleague and rival Pierre Janet became a half-forgotten figure for decades. It was Janet's, not Freud's, researches into hysteria and especially dissociation and the ensuing 'double consciousness' that attracted wide academic as well as popular attention at the turn of the twentieth century. Janet was the first academic psychologist to study what almost a century later became known as 'multiple personality disorder' (a controversial diagnosis that was never accepted by many psychiatrists). Janet was of the opinion that Freud's psychoanalysis was nothing but a copy of his own psychological analysis (Shamdasani 2005; Hacking 1995).

Freud and psychoanalysis

Sigmund Freud's psychoanalysis grew out of the increase in and cultural visibility of less severe mental health problems commonly grouped together as neuroses (on the history of psychoanalysis, see Makari 2008). The majority of Freud's clientele consisted of the upper-middle-class members of the Jewish and gentile bourgeoisie, who were initially mostly Viennese. When Freud became world famous after World War I, he was sought after by wealthy individuals from many parts of Europe and especially from the United States. Freud also created the diagnosis of anxiety neurosis, which became a major mental malaise and a sort of psychopathological symbol of twentieth-century modernity. For more than half a century, psychoanalysts assumed the role of neurosis experts par excellence. American maverick psychoanalyst John Rosen made this point clearly in his assertion that he had never met truly neurotic persons who could have been able to control their behaviour without the help of a psychoanalyst (Rosen 1968, 68).

Freud was a theoretical innovator, but he did not invent talk therapy. A pioneer 'psychotherapist' was the now-forgotten Austrian medical doctor and poet Ernst von Feuchtersleben (1806–49). In 1844, Feuchtersleben gave the first lecture course on psychiatry at the University of Vienna, and he wrote an immensely popular book, *On the Dietetics of the Soul* (*Zur Diätetik der Seele*, 1838), of which there are no fewer than 46 editions. Another major publication of his was *The Principles of Medical Psychology* (*Lehrbuch der ärztlichen Seelenkunde*, 1845), in which he was perhaps the first to discuss the later psychiatric key-terms 'psychopathy' and 'psychosis'. Feuchtersleben saw mental disorders as dynamic processes in which personal adversities and misfortunes leave their marks on the mind, triggering mental disorders later in life. He favoured 'soft' therapies, such as comforting talk and a soothing voice, and he paid close attention to his patients' sleep and dreams, because he believed that psychopathological conditions are related to these twilight states of consciousness (Pisa 1998). Feuchtersleben died in his early forties and his therapeutic ideas had no influence on Freud when, decades later, the latter was developing his psychoanalysis. Freud's older Viennese colleague and early mentor Josef Breuer (1842–1925) had a much greater impact on the development of psychoanalysis. In the early 1880s, Breuer treated a young hysterical patient, Anna O. (Bertha Pappenheim), just by letting her talk. He used the Greek term *katharsis*, meaning 'purification' or 'purgation' of emotions resulting in renewal, to describe his therapy. Then, about a decade later, Breuer and Freud published *Studies on Hysteria* (*Studien über Hysteria*, 1895), in which they presented five clinical cases and developed a theory of hysteria and psychotherapy. Although Freud was not Anna O.'s therapist himself, Anna O. is an archetypal figure in the history of psychotherapy in that her patient role was *active*: she was the one who did the talking, and the role of the doctor was to listen and interpret the patient's utterances. In the case of Anna O., the rudimentary talk therapy did not have notable therapeutic effects. In fact, she grew worse and had to be institutionalized. Fortunately, she later recovered, led a productive life and became a pioneer in the field of social work (Breuer & Freud 1995; on Anna O., see Borch-Jacobsen 1996).

I will not go into the details of Freud's psychoanalysis and its developmental history. Suffice it to say here that Freud was not particularly interested in psychoanalysis as a method of treatment. Rather, his focus was on building an original theoretical construction of human nature, no less. What turned out to be a serious obstacle to Freud's heroic goal was his own reluctance to develop psychoanalytic theory as part of the emerging academic fields of psychology and psychopathology. Freud was so preoccupied with making psychoanalysis his own science of the mind that his and his intellectually inferior disciples' work was isolated from academic research on the human mind and behaviour. To his detriment, Freud did not even try to connect his relevant observations of the irrational, the unconscious and the psychic drives to the human sciences or to evolutionary theories, even though he revered Darwin and argued that unconscious mental processes have a biological and physiological matrix. When an American psychiatrist dared to ask the elderly Freud about the scientific basis of his Lamarckian biological assumptions, Freud retorted: 'But we can't bother with the biologists [. . .] We have our own science' (Wortis 1994, 84).

218 The Golden Age of the asylums

The key ideas of psychoanalysis, such as the Oedipus complex or the psycho-sexual stages of a child's development, were based on theories and assumptions that were considered increasingly outdated, false or redundant in the early twentieth-century academic community and medicine. These included the Lamarckian theory of the inheritance of acquired characteristics, speculative interpretations of the origins of religion and morality and, at times, bizarre conjectures about mental disorders and their treatment. One such conjecture was put forward by Freud's one-time friend and colleague Wilhelm Fliess (1858–1928), whose theory of 'nasal reflex neurosis' described a pathological condition in which there was a physiological link between the nose and other parts of the body, especially the genitalia. Fliess dedicated a whole book to the relationship between the nose and the female sexual organs, and he was influenced by Freud's key-idea that nervous disorders are of sexual origin. Freud in turn approvingly referred to Fliess' theory, which predicted that, for example, gastric pains can be relieved by anaesthetizing with cocaine the 'gastric spot' within the interior of the nose (Freud 1905/1981, 78).

Freud was a private practitioner who made his living by treating (mostly) upper-middle-class members of the bourgeoisie. In 1910, when psychoanalysis was becoming more widely known as a theory and therapy, Freud was charging as much as 1,500 dollars an hour in current value (LeBlanc 2013, 98). Most of his patients were women who suffered from hysteria, neurasthenia or some other kind of neurosis, but he also had male patients and patients whose mental afflictions were more serious (such as manic-depression). They were predominantly affluent people who spent time in sanatoria, rest homes and spas across Europe and who consulted private nerve doctors such as Dr Freud. As patients, they were receptive to new therapeutic currents, especially those that were non-authoritarian, indi-vidualistic and elitist in the sense that patients had to be not only relatively well off; they also had to be able to articulate their mental problems verbally. Freud's psychoanalysis easily fulfilled these criteria, and what was particularly innovative in Freud's therapy was, first, that he let the patients do most of the talking, and, second, that he shifted the responsibility for cure on to his patients – if they did not reveal to the analyst all that was necessary for him/her to know about their innermost feelings and worries, it was the patient's fault if the treatment failed. To Freud, the 'ideal situation for analysis is when someone who is otherwise his own master is suffering from an inner conflict which he is unable to resolve alone, so that he brings his trouble to the analyst and begs for his help', but who otherwise thinks and acts in an organized manner (Freud 1920/1981, 150). 'Good' patients are also able to give a verbal account of their distress and thereby help the doctor to find a proper therapeutic key to solve the inner conflict. Presumably, ideal patients for psychoanalytic therapy are both sufficiently intelligent and mentally balanced to talk about their inner conflicts in a way that enables the analyst to utilize their verbalizations therapeutically.

Freud continued to see patients until his death in exile in London in 1939. The empirical basis of his theories was in the discussions he had with his patients. Although he had hundreds of patients during his long career as a psychotherapist, he published only a handful of case studies in which he gave a more detailed account of his patients' psychic afflictions and of his treatment of the case. What may be surprising to those unacquainted with the history of psychoanalytic therapy is that there is no evidence that Freud ever actually cured any of his patients. Historian Mikkel Borch-Jacobsen has studied Freud's patients for years, and he estimates that, of the 31 patients about whom he could find sufficient information, only 10 per cent (three) recovered as a direct result of Freud's treatment. Many of Freud's patients grew worse, two of his early patients died and three others killed themselves; one committed suicide by jumping from an upper floor of Freud's house down into the street. A general conclusion that can be drawn is that Freud was not much of a healer (Borch-Jacobsen and Shamdasani 2013).

Freud's decision to publish some of his cases is to some extent due to the inconvenient fact that he had no choice: as he had already worked for several years as a psychoanalyst without publishing any case studies, around 1905 he simply had to make an effort to demonstrate to his sometimes sceptical colleagues that psychoanalysis worked as a therapy. It was only much later, when his reputation and popularity were firmly established, that he dared to hint at his less than remarkable healing gifts (Crews 1998, 144). Despite its meagre therapeutic results, psychoanalysis became an increasingly popular and respected form of psychotherapeutic treatment, and after World War II it started to make inroads into academic psychiatry, particularly in the United States (Hale 1995; Samuel 2013).

In defence of Freud and anyone who treats mental afflictions, it is fair to point out that a survey of the history of neuroses and their treatment shows that it is exceedingly difficult to cure individuals who are unhappy, anxious and severely depressed. What psychotherapy, medication and social support can do is to alleviate or, in some cases, even remove the symptoms, but what the history of mental suffering suggests is that distressed individuals recover anyway with the help of near and dear ones, as a result of a changed life situation, or simply with the passing of time.

Patients were important to Freud as a source of income, but he also used both his own and his disciples' patients as 'clinical evidence' for his theories. It was important for Freud to convince the scientific community that psychoanalysis was based on robust empirical observations of the mental lives of his patients. As a philosophical positivist, Freud emphasized the importance of 'psychic facts' that an astute observer could detect regardless of the possible weaknesses of his theory. The strong assumption that the psychoanalyst can objectively see the facts of mental reality goes like a red thread through Freud's writings. With the help of his theories, Freud did not merely interpret the verbal utterances and bodily expressions of his patients; he also controlled, directed and manipulated their own interpretations. He did not so much illustrate and clarify case histories as build whole new histories that supported his psychoanalytic ideas. Together with his patients, who were often vulnerable and receptive to his interpretations, Freud constructed case histories, in which psychoneuroses, phobias, neurotic obsessions, hysteria and other mental maladies made sense only in his psychoanalytic explanatory framework.

Freudian psychic reality is a mythical place. There, small children have incestuous feelings towards their parents and siblings; there, boys suffer from Oedipal castration anxiety because of their fathers, while girls suffer from penis envy because they do not have the male sex organ, like their father and brothers have. Furthermore, on 'Planet Freud' girls feel resentment towards their mothers because mothers frustrate their attempts to 'conquer' their fathers. There, children suffer from witnessing the 'primal scene', such as sexual intercourse between parents or other adults – and even if such an *Urszene* is just a product of imagination, it may give rise to psychic symptoms later in life. There, disturbances in the psychosexual development of the child can result in a neurotic or psychotic disorder. I call this Freudian reality a mythical place or Planet Freud because contemporary cutting-edge research on developmental psychology, parent–offspring conflict, parental investment and other issues addressed by psychoanalysis has decisively abandoned the theoretical constructions of Freud and later Freudians (see e.g. Pinker 1997; Rodgers 2001; Trivers 2002).

The fate of psychoanalysis after Freud

Freud used ingenious copyright tactics to bind psychoanalysis to his own person. Unlike the great majority of researchers who integrate their findings into a larger theoretical or programmatic framework, Freud insisted that, because he alone had created psychoanalysis, only those medical doctors who were approved of and certified by Freud could in principle become professional psychoanalysts. Whereas 'psychotherapy' became a general term for a certain kind of psychomedical treatment, psychoanalysis was tightly linked to Freud, and, later, to Freud's disciples, and then disciples of Freud's disciples, and so forth – psychoanalysis became a 'guild-controlled ascription' (Gellner 1993, 77). As Freud began to have disciples and supporters from many European countries and from North America, psychoanalysis gained ground as an international movement. Its popularity was increased by the overall therapeutic trend away from the neurological language of nerves and nervous disorders and towards emphatically psychological disorders and psychotherapeutic language and practices.

During the 1920s and the 1930s, nerve doctors began to call themselves psychotherapists, and as such they did not treat weak or strained nerves but psychic conflicts, complexes (such as inferiority complex) and unconscious drives. This was the language of dynamic psychology, which was derived from the 'depth psychological' doctrines of Freud, Carl Gustav Jung, Alfred Adler and Pierre Janet. Psychotherapy began to be administered even at some mental hospitals. Among asylum doctors, an important pioneer in psychodynamic psychiatry was Eugen Bleuler, chief physician of the famous Burghölzli Mental Hospital in Zurich, Switzerland. Bleuler, the father of the schizophrenia diagnosis, had a young and energetic colleague, C.G. Jung, who became Freud's 'crown prince' and then, after his break with Freud in 1913, a creator of his own brand of dynamic psychology called 'analytical psychology'. During the first decade of the twentieth century, Bleuler and Jung were the first academic psychiatrists to apply psychoanalytic methods to the treatment of the more seriously ill asylum patients (Kerr 1993).

There were two major obstacles to a more widespread use of psychotherapy, psychodynamic or otherwise, in hospital settings. First, asylum psychiatrists seldom had time to engage in private psychotherapeutic discussions with their numerous patients. One solution to this problem was the introduction of the more cost-effective group therapy sessions in post-World War II asylum psychiatry, but anyone who has seen the film *One Flew Over the Cuckoo's Nest* (1975) may well remember how so-called group therapy could be used by the staff as a disciplinary method with the aim of controlling the patients. Sometimes the patients had to 'confess' their misdemeanours, real or imaginary, in front of other patients, not unlike in Stalin's show trials in Moscow in the late 1930s. Another and more serious problem with psychotherapy was its relative ineffectiveness in the treatment of psychotic patients, who constituted a majority in most mental hospitals. Freud himself was of the opinion that psychoanalysis was not much use in the treatment of schizophrenia. He was right, even though it would have been more accurate to say that psychoanalysis was inefficient in the treatment of all except (mildly) neurotic patients.

In the western cultural sphere, psychoanalysis was most warmly received in the United States, not least because many European Jewish psychoanalysts emigrated there between 1933 and 1945. In their new home country they were often revered as representatives of a superior intellectual and scientific culture (the United States became a scientific superpower only after World War II). Particularly between the end of World War II and the 1970s, psychoanalytic therapy was widely used and also much discussed in the American media. The psychodynamic approach to the war neuroses of the American troops during and after the war paved the way for the widespread endorsement of psychoanalysis in post-war American psychiatry and popular culture. Most psychoanalysts worked as private practitioners or in private clinics or hospitals, but a great many academic psychiatrists were also either psychoanalysts themselves or at least sympathetic to psychoanalytic theories. Psychoanalysis was something that could offer insights to almost everybody: it was easy to learn the basic Freudian tenets about the unconscious, the superego and psychic conflict, but it was also attractive to ambitious academics who wanted to master the more sophisticated theories and complex details of psychoanalysis.

By the end of the twentieth century, psychoanalytic therapy had lost its hegemonic position in the psychocultural market. Its major drawback was that therapy sessions for each patient often continued for years, sometimes for decades. No wonder insurance companies in the United States and national health services in Europe began to look for other therapeutic options, such as cognitive behavioural therapy (CBT), which increased in popularity at the turn of the twenty-first century. Unlike psychoanalytic therapy, CBT is cost-efficient and pragmatic as it prefers to find solutions in the here and now rather than lingering in the patient's past. The therapeutic ethos of CBT tallies well with the aspirations of modern, evidence-based medicine, and it also harmonizes with the present cultural ideals

222 The Golden Age of the asylums

and assumptions, such as the premium put on quick-fix solutions, efficiency and the well-adjusted, self-directed personality. It is important for the modern 'protean self' effortlessly to adapt to new demands in the labour market and, on a more general level, to flourish in society where networking abilities, career management and marketing one's personality have become increasingly important assets (Brinkmann 2008).

Psychosomatic medicine

In recent decades, psychoanalysis has become marginalized as a therapy and theory, but one medical field in which its legacy is still visible is *psychosomatic* medicine. In the 2010s, the intricate relationship between mind and body is again on the agenda of many research groups all over the world. Psychosomatic medicine, which focuses on the impact of mental stress or psychological problems on physiology and bodily functions, has made a comeback of sorts, particularly in association with the growing interdisciplinary research on stress factors and the long-term effects of chronic stress. During the interwar years, psychoanalysis was an important, albeit not hegemonic, theoretical framework for psychosomatic medicine.

Since Classical Greek antiquity, if not earlier, physicians have been aware that the mind affects the body in a number of ways. A more systematical study of the mind–body relationship started in early nineteenth-century German psychiatry. Some psychiatrists emphasized the power of the mind over the body, while others saw the causal mechanism working both ways. Perhaps the first recognizably psychosomatic illness of all time was *spinal irritation* in the 1820s. This diagnosis, which flourished until the last decades of the century, referred to a 'sensitivity to sensation in the general area of the back ("the spine"), as well as the belief that far-distant peripheral symptoms were caused by an invisible but nonetheless real disease of the spinal cord' (Shorter 1992, 25). Spinal irritation was a useful drawing card to European water cure clinics, spas and sanatoria, because it was a vague and relatively harmless illness that particularly afflicted many upper-middle-class women, who (may have) preferred to think that their spines were irritated rather than that their malady was psychological in nature. In the latter half of the century, the pseudodiagnosis of spinal irritation gave way to the diagnosis that was even more suspicious-looking: *reflex neurosis*. This strange illness appeared to cause a network of organic irritations as any irritated organ in the body could cause irritation in any other organ, including the brain and genitalia (Shorter 1992, 40–68). One rather flamboyant form of this illness was nasal reflex neurosis, the main symptom of which was irritation in genitalia caused by the mucosa of the nose. Freud's one-time friend and colleague Wilhelm Fliess was the best-known advocate of nasal reflex neurosis (Sulloway 1992, 139–40).

The Swedish nerve doctor Axel Munthe (1857–1949) described in his memoirs (*The Story of San Michele*, 1929) how he treated society ladies in late nineteenth-century Paris. The majority of these upper- and upper-middle-class patients were not ill, rather they were distressed or bored for various reasons, and the Parisian medical market was keen to provide proper cures for these 'worried well'. Appendicitis, one widely used diagnosis among nerve doctors, lost its appeal to the privileged members of the Parisian *haute bourgeoisie* when the rumour spread that American surgeons had begun to cure appendicitis by cutting out the appendices. Munthe and other society doctors realized that as their patients did not want surgical operations,

> a new complaint had to be discovered to meet the general demand. The Faculty was up to the mark, a new disease was dumped on the market, a new word was coined, a gold coin indeed, COLITIS! It was a neat complaint, safe from the surgeon's knife, always at hand when wanted, suitable to everybody's taste. Nobody knew when it came, nobody knew when it went away. I knew that several of my far-sighted colleagues had already tried it on their patients with great success [. . .] Colitis spread like wildfire all over Paris.
> (Munthe 1975, 28–9)

Munthe confesses in his memoirs that, as a disease, colitis was as illusory as appendicitis; it was nothing but a nervous complaint. He realized that doctors can turn healthy people into patients, and that some people even want to become ill:

> Many were not ill at all, and might never have become so, had they not consulted me. Many imagined they were ill [. . .] They seemed quite upset when I told them that they looked rather well and their complexion was good, but they rallied rapidly when I added that their tongue looked rather bad – as seemed generally to be the case.
> (Munthe 1975, 23)

The complaints of Munthe's wealthy clientele seemed to be psychosomatic in the sense that they were probably psychological or *psychogenic* in origin. Yet, psychosomatic medicine did not really take off in the nineteenth century, when scientific medicine truly emerged and became differentiated into various subfields, including internal medicine, surgery, neurology and psychiatry. It was with Freud and his disciples that the psychosomatic approach to mental afflictions became more pronounced in the early decades of the twentieth century.

Freud connected the term 'conversion' with the diagnosis of hysteria and created 'conversion hysteria', a psychosomatic illness in which the unconscious conflicts 'converted into' somatic symptoms. Although Freud himself was not particularly interested in physical symptoms, psychoanalysts contributed the most to psychosomatic medicine during the first half of the twentieth century. In the early 1920s, Freud's early disciple Wilhelm Stekel (1868–1940) began to use the term 'somatization' (*somatisieren*) to refer to the conversion of emotional states into physical symptoms. Thus, heart symptoms, an upset stomach, asthma and headaches were often interpreted by Stekel and like-minded psychosomatists as conversions of psychic conflicts into physical symptoms. Stekel claimed that physicians did not pick up this conversion, because they did not understand the 'organic language of the soul'. In his view, the neurotics had an ability to express their mental states in the symbolic language of bodily organs. An example of such a conversion was a male patient who had a swollen knee. Stekel saw the knee as a symbol of the swollen head of the man's father who died after a fall. The swollen knee functioned like a memento to the patient: it constantly reminded him not to forget his dead father (Berrios & Mumford 1995, 463). Even more extravagant psychosomatic claims were put forward by the German nerve doctor and maverick psychoanalytic theorist Georg Groddeck (1866–1934). Groddeck believed that the unconscious cunningly selects somatic symptoms or accidents in order to make its conflicts visible. 'Illness has a purpose', proclaimed Groddeck and continued:

> Whoever breaks an arm has either sinned or wished to commit a sin with that arm, perhaps murder, perhaps theft or masturbation; whoever grows blind desires no more to see, has sinned with his eyes or wishes to sin with them; whoever gets hoarse has a secret and dares not tell it aloud.
>
> (Groddeck 1961, 101)

To Groddeck, there was no such thing as chance – everything could be explained by the cunning power of the unconscious psyche (Dolnick 1998, 25). Groddeck was not, however, considered a serious medical researcher, and his wild ideas did not have much influence on psychosomatic medicine.

Far more prestigious psychosomatic researchers were the German-American psychoanalyst Franz Alexander (1891–1964) and his colleagues at the Chicago Psychoanalytic Institute. They found psychosomatic components in a wide variety of diseases, including gastrointestinal disturbances (such as a peptic ulcer, anorexia nervosa and bulimia nervosa), respiratory disturbances (especially asthma), cardiovascular disturbances (including essential hypertension), skin diseases (including neurodermatitis), metabolic and endocrine disturbances (such as hyperthyroidism), disturbances of the joints and skeletal muscles (especially rheumatoid arthritis) as well as sexual disturbances (such as impotence, ejaculation praecox, homosexuality and frigidity). This was a long list of diseases and symptoms, but that was only how it should be, because, as Alexander assured the readers of his influential *Psychosomatic Medicine* (1950), the 'psychosomatic approach [. . .] can be applied to every phenomenon which takes place in the living organism' (Alexander 1950, 12).

From the late 1930s onwards, Alexander and his associates attempted to show that persons who suffered from one of these allegedly psychosomatic illnesses were often experiencing certain kinds of psychic conflicts, or, alternatively, their psychic structure was manifested through these afflictions. An Asthma attack, for example, was explained in this psychosomatic framework as a suppressed cry or desire for the mother, and it represented 'a retreat from action into a dependent, help-seeking attitude'. Parkinson's disease was seen as the result of the individual's anger that has not found another outlet for expression. The psychodynamic roots of anorexia nervosa in turn could be found in the 'unconscious aggressive posses-sive impulses such as envy and jealousy', which, 'if inhibited by the conscience, may lead to severe inhibitions of eating'. Alexander became famous for his theory of 'psychosomatic specificity', by which he meant that 'every emotional state has its own physiological syndrome' (Alexander 1950, 63–8, 91, 139). According to this sweeping theory, repressed aggression, frustration, guilt feelings or erotic impulses are present in somatic disorders.

As a psychoanalyst, Alexander had a ready-made recipe for psychosomatic ail-ments: cooperation of the psychiatric and non-psychiatric specialist. If the patient suffers from bronchial asthma, a medical specialist in respiratory disturbances cooperates with the (psychoanalytic) psychiatrist, who addresses the psychic aspects of the affliction; in the case of a peptic ulcer, a specialist in gastric disorders coop-erates with a (psychoanalytic) psychiatrist; in the case of essential hypertension, a cardiologist cooperates with a (psychoanalytic) psychiatrist, and so forth. This is a textbook example of how to expand your professional jurisdiction to cover new areas of expertise, in this case new disease entities. For psychoanalysts and psychotherapists, Alexander's ideas must have been heaven sent. As he reminded his readers at the end of his book, 'it must be borne in mind that the fundamental personality problems [underlying somatic disturbances] can be resolved only by consistent psychoanalytic therapy aimed at the resolution of the basic conflicts' (Alexander 1950, 268). To illustrate Alexander's point, psychoanalysts contributed to the treatment of asthma attacks by giving the patient an 'opportunity to "con-fess" his repressed ego-alien tendencies in a few psychotherapeutic interviews' (Alexander 1950, 268–70).

After the 1960s, psychoanalytically oriented psychosomatic medicine lost much of its scientific credibility, but medical interest in the mind–body problem per-sisted. The somewhat tarnished term 'psychosomatic' began to be avoided, while the idea of *somatoform* illnesses gained in popularity. In the 1970s, medical doctors observed that many psychiatric patients in developing countries in Africa, India and the Near-East had somatic symptoms. This observation revived the term *soma-tization*, introduced by Stekel, in comparative psychiatry and medical anthropol-ogy. The American psychiatric anthropologist Arthur Kleinman studied mental illness in China in the 1970s, and he interpreted somatization as an expression of private and public distress in a culture that disposes people to talk about their psychiatric problems in terms of physical symptoms in order to be entitled to medical services (Kleinman 1986). The Polish-born physician Zbigniew Lipowski (1924–97) was a key figure in the revival of somatization disorder, and he built his psychosomatic medicine not on psychoanalysis but on the more diffuse and inclusive holistic tradition. Thus, Lipowski's framework included all the physical symptoms in the involuntary (autonomic) and voluntary (somatic) nervous sys-tems produced by mental activity. In this holistic view, psychosomatic illness was again conceptualized very broadly as any disturbance in the mind–body relation-ship (Shorter 1995, 479). This sort of psychosomatic research is now more relevant than ever, as can be seen in studies that explore the mind–body relationship, for

226 The Golden Age of the asylums

example in stress reactions, depression and cardiovascular diseases, as well as in epidemiological studies of the links between socio-economic status and ill health (see Marmot 2004; van Lenthe et al. 2004).

Bibliography

Alexander, F. (1950) *Psychosomatic Medicine, Its Principles and Applications*, New York: Norton.

Benedetti, F. (2009) *Placebo Effects. Understanding the Mechanisms in Health and Disease*, Oxford: Oxford University Press.

Berrios, G.E. and Mumford, D. (1995) 'Somatoform disorders – clinical section', in G.E. Berrios and R. Porter (eds) *A History of Clinical Psychiatry: The Origin and History of Psychiatric Disorders*, London: Athlone.

Borch-Jacobsen, M. (1996) *Remembering Anna O.: A Century of Mystification*, London: Routledge.

Borch-Jacobsen, M. and Shamdasani, S. (2013) *The Freud Files: An Inquiry into the History of Psychoanalysis*, Cambridge: Cambridge University Press.

Braid, J. (1843) *Neurypnology or the Rationale of Nervous Sleep Considered in Relation with Animal Magnetism Illustrated by Numerous Cases of Its Successful Application in the Relief and Cure of Disease*, London: John Churchill.

Breuer, J. and Freud, S. (1995) *Studies on Hysteria*, orig. German edn 1885, *The Standard Edition of the Complete Psychological Works of Sigmund Freud*, Vol. 2, ed. J. Strachey, London: The Hogarth Press, 1–335.

Brinkmann, S. (2008) 'Changing psychologies in the transition from industrial society to consumer society', *History of the Human Sciences*, 21: 85–110.

Crabtree, A. (1993) *From Mesmer to Freud: Magnetic Sleep and the Roots of Psychological Healing*, New Haven, CT: Yale University Press.

Crews, F. (ed.) (1998) *Unauthorized Freud. Doubters Confront a Legend*, New York: Viking.

Dolnick, E. (1998) *Madness on the Couch: Blaming the Victim in the Heyday of Psychoanalysis*, New York: Simon & Schuster.

Dubois, P. (1905) *The Psychic Treatment of Nervous Disorders*, trans S.E. Jelliffe and W.A. White, orig. French edn 1904, New York: Fund & Wagnalls Company.

Ellenberger, H.F. (1994) *The Discovery of the Unconscious*, 1st edn 1970, London: Fontana Press.

Freud, S. (1905/1981) 'Fragment of an analysis of a case of hysteria', in *The Standard Edition*, Vol. 7 (1901–5), trans. and ed. J. Strachey, London: The Hogarth Press.

Freud, S. (1920/1981) 'The psychogenesis of a case of homosexuality in a woman', *The Standard Edition*, Vol. 18 (1920–22), trans. and ed. J. Strachey, London: The Hogarth Press.

Gauld, A. (1992) *A History of Hypnotism*, Cambridge: Cambridge University Press.

Gellner, E. (1993) *The Psychoanalytic Movement: The Cunning of Unreason*, 1st edn 1985, London: Fontana Press.

Groddeck, G. (1961) *Book of the It*, orig. German edition 1923, New York: Vintage.

Hacking, I. (1995) *Rewriting the Soul: Multiple Personality and the Sciences of Memory*, Princeton, NJ: Princeton University Press.

Hale, N.G. (1995) *The Rise and Crisis of Psychoanalysis in the United States: Freud and the Americans, 1917–1985*, Oxford: Oxford University Press.

Kaptchuk, T. (2009) 'Placebo controls, exorcism, and the devil', *The Lancet*, 374, October 10: 1234–5.

Kerr, J. (1993) *A Most Dangerous Method*, New York: Alfred A. Knopf.

Kirsch, I. (2009) *The Emperor's New Drugs. Exploding the Antidepressant Myth*, London: The Bodley Head.

Kleinman, A. (1986) *Social Origins of Distress and Disease: Depression, Neurasthenia, and Pain in Modern China*, New Haven, CT: Yale University Press.

LeBlanc, A. (2013) 'Review of M. Borch-Jacobsen, *Les Patients de Freud: Destins, Journal of the History of the Behavioral Sciences*, 49: 98–9.

van Lenthe, F.J., Schrijvers, C.T.M., Droomers, M., Joung, I.M.A., Louwman, M.J. and Mackenbach, J.P. (2004) 'Investigating explanations of socio-economic inequalities in health. The Dutch GLOBE study', *European Journal of Public Health*, 14: 63–70.

Makari, G. (2008) *Revolution in Mind. The Creation of Psychoanalysis*, New York: Harper.

Marmot, M. (2004) *Status Syndrome: How Social Standing Affects Our Health and Longevity*, London: Bloomsbury.

Munthe, A. (1975) *The Story of San Michele*, 1st edn 1929, London: John Murray.

Pietikainen, P. (2007) *Neurosis and Modernity. The Age of Nervousness in Sweden*, Leiden: Brill.

Pinker, S. (1997) *How the Mind Works*, New York: W.W. Norton.

Pisa, K. (1998) *Ernst Freiherr von Feuchtersleben – Pionier der Psychosomatik*, Vienna: Böhlau.

Rodgers, J.E. (2001) *Sex: A Natural History*, New York: W.H. Freeman.

Rosen, J.N. (1968) *Selected Papers on Direct Psychoanalysis*, New York: Grune & Stratton.

Samuel, L.R. (2013) *Shrink: A Cultural History of Psychoanalysis in America*, Lincoln: University of Nebraska Press.

Schott, H. and Tölle, R. (2006) *Geschichte der Psychiatrie*, Munich: C.H. Beck.

Shamdasani, S. (2005) '"Psychotherapy": the invention of a word', *History of the Human Sciences*, 18: 1–22.

Shorter, E. (1992) *From Paralysis to Fatigue: A History of Psychosomatic Illness in the Modern Era*, New York: The Free Press.

Shorter, E. (1995) 'Somatoform disorders – social section', in G.E. Berrios and R. Porter (eds) *A History of Clinical Psychiatry: The Origin and History of Psychiatric Disorders*, London: Athlone.

Sulloway, F.J. (1992) *Freud, Biologist of the Mind*, 1st edn 1979, Cambridge, MA: Cambridge University Press.

Trivers, R. (2002) *Natural Selection and Social Theory*, Oxford: Oxford University Press.

Wortis, J. (1994) *My Analysis with Freud*, Northvale, NJ: Janson Aronson.

Yeates, L.B. (2013) 'James Braid: Surgeon, Gentleman Scientist, and Hypnotist', PhD Diss., Sydney: University of New South Wales.

11

WAR AND MADNESS

This chapter explores madness and war. I will describe shell-shock in the Great War (1914–18) and war neuroses in World War II (1939–45). In addition, I will discuss perhaps the darkest chapter in the history of madness, the mass murdering of institutionalized mental patients and the feebleminded in National-Socialist Germany between 1939 and 1945. The chapter ends with a short account of the more recent war-related diagnoses as well as our contemporary cultural infatuation with trauma.

Psychiatric casualties in World War I

Life in the front line may exacerbate mental health problems, and prisoners of war (POWs) have suffered from transient 'reactive psychoses' related to the shock of imprisonment and the brutality that POWs have often seen and experienced. Yet, researchers have not found that wars would increase mental disorders in the civil population or in the army. Wars in themselves do not drive soldiers or civilians insane, but they do increase their nervousness, anxiety and depression. Violent conflicts and social unrest increase general anxiety, but they may also arouse ideological fervour and patriotic enthusiasm, especially initially. This, of course, is what happened in the early days of the Great War. A few years later, the massive self-deception of European war-mongers had been transformed into disillusionment, apathy or fatalism. The horrors of the trenches of the Great War have come to symbolize the cultural and existential wasteland, the western disillusionment with progress and enlightenment.

War-related traumas became familiar to the medical community with the phenomenon of *shell-shock* during the Great War. However, the epidemic nervousness of soldiers was known before the twentieth-century world wars. During the Napoleonic wars of the early nineteenth century, a number of British soldiers were treated in a mental hospital for nervous breakdowns, and such breakdowns were also witnessed in the American Civil War (1861–5). During the conflict-ridden twentieth century, war-related psychiatric suffering had different names and diagnoses at different times. In World War I, the terms 'shell-shock', 'traumatic neurosis' and 'male hysteria' were all common, while in World War II the term 'war neurosis' was widely employed. After the Vietnam War, 'post-traumatic stress disorder' became an official diagnosis (codified in DSM-III), and in the 2000s this term has been used interchangeably with 'combat stress reaction' or 'combat fatigue' (Pizarro, Silver & Prause 2006).

The first case of 'modern' war neurosis was reported in early 1915 by the British Army in France. The victim was a 20-year-old private soldier who was caught in barbed wire while moving from one front-line trench to another. When he tried to disentangle himself he was spotted by the German artillery:

> Immediately after one of the shells burst in front of him, his sight, he said, became blurred. Another shell, which then burst behind him gave him a greater shock, 'like a punch on the head without any pain after it'. The shell in front cut his haversack clean away and bruised his side.
>
> (Shephard 2002, 1)

His comrades managed to drag the soldier back to the trenches, from where he was taken, crying and shivering, to a dressing station and then to the base hospital at Le Touquet. There, he was interviewed by the Cambridge psychologist C.S. Myers, who was so mystified by the soldier's symptoms that he promptly wrote an article in which he introduced a term that was already current in the Army: 'shell-shock'. In winter 1915, similar cases arrived at the hospitals and casualty clearing stations of the British Army in France. These shell-shocked soldiers were not wounded, but they had trouble seeing, speaking, standing up, urinating or defecating. Some men vomited uncontrollably while others had lost their memories. Many were shaken, trembling, anxious and semi-paralysed. Shell-shock arose from the trenches (Shephard 2002; Leese 2002; Reid 2011).

The Great War was the great collective experience of megadeath of history. The death toll is simply staggering: more than 9 million combatants were killed, and altogether more than 38 million people were killed, wounded or missing. The most devastating day of the war was at the Battle of the Somme in France on 1 July 1916, when 60,000 soldiers were killed or wounded, most of them British. This and similar catastrophes resulted from trench warfare, which was employed on the Western Front until the last weeks of the war in November 1918. With a huge number of casualties and no reinforcements forthcoming, the majority of soldiers had to serve long periods in poor or appalling conditions. In the trenches, one could not escape the reality of the war, as one British lieutenant noticed when he arrived at the front line in August 1915:

> I must say it is a devilish affair altogether. You sit like rabbits in a burrow and just wait for something to come and blow you to hell. You don't see the

230 The Golden Age of the asylums

> enemy and you kill very few of them. But you shell them very often. They do the same [. . .] Nerves seem to be the one vital thing for a soldier, nerves good and strong and better still no nerves.
>
> (Shephard 2002, 33)

What added to the anxiety was the use of poisonous gases, which was started by the Germans in 1915 and subsequently used by the British and the French. The most painful and dreaded gas was mustard gas, developed by the German chemist Fritz Haber in 1917 (Haber was awarded the Nobel Prize in Chemistry in 1918, but not for his work on poisonous gases). Haber's devilish innovation in gas was lethal 'only' in about 1 per cent of cases, but its incapacitating and psychological effect was considerable. Soldiers wearing gas masks were not protected against absorbing the gas through their skin, which caused blistering. Within 24 hours of exposure to mustard gas, victims experienced intense itching and skin irritation, which gradually turned into large blisters, very painful and debilitating chemical burns. Severe mustard gas burns were often fatal, and even mild or moderate exposure to the mustard agent required lengthy periods of medical treatment and convalescence. Moreover, due to the mutagenic and carcinogenic effects of mustard agent, even victims who recovered from mustard gas burns had an increased risk of developing cancer in later life. The intensity of pain and discomfort suffered by the victims horrified even the experienced nurses working in field hospitals. One British nurse noticed that the victims

> cannot breathe lying down or sitting up. They just struggle for breath, but nothing can be done. Their lungs are gone – literally burnt out. Some have their eyes and faces entirely eaten away by gas and their bodies covered with first-degree burns. We must try to relieve them by pouring oil on them. They cannot be bandaged or touched. [. . .] One boy today, screaming to die, the entire top layer of his skin burnt from face and body. I gave him an injection of morphine. He was wheeled out just before I came on duty. When will this end?
>
> (van Bergen 2009, 184)

Who could have stayed calm in these circumstances?

At first, shell-shock perplexed psychiatrists and neurologists. Was it caused by a physical lesion in the nervous system or some sort of emotional shock? Gradually, shell-shock began to be associated with nervous disorders, such as neurasthenia, traumatic neurosis or, most disparagingly, male hysteria. Shell-shock was placed in this continuum as a nervous illness that was triggered by nerve-wracking circumstances in the front line. The diagnosis was anything but warmly received in the Army, which naturally emphasized martial masculine values, such as fortitude, honour, discipline, self-control, duty and hierarchy. In such an environment, men who lost their nerve were often treated with scorn rather than with empathy and understanding, especially when they encountered officers and representatives of military medicine.

One of the dark chapters of World War I was the way in which the military command both in the Axis and Allied powers approached war neuroses. If the traumatized men were given psychiatric treatment, the preferred method was often the administration of electricity. This method was applied especially by the German military psychiatrists, but also in France and other Allied countries (on German military psychiatry during World War I, see Lerner 2003). Depending on the specific situation, the seriousness of the symptoms and the attitude of physicians, the administered voltage could be small, moderate or excessive, in which case it was no longer therapy but torture. Most infamously, the Austrian psychiatrist Julius Wagner-Jauregg was keen on 'treating' his 'male hysterics' with painful electric shocks and other brutal methods, such as confinement to a small cell for weeks. The aim of such treatment was to strengthen the weak will of the neurotics and send these dishonoured soldiers back into battle. After the war, the possible malpractices at Wagner-Jauregg's clinic in Vienna were examined, but the Maestro was exonerated from all blame. His Viennese colleague Sigmund Freud defended him against an accusation of mistreating soldiers during the war. His assistant Dr Kozlowski, whose treatment of soldier-patients had been more than a little sadistic, was reproached for 'excessive zeal' (by then, Kozlowski had returned to his native Poland) (Shephard 2002, 135–8). Wagner-Jauregg in turn received the 1927 Nobel Prize for Medicine for his discovery of malaria fever therapy for the treatment of neurosyphilis (see Chapter 8).

Official reactions to the psychosomatic symptoms of soldiers varied, but high command particularly, which had little insight into the reality of trench warfare, tended to have a highly judgemental attitude towards shell-shocked soldiers. But as the war lingered on, this problem began to be approached a bit more subtly as it dawned on (some) physicians and psychologists that they were dealing with an emotional or psychological wound that required psychotherapeutic rather than disciplinary intervention. Some extremist military psychiatrists refused to see shell-shocked soldiers as victims rather than cowards or 'querulants' who kept on complaining on manifestly unfounded grounds. Perhaps the most appalling approach to the problem of war neuroses was taken by the French military commanders for whom the mental sufferers appeared as simulators, querulants and malingerers. (Shephard 2002, 101–12). In light of what we know of the high-ranking French officers' attitude towards the common foot soldier, Stanley Kubrick's classic film *Paths of Glory* (1957), which portrays the corruption and indifference of the French high command towards the loss of their own soldiers' lives, hits the target (the film was not shown in France until 1975). After the war, veterans who had suffered from mental problems faced hard reality everywhere in Europe, and they had to struggle to receive disability benefits or even official acknowledgement of their suffering. Historian Peter Barham, who has studied the 'forgotten lunatics' of the Great War, has written about the way in which these men were silenced and buried in a 'cultural mass grave' in Britain (Barham 2004, 5–7).

232 The Golden Age of the asylums

Heart of darkness: the euthanasia programme in the Third Reich

Hitler's rise to power in early 1933 signalled hard times for the mentally ill and the feebleminded in Germany. The first step was the enactment of the Sterilization Law in July 1933. The law allowed the forced sterilization of any citizen who in the opinion of a 'Genetic Health Court' was tainted by a putatively genetic disorder, such as schizophrenia, manic-depressive insanity or congenital mental deficiency. The medical leader of German racial hygiene was the psychiatrist Ernst Rüdin, who in 1932 had become President of the International Eugenic Society and who acted as an expert in the preparation of race legislation. Compared to other professions, physicians were over-represented in the National Socialist Party: about 45 per cent of German doctors belonged to the Party (Schott & Tölle 2006, 172). During the first year (1933–4) at least 56,000 Germans were sterilized, and by 1937 the number had increased to 200,000. Thereafter statistics were no longer published, but researchers have estimated that between 350,000 and 400,000 Germans were sterilized. About a quarter of them were diagnosed as schizophrenics and 14 per cent as manic-depressives; more than half (52.9 per cent) were suffering from congenital feeblemindedness, a vague classification that could be used in many different situations (Lindert et al. 2013, 4).

The culmination of German racial hygiene was the so-called euthanasia programme, unleashed at Hitler's order in September 1939. The first victims of this murderous campaign were the approximately 2,000 patients at the Polish mental hospital in Kocborowo (Conradstein). The SS (the *Schutzstaffel*; a powerful paramilitary Nazi organization) murdered the director and the medical personnel and transported the patients (including 130 children brought in from an affiliated clinic) to the nearby forest, where they were shot. The euthanasia programme continued until August 1941, by which time the German Army had begun its military offensive into the Soviet Union (Klee 1999, 2001; Burleigh 2002). In less than two years, 70,273 psychiatric and mentally disabled patients were killed in gas chambers in six German and Austrian mental institutions turned into death centres (one of them was a prison). Not included in these figures are the murdered children and mentally ill criminals who were killed in concentration camps. The most well-known 'murder factory' was in the small town of Hadamar, where the inhabitants became accustomed to seeing the black smoke arising from chimneys when the bodies of the victims were burned in ovens.

The euthanasia programme was named Aktion T 4 after the administrative office at Tiergartenstrasse 4 in Berlin. Aktion T 4 was constructed quickly and without any administrative preparation, and it was largely based on a network of personal relations and a hierarchical chain of orders. One of the leaders of the programme was Hitler's personal physician, Dr Karl Brandt, who was authorized to carry out 'mercy killing' (a travesty of language if there ever was one). At first, the programme functionaries persecuted disabled children, an easy prey to Nazi machinery. Approximately 5,000 children were murdered by 1941, usually by an

FIGURE 11.1 A Nazi (NSDAP) Party poster showing how disabled people cost money and promoting eugenics and euthanasia of the disabled.
Source: © CBW/Alamy

overdose of morphine and barbiturates (Schott & Tölle 2006, 175–6). Next in line were adult mental patients and the mentally disabled. They were gathered by buses from local mental hospitals to one of the six death centres, where they were undressed, gassed to death with carbon monoxide and then burned. For every victim, a fake death certificate was prepared to fool the relatives. The certificate was sent to the family together with an urn of ashes – random ashes, of course, since the victims were cremated en masse. Doctors operating the centres spent most of

234 The Golden Age of the asylums

their working days preparing falsified death certificates. The most widely used false diagnosis was pneumonia.

An implementation of such a large-scale killing programme required both unconditional obedience to the orders given from above and a logistic machinery, which enabled an efficient transportation of 'material' from one place to another. This mentality, in which human beings were treated as cargo that posed only logistic problems, became more pronounced over the years, culminating in the Holocaust or the Final Solution (*die Endlösung*), the systematic killing of Jews and Roma (Gypsies). The Final Solution, which began as 'Operation Reinhardt' in January 1942, grew out of Aktion T 4. What also characterized the euthanasia programme was the conscious perversion of language. There are no documents that use such direct words as 'killing' or 'gassing'. Instead, the executioners used the cover word *Behandlung*, meaning 'treatment'. In medical reports there were typically sentences such as 'the child can be treated' (*das Kind kann behandelt werden*). Victims were selected by psychiatrists working in mental hospitals and institutes for the disabled. Their duty was to list the patients who were the most 'useless' and the greatest burden to the national economy. Such persons were often chronically ill patients, those who required care and attention as well as those who were 'unusable' for any productive work (Klee 2001, 102–4).

Unfortunately, there is not much we know about the victims. They were typically of working-class background, lacked education and did not have a permanent job or family. From 1933 onwards, the criteria for incarceration in a mental hospital included alcoholism, antisocial behaviour, homosexuality, political dissent, prostitution, vagrancy and disinclination to work (Schott & Tölle 2006, 177). What we do know is that victims often became research objects, presenting precious material for unscrupulous researchers. One such was the Heidelberg psychiatrist Carl Schneider, who collected the brains of murdered Jews, disabled children and other victims for research in his clinic and for teaching. A member of the Nazi Party since 1932, Schneider coined the term 'national therapy' for the policy of eliminating the individuals tainted by genetic and blood contaminants, which in his view threatened the psychological and physical health of the Aryan *Volk* (people). After the war, Schneider hanged himself in his prison cell when he was prosecuted in the Doctors' Trial, an American military tribunal in Nuremberg (Remy 2002, 118). The brains, eyes or intestines of the victims were often removed and sent to researchers working in prestigious research institutes, such as the Kaiser Wilhelm Institute for Psychiatry in Munich. This practice was continued during the years of Holocaust, when cadavers of Jewish and Roma victims provided material for researchers. There were also atrocious medical experiments conducted in concentration camps such as Dachau and Auschwitz, including high-altitude experiments in a low-pressure chamber, mustard gas experiments, freezing or cold water immersion experiments that caused hypothermia, and Josef Mengele's sadistic experiments on twins (Weindling 2005).

The Aktion T 4 programme was officially closed in August 1941. One reason for the closure were the protests from some concerned parents and from churchmen, both Protestant and Catholic. Another, probably more important, reason was that there were now enough empty institutions to be used for the wounded *Wehrmacht* soldiers, many of whom were invading Russia at that time. Yet, the 'mercy killings' continued in many hospitals in Germany and occupied regions in eastern Europe in a decentralized, less systematic fashion until the end of the war. Between 1941 and 1945, countless victims were overdosed by drugs, starved to death or killed by injecting air into the blood circulation, which can cause sudden cardiac arrest or stroke. All in all, by 1945 perhaps as many as 400,000 mental patients and patients with disabilities had been murdered, most of them as a result of 'wild euthanasia' (Lindert et al. 2013, 7). In the Meseritz-Obrawalde Hospital in Prussia alone 10,000 inmates were killed by the staff. The administrative director of the hospital was Walter Grabowski, a former salesman and fanatical Nazi, whose attitude towards mental suffering was cruel. Although not responsible for medical treatment, he was instrumental in the project of 'mercy killings' that emptied the hospital of patients. In most cases, inmates were murdered by an overdose of barbiturates and then buried in Obrawalde's own cemetery (Benedict & Chelouche 2008). The notorious SS Einsatzgruppen, paramilitary death squads following the invading troops of the *Wehrmacht* (German Army) in the Soviet Union and eastern Europe, also slaughtered tens of thousands of mental patients between 1941 and 1945.

After the war, only 20 medical doctors (plus three others) were prosecuted in the Doctors' Trial in Nuremberg. Seven of them were acquitted, seven received death sentences and the remainder were sentenced to prison, some for life. One of those who were sentenced to death by hanging was Karl Brandt, the director of Aktion T 4. The only 'euthanasia doctor' who received a death sentence in a West German court was the psychiatrist Hilda Wernicke, a member of the National Socialist Party who had worked at the above-mentioned Meseritz-Obrawalde Hospital during the 'wild euthanasia' phase (Benedict & Chelouche 2008). Many Nazi doctors managed to avoid prosecution, some of them becoming successful physicians in post-war West Germany. One of them was Werner Catel, who was involved in child euthanasia, and who became Professor of Paediatrics in 1954. When he died after a long and successful career in 1981, his obituary stated that Catel had acted 'in many ways, to the welfare and well-being of sick children' (Petersen & Zankel 2003). In 1990, an author of the historical survey of the Max Planck Institute (formerly the Kaiser Wilhelm Institute) noted quite excitedly how the 'mass killing of the mentally ill also opened up new research opportunities both to the Psychiatric and the Brain Research Departments of the Institute' (Klee 2001, 379; my translation). This is an indisputable yet deeply troubling fact.

Psychiatric casualties of World War II and beyond

During World War II, military command, physicians, politicians and the home front were more prepared for the possibility of psychological injuries than had been the case in World War I. 'Combat fatigue' was the phrase that was commonly used in the British and American Armies. Most importantly, war neuroses were stigmatized to a much lesser extent than during the Great War. To some degree, the military and civil authorities had learned their lesson, and the recruitment of new medical specialists, military psychiatrists, signified a more professional and concerted effort both to prevent and to treat the mental wounds of the soldiers. In the United States, there was an effort to find 'mental cases' in draft offices, and American military psychiatry was most developed in the psychotherapeutic treatment of war neuroses, which was an indication of the increasingly psychological and psychodynamic orientation of American psychiatry. Above all, American psychiatrists realized in the course of the war that selection and indoctrination of an anti-Nazi mentality were not enough – what was needed was a strengthening of the ties that bind the GI to his buddies. Consequently, to motivate the soldier the behaviour experts as well as the military officers had to reinforce the GI's fundamental loyalty to his primary group. Such reinforcement would prevent the GIs from breaking down and becoming mental invalids. Another valuable insight was that because everyone becomes mentally and physically exhausted in the end, there needed to be a replacement system to make sure that soldiers have a chance to rest and recuperate after roughly 210 combat days. These were important practical suggestions, but they were inadequately implemented due to the managerial dogmatism of the Pentagon. Later, when American soldiers served in Vietnam, the idea of the one-year tour of duty was accepted and put into practice, but perhaps the more important principle of sustaining group loyalty was sadly ignored (Shephard 2002, 243–5).

In the end, regardless of whether the soldiers fought in the American or European Army, the symptoms of war neurosis were more or less the same. A typical case is that of Private Usko M., a 26-year-old Finnish farmer who had been regarded as unfit for front-line service but who was serving in the heat of battle against the Soviet troops in June 1944. Before the war broke out in 1939, Usko had suffered from sleeplessness and a 'difficult nervous disorder'. He had always been shy and sensitive, and although he abhorred seeing blood and wounds, he had to serve as a field medic in the summer offensive of 1941. Unable to fulfil his duties, he was first hospitalized and then sent home, from where he was called back to service two years later. His unit was fortifying a defensive line behind the front line when the terrifying Soviet offensive was unleashed in June 1944. The area around Usko's fortification unit was heavily bombed, which made Usko run to the woods in panic. When he was taken to the psychiatric department of a military hospital, he was crying and trembling. He told his doctors how 'he had seen a "monster" sitting by a tree and telling him that tomorrow he would be shot' (Kivimäki 2013, 153). Otherwise, he could remember hardly anything, not even his date of birth. Transferred to another military hospital, Usko was described as 'a neurotic laggard and phobic type' by the psychiatrists. He was given electroshocks, which he feared and loathed, and some months later he was sent home as a feebleminded neurasthenic.

As the historian Ville Kivimäki found out when he studied the war neuroses in the Finnish Army,

> besides nightmares, some psychiatric patients saw and heard non-existent enemies sneaking around them or had the tumult of war constantly in their ears. At the extreme end were the soldiers who had such strong and vivid hallucinations that they indicated a serious mental illness: a soldier who was haunted by a 'small, evil black man with a knife'; another one whom the 'devil' forced to jump from a window; a third one who had been shocked by artillery barrages and air raids and then started to see headless people and strange creatures. Nevertheless, even though the symptoms leading to psychiatric hospitalization were usually quite severe, full-fledged psychotic disorders, most importantly schizophrenia, were relatively rare.
>
> (Kivimäki 2013, 153–4)

Kivimäki's research confirms the already well-established view that even if war is madness, it does not increase severe mental illnesses such as schizophrenia. But there are exceptions, only then we are no longer referring to the soldiers but to the civilian victims of Nazi genocide. In his landmark study of concentration camp survivors, the Jewish psychiatrist Leo Eitinger argues that in extremely inhumane conditions humans may lose their minds and become permanently mentally damaged. In the late 1950s and early 1960s, Eitinger studied almost 600, mostly Jewish survivors in Israel and Norway, where he had immigrated in 1939. His conclusion is that, in the case of many former concentration camp inmates, schizophrenia was caused by their horrendous environment in Auschwitz, Buchenwald, Bergen-Belsen and other hellholes. Eitinger could easily identify with the tragic stories of these survivors: after Norway, his new home country, was occupied by the German Army, he was one of 762 Jews deported to concentration camps. Interned in Auschwitz in 1943, Eitinger survived the camp, as did only 22 other Jewish prisoners from Norway.

This is the abridged version of the sad story of one of the survivors who was hospitalized in an Israeli asylum:

> A man, born in 1928, in Poland. His father died early and the mother moved back to her parents where the boy lived until the outbreak of war [. . .] During the war, the family was moved first into the [Warsaw] ghetto, later during an 'action' [resistance] the grandfather was captured, and the boy saw how the Germans first scorched his beard off and then killed him. He rapidly developed an uncanny gift for hiding during all the raids, and managed to stay alive for 4 months alone after the ghetto had been liquidated. He 'lived like a rat', came out of his hiding place in the ruins during the night, and stole what he could find. He was finally caught, however, and taken to Auschwitz.
>
> (Eitinger 1964, 150)

238 The Golden Age of the asylums

In Auschwitz, the boy did all he could to stay alive, helping the *kapos* (prisoners in concentration camps who were assigned by the SS guards to supervise forced labour) by dragging the corpses out of the block and sorting out the belongings of those killed in the camp. Like many other survivors, he described himself as a 'living corpse' during his imprisonment in Auschwitz. From there he was evacuated to Mauthausen, another concentration camp (in Austria), where he also managed to survive. After the war, he tried to get to Palestine illegally, but was caught and interned on Cyprus, from where he was able to come to Israel in 1948. He immediately volunteered for the military forces and was subsequently regarded as a good soldier, even though he was reckless and badly disciplined. Between the late 1940s and the mid-1950s, he was injured three times during the fighting, but survived. After demobilization, he was totally unable to adjust himself to civilian life. He stole, lied and cheated and could not hold a job. His condition worsened and eventually he was confined in a mental hospital. When Eitinger interviewed him in 1962,

> he appeared cynical and reserved. He looked upon the whole world as a concentration camp. 'They all behave exactly as they did in the camp, everyone thinks of himself, they just grab all they can lay hold on. The only difference is the way they speak and their clothes' [. . .] He only laughed when asked if there was anyone he trusted, and on being put the question whom he hated here, the answer came like the lash of a whip: 'Everyone'.
>
> (Eitinger 1964, 151)

This man was so badly damaged by what he saw and experienced during the war as a child that he had lost his essential humanity. His case is at the extreme end of the continuum including all sorts of mental suffering, as Eitinger's book so convincingly demonstrates. It is hardly surprising that the persecutory delusions of the disordered concentration camp survivors centred around the SS and the Gestapo, or that the typical symptom of these sufferers was a hopeless and apathetic depression. They were often individuals who had given up, who lived in a grey haze of disenchantment, who had lost the spark of life. As one Polish-born patient, who spent three years of her life in Auschwitz and other camps as a young woman, told Eitinger,

> it's no good, doctor, we can talk about it as long as the doctors want to, I can take all the pills in the world, I still can't enjoy anything, nothing has any meaning for me, I'm alive, I'm married, I have children, but I'm just not there.
>
> (Eitinger 1964, 171)

What this woman and countless other Jews and Roma people had to endure in the camps is almost beyond the limits of understanding. If we want to end this sad chapter on a slightly lighter note, we can look at the post-war development of war neuroses and see that the attitude of the military and civil authorities towards psychiatric casualties of war became more humane and understanding. One indication of this development was the emergence of post-traumatic stress disorder (PTSD) in the aftermath of the demoralizing Vietnam War. This malady was adopted by the American Psychiatric Association as part of its official diagnostic system (DSM-III) in 1980, and in the 1980s the diagnosis and the whole idea of traumatic memory attracted the attention of psychiatrists and other behaviour experts in Europe, Australia and Israel. Interestingly, the acceptance of PTSD as an official diagnosis followed a political struggle waged by psychiatrists and activists on behalf of the large number of Vietnam War veterans who were troubled by recurring nightmares, intense anxiety and other psychological effects of war-related trauma. PTSD became a sort of social-political warranty that guaranteed much-needed benefits to the veterans (Young 1997). In the recent wars in Iraq and Afghanistan, the distress of the American soldiers has been medicalized and individualized to the extent that the soldier-patients may easily feel that they are on their own and that their war-related suffering is related only to their individual psyches, which are then 'fixed' by psychiatric drugs, such as neuroleptics, sedatives, stimulants and antidepressants. From 2005 to 2011, there was almost a 700 per cent increase in the number of psychoactive drugs prescribed to American troops in Iraq and Afghanistan. What is even more alarming, more active-duty soldiers committed suicide than died in battle in 2012 (Healy 2012, 108; Friedman 2013).

As often happens when new psychiatric diagnoses are introduced, symptoms of PTSD began to be detected in individuals who had never been to war or who had never been placed in life-threatening situations. By the 2000s, it could be enough to learn about shattering experiences of other people (i.e. the 9/11 terrorist attacks) to become traumatized oneself. Defined too broadly in recent decades, PTSD has become the common diagnosis all over the world, 'the lingua franca of human suffering, following wars and natural disasters' (Watters 2010, 2). The British psychologist Stephen Joseph has argued that our culture's endorsement of PTSD has gone too far, and that the western world is now suffering from an over-medicalization of painful experiences that should be considered a normal part of the human condition (Joseph 2011). Indeed, westerners appear to have a cultural obsession with trauma. In the 2000s, such obsession has become an insidious export as mental health professionals, especially in the United States, spread this western 'anti-gospel' of trauma to different regions in the world. Such a globalization of the western notions of mental illness has resulted in a pathologization of 'traumas' and other problems of local people, whose own culturally specific beliefs about illness and healing are disregarded (Watters 2010). A critic might call it psychomedical imperialism (Lauterbach 1977).

* * *

Since World War II, the great majority of victims in global wars and other armed conflicts have been civilians – men, women and children. The renowned

240 The Golden Age of the asylums

historian Eric Hobsbawm called his 1994 study of the twentieth century *The Age of Extremes*, which is an apt title for a book that chronicles both extremes of the era: increasing affluence and the advance of democracy and human rights as well as bloody wars, violent ideologies and the rise of totalitarian regimes. In a way, the worst aspects of twentieth-century madness were not to be found in asylums but in the trenches, concentration camps, torture chambers and killing fields across the world. Hobsbawm's age of extremes was simultaneously an age of extreme political, social and ideological madness.

Bibliography

Barham, P. (2004) *Forgotten Lunatics of the Great War*, New Haven, CT: Yale University Press.

Benedict, S. and Chelouche, T. (2008) 'Meseritz-Obrawalde: A "wild euthanasia" hospital in Germany', *History of Psychiatry*, 19: 68–76.

van Bergen, L. (2009) *Before My Helpless Sight: Suffering, Dying and Military Medicine on the Western Front, 1914–1918*, Farnham: Ashgate.

Burleigh, M. (2002) *Death and Deliverance: 'Euthanasia' in Germany c. 1900–1945*, London: Pan.

Eitinger, L. (1964) *Concentration Camp Survivors*, London: Allen & Unwin.

Friedman, R.A. (2013) 'Wars on drugs', *New York Times*, 7 April.

Healy, D. (2012) *Pharmageddon*, Berkeley: University of California Press.

Joseph, S. (2011) *What Doesn't Kill Us: The New Psychology of Posttraumatic Growth*, New York: Basic Books.

Kivimäki, V. (2013) *Battled Nerves. Finnish Soldiers' War Experience, Trauma, and Psychiatry, 1941–44*, Turku: Åbo Akademi University.

Klee, E. (1999) *'"Euthanasie" im NS-Staat: Die "Vernichtung lebensunwerten Lebens"'*, Frankfurt am Main: S. Fischer.

Klee, E. (2001) *Deutsche Medizin im Dritten Reich. Karrieren vor und nach 1945*, Frankfurt am Main: S. Fischer.

Lauterbach, A. (1977) 'Changing concepts of imperialism', *Review of World Economics*, 113: 322–47.

Leese, P. (2002) *Shell Shock. Traumatic Neurosis and the British Soldiers of the First World War*, Basingstoke: Palgrave Macmillan.

Lerner, P. (2003) *Hysterical Men: War, Psychiatry, and the Politics of Trauma in Germany, 1890–1930*, Ithaca, NY: Cornell University Press.

Lindert, J., Stein, Y., Guggenheim, H., Jaakkola, J.J.K. and Strous, R.D. (2013) 'How ethics failed – the role of psychiatrists and physicians in Nazi programs from exclusion to extermination, 1933–1945', *Public Health Reviews*, 34: 1–26.

Petersen, H.C. and Zankel, S. (2003) 'Werner Catel – ein Protagonist der NS-"Kindereuthanasie" und seine Nachkriegskarriere', *Medizinhistorisches Journal. Medicine and the Life Sciences in History*, 38: 139–73.

Pizarro, J., Silver, R.C. and Prause, J. (2006) 'Physical and mental health costs of traumatic war experiences among civil war veterans', *Archives of General Psychiatry*, 63: 193–200.

Reid, F. (2011) *Broken Men: Shell Shock, Treatment and Recovery in Britain 1914–30*, London: Continuum.

Remy, S.P. (2002) *The Heidelberg Myth: The Nazification and Denazification of a German University*, Cambridge, MA: Harvard University Press.

Schott, H. and Tölle, R. (2006) *Geschichte der Psychiatrie*, Munich: C.H. Beck.

Shephard, B. (2002) *War of Nerves. Soldiers and Psychiatrists, 1914–1994*, London: Pimlico.

Watters, E. (2010) *Crazy Like Us: The Globalization of the American Psyche*, New York: Free Press.

Weindling, P.J. (2005) *Nazi Medicine and the Nuremberg Trials: From Medical War Crimes to Informed Consent*, Basingstoke: Palgrave Macmillan.

Young, A. (1997) *The Harmony of Illusions: Inventing Post-Traumatic Stress Disorder*, Princeton, NJ: Princeton University Press.

12

SHOCKS AND SURGERIES

Somatic treatments of the twentieth century

Above in this book, I mentioned the early nineteenth-century shock methods, such as plunging hapless patients headlong into ice-cold water or revolving them at high speed in rotating chairs. In this chapter, I will examine new somatic treatments that were introduced between the two world wars – it is a story of the use of rough methods in tough times. I will focus on the four most widely used treatments, namely insulin coma therapy, convulsive shock therapy, electroconvulsive therapy and psychosurgery. The principal question I will ask in this chapter is whether the most important therapeutic goal in the Age of the Asylum was the pacification of mental patients so that they would become easy to manage in the context of mass-produced institutional care. I will discuss the idea that what was meant by treatment was largely an intervention aimed at calming the patients in order to adjust them to the demands of a strictly regimented institutional life in the hospital or, if the therapy was efficient enough, to life in the outside world. Related to this idea, I will explore the question of who were the true beneficiaries of these therapeutic interventions into the body and mind of mental patients.

Before shock treatments, the therapeutic arsenal in mental asylums was rather meagre. The Austrian psychiatrist Julius Wagner-Jauregg started treating general paralysis of the insane (neurosyphilis) with malaria fever in 1917 (see Chapter 8), and in the 1920s the Swiss psychiatrist Jakob Klaesi (1883–1980) treated schizophrenic patients with sleep treatment (*Dauernarkose*), with poor results and relatively high risks, because it was difficult to make the patients fall asleep and then equally difficult to wake them up. Klaesi used barbiturates, which involved the risk of overdose, which in turn could mean coma and death. Perhaps the most extravagant physiological therapy of the time was the endocrine treatment of schizophrenia. This treatment was based on the speculations about schizophrenia being caused by thyroid deficiency, or by abnormalities in sex hormones. When these ideas were transferred to therapy, it meant that the patients were given pituitary glands, powders of dried thyroid glands and, most controversially, testicular or ovarian extracts. When the theory dictated that in schizophrenic patients there was lack of glandular function of the opposite sex, the male patients received ovarian extracts, while testicular extracts were administered to the female patients. Some patients were also sterilized and castrated, and an 'extract of normal glands derived either from other human beings or from animals was implanted in their body' (Hoff 1959, 7). These therapeutic experiments were a gross failure; not only did they not cure anybody, they caused unnecessary suffering and disability (castration) to the patients.

Insulin coma therapy

The first modern shock treatment was insulin coma therapy (ICT). Its invention was made possible by the extraction of purified insulin hormone that was suitable for use on human patients. This signified a breakthrough in the treatment of diabetes in the early 1920s. Psychiatric insulin treatment was developed by the Viennese physician Manfred Sakel (1900–57) in the early 1930s, even if he was not the first to use insulin in the treatment of mental illness: a number of psychiatrists had used it to combat malnutrition and anorexia in psychotic patients (Wortis 1959, 20). In his early medical career in Berlin, Sakel had treated a famous actress who suffered from drug addiction and diabetes. Once, Sakel accidentally gave his patient an overdose of insulin, which made her fall into a light coma. This happened because insulin lowers the level of glucose in the blood. If the insulin dose is large enough, it leads to pathologically low glucose levels (hypoglycemia), which in turn produces coma and sometimes convulsions. Sakel noticed that after the actress had regained consciousness she was no longer addicted to drugs. This prompted Sakel to treat all drug addict patients with large doses of insulin. What encouraged him to administer insulin to *mental* patients was an overdose of insulin that he accidentally gave to a drug addict who was also psychotic. Predictably, his patient fell into a coma, and when Sakel terminated coma by an intravenous injection of glucose, he noticed his patient's improved mental condition. Back in Vienna, Sakel became extremely interested in insulin, and he started crude insulin experiments with animals in his own kitchen. Satisfied with the results, he began to produce insulin-induced comas in his schizophrenic patients. In 1936, he reported that his 'insulin shock treatment' was efficacious in as many as 88 per cent of his patients – more than 70 per cent of the cases responded with full remission. Such a result was nothing short of phenomenal at a time when schizophrenia was typically considered an incurable illness (Valenstein 1986, 46–7).

Sakel's positive reports aroused great interest in the international psychiatric community, and soon curious psychiatrists from all over the world began to visit his clinic in Vienna. Insulin coma therapy was widely regarded as a glimmer of hope in the therapeutic darkness of mental medicine, and it was adopted with

244 The Golden Age of the asylums

great enthusiasm, although there were also sceptics who preferred the psychological approach to the disordered mind. European psychiatric thinking was predominantly organic and physiological and therefore more receptive to Sakel's method than the 'psychobiological' psychiatry prevailing in the United States (Wortis 1959, 29–32). Still, even American asylum psychiatrists were in desperate need of therapies that worked, and Sakel was invited to the United States in 1936. ICT became a standard treatment in mental health care all across the world for more than two decades.

Therapy with large doses of insulin required time, space and personnel. Therefore, comas began to be produced in specific treatment rooms which were darkened, warm and quiet. In these rooms, patients were given the appropriate doses of insulin subcutaneously, and the goal was to obtain a prolonged hypoglycemic reaction of drowsiness or sleep, often accompanied by convulsions. After one to two hours, the coma was terminated by the administration of glucose, usually via a nasogastric feeding tube into the stomach. It was common to produce at least 50 insulin comas in the patients in a period of six to eight weeks. Bigger hospitals sometimes had fully equipped insulin units and small wards that differed considerably from the other wards in that they were not noisy, smelly or disordered. One Finnish psychiatrist drew attention to this fact in 1947 when he wrote that 'as necessary as the operation room in the surgical hospital is the insulin treatment room in the mental hospital' (Kalpa 1947, 631). The length of the coma was crucial: if it was too short, the therapeutic results were poor, but if the coma could not be interrupted in time, it could result in brain damage or death. At the Pitkäniemi Hospital in Finland there were very few fatalities in the ten-year period 1937–47 (1.2 deaths per 10,000 shocks), which indicates that even if insulin therapy was risky, very few patients died as a result of complications caused by a prolonged coma (Kalpa 1947, 631). On the other hand, one large American survey from the early 1940s gave more alarming figures; about 5 per cent of the patients died (Moncrieff 2009, 29).

In a few years it became clear to the psychiatric community that the best therapeutic results were obtained in acute conditions with marked anxiety and panic reactions, and in catatonic schizophrenic excitements. Chronic patients who had been ill for more than a decade before they were given insulin shocks were beyond the pale of psychiatric help. Often, ICT had to be continued for three months before it could be determined whether the treatment was truly beneficial. What also became evident quite soon was that the cures were not permanent. Patients released from asylums relapsed over the years, and one ten-year follow-up study showed that there were no great differences between those who had received ICT and those who had not. Still, in those dark therapeutic times such remissions, sometimes lasting for years, were regarded as a major therapeutic accomplishment as well as a medical breakthrough of major importance. Sakel was honoured not only as the inventor of a new and efficient treatment, but also as the first successful advocate of a strictly physiological approach to the treatment of psychoses (Wortis 1959, 27; Shorter & Healy 2007, 11–21).

Sakel's explanation of the curative effect of ICT went something like this: in the state of induced coma, sick and defective cell connections in the brain would be disconnected. The reason for these cells becoming defective was that psychological determinants exerted a detrimental influence on the brain cells, which were prone to such defective connections due to hereditary factors. After the chemical separation of cell connections during the coma, which Sakel called 'blocking the nerve cell',

> vital processes transforming energy will be slowed down and the nerve cell will be given a chance to rest. If the damage has not been too severe, the self-restorative processes in the nerve cell will come into play and will soon accumulate sufficient strength to withstand the noxa [something that exerts a harmful effect on the body] and repair any damage done.
>
> (Sakel 1958, 208)

Sakel believed that the damaged cells were located in the part of the brain that was evolutionarily younger, as a result of which the older, more primitive parts of the brain began to dominate mental activity. ICT weakened the power of the 'primitive brain' and enabled the reactivation of the more developed part of the brain in the frontal lobes. To defend his speculative theory, Sakel claimed, quite rightly, that possible errors in the theory should not be used against ICT, because what counted was the efficiency of the treatment (Valenstein 1986, 54–6).

In 1950, the young neuropsychologist Elliot Valenstein (b. 1923) observed an insulin unit in action. The ICT ward was a dimly lit room with approximately 30 patients, who were lying in beds, tightly wrapped in sheets to prevent them from falling out of bed during the coma. Beside each bed there was a small cabinet containing a jar of sweetened orange juice or 40–50 per cent solution of glucose as well as a syringe and needles. This is how Valenstein described the treatment:

> Shortly after the injection, the patients became quiet as the insulin began to lower blood sugar and deprive the brain of energy. Some of the patients started to perspire and salivate, drooling down their chins. By the end of the first hour, the patients who had higher insulin doses had lapsed into a coma; many were tossing, rolling, and moaning, their muscles starting to twitch; and some had tremor and spasms. Here and there an arm would shoot up uncontrollably. Some of the patients started to grasp the air, reflexively. I noticed other primitive movements, including rapid licking of the lips. Patients furthest along in the treatment series, with the highest insulin doses, might be having violent convulsions. With all these people – tossing, moaning, twitching, shouting, grasping – I felt as though I were in the midst of Hell as drawn by Gustave Doré for Dante's *Divine Comedy*.
>
> (Valenstein 1986, 56–7)

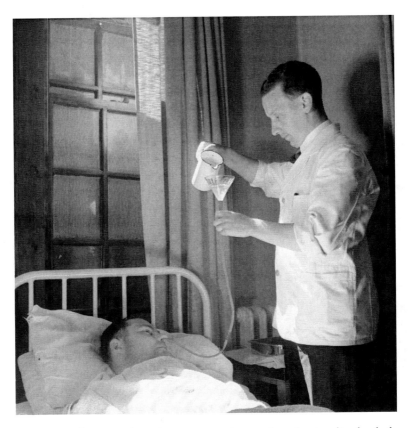

FIGURE 12.1 A male nurse gives glucose to a patient undergoing insulin shock therapy at Runwell Hospital in Essex, England, in 1943. The glucose is being poured from a jug into a funnel and down a tube which goes into the patient's nose.
Source: © Imperial War Museums (D 14313)

To understand how ICT worked, it is important to understand why it was experienced as an effective therapy in those particular geographic areas called the 'insulin unit' or 'insulin ward' (Doroshow 2007, 219–21). First of all, the ICT staff aimed to keep patients physically comfortable by creating a sense of peace, calm and safety. Second, insulin patients were given much positive attention: when they were 'woken up' by sugar solution, they were surrounded by nurses and physicians who were watching them closely, ready to offer them care and encouragement and concerned about their well-being for as long as they remained in the ward. Third, there prevailed a spirit of comradeship among the patients, who were brought together by their shared sense of having experienced something unique and dramatic in the otherwise grim and dull reality of the mental hospital. This helped create strong bonds between the staff and the patients, who were both aware of the risks involved in the somewhat unpredictable treatment. In some hospitals, insulin patients regularly gathered together to talk about their experiences, particularly about the experience of 'struggling to come back to life, really, from death's door in the coma' (Doroshow 2007, 238). In the local, closed world of the mental hospital, ICT often appeared to be an effective therapeutic intervention, especially as the mental state of patients post-coma was often different: they were calm, their behaviour was more organized and they seemed to become more like themselves.

There is no doubt that a number of patients benefited from ICT, at least temporarily. This was better than nothing at a time when there was a chronic lack of therapies that worked even in the short term. Even if many insulin patients had to return to psychiatric institutes after the therapeutic effect had disappeared, ICT brought much-needed light to the therapeutic darkness, and it cetainly increased the professional self-esteem of psychiatrists, who could feel that they did something positive for their patients. Even a promise of the partial efficiency of a specific treatment was welcomed in the asylums where the medical staff was in charge of hundreds or even thousands of patients. As the American psychiatrist Joseph Wortis reminisced of the time when ICT was introduced: 'It was a wonderful period, full of excitement, with an atmosphere of great events surrounding it. Something really new and good was coming into psychiatry' (Wortis 1959, 33).

The fall of insulin coma therapy

ICT was widely used in western mental health care from the late 1930s to the late 1950s, when it declined. One important reason for the decline was the observation that the long-term results of the treatment were uncertain and conflicting. In 1953, the young British psychiatrist Harold Bourne published a much-discussed article about 'The Insulin Myth', in which he argued that the medical effect of the insulin shock itself was negligible. The relatively beneficial short-term effects of ICT were due to its strong psychological effects on the patient, the enthusiasm of the dedicated 'insulin staff' and the positive group spirit prevailing in the insulin ward (Bourne 1953). Leading psychiatrists in Britain rushed to renounce Bourne's critique, but the damage was already done. In another article published five years later, Bourne called ICT an 'irrational and hazardous therapy' and was happy to note that 'this fallacy has been exploded in the last decade' (Bourne 1958, 1015–16). By the end of the 1950s, a number of critical studies had been published, one of them arguing that the therapeutic results of ICT were no better than those achieved by barbiturate narcosis (Ackner, Harris & Oldham 1957). In Denmark, the psychiatric community had already became disillusioned in the early 1940s, when a Danish follow-up study revealed that, four months after the termination of insulin therapy, only 4 out of 162 schizophrenic ICT patients had fully recovered. One Danish psychiatrist later recalled that the results of this study were 'an anticlimax, an ice-cold douche' to great expectations (Kragh 2010b, 359). The downfall of ICT was also precipitated by its costs – running a separate insulin unit was a labour-intensive and rather expensive activity. When psychopharmaceuticals were

248 The Golden Age of the asylums

introduced in the mid-1950s, drugs began to replace such invasive therapies as ICT and psychosurgery.

Still, as even Harold Bourne admitted, there is no doubt that ICT had at least some short-term beneficial effects; the problem was that the effects were probably psychological rather than physiological. Some psychiatrists referred to the risk of death as a therapeutic feeling. When ICT patients were induced into a coma, they fell in the twilight zone between life and death, and such an extreme experience caused them to feel a strong emotional bond to the psychiatrists and the attending nurses (Collins 1988, 94). Others surmised that the experience of fear was in itself therapeutic. When ICT patients were told that they would receive another insulin shock, such information was received as a *threat*, which induced fear and spurred (some) patients onto the path of speedy recovery (Pressman 1998, 159). This was the same explanation that had been used by the advocates of the early nineteenth-century shock treatments: an instigation of fear and terror has therapeutic effects on the insane. It has also been conjectured that the prolonged hypoglycaemia and anoxia (an absence of oxygen supply to an organ or a tissue) produced by insulin coma and convulsions may have caused slight brain damage. One psychiatrist observed in the early 1950s that ICT patients appeared demented and confused for days after the coma. Or, ICT may have worked simply through a placebo effect.

'As if you were burned by an invisible fire': convulsive shock therapy

Soon after Manfred Sakel had introduced ICT, his Hungarian neurologist colleague Ladislas von Meduna (1896–1964) invented another type of shock treatment known as convulsive shock therapy or Cardiazol treatment. It was based on Meduna's observations of the slight differences between the brains of schizophrenics and epileptics. From this observation, Meduna drew a contested conclusion that there prevails a mutual antagonism between schizophrenia and epilepsy: epileptics could not become schizophrenics, and vice versa. Strangely enough, Meduna's unwarranted claim did not arouse much opposition among his colleagues, even though many asylum doctors knew very well that one and the same patient could suffer from both epilepsy and schizophrenia. Still, Meduna's speculations were accepted at least partly because epileptic convulsions were widely regarded as antagonistic to schizophrenia. Meduna believed that the epileptic convulsions themselves might have therapeutic effects on schizophrenics (von Meduna 1937, 7).

In 1934, Meduna introduced Cardiazol shock treatment to produce epileptic convulsions in his schizophrenic patients. Cardiazol (Metrazol in the United States) was a synthetic preparation that was used as a circulatory and respiratory stimulant and that in high doses caused convulsions. After treating a handful of patients with Cardiazol, Meduna did not waste time in declaring that he had discovered a new psychiatric therapy. Meduna's superior at the Brain Research Institute in Budapest thought his treatment was nothing but humbug, but Meduna was obstinate. In 1935 he published a report in which he claimed that of his first 26 patients treated with convulsive therapy, ten had completely recovered. When his Hungarian colleagues published similar, very encouraging reports the following year, central European psychiatrists began to try the method. Like Sakel, Meduna was a tireless promoter of his therapeutic invention, and, also like Sakel, he moved to the United States, where his method became widely known in the late 1930s. Cardiazol appeared to be an effective short-term treatment for acute catatonic schizophrenia, and it was later claimed that Cardiazol convulsions were also effective in the treatment of involutional melancholia (McCrae 2006, 72–6). For a few years in the late 1930s and the early 1940s, Cardiazol treatment was widely used in western psychiatry, and more than 1,000 articles were published on this method.

An uncomfortable problem with Cardiazol treatment was that many patients hated it. This was because the injection produced a violent convulsion, which lasted about a minute. When the tonic contractions began, patients lost consciousness, but between injection and seizure there was about a ten-second period of intense purgatory during which patients often felt extreme anxiety and fear of death. During the seizure itself, clonic jerks and spasms quickly came on, the skin turned blue, the pupils would widen and incontinence was common. After about 40 seconds of convulsions, patients fell into a comatose sleep for ten minutes or so. One psychoanalyst aptly called Cardiazol therapy 'a violent thunderstorm' (McCrae 2006, 81). Although the risk of death was small, convulsions could be physically risky, because they caused severe stress on the musculoskeletal system. Extreme contractions could cause joint dislocations, bone fractures and obstruction of the blood vessels. Another risk was that the epileptic condition did not end, but lingered on (this was called *status epilepticus*). If the treatment continued for a longer period of time, there was an additional risk of lasting cognitive impairment – it could impair the mental functioning of patients. As this risk became known to psychiatrists, the administration of Cardiazol became more class specific: it was considered less risky for uneducated people who did not have to rely on intellectual function in their work (McCrae 2006, 78). The same criterion was applied to the selection of suitable patients to psychosurgical treatment.

In a letter to his family, a Danish male patient described what happened about ten seconds after he had received the Cardiazol injection:

> [It] is as if you are pulled out of yourself and into another world [. . .] It is utterly unbearable and quite impossible to get out of. [. . .] The room you are lying in begins to look like Hell, and it is as if you are burned by an invisible fire.
>
> (Kragh 2010b, 351)

The patient described the experience as very scary. Presumably, this description was too much for the medical staff, who confiscated the letter.

Patients did not have any recollections of the convulsions, but what they could not forget was the ten-second purgatory after the injection of Cardiazol. If the dose was too small to produce the seizure, it still managed to produce anxious

250 The Golden Age of the asylums

tension in the patient. No wonder patients did not eagerly line up to receive such shocks, and there are stories of nurses and attendants chasing terrified patients running down the corridor and trying to escape the treatment table. Some patients tried to escape the injection by 'jumping through the ward window, climbing on to the hospital roof, and suicidal acts' (McCrae 2006, 79). One Danish patient said that, just before the convulsions started, she felt as if 'fire was spreading through my entire body'. Another patient felt that her 'brain was trembling' (Kragh 2010b, 352). Some patients compared the treatment to electrocution, others described the experience as worse than death. When psychiatrists considered the curative aspect of the treatment, some suggested that the fear and severity of seizure had a therapeutic psychological impact on patients, who struggled to behave in a more organized and rational manner in order to avoid further exposure to the dreadful Cardiazol treatment (McCrae 2006, 85). Still, there also were patients who reacted positively to this treatment. One female patient in the Danish state mental hospital in Vordingborg wrote in a letter to her family that her condition had been improved, because it 'helps to get injections every second day, it clears up my thoughts so well'. Sometimes the staff at Vordingborg received letters from grateful patients who had been discharged and who appreciated the treatment they had received at the hospital (Kragh 2010b, 355–6).

By the early 1950s, Cardiazol treatment was more or less replaced by electroconvulsive therapy. Using electricity rather than an injection made the production of epileptic convulsions easier, more efficient and less risky. Some psychiatrists and mental hospitals abandoned Cardiazol because patients had an intense aversion to it, others because there was a risk of spinal fractures. Nobody could come up with a satisfactory explanation of the usefulness of Cardiazol. What became evident was that, like electroconvulsive therapy, Cardiazol therapy was moderately successful in the treatment of severe depression. But Meduna was wrong in assuming that epilepsy and schizophrenia were somehow antagonistic illnesses. He later turned his attention to carbon dioxide treatment, a therapeutic dead end if ever there was one.

Shocking the mind: electroconvulsive therapy

Treatment with electricity started in the second half of the eighteenth century, especially in the treatment of melancholia. A century later, mild electric shocks were given to neurasthenic patients whose 'nervous battery' had been exhausted. George Beard (1839–83), father of neurasthenia, wrote a 600-page tome on the therapeutic application of electricity together with his colleague A.D. Rockwell (*A Practical Treatise on the Medical and Surgical Uses of Electricity*, 1871). In the book, direct current was described as soothing and alternating current as stimulating treatment. In the late 1930s, these soft forms of electrotherapy were replaced by the much more violent and dramatic electroshock.

Electroconvulsive therapy (ECT) was the third widely used form of shock therapy, and the only one still in use today. ECT was invented by two Italian psychiatrists, Ugo Cerletti (1877–1963) and his young colleague Lucio Bini (1908–64) at Rome University. Like Meduna, who invented Cardiazol treatment, Cerletti was interested in epileptic fits and especially in the speculative idea that in extreme stress situations the body produces so-called 'acro-amines'. Cerletti became convinced that, as a response to the stress of an epileptic convulsion, this 'vitalizing substance' had a therapeutic effect on the mentally ill. He and Bini decided to produce acro-amines by giving electroshocks to animals. They started their experiment by placing electrodes in the mouth and rectum of dogs. While it was easy to produce epileptic fits, these early electroshocks had one unpleasant 'side effect': many of these dogs died of cardiac arrest. Bini realized that deaths were not produced by seizures but by the electric current running through the heart. When they placed both electrodes on the sides of the head, the animals survived. Meanwhile, Cerletti (or Bini and his assistants) visited a municipal slaughter house in Rome, where he noticed that, before their necks were slashed, the pigs were given electric shocks, which made them lose consciousness without killing them. Cerletti and Bini concluded that electric currents had to be of very short duration – about half a second – and the dose had to be large enough without being fatal so that it would produce a shock without damaging the brain cells (Valenstein 1986, 50–1; Shorter & Healy 2007, 32–7).

By spring 1938, Bini had constructed a machine that produced electroshocks. He and Cerletti were given an opportunity to test the machine on a human guinea pig when the Roman police found a middle-aged man walking around the central railway station in a state of confusion. Deemed psychotic, he was brought to Cerletti's clinic. According to the official story, Cerletti and Bini decided to use electroshock on this anonymous patient after assessing him. Their curious and doubting colleagues watched as they administered a 70-volt discharge for 0.2 seconds to the patient. The man jumped on his bed and his muscles tensed for a very short time. Instead of losing consciousness, the patient started to sing at the top of his voice. It was clear to Cerletti and Bini that the current had been too low, and they decided to give another electroshock to the man the following day. When the patient heard what the doctors around him were saying, he exclaimed: 'Not another one! It will kill me!' (*Non una seconda. Mortifiera!*). Upon hearing these comprehensible words, Cerletti decided, against the opinion of his colleagues, to repeat the electric shock. The electrodes were reapplied, and a 110 volt discharge was sent through the patient for 0.5 seconds. At first, a short cramping of the muscles occurred, and then, after a brief pause, an epileptic fit followed. Nervously, Cerletti and his colleagues witnessed a gradual awakening:

> The patient sat up of his own accord, looked about him calmly with a vague smile, as though asking what was expected of him. I asked him 'what has been happening to you?' He answered, with no more gibberish: 'I don't know; perhaps I have been asleep'.

> (Cerletti 1950, 90–1)

252 The Golden Age of the asylums

The patient received about ten additional electroshocks over a two-month period before he was released from the hospital in complete remission. However, what Cerletti and Bini failed to disclose was that the second shock was not given immediately after the first one, but more than a week later. Besides, the patient did not fully recover but had to be readmitted to a mental hospital in Milan two years later (Shorter & Healy 2007, 37–43). Such a concealment of therapeutic failures and, conversely, an exaggeration of the therapeutic efficiency have been very typical in the history of psychiatry. A convenient whitewashing of clinical evidence has been used to portray a rosy picture of psychiatry when the reality has been much more complicated and often disappointing (Valenstein 1986, 49–50). It is easy to see why electroshocks did not cure the first, apparently schizophrenic patient: it was later discovered that severely depressed, non-schizophrenic patients responded most positively to ECT.

Cheap and easy to apply, ECT became a widely used psychiatric treatment in the 1940s, and has been a part of the therapeutic arsenal ever since. For decades, electroshocks have been given mostly to severely depressed patients whose mental pain could not be alleviated by drugs or psychotherapy. The maximum voltage used has usually been 170 volts, which produces an epileptic seizure lasting from 30 seconds to 1 minute. Despite its dubious reputation, the therapeutic benefits of ECT in severe depression are indisputable. Yet those indisputable therapeutic benefits remain, in turn, problematic. One patient who was happy to receive electroshocks was a Finnish novelist who suffered from manic-depression in the early 1990s.

> Miracle happened right away: after a few electroshocks, the Great Unknown pulled the sword out of my heart. It was simply no longer there. [. . .] Nowadays ECT is given to patients when they are anesthesized. That's why it is so wonderful to receive it. It is a dream.
>
> (Sirola 1996, 72–3; my translation)

As a young woman, Sirola's mother had also received electroshocks. Obviously, his mental pain was such that he was grateful for a treatment that alleviated his agony, at least temporarily. Unfortunately, the gifted writer committed suicide five years after writing these words. What is also unfortunate is that the beneficial effects of electroshock vanish in a few weeks. Some overzealous psychiatrists have applied ECT too frequently, while others have used it as a punishment to recalcitrant patients. Like insulin shocks and convulsion therapy, ECT may cause a mild and transient brain injury, which manifests itself as a sedated or calm behaviour, which in turn is misinterpreted as clinical improvement (Moncrieff 2009, 34–40). The most common adverse effect of ECT is the impairment of short-term memory, which is usually temporary, but in some cases it may lead to more permanent memory problems. There are profoundly conflicting opinions about the treatment, and the jury is still out on the effects of ECT. What is indisputable is that many seriously depressed people are willing to pay the price of mild cognitive impairment for finding even a temporary relief from their agony. (For a partisan approach to ECT, see Shorter & Healy 2007.)

I will give the last word to William Moore, an American mental patient who became a civil rights activist and a victim of a racist killing in Mississippi (see Chapter 13). When he was in a mental hospital in the early 1950s, William was treated with electroshocks, although he was diagnosed with schizophrenia, not with depression. Nevertheless, William had a relaxed attitude towards ECT. When the doctor administering the shocks told him 'we'll knock those [delusional] ideas out of your head', William said to himself:

> You think so, doctor? Well, I don't want them to be knocked out, because they are true ideas. Why, I bet you couldn't knock them out with a dozen shock treatments! Which turned out to be true, too.
>
> (Moore 1955, 10)

William was not a stranger to insulin shocks either:

> Everyone should take insulin treatment. Then they will know beforehand what all my life I have wondered about – how it feels to die, what it is like to pass from this life into the next.
>
> (Moore 1955, 269)

William knew what he was talking about – he received 70 insulin shocks.

Pacifying the wards

Sooner or later it became apparent to all involved that shock methods did not cure patients. Still, there is no denying the significant aspect of these treatments, namely the fact that, in some cases, they calmed the wards and pacified the often restless and agitated, occasionally also aggressive and combative, patients. After the treatment, some patients became more interested in external reality, treated their family members in a friendlier manner and, in general, tended to behave in a more rational and organized manner – at least for a period of time. When inmates became more manageable, it improved the therapeutic atmosphere of the wards and relieved the workload of the medical staff and the attendants. One American psychiatrist put it aptly in 1943 when he wrote that 'one may question whether shock treatments do any good to the patients, but there can be no doubt that they have done an enormous amount of good to psychiatry' (Pressman 1998, 191).

The pacification of wards was seen in the not unproblematic statistics: violence in hospitals began to decline after the introduction of shock treatments. Sometimes these methods worked so well to pacify patients and make them docile that they were discharged from the hospital, and they often improved the patient's condition at least temporarily. Psychiatrists could claim that they had efficient interventions in their therapeutic tool box. To some, it was close to a miracle to

254 The Golden Age of the asylums

see delusional and anxious patients calming down and behaving in a responsive and lucid manner. As one relieved Finnish psychiatrist noted in 1947: 'There is no longer any need for therapeutic nihilism' (Kalpa 1947, 632).

In addition to shock treatments, another and more sinister therapy entered the psychomedical scene in the 1930s: lobotomy.

The introduction of psychosurgery

The first so-called psychosurgical operations were conducted in the latter half of the nineteenth century. Early gynaecologists in particular attempted to cure nervous illnesses through surgical operations, mainly on women, whose illnesses the medical authorities readily attributed to the 'female nervous temperament'. The first gynaecologists won medical attention with their surgical interventions, starting with ovariotomy or 'castration' (the removal of one or both of the patient's ovaries), which became a cornerstone of gynaecological surgery (Daly 1991). Other, more extreme interventions into the 'hysterogenic zones' had such technical names as 'clitorectomy' and 'vaginal hysterectomy', and they amounted to a cauterization or outright extirpation of the clitoris, ovaries or womb. Surgical treatment was also recommended as a solution to masturbation (Fishman 1982). The surgical frenzy of nineteenth-century gynaecology constitutes a dark chapter in the annals of modern medicine. Still, it is even more painful to read about a certain Dr Cotton and his mad surgical operations on his mental patients.

Henry Cotton (1876–1933), an American psychiatrist, is a protagonist and sort of anti-hero in the sociologist Andrew Scull's book *Madhouse* (2005). Cotton's psychiatric obsession was the idea that mental disease was caused by local infections wreaking havoc in other parts of the body. Influenced by cutting-edge bacteriological research, the doctrine of focal sepsis asserted that chronic but hidden infections in various organs released toxins into the bloodstream which could reach other organs, including the brain. Cotton reasoned that if the site of infection was cut out, the cause of the disease was removed and the patient became well. In itself, the doctrine of focal sepsis was not extreme or unscientific in early twentieth-century medicine. What made Cotton's clinical work senseless was his blind determination to continue on the surgical path regardless of the disastrous consequences of his treatment. In short, his *furor therapeuticus* destroyed the lives of many of his patients. As the superintendent of Trenton State Hospital in New Jersey from 1907 onwards, he was given almost unlimited power to realize his therapeutic vision.

Cotton started out by extracting the allegedly infected teeth of his patients in 1916. After the removal of their teeth, hundreds of patients at Trenton could no longer speak clearly or even eat properly. Next, Cotton began to remove diseased tonsils, and to look for gastroenteritis by taking X-rays of his patients. But far worse was yet to come. Together with his assistants, Cotton began to extend his 'programme of defocalization' by operating on the colon, appendix, thyroid and stomach. These abdominal surgeries and other risky operations were often fatal to the patients: the mortality rate was between 25 and 30 per cent – at least a quarter of his surgical patients died! Typically, the cause of death was peritonitis, an inflammation of the peritoneum (the thin tissue that lines the inner wall of the abdomen and covers most of the abdominal organs). Female patients were especially prone to become targets of Cotton's surgical assault. Almost 78 per cent of the patients undergoing colectomy (colon surgery) were women; of surgical treatment of peritonitis as many as 83 per cent.

Apparently, the great majority of physicians either accepted Cotton's 'innovative' methods despite their risks or criticized them only in closed collegial circles without any intention of condemning his operations in public. When the Board of Trenton Hospital finally commissioned a medical inspection of Cotton's therapeutic results, the commissioner came to the horrifying conclusion that of 309 patients whose colons had been operated on (colectomies), no less than 45 per cent (138 patients) died and one-third were still in hospital. The most damning finding for Cotton was that the majority of deaths were the direct result of botched surgical operations. All in all, approximately one-third of the unfortunate victims of Cotton's gross medical malpractice died. Yet, even this report failed to create a stir in the medical community; this horror story came to an end in 1933 when Cotton died of a heart attack (Scull 2005, 264–5). A local newspaper wrote a moving obituary to Cotton:

> Thousands of people who have suffered mental affliction owe [Dr Cotton] an enduring debt of gratitude for . . . displacing confusion and despair with hope and confidence. [All must lament the loss of] this great pioneer whose humanitarian influence was, and will continue to be, of such monumental proportions.
>
> (Scull 2005, 270)

If this was the psychosurgical scene in 1933, what could possibly make such a 'dementia psychiatrica' more respectable to the medical community and less fatal to the patients?

The invention of modern psychosurgery

In 1935, the Portuguese neurologist Egas Moniz (1874–1955) attended a neurological congress in London. One of the presentations there was given by the American physiologist Carlyle Jacobsen, who together with his colleague John Fulton at Yale University had conducted psychosurgical experiments with two female chimpanzees, Becky and Lucy. Fulton and Jacobsen had noticed that Becky and Lucy had distinctly different temperaments; Becky was easily frustrated and had temper tantrums during learning tests, while Lucy's character was calmer and emotionally stable. On the basis of this observation, Fulton's group decided to make a radical surgical experiment: they removed the frontal lobes of both Becky's and Lucy's brains in order to see how the removal would affect their problem-solving capacities. What they discovered surprised them. The operation did not seem to lower

256 The Golden Age of the asylums

the apes' intelligence, but their responses to learning tests changed dramatically. The formerly 'neurotic' Becky began to display more controlled behaviour, while the formerly serene Lucy lost her temper much more easily than was the case before the operation. Apparently, this presentation made Moniz think long and hard (El-Hai 2005, 97; Valenstein 1986, 77–9).

Back in Lisbon, Moniz began psychosurgical experiments with mental patients sent to him from the local state mental hospital. Moniz did not go so far as to remove the frontal lobes of his patients. Instead, he hired a neurosurgeon and attempted the technique first on the brain of a cadaver. Then they began to use a method called 'leucotomy' ('cutting white matter'), in which they drilled two holes in the top of the patient's skull directly over the frontal lobes. Moniz started to use a surgical instrument he named 'leucotome', which was used to cut 1-centimetre-wide cores of brain tissue (white neural fibres) in the area between the frontal lobes and other regions of the brain. Soon after the first, allegedly successful, leucotomies, Moniz named his therapeutic innovation 'psychosurgery' (Pressman 1998, 48–50; El-Hai 2005, 101–2).

Moniz hurried to report on his first 20 leucotomized patients at the meeting of the Academy of Medicine in Paris in spring 1936. According to Moniz, more than a third of the patients were cured, another third were helped and only 30 per cent remained the same after leucotomy. Once again, the inventor of a psychiatric treatment painted an over-optimistic picture of the efficiency of his therapy. Moniz admitted that leucotomy did not remove hallucinations and delusions, but he argued that his method alleviated the emotional symptoms and muted the patients' emotional responses to their psychotic symptoms. Leucotomized patients became calmer and more composed, which enabled their discharge from hospital. Moniz also claimed that leucotomy did not affect intelligence, but he did not give any evidence for his assertion (El-Hai 2005, 101–2). Vigorously promoting his new method through articles, presentations and a book that was published simultaneously in several languages (*Prefrontal Leucotomy*, 1937), the international medical community became aware of Moniz's psychosurgical innovation within a few years.

Walter Freeman, the Ambassador of Lobotomy

The American neurologist Walter Freeman (1895–1972) was so impressed by Moniz's initial reports that he promptly decided to try leucotomy on his own patients. From the mid-1930s to the mid-1960s he did more than anyone else to promote psychosurgery. When he first tried Moniz's method together with the young neurosurgeon James Watts (1904–94) in the autumn of 1936, Freeman was an ambitious Professor of Neurology and Chairman of the Neurology Department at the medical school of George Washington University in Washington, DC. He was an energetic go-getter who had little patience with time-consuming psychotherapy, clinical trials or ethical aspects of clinical work. Well disposed to somatic treatments and biological theories of insanity, he saw psychosurgery as a very efficient and dramatic therapeutic intervention that appealed to his medical vision as well as to his burning ambition to find a psychiatric treatment that worked.

To differentiate their method from leucotomy, Freeman and Watts introduced the term 'lobotomy' from the ancient Greek words *lobos* ('lobe' of the brain) and *tome* ('cut, slice'). In contrast to Moniz, who targeted the white matter (the tissue through which messages pass between different areas of grey matter within the nervous system), Freeman's and Watt's lobotomy was targeted on the frontal lobes. Nonetheless, Freeman had a high regard for Moniz, and he nominated him for the Nobel Prize in Medicine or Physiology in the 1940s. He and a group of Portuguese and Brazilian physicians achieved their goal in 1949 when Moniz won the Nobel Prize 'for his discovery of the therapeutic value of leucotomy in certain psychoses' (El Hai 2005, 226–7; The Nobel Foundation 1949).

By the time Moniz received the Nobel Prize, it was Freeman who had become the world's leading advocate of psychosurgery. Freeman was careful not to make claims that were too extravagant about the method, and instead of declaring that he and Watts cured their psychotic patients with lobotomy, he made the more modest claim that lobotomy relieved the emotional symptoms, such as anxiety, nervous tension, apprehension and insomnia. Quite surprisingly, it could also alleviate intractable pain. In Freeman's own words, it is as if the 'emotional nucleus of the psychosis is removed, the "sting" of the disorder, is drawn' (Freeman & Watts 1950, xiii). Startlingly, a number of lobotomy patients told Freeman that 'they accepted the operation in the hope that it would kill them' (Freeman & Watts 1950, 113).

After a few years, Freeman and Watts began to use local anaesthesia when they operated on patients who were less psychotic. In other words, such patients were awake when their brains were operated on. During the operation, Freeman and Watts talked with the patients to determine when the instrument had cut the brain tissue deep enough. When this happened, the patients' utterances became more confused, or they became silent. Occasionally they were asked to say their prayers, which did not necessarily put the usually rather highly strung patients at ease. As Freeman and Watts wrote in their book *Psychosurgery* (1942/1950), many patients were already on the verge of panic at the beginning of the operation when the holes were drilled. This was probably due to the actual pressure on the skull and to the grinding sound that is as distressing, or more so, than the drilling of a tooth. During this part of the procedure the mouth is dry, the heart beats rapidly and the hands are cold, all signalling an emotional tension of which the patients themselves are quite aware (Freeman & Watts 1950, 115).

Sometimes the patient found exactly the right words for the moment. When Freeman and Watts asked an 'extremely serious-minded individual' what was going through his mind, the patient replied after a long pause: 'A knife' (Freeman & Watts 1950, 116).

Below is an excerpt from a discussion between Freeman and a male schizophrenic patient who had tried to commit suicide (he thought he had syphilis and that he was being followed by the FBI).

Freeman: How do you feel?
Patient: Not too bad, Doc. I feel like I was slit in two . . .

[later]

Freeman:	What is happening now?
Patient:	Don't they believe in this stuff? God, that hurts!
Freeman:	What's going on?
Patient:	I'm being operated on. Doctor Watts, isn't it?
Freeman:	Any comments?
Patient:	Only that it hurts. Nothing much to do about it.
Freeman:	They're sewing up. Are you glad it's over?
Patient:	Uh-huh. That's the end of it – whew!

(Freeman & Watts 1950, 127–30)

For weeks after the standard prefrontal lobotomy, patients resembled helpless children. After this initial postoperative condition of relative confusion, patients were supposed to get better and, ultimately, to be able to take care of themselves or even return to their former occupations (Freeman & Watts 1950, 191). Such progress was sometimes indeed possible in the case of depressed or anxious patients, whose symptoms were alleviated by the operation. Psychotic patients fared considerably worse, and it dawned upon Freeman and Watts that lobotomy worked best for patients with emotional afflictions, such as obsessive tension states, but it was much more difficult to help schizophrenic patients with lobotomy. Some patients were operated on twice or even three times. Freeman and Watts estimated in 1950 that 'one-third of the patients recover, one-third are improved, and one-third are unimproved' (Freeman & Watts 1950, 202). If we regard these figures as reliable, then it means that two-thirds of the patients were helped by lobotomy. This sounds like a great achievement, but it is very much dependent on how they defined 'recovery' and 'improvement'. As one psychiatric opponent of lobotomy asked, 'is the quieting of the patient a cure?' He went on to warn that lobotomies 'should be stopped before we dement too large a section of the population' (El-Hai 2005, 211).

Still, there is no doubt that lobotomy did help some patients (on the question of why patients and their family members came to accept this invasive treatment, see Raz 2013). What could be the explanation for even such a mild therapeutic success? Freeman and Watts found it in the connection between thalamus and the frontal lobes. Today, the thalamus is seen as a kind of switchboard of information, but in the heyday of lobotomy it was regarded as an organ that regulated emotions. Freeman surmised that, in mentally ill people, the thalamus exerted too much control over their frontal lobes and thereby over their higher mental functions, especially intelligence and will. When the connections between the thalamus and the frontal lobes were severed, claimed Freeman, the supremacy of emotion over reason was broken (El Hai 2005, 169). This was sheer speculation, but at least it offered a plausible justification for inflicting brain damage.

Freeman and Watts as well as other pioneers of lobotomy quickly realized that the operation could cause irreparable damage to the brain. The behaviour of lobotomized patients could become uncontrolled or uninhibited, their mental state could betray childish cheerfulness or they had motor disturbances of the limbs. They could also lose their initiative and judgement and behave inappropriately on social occasions. Worst of all, lobotomized patients lost their creativity and their imagination went dull. As Freeman and Watts pointed out in *Psychosurgery*, 'in order to relieve a confirmed schizophrenic prefrontal lobotomy has to be done far back enough so that practically the whole imaginative life of the individual has to be sacrificed in order to get rid of the pathologic fantasy'. The personality of lobotomized patients tended to become shallow, and their creative capacity was ruined, but the 'prerequisite for success [. . .] is destruction of fantasy life' (Freeman & Watts 1950, 131, 236–8). In short, lobotomy patients became individuals whose souls had been amputated, as the Swedish psychiatrist (and Freeman's friend) Gösta Rylander memorably put it.

The post-lobotomy patients often lived their lives without tears of joy or sorrow, without the ups and downs and the mood swings that characterize human life. Such a mental amputation was a heavy price indeed, but many patients and their families were glad to get rid of symptoms that could make their life sheer torment to all concerned. After the operation, many patients were relieved of their mental pain, or at least they no longer *cared* about their pain. And what was often a relief to the family and the community was that the impulsive, unpredictable patients became effortless and obedient, more 'adjusted' to the demands of society.

As the years went by, Freeman became increasingly frustrated by the limits of standard prefrontal lobotomy, which was too expensive and impractical for state mental institutions to be a really widely used and effective form of treatment. Furthermore, the operation involved risks to the patients – too many operations ended in a failure of some degree as the patient's personality changed and their health deteriorated. In his unpublished autobiography, Freeman admitted that 'it took a number of dramatic instances of severe personality downgrading in well-preserved patients to make me realize that the standard or radical lobotomy was too damaging' (El Hai 2005, 179). In order to avoid the pitfalls of standard prefrontal lobotomy, in 1946 Freeman developed a simplified surgical procedure called 'transorbital lobotomy'. What was innovative in this method was that there was no longer any need for neurosurgeons or operation rooms, because psychiatrists could perform the operation in their own offices. This is how Freeman described the new, cost-effective method to his son: transorbital lobotomy.

> consists of knocking them [patients] out with a shock [electroshock] and while they are under the "anesthetic" thrusting an ice pick up between the eyeball and the eyelid through the roof of the orbit, actually into the frontal lobe of the brain, and making the lateral cut by swinging the thing from side to side.
>
> (El Hai 2005, 184)

260 The Golden Age of the asylums

This 'ice pick' lobotomy lasted for less than ten minutes, and, compared to the time-consuming standard lobotomy, it was less risky to the patients, who left Freeman's office with just swollen eyes and a temporary headache. Electric anaesthesia guaranteed that the patients usually did not remember anything about their pre-operation state of fear and anxiety. Freeman admitted that, for all its advantages, the procedure was 'definitely a disagreeable thing to watch' (El-Hai 2005, 184). His neurosurgeon-partner James Watts disliked transorbital lobotomy and ended his collaboration with Freeman, although he himself performed nearly 30 transorbital lobotomies in the years to come (and they remained on good terms on a personal level).

Whereas standard lobotomy was in principle reserved as a treatment of 'last resort' when all other treatments had failed, Freeman conceived of transorbital lobotomy as an early intervention aimed at preventing the worsening of moderate symptoms into severe psychotic ones. From 1946 until his last operation in 1967, Freeman single-handedly performed 2,400 operations, either in his office or during his many travels across the United States when he visited mainly state mental hospitals and, as if working on an assembly line, operated on a number of patients in a row. Once he operated on 25 female patients in one day – this must be the world record for the number of brain surgeries performed by a single physician in a single day. Freeman claimed that no less than 85 per cent of his lobotomized private patients recovered, and of the more severely ill mental hospital patients almost 50 per cent got better. These are truly impressive results, but we should bear in mind that the targets of transorbital lobotomy were mostly patients with affective disorders – depression, anxiety, nervousness – and what characterizes the symptoms of such afflictions is that they often disappear in time, even without any clinical intervention. It was a much more formidable challenge to successfully treat chronic and severely ill psychotics, who were initially the targets of leucotomy and standard lobotomy.

One explanation for Freeman's preference for transorbital lobotomy was his inclination to 'show off' his talents and his desire to receive attention from the media as well as from his medical peers. In 1948, a student nurse watched Freeman perform a transorbital lobotomy at a state hospital in Virginia. After several operations, the Grand Lobotomist, wearing no gown, mask or gloves,

> enlivened the demonstration by cutting nerve fibers on both sides of the brain simultaneously. 'Then [recalled the nurse decades later], he looked up at us, smiling. I thought I was seeing a circus act. He moved both hands back and forth in unison, cutting the brain identically behind each eye. It astonished me that he was so gay, so high, so "up".' Derian [the student] recalled the sequence of events as a living nightmare, a deeply disturbing performance.
>
> (El-Hai 2005, 245)

Freeman also operated on children, one of whom was the 12-year-old boy, Howard Dully, who years later as a middle-aged man started to investigate

Freeman's psychosurgical activities and his own transorbital lobotomy (Dully 2007). Children were also operated on in Nordic countries and probably elsewhere too; in Denmark, for example, at least 20 children were lobotomized, some of them mentally disabled children between the ages of six and eight (Kragh 2010a). In Finland, too, a number of mentally disabled children were lobotomized (Salminen, forthcoming).

To Freeman's consternation, by the early 1960s the heyday of lobotomy was definitely over. New psychiatric drugs pacified the patients much more quickly, cheaply and safely than lobotomy, and there were an ever-increasing number of follow-up studies revealing that psychosurgery had produced a great number of more or less mentally handicapped patients. Also, the 1960s was a decade of cultural radicalism and anti-psychiatry, and such invasive methods as lobotomy began to look increasingly outdated, barbarous and shameful. The popularity of psychoanalytic psychiatry in the United States further undermined lobotomy's reputation, particularly among academic medical circles. Last but not least, the development of neuroscience contested the simple idea championed by Freeman, according to which emotional life is regulated by the connections between the thalamus and the frontal lobes. It became increasingly evident to the researchers that the brain is not a two-stroke engine but a very complicated network of nerve cells and synapses, and that the regulation of emotions is located in all of the limbic system, which is a complex set of brain structures that lies on both sides of the thalamus. From the 1940s onwards, neurosurgeons developed more refined stereotactic operations, which made it possible to locate the exact coordinates in the cerebral cortex more accurately. What is ironic in this context is that it was Freeman's and his colleagues' psychosurgery that initially provided the researchers with the necessary knowledge about the functions of the limbic system, which helped neuroscience to establish itself as a scientific specialty.

Freeman's career as a lobotomist came to an end in 1967, when he operated on a woman who had already been his patient twice, on her own initiative. This time the operation failed, and the patient died of a haemorrhage. Soon afterwards, the hospital refused to continue Freeman's operating room privileges. Ill with cancer, disappointed and marginalized by the medical community that had once revered him (albeit not without reservations), Freeman died at the age of 76 in 1972 (El-Hai 2005, 292–304). Since his death, most psychiatrists have wanted to erase his memory, and consign lobotomy to the Orwellian memory hole to be speedily forgotten.

All in all, more than 40,000 lobotomies were performed in the United States between 1936 and 1967. The golden age of lobotomy was the approximately ten-year period between the end of World War II and the introduction of modern psychiatric drugs in the mid-1950s. In Europe, lobotomy was used in most countries, and some individual enthusiasts played a crucial role in promoting the method as well as using it themselves. One such enthusiast was the London-based British doctor Wylie McCissock, who had performed more than 1,300 leucotomies by 1950 – more than Freeman or any other lobotomist at that point (El-Hai 2005, 219).

262 The Golden Age of the asylums

In Japan, lobotomy became quite fashionable after World War II, and the method was used on a large scale in South America (Brazil and Venezuela), Canada, New Zealand and the Nordic countries. In the post-war German psychiatric community, wary of the international condemnation of the unspeakable atrocities of the Nazi medical experimenters, lobotomy did not win approval. In the Soviet Union, psychosurgery was banned soon after the creation of the 1947 Nuremberg Code of Medical Ethics.

Wanted: easy-to-handle patients

What can be concluded from the history of shock methods and psychosurgery is that the mental health care system was geared towards adjusting patients to institutional life in the asylums. With the introduction of these somatic treatments in the 1930s, the idea that well-adjusted patients could be discharged from the hospital brought much-needed hope to the asylum psychiatrists as well as to the hospital boards and policy makers. To keep people, mainly adults, in a hospital, sometimes for years, meant that these people were unproductive citizens and a heavy burden to society in that they did not work or study, and somebody had to pay their hospital bills. In Europe, it was usually the state or municipalities that bankrolled mental hospitals, and in the United States there were both private and public hospitals, the latter owned by the states.

To understand the widespread use of treatments that in our opinion were brutal and unnecessary, we need to be aware of the acute problem of overcrowding and therapeutic impotence that haunted institutional mental health care in all of the western world. Mental hospitals often resembled human warehouses that stored the insane, the elderly, the demented, the misfits (often diagnosed as psychopaths) and people who suffered from non-psychiatric afflictions, such as epilepsy, alcoholism and drug addiction. Restless, noisy and violent patients were particularly difficult to manage before the introduction of modern psychiatric drugs. And it seems to be the case that these 'difficult' patients were more easily singled out for psychosurgery, which was known to change the personality in a way that made the management of these patients easier. What probably appealed to psychiatrists, superintendents and hospital boards was the fact that lobotomized patients could often be discharged from hospital. A more rapid turnover of patients both reduced the costs and demonstrated to the world that mental health professionals were able to cure their patients or at least to alleviate their symptoms to the extent that they could live with their illness independently, even if they could not earn their own living. In psychiatry, social recovery was a therapeutic achievement in itself.

Patients who were selected for lobotomy were often restless, disorderly and difficult. Hence, it was not so much the diagnosis itself which dictated who was going to be operated on, but how the schizophrenic or psychoneurotic patient behaved. To be sure, the majority of lobotomized patients were schizophrenic, but among the patients in this diagnostic group there was a wide variety of symptoms and behaviours. 'Difficult' schizophrenics, who for example soiled themselves with faeces or disturbed other patients and the staff, were probably much more likely to become candidates for psychosurgery than the quiet, withdrawn or more organized patients. There is no doubt that, to some extent, psychosurgery made the wards quieter and the daily routines of the staff easier. The discharge of lobotomized patients as recovered or improved also made hospital beds available for new patients. In some cases the patients themselves wanted to have psychosurgery, or their relatives suggested the operation. Obviously, such 'bottom-up' initiatives were much more common in the early years of lobotomy when very little was known about the long-term consequences of the operation.

In the mid-twentieth century, there were patients from all social classes in mental hospitals, and psychosurgeries were performed on unskilled workers, middle-class teachers and members of elite groups (such as John Kennedy's sister Rosemary). Nevertheless, the majority of the lobotomy patients were members of the working class and lower middle class (artisans, shopkeepers, clerks). In Nordic countries, there were many uneducated women among lobotomy patients. Presumably, upper-middle-class psychiatrists were concerned about the consequences of psychosurgery on the work ability of the educated class, because they soon learned that lobotomy affected cognitive abilities and the whole personality of patients. Manual labourers, on the other hand, could still earn their living even if their imagination and powers of reasoning were destroyed or damaged by psychosurgery (Pressman 1998, 233–4). Moreover, in the eyes of psychiatrists, working-class patients were less capable of controlling themselves, and their general 'patterns of behaviour' were crude, unrefined and sometimes uncanny. This socio-economic, cultural and psychological abyss between the medical staff and the majority of patients contributed to the selection of potential lobotomy patients: since nobody seemed to expect much from the people of the lower classes, it was easier to pick them out for drastic medical interventions, including psychosurgery, shock methods and, later, over-prescription of psychiatric drugs. Conversely, middle-class and upper-middle-class patients were more likely to receive psychotherapy (Myers & Bean 1968, 105, 202–3).

Today, psychosurgery is in very limited use, and it does not resemble the stone-age techniques of early lobotomists. The most well-known new method is called *deep brain stimulation* (DBS), and it refers to a surgical treatment in which a medical device called a brain pacemaker is implanted deep in the brain (exact site depends on the symptoms the device aims to alleviate). From there, the device sends electrical impulses to specific regions in the brain. DBS has proved to have therapeutic effects on difficult movement and affective disorders such as dystonia, Parkinson's disease, chronic pain and severe depression. Compared to even the most sophisticated psychosurgical techniques, DBS influences brain activity in a controlled manner, and its effects are reversible. However, its underlying principles and mechanisms are still unclear, and some critics argue that commercial interests have brought the method to the medical limelight prematurely, since robust scientific evidence of the therapeutic efficacy of DBS is still lacking (Carey 2011). Moreover, the method is so expensive and invasive that it is hard to believe that it will replace more traditional and less risky therapies, at least in the near future.

264 The Golden Age of the asylums

During the time of civil unrest in the late 1960s, some American brain researchers suggested that psychosurgery could be used to pacify the leaders of urban riots. In their book *Violence and the Brain* (1970), the neurosurgeon Vernon Mark and the neuropsychiatrist Frank Ervin discussed 'surgery of violence', by which they meant stereotactic psychosurgery for the purpose of controlling the behaviour of violent patients. They pointed out that

> something must be done. The need for finding some way to curb violence and to identify abnormal and potentially violent individuals grows ever more acute as technological advances in bacteriology and chemistry make it more and more possible for a single abnormal person to kill great numbers of people.
>
> (Mark & Ervin 1970, 147)

Their proposal was not implemented, but the mere possibility that such invasive medical methods could be used for social purposes should keep us alert to the potential abuses of any method that meddles with our thoughts and feelings. This, I believe, is the ultimate problem with lobotomy and other radical interventions into the depths of our being: we may become alienated from ourselves, our ideals, idiosyncrasies and aspirations. You may remember that, in French mental medicine, alienation used to be a synonym for insanity.

Bibliography

Ackner, B., Harris, A. and Oldham, A.J. (1957) 'Insulin treatment of schizophrenia, a controlled study', *Lancet*, 1: 607–11.

Beard, G.M. and Rockwell, A.D. (1871) *A Practical Treatise on the Medical and Surgical Uses of Electricity: Including Localized and General Electrization*, New York: Wood.

Bourne, H. (1953) 'The insulin myth', *Lancet*, 262: 964–8.

Bourne, H. (1958) 'Insulin coma in decline', *American Journal of Psychiatry*, 114: 1015–17.

Carey, B. (2011) 'Wariness on surgery of the mind', *New York Times*, 14 February. Online. Available HTTP: <www.nytimes.com/2011/02/15/health/15brain.html?_r=0 > (accessed 26 August 2013).

Cerletti, U. (1950) 'Old and new information about electroshock', *American Journal of Psychiatry*, 107: 87–94.

Collins, A. (1988) *In the Sleep Room. The Story of the CIA Brainwashing Experiments in Canada*, Toronto: Lester & Orpen Dennys.

Daly, A. (1991) *Women under Knife: A History of Surgery*, London: Routledge.

Doroshow, D.B. (2007) 'Performing a cure for schizophrenia: Insulin coma therapy on the wards', *Journal of the History of Medicine and Allied Sciences*, 62: 213–43.

Dully, H. (2007) *My Lobotomy*, New York: Crown.

El-Hai, J. (2005) *The Lobotomist*, Hoboken, NJ: John Wiley & Sons.

Fishman, S. (1982) 'The history of childhood sexuality', *Journal of Contemporary History*, 17: 278-330.

Freeman, W. and Watts, J.M. (1950) *Psychosurgery in the Treatment of Mental Disorders and Intractable Pain*, 1st edn 1942, Springfield, OH: Charles C. Thomas.

Hoff, H. (1959) 'History of the organic treatment of schizophrenia', in M. Rinkel and H.E. Himwich (eds), *Insulin Treatment in Psychiatry*, New York: Philosophical Library.

Kalpa, I. (1947) 'Sokkikäsittelyn vaikutuksesta mielisairaalan toimintaan', *Duodecim*, 63: 621–32.

Kragh, J.V. (2010a) *Det hvide snit. Psykiatri og psykokirurgi i Danmark 1922–1983*, Odense, Denmark: Syddansk Universitetsforlag.

Kragh, J.V. (2010b) 'Shock therapy in Danish psychiatry', *Medical History*, 54: 341–64.

Mark, V. and Ervin, F. (1970) *Violence and the Brain*, New York: Harper & Row.

McCrae, N. (2006) '"A violent thunderstorm": Cardiazol treatment in British mental hospitals', *History of Psychiatry*, 17: 67–90.

von Meduna, L. (1937) *Die Konvulsionstherapie der Schizophrenie*, Halle, Germany: Carl Marhold.

Moncrieff, J. (2009) *Myth of the Chemical Cure*, Basingstoke: Palgrave Macmillan.

Moore, W.L. (1955) *The Mind in Chains: The Autobiography of a Schizophrenic*, New York: Exposition Press.

Myers, J.K. and Bean, L.B. (1968) *A Decade Later: A Follow-up of Social Class and Mental Illness*, New York: John Wiley and Sons.

Pressman, J.D. (1998) *Last Resort: Psychosurgery and the Limits of Medicine*, Cambridge: Cambridge University Press.

Raz, M. (2013) *The Lobotomy Letters: The Making of American Psychosurgery*, Rochester, NY: University of Rochester Press.

Sakel, M. (1958) *Schizophrenia*, New York: Philosophical Library.

Salminen, V. (forthcoming) 'Psykokirurgian historia Suomessa [History of Psychosurgery in Finland]', PhD Diss., Oulu, Finland: University of Oulu.

Scull, A. (2005) *Madhouse. A Tragic Tale of Megalomania and Modern Medicine*, New Haven, CT: Yale University Press.

Shorter, E. and Healy, D. (2007) *Shock Therapy. A History of Electroconvulsive Treatment in Mental Illness*, New Brunswick, NJ: Rutgers University Press.

Sirola, H. (1996) 'Kaikki mitä muistan kolmen vuoden kuolemasta', *Image*, 5: 62–78.

The Nobel Foundation (1949) 'The Nobel Prize in Physiology or Medicine 1949'. Online. Available HTTP: <www.nobelprize.org/nobel_prizes/medicine/laureates/1949> (accessed 27 October 2013).

Valenstein, E.S. (1986) *Great and Desperate Cures*, New York: Basic Books.

Wortis, J. (1959) 'The history of insulin shock treatment', in M. Rinkel and H.E. Himwich (eds) *Insulin Treatment in Psychiatry*, New York: Philosophical Library.

PART IV

Madness in the Cold War era and beyond

13

MIND CONTROL, POLITICAL PSYCHIATRY AND HUMAN RIGHTS

Recently, American researchers examined archival medical records of more than 1,000 hospitalized mental patients at the same state psychiatric facility in Pennsylvania. From a sample across a 100-year period, researchers examined types of delusion content characteristic of these psychotic patients at different times. Their main discovery was that persecutory delusions were the most common delusion category (76 per cent), followed by religious (38 per cent) and somatic (28 per cent) delusions. Next came delusions of poisoning (25 per cent) and grandiosity (20 per cent). Interestingly, after 1950 more patients believed that they were being spied upon, which is consistent with the advent of the Cold War and the ensuing cultural atmosphere of suspicion. Comparative studies have shown that persecution is the most common delusion type in different parts of the world.

In the early twentieth century, most delusions at the Pennsylvania Hospital revolved around syphilis, religion and grandiosity. During World War II, the 'main characters' of delusions were Germans, and, in the ensuing Cold War era, Communists. After the 1950s, persecution and spying were the most common theme, whereas today's delusions are more and more preoccupied with the Internet, computers and computer games. A similar study in Slovenia gave the same results, and researchers there found out that historical events influence delusional content. For example, at the time when radio and TV became more common, delusions related to control and 'action at a distance' also became more common: patients often received messages and orders through radio or TV (Cannon & Kramer 2011). To some extent, then, delusional content seems to reflect changing socio-cultural factors, collective mentality and anxieties of the associated time period.

After World War II, the western world entered into an era of economic growth, but it also entered into a prolonged state of political and military tension with the Soviet Union and its Communist allies in the so-called Eastern bloc. This period lasted from around 1947 to the collapse of the Soviet Union in 1991, and it

270 Madness in the Cold War era and beyond

is known as the Cold War. It was 'cold' because the tensions between the US-led Western bloc and the Eastern bloc did not culminate in large-scale fighting, even if there were a number of regional wars in Korea (1950–3), Vietnam (1955–75) and Afghanistan (1979–89). More than anything else, the Cold War era was characterized by preparation for a potentially apocalyptic nuclear war between the two superpowers. This nuclear arms race was predicated on the fact that each side had a nuclear deterrent that discouraged an attack by the enemy side, because such an attack would have enormous costs to the attacker. This doctrine of mutually assured destruction had a fitting acronym MAD. Indeed, with the benefit of hindsight, this doctrine and the whole nuclear arms race, which led to the development of gigantic hydrogen bombs of more than 10 megatons that no longer had practical military value, were a symbol of a mad era in world history (Rhodes 2005).

In addition to MAD and the deployment of conventional military forces, the Cold War was fought on many different fronts around the world, including proxy wars, propaganda and espionage as well as psychological warfare in which physicians and behaviour experts were recruited by governments to develop methods and tools of interrogation, terror, torture and what became known as 'brainwashing'. This chapter examines the ways in which psychiatry was used for political and military purposes during the Cold War in North America and the Soviet Union. The North American case represents the CIA-led project of 'mind control', while the Soviet case shows how the Russian psychiatric community became involved in the authorities' attempt to discredit and silence internal critics of the political system. I will end the chapter with a short discussion of the civil rights activism of an exceptional ex-psychiatric patient in the United States.

Ewen Cameron and mind control

A strange but revealing episode concerning the political and military uses of psychiatry during the Cold War revolves around the Scottish-born American psychiatrist Ewen Cameron (1901–67). In the mid-1950s, the CIA (Central Intelligence Agency) decided to start bankrolling Cameron's allegedly therapeutic but in fact experimental and highly dangerous methods of treatment. In those days, executives at the CIA were looking for physiological and psychological methods that could be useful in the difficult art of brainwashing. The term 'brainwashing' entered the English language in 1950, when the journalist Edward Hunter referred to a powerful technique pioneered by the Chinese Communists with help from their Soviet comrades. Hunter claimed that brainwashing was a new secret weapon that combined scientific laboratory techniques with ancient Chinese coercion methods. Hunter was a psychological warfare specialist for the US Office of Strategic Services and later the CIA, and it seems his mission was to pique the reading public's interest in this new Cold War concept. He succeeded quite well, because in a few years the word 'brainwashing' had become familiar in the English-speaking world. What increased its visibility in the early 1950s was the Korean War. When American prisoners of war in Korea publicly confessed to supposed germ warfare conducted by American troops, refused repatriation or, upon returning to their home country, kept on denouncing the American military and praising communism, the CIA and the military command drew the conclusion – or, consciously promoted the useful message – that these soldiers were somehow 'brainwashed' to believe in the Communist propaganda of the Chinese and the Soviets.

Having decided that brainwashing was the real thing, the CIA took action. In 1953, Allen Dulles, the unscrupulous director of the CIA, launched a secret mind control programme dubbed MKULTRA. The idea of the programme was to find and develop all potential brainwashing techniques that could function the same way as the 'psychological nuclear bomb' purportedly possessed by the Chinese and the Soviets. It is doubtful whether the CIA and the US Army truly believed that their Communist enemies had a powerful psychological weapon at their disposal, but what was beyond doubt was that the CIA could easily use this threat as a way of legitimizing their own mind control programme. MKULTRA, which was preceded by two other mind control programmes, BLUEBIRD and ARTICHOKE, was in operation for ten years, and its principal modus vivendi was to support psychological and psychiatric research on human guinea pigs, who were given LSD, mescaline, magic mushrooms, sodium amytal and other barbiturates, electroshocks and nitrous oxide. The CIA operated through various 'charitable' front organizations, such as the Society for the Investigation of Human Ecology and the Geschickter Fund for Medical Research. In the projects funded by MKULTRA, there were 185 researchers from 80 institutes, many of them top universities. The goal of their human experiments was to develop brainwashing techniques with the intention of turning enemy agents against their own government and getting them to start working for the CIA (Streatfeild 2008; Marks 1979).

MKULTRA tested the idea of whether the individual's values, beliefs and ideals could be wiped out and replaced with new ones. It was a question of using knowledge of the mind, elicited by human experiments, for mental torture, creation of a new psyche and, more generally, for the manipulation of the mind through psychological, somatic and chemical tools. In the 1950s, there was a strong faith in the United States in the power of the behavioural sciences (psychology, psychobiology, social psychology) to reveal the hidden corners of the human mind and to provide the authorities with useful instruments for controlling and conditioning people. One annoying obstacle for human experiments was that they were clearly considered unethical even in the careless atmosphere of the early Cold War era. For this reason, the CIA favoured experiments conducted outside the United States. Canada was a friendly and culturally similar neighbouring country, and, as it happened, there was a certain American psychiatrist in Canada who was doing interesting things with his patients.

Ewen Cameron was the Director of the Allan Memorial Institute and Professor of Psychiatry at McGill University in Montreal. He was contacted by the CIA on account of his idiosyncratic therapeutic method called 'psychic driving'. What this originally meant was that Cameron taped his conversations with the patients, who were then played the key parts of the conversation. Next, Cameron began to tape

272 Madness in the Cold War era and beyond

key sentences that he himself had invented after his interviews with the patients. At first, the patients heard repeated sentences containing negative messages, and when the minds of the patients were sufficiently irritated, they were played positive messages. To ensure that patients could not avoid listening to the messages, a 'dormiphone' was placed under their pillow, or the tapes were played through earphones. Needless to say, the patients' own opinions about the procedure were routinely discounted. All in all, during one round of psychic driving the patients were subjected to a stream of negative and positive messages between 250,000 and 500,000 times. Cameron also intentionally disorganized the patients' thinking during psychic driving by giving them LSD or other drugs, by putting patients into artificial sleep and by hypnotizing or isolating them. One female patient had to listen to the same positive messages continuously for 101 days. Cameron estimated that after about ten repetitions, the patient began to feel uncomfortable. If the goal was to break the individual's psychic defence, a repetition of a 30-minute psychic driving was usually enough. Sometimes the patient had to listen to repeated messages for 10 or 12 hours a day. As Cameron wrote in his 1956 article on this method, psychic driving 'is a potent procedure – it invariably produces responses in the patient, and often intense responses' (Cameron 1956, 508). It was the publication of this article that prompted the CIA to contact Cameron and to start supporting his experiments. Cameron was an ideal researcher for the CIA: a respected, powerful and ambitious psychiatrist who had no scruples about pushing his patients' mental endurance to the limit, and, if necessary, beyond.

On the basis of psychic driving, Cameron began to create new methods to unlock the patient's mind. In the last analysis, what was needed was to create a new identity for the patient. The patient's disturbed mind had to be turned into a blank slate onto which the behaviour expert wrote the traits of a new and improved personality. From the mid-1950s to the early 1960s, at least 100 patients at Allan Memorial were used as psychiatric guinea pigs. One of them was Velma 'Val' Orlikow, wife of a member of the Canadian Parliament, who suffered from 'character neurosis'. Together with eight other Canadian ex-patients, Orlikow sued the CIA in 1984 for subjecting them unknowingly to experimental mind control techniques developed by Cameron. The CIA settled out of court in 1988 but maintained that the settlement was not an admission of guilt. In the latter half of the 1950s, Orlikow was one of the patients who was repeatedly given LSD and forced to undergo psychic driving. She reacted to the injections of LSD with panic and fear, feeling that all her bones 'were melting' (Collins 1988, 14). After the fourteenth and last shot, Orlikow fell into a 'black hole'. Some days later, when Cameron and his entourage entered her room, she escaped to the washroom and, in front of Cameron's colleagues, categorically refused to take the LSD shot. Indignantly, the revered doctor turned on his heel and left the room. Soon after this incident, she was discharged from the hospital, but in 1963 she had to return. Again, she was subjected to psychic driving and drug treatment (though not LSD) (Collins 1988, 18–21).

Fortunately, Val Orlikow was not confined in the so-called sleep room, where patients were drugged into narcosis for days, played tapes through speakers placed under their pillows and given repeated electroshocks two or three times a day until they became totally dazed and disoriented. Cameron called this toxic mixture of interventions 'depatterning', and its goal was to produce 'differential amnesia' through 'the extensive breakup of the existing patterns of behavior, both normal and pathologic' (Cameron 1960, 26). The therapeutic idea behind depatterning was to change the patients' psychotic behaviour by making them first lose their recent memory and, eventually, forget their former selves altogether. Then, through the stages of 'depatterning in reverse', the patients would recover with their schizophrenic symptoms gone. At the end of treatment, the patients were supposed to 'enjoy' either differential or total amnesia regarding the time when the symptoms appeared. In other words, the recovered patients would not remember anything about the onset of their illness. In reality, depatterning created neurological symptoms and shrank individuals into a shadow of their former selves. This, of course, was the whole point of depatterning, because Cameron claimed that, at the end of the treatment, these damaged individuals no longer suffered from anxiety and other mental symptoms (Cameron 1960). According to a retired CIA agent, to produce amnesia was the central objective of the Agency's department of research and development. From the CIA's perspective, then, Cameron's treatment of one of his female patients was successful: after receiving over a hundred electroshock treatments and almost three months of sleep therapy, she had no memory of anything that had happened to her before her confinement in Allan Memorial. What was more, she was also 'unable to recognize either her husband or her children' (Streatfeild 2008, 230).

It is not clear whether Cameron knew for sure that his work was (partly) funded by the CIA, but what is beyond doubt is that he saw psychic driving and depatterning as forms of brainwashing. One of his assistants told the *New York Times* that Cameron and his co-workers had called these treatments 'brainwashing' (Collins 1988, 132–3).

Patients in a box

In addition to psychic driving and depatterning, Cameron also experimented with sensory deprivation, a devilish method developed in the early 1950s by the psychologist Donald Hebb, who was Cameron's colleague at McGill University. The basic idea of the sensory deprivation experiment was to strip an individual of all sensory stimulation in order to see what happens to their psychological faculties in total isolation. For this purpose, Hebb constructed a number of small air-conditioned isolation cells, and doctoral students were paid 20 dollars to act as volunteers. They were told to stay in the cell for as long as they could. What Hebb soon found out was that the students found the isolation experience hard and unsettling, only a few of them lasted for more than two days in the cells. Most alarmingly, some of the subjects began to hallucinate and report feelings of paranoia, while others could not distinguish between sleep and waking. One subject became convinced that he was not alone in the box. In a state of panic, he thought

274 Madness in the Cold War era and beyond

there were two 'hims' who began to overlap, and he was incapable of determining which him was himself (Streatfeild 2008, 111–12). Startled, Hebb concluded that his experiments were 'very unsettling' – he certainly did not anticipate that sensory deprivation would result in hallucinations, paranoia, fear and disturbances of personal identity. Evidently, healthy young people found isolation for prolonged periods intolerable. What Hebb had invented was partly a mechanism of brainwashing, but the more lasting significance of his work was that it offered a very useful and effective method of torture and interrogation in which the damage was mostly 'self-inflicted' (McCoy 2007, 32–59; on sensory deprivation, see also Salomon et al. 1957).

Intrigued by sensory deprivation experiments, Cameron constructed a box in his 'behaviour laboratory' and began to lock patients into it for days at a time. One woman, who suffered from menopausal anxiety, was kept in the box for more than a month. Cameron had already 'treated' her with depatterning and psychic driving, which had lasted for more than three months, after which the patient was already so confused that even a record-long isolation did not change her condition. Cameron made his 'creative' variation of the experiment by subjecting his 'boxed' patients to psychic driving: he played tapes to them. He also injected his patients with curare before putting them into the box, presumably because he wanted to make the patients as immobile as possible. On top of all this, he did not tell his human guinea pigs how long they would be kept in the state of sensory deprivation, which increased their feelings of anxiety and insecurity.

Cameron's psychiatric work is reprehensible for at least two reasons. First, by recklessly combining invasive methods and techniques, such as electroshocks, drug treatment, psychic driving and sensory deprivation, he risked his patients' lives, exposed them to nothing less than psychological torture and exacerbated their mental ill health, which is quite ironic given the fact that his patients were by definition already mentally damaged individuals to some degree. Second, he did not tell his patients that they were guinea pigs in human experiments rather than mental patients who were entitled to humane and medically approved treatment. In fact, his most abusive methods were developed after 1955, when the World Medical Association adopted ethical guidelines regarding human experimentation. Related to these two moral and professional crimes is the question of false collegiality: among Cameron's colleagues, associates and assistants there was not a single person who would have blown the whistle and exposed his psychological torture to the medical community and to the outside world. It was not only that everybody decided to keep quiet, there were also colleagues who used the same methods (e.g. depatterning) as the Chief, even after Cameron had left Montreal. Even Donald Hebb, who profoundly disliked Cameron's irresponsible way of using his method of sensory deprivation, failed to speak out while Cameron was still alive (he died in 1967). It was only when Cameron's work was under investigation in the mid-1980s that the elderly Hebb disclosed in an interview that Cameron was 'criminally stupid' (Weinstein 1990, 122).

In 1964, Cameron retired from his post at Allan Memorial and moved back to the United States to work at the Veterans' Administration Hospital in Albany,

New York, where he continued with his old research topic, memory (his book *Remembering* had been published in 1947). One probable explanation for his retirement is the total failure of his methods as a form of therapy and as a research tool. Indeed, Cameron himself publicly acknowledged his failure when he told a prestigious audience in New York in 1963 how he had made 'a wrong turn' when he decided to do experimental research on personality change. By that time, the CIA no longer bankrolled his work. Disillusioned, officials at the Agency concluded that Cameron's experimental research on brainwashing was only half successful: the method of depatterning indeed wiped out the contents of the mind, but Cameron could not 're-programme' the mind and create new patterns of behaviour. In the end, the CIA understood that it was nothing but a pipe dream to create a New Man, a sort of psychomedical Frankenstein. Rather than supporting research on the complicated techniques of brainwashing, CIA officials began to think that, after all, enemy agents can be 'treated' the way the Russians and the Chinese did it: isolate the individual, monitor and control him at all times and, most importantly, break his will. Straightforward, brutal interrogation techniques triumphed over psychotechnical mind control. Sidney Gottlieb, who was in charge of the MKULTRA programme, told a Senate hearing that supporting Cameron was 'a foolish mistake. We shouldn't have done it. I'm sorry we did.' Indeed, the whole MKULTRA project was really 'much ado about nothing'. Gottlieb confessed in public that MKULTRA 'had not yielded any results of real positive value to the Agency' (Streatfeild 2008, 111–12; Weinstein 1990, 143).

In the last analysis, Cameron's psychological torture remains inexplicable. Was he driven by blind ambition to conquer mental illness at any price? Was he driven by anti-communism and a patriotic duty to help the 'American cause'? Or was it all due to his extraordinary insensitivity to the suffering of his patients? To me, Cameron is an archetypal example of what in 1937 the great Austrian writer Robert Musil called 'higher stupidity'. Individuals who represent such stupidity or folly are typically clever and rational, but they are overwhelmed by some all-important idea or conviction, which makes them immune to all contrary ideas and lose all sense of moderation and proportion (Musil 1990). Cameron suffered from this Musilian moral malady in his unbounded hubris, therapeutic fanaticism (*furor therapeuticus*) and indifference to the well-being of his patients. Although his medical practice did damage to many of his patients, he never had to face the consequences of his malpractice. Instead, upon his death he was eulogized by a colleague as a 'man who was vitally concerned with the well-being of men everywhere' (Silverman 1967).

In 1964, when Cameron decided he was stuck in a blind alley and left Montreal for good, strange things in psychiatry were happening on the other side of the Iron Curtain. In the Soviet Union, the authorities were persecuting dissident political thinkers and those deemed enemies of the state. Whereas the CIA recruited psychiatrists, neurologists and psychologists to experiment with brainwashing techniques, Soviet officials turned psychiatry into an instrument of political repression.

276 Madness in the Cold War era and beyond

The price of conviction: political psychiatry in the Soviet Union

This section focuses on Russian political psychiatry in the 1960s and the 1970s, but I will first briefly refer to the fact that even in Imperial Russia one could be labelled mad if one gave expression to politically dangerous ideas. The Russian philosopher Peter Chaadayev (1794–1856) was a 'westernizer' and a leading figure of the English Club in early nineteenth-century Moscow. In 1836, he published a 'Philosophical Letter' in the periodical *Teleskop*. In the letter, written in French, Chaadayev argued that Russia belonged neither to the west nor to the east; in fact, Russia did not represent any civilization of its own. This was too much for the Tsar Nicholas I and the authorities: *Teleskop* was closed down, its publisher N.L. Nadezhdin (professor of archaeology) was exiled and:

> the Tsar personally ordered that Chaadayev should be considered mad and should be regularly inspected by a doctor. After some months of this humiliating treatment he was left alone and continued to live in Moscow for another twenty years, always taking care not to become involved in any political activity.
>
> (Seton-Watson 1967, 258)

Later, when the Soviet Union was born in the bloody aftermath of the Russian Revolution in 1917, dissidents and other difficult individuals were usually taken care of by jailing or killing them, or deporting them to the endless forests and steppes of Siberia. During Stalin's dictatorial reign, 'enemies of the people' were languishing in a huge network of forced labour camps across the Soviet Union (about 14 million people were sent to these Gulag labour camps between 1929 and 1953). After Stalin's death in 1953, political prisoners began to be released, and the Gulag institution was closed in 1960 (Applebaum 2003; Khlevniuk 2004; on psychiatry in Stalin's Soviet Union, see Zajicek 2009). Nevertheless, forced labour colonies continued to exist, and during the reign of Nikita Khrushchev, leader of the country from 1956 to 1964, a new or reinvented (see Chaadayev's case above) instrument of political repression was instated. The ideological justification for political psychiatry was given by Khrushchev in 1959 when he declared in a speech that:

> a crime is a deviation from the generally recognized standards of behaviour frequently caused by mental disorder. Can there be diseases, nervous disorders among certain people in Communist society? Evidently yes. If that is so, then there will also be offences that are characteristic for people with abnormal minds [. . .] To those who might start calling for opposition to Communism on this basis, we can say that [. . .] clearly the mental state of such people is not normal.
>
> (van Voren 2013, 6–7)

One such 'abnormal' Soviet citizen was the molecular biologist Zhores Medvedev (b. 1925). In April 1970, he was invited to an urgent meeting with the

In the same year (1970), Solzhenitsyn was awarded the Nobel Prize in Literature, and in 1974 he was arrested and deported as an 'enemy of the state'. Meanwhile, Zhores and Roy Medvedev together wrote *A Question of Madness* (published in London in 1971), in which they gave a detailed account of Zhores' ordeal and its political, scientific and medical context. In 1971, Medvedev was given a job at the Institute of Physiology and Biochemistry of Farm Animals in Borovsk (in the Kaluga region), and the following year he moved to London with his family to work at the National Institute for Medical Research as a visiting researcher. While in the UK, Medvedev was stripped of his Soviet citizenship and his passport was confiscated. He remained in London and worked at the same institute until his retirement in 1991, the year when the Soviet Union ceased to exist.

The scope of political psychiatry included all who were considered dissenters regardless of their education and background. The establishment of a 'Psychiatric Gulag' had started during the reign of Khrushchev, and when he was dethroned by Leonid Brezhnev in 1964, the connection of political opposition with mental disorder became more systematic. In 1967, Yuri Andropov became Chairman of the KGB, and he began to develop a medical machinery to deal with political opposition (after the death of Brezhnev in 1982, Andropov became General Secretary of the Communist Party; he died in 1983). Using all the power of the state apparatus, Andropov wanted to destroy dissent in all its forms, one of which was the struggle for human rights and freedom of expression. To treat the problem of political opposition psychiatrically made it possible for the authorities to avoid the taint of public trials and to demonstrate that the ideas and deeds of dissidents had their source in the delusions of the sick mind. Andropov suggested the establishment of a network of mental hospitals to defend the 'Soviet Government and socialist order' from dissenters. In most cases, political opponents were officially examined in Moscow at the Serbsky Central Research Institute for Forensic and General Psychiatry, which evaluated the dissidents and sent indictees for involuntary treatment to special hospitals operated by the Ministry of Internal Affairs. The majority of such incarcerations took place between the late 1960s and the early 1980s.

As the centre of Russian forensic psychiatry, the Serbsky Institute became a notorious persecutor of dissidents. Georgi Morozov, Director of the Institute, was reported to have said, 'why bother with political trials when we have psychiatric clinics?' (Medvedev & Medvedev 1971, 67). One reason for the abuse of psychiatry was the almost total isolation of Soviet psychiatry from developments in world psychiatry, and another was the monopolization of psychiatry by the 'Moscow School', which was instrumental in creating the procedure and framework for the use of psychiatry for political purposes. KGB offices in places like Ukraine were given instructions on how to use psychiatry either as a 'preventive measure' or as a tool to eliminate a 'hostile element' from society (van Voren 2013, 8).

The attention of the western world was first drawn to the sinister side of Soviet psychiatry by the Ukrainian writer Valery Tarsis with his autobiographical novel *Ward 7* (*Palata No. 7*), which depicted life in a Soviet mental asylum. Tarsis himself had been committed to a mental institution in 1963 after his book *The Bluebottle* had been smuggled out of the Soviet Union and published in the west in 1962 (the novel described the predicament of writers and other intellectuals under the Khruschev regime). *Ward 7* was published three years later (1965). In Tarsis' asylum, all but one of the patients were sane – sane but troublesome to the authorities. Tarsis referred to one group of young, 'maladjusted' and 'rebellious' male patients who did not want to go into the Army (military service was compulsory in the Soviet Union), and for whom a stay at a psychiatric hospital meant exemption from military service (Tarsis 1965, 23). A year after the book was published, Tarsis was permitted to emigrate to the West (van Voren 2010). Soon thereafter, he was deprived of his Soviet citizenship, and the revengeful KGB had plans to compromise Tarsis' literary career abroad by labelling him as insane.

In 1963, when Tarsis was incarcerated in a psychiatric hospital in Moscow, the authorities accused the poet Joseph Brodsky (1940–96) of being a 'loafer'. He was taken to a psychiatric clinic in Moscow, where he was examined for several days. Some weeks later, Brodsky was arrested again, put to trial and hospitalized against his will, this time in Leningrad (now St Petersburg). His crime was that he was a poet who 'pursued a parasitic way of life'. In his trial, he was called a 'pseudo-poet in velveteen trousers' who failed to fulfil his 'constitutional duty to work honestly for the good of the motherland' (McFadden 1996). Brodsky was sent for psychiatric examination to the Psychiatric Hospital No. 2, where he was kept for about three weeks. In the hospital, Brodsky was given neuroleptics, wakened in the middle of the night and immersed in cold water. The most horrendous treatment was the abusive use of the wet pack: wrapped in a wet sheet, Brodsky was put next to the heater so that the sheet would cut into his body and cause him considerable pain and breathing difficulties when it dried and shrank. These two incarcerations in psychiatric establishments inspired him to write his poem 'Gorbunov and Gorchakov' (1970) about two patients confined in a mental asylum near Leningrad. For his 'parasitism', Brodsky spent 18 months in harsh conditions on a village farm located in the Arctic Archangelsk region. In 1972, when the authorities wondered whether the onerous Brodsky should be exiled, they consulted Andrei Snezhnevsky, the Director of the Institute of Psychiatry of the USSR Academy of Medical Sciences and the most eminent psychiatrist in the country. Snezhnevsky, who was the inventor of the diagnosis of 'sluggish schizophrenia', diagnosed Brodsky as schizophrenic without examining him personally. He concluded that Brodsky was 'not a valuable person at all and may be let go'. In 1972, Brodsky was put on a plane headed for Vienna, and he never returned to his home country. Fifteen years later, he was awarded the Nobel Prize in Literature.

It has been estimated that the number of the victims of Soviet political psychiatry is somewhere between 15,000 and 20,000. These 'dissident' individuals were confined in the archipelago of prison-hospitals purely for political reasons, and the point of their confinement was to isolate, punish and silence these enemies of the state. Their condition 'improved' markedly when they told their psychiatrists in no uncertain terms that they were now aware of their political madness and that they no longer suffered from anti-Soviet delusions. Some victims were permanently damaged either physically or mentally, and some (like the Ukrainian mineworker Aleksei Nikitin, who established the Free Trade Union of the Soviet People) perished in the hospitals. Political psychiatry as a form of systematic persecution was abandoned during Gorbachev's regime (1985–91), but there is strong evidence that the abuse of psychiatry has continued even in post-Soviet Russia. In 2012, for example, three members of Pussy Riot, the feminist protest rock group, were put on trial and convicted of 'hooliganism motivated by religious hatred'. The three women underwent a court-ordered psychiatric examination, and in the report presented by the prosecution they were described as suffering from 'personality disorders', which meant that the women should be isolated from society (van Voren 2013, 17). Fortunately, they were 'only' sentenced to two years in a penal colony and freed in December 2013 under an amnesty initiated by President Putin.

Between the 1960s and the 1980s, psychiatry was also turned into a tool of repression in the Socialist dictatorships in eastern Europe, especially in Romania and what was then Yugoslavia. As can be imagined, psychiatry was abused also in non-Communist dictatorships, such as Chile and Argentina (where some individual psychiatrists were involved in developing effective forms of torture), and in South Africa psychiatry was seriously compromised by the racially discriminatory policy of apartheid. After the fall of dictatorships in eastern Europe and South America, and after the end of apartheid in South Africa, psychiatry was no longer used for directly political purposes. In the 2000s, the question of political abuse of psychiatry in China has been discussed within the international psychiatric community, but there is still very little foolproof evidence of such an abuse. Nevertheless, there is hardly any doubt that human rights activists have been incarcerated and 'treated' in mental hospitals in China (Munro 2006).

When we evaluate whether, and to what extent, psychiatry is used as a tool of repression, we simultaneously evaluate the degree of democracy and openness of societies. In the countries where undemocratic and authoritarian groups, be they oligarchies, dictatorships or monarchies, have had political power, political opponents and other 'enemies of the state' have been persecuted and locked up in prisons, interrogation centres and mental institutes. In authoritarian states, psychiatry and all other sciences, especially if they did research on humans, were easily drawn into the trajectory of politics, power and intrigue. We could see this phenomenon in Soviet psychiatry, but even in liberal democracies such as the United States the human sciences were not just doing their own thing regardless of politics; as the story of MKULTRA and Ewen Cameron reveals, part of North American psychiatry was definitely in the service of the state and its intelligence agencies.

When we read about political psychiatry or mind control experiments, we may be tempted to doubt the sanity of the mental health professionals who were involved in the abuse of psychiatry. On the other hand, when we read about the ideas and deeds of the so-called insane, we may marvel at their moral courage or their refusal to comply with the rules of inegalitarian and repressive societies. This, at least, is what happened to me when I learned about the life and death of certain Mr Moore.

282 Madness in the Cold War era and beyond

'Mississippi or Bust': from a mental patient to a civil rights warrior

> I always dreamed of Utopia and I was not content merely to dream. Therefore my story.

So begins *The Mind in Chains*, a remarkable book by a remarkable man who spent 18 months in a mental hospital in the early 1950s. This is how he continues his story:

> You are one person; I am another. I have thought long and hard about this world we live in; I have dreamed wild dreams – crazy dreams, if you will – in the hope of being able to make this life a better thing for us all. And that is why all windows are barred, all doors are locked, all exits are guarded. I would save the world; therefore I am locked up to save the world from me.
>
> (Moore 1955, 7)

The story of William Moore (1927–63) is worth telling, because he was someone who tried to fulfil his 'Utopian' dream. Born in Binghamton, New York, he joined the Army in 1945 and was sent to Guam in the Pacific Ocean, where he was spared from participating in the last battles of the war. After returning from military service in 1949, he enrolled in college, studying economics, sociology, English and political science. In the early 1950s, he attained his degree and applied to Johns Hopkins University for graduate study in economics. At this point, he developed a delusion about a conspiracy spinning around him (not *against* him), as a result of which his family committed him to Binghamton State Mental Hospital. He spent a year and a half on the overcrowded schizophrenia ward before he was discharged in August 1954. During his confinement, he wrote a book that he managed to get published after his discharge (*The Mind in Chains*, 1955). In the last chapter, written in January 1955, William envisions his life at the 'beginning of a new year for me – a new full year of freedom from imprisonment, from treatments [e.g. insulin shocks] that knock me cold, from life among the mad and the supposedly insane' (Moore 1955, 294). Musing on his older dream of working for world government through the newly founded United Nations, he admits that 'I was not made quite normal, I was made to wish for more – more than the mere possible or even the probable. I must pursue the impossible' (Moore 1955, 307).

The 'impossible' path that William chose was that of a civil rights activist. He stayed in Binghamton, married a single mother, joined local pacifist organizations and started to attract the attention of the town dwellers – not because of his 'madness', but because he began to organize one-man protest marches against military armament, school prayers and other forms of socially sanctioned foolishness. He became known as a pacifist, atheist and anti-racist, which separated him from his community. Convinced that ex-patients needed a self-help network such as Alcoholic Anonymous, he created a group called Mental Health Anonymous. He was inspired by Clifford Beers, an early twentieth-century ex-patient turned mental health activist whose autobiographical book *A Mind that Found Itself* (1907) was instrumental in turning the psychiatric community's attention to the predicament of institutionalized mental patients. Beers' noble ambition had been to improve conditions in mental hospitals, and to strengthen the rights of patients. Unfortunately, in the manipulating hands of the eugenically oriented leaders of the National Committee for Mental Hygiene that he founded together with Adolf Meyer, an eminent professor of psychiatry, his bottom-up suggestions for radical reforms were diluted and transmogrified so that mental hygiene became a top-down programme and an ideology that aimed at the prevention of mental disorders and other forms of 'deviant' behaviour by guidance and eugenic methods. What was conveniently forgotten by 'mental hygienists' was the improvement of the conditions of institutionalized patients, who continued to be routinely abused and mistreated (Beers 2007; Grob 1994, 152–8).

In the early 1960s, William moved to Baltimore, where he found a job as a mailman. He continued his activism, which once led to a confrontation with the police: together with a group of African American students, he protested against the segregation policy of a local cinema, as a result of which picketing spread from the theatre to the community and the nearby college, which finally, after arrests of some activists, prompted the owner to desegregate the theatre. At that time, segregation and racism were still rampant in the Southern states, and many Southerners angrily dismissed the demands of desegregation made by the increasingly popular civil rights movement. One of these opponents of desegregation was William's father, who on several occasions told William's wife how he was disgusted with his son's 'nigger-loving' activities (Stanton 2010, 43–9).

With his experience as a social activist, William was well-prepared to work for the civil rights movement. In 1963, he decided to undertake a freedom walk in the South and take a letter to the governor of Mississippi. The simple message in his letter was: stop segregation and give the blacks the civil rights already possessed by the Constitution. Mississippi is in the deep South, where the policy of segregation also ran deep and where the Ku Klux Klan was still active. William had practised freedom walking by taking a letter to President Kennedy in Washington, DC just one month before his 'Mississippi or Bust' trek (he gave his letter to the guardians of the White House). In April 1963, he set out on his trip in Chattanooga, Tennessee. He knew the risks involved in walking alone for roughly 350 miles through areas suffused with the ethos of white supremacy and 'nigger-hating' attitudes, but he regarded his walk as an act of conscience, and as such he could not give primacy to his personal security. He carried a board sign, on the front panel of which he had written, 'End Segregation in America, Eat at Joe's – Both Black and White', and, on the back, 'Equal Rights for All (Mississippi or Bust)'.

William walked to the state border of Alabama without serious incidents, but after crossing the border he had an argument at a grocery store-service station on Highway 11. The owner of the grocery was a man named Floyd Simpson, a pure-bred redneck and member of the Ku Klux Klan, who wanted to know if William was 'part of that nigger preacher's [Martin Luther King] crew in Birmingham'

284 Madness in the Cold War era and beyond

(Alabama). Later that day, Moore was stopped by Simpson and his friend, who had hopped into a car and followed William. This time the atmosphere in the discussion was more ominous, as both men questioned William about his provocative beliefs. In the evening of the same day, William was shot twice in the head on the side of the road where he was walking. He died on the spot (Stanton 2010, 61–73).

President Kennedy, irritated at the segregationist and anti-federalist stance of the Southern states, made the murder of a civil rights activist famous across the nation by giving a press conference in which he called the murder an 'outrageous crime'. It did not take long for the police to find out that the rifle belonged to Floyd Simpson, who was charged with murder, but then, inexplicably, freed by the jury of 17 whites and 1 black man in Etowah County, Alabama. Then again, maybe the release of Simpson was not that inexplicable. It was 'just' a case of a Southern white jury refusing to indict an ordinary white man for killing a dangerous agitator and a godless race mixer. In the 1950s and 1960s, members of the Ku Klux Klan often forged alliances with police departments in Alabama and other Southern states; or with governor's offices, most notoriously with George Wallace of Alabama. Maybe it is not that surprising that no-one was ever indicted for the murder of William Moore.

A group of young civil rights activists decided to continue William's freedom walk, but they were stopped and taken to county jail by the police as soon as they crossed the state line into Alabama. This arrest might have saved them from something much worse, because they were confronted by more than 1,000 angry, bloodthirsty Alabamians. One freedom walker carried William's bloodied sign when he led other walkers into Alabama. As he crossed the border, hell broke loose:

> 'Throw them niggers in the river', somebody shrieked. 'Kill the white men first'. A white woman with her hair set in pink plastic curlers yelled. 'Kill him! Kill him! Kill him!' to nobody in particular. The troopers tackled [the freedom walkers] Zellner and Eric Weinberger first, electroshocking them with three-foot cattle prods before tossing them into a police car. 'That's white men dealing with you, brother!' a young man jeered. Bottles and rocks flew through the air, many hitting the walkers, as each was arrested the moment he stepped into Alabama.
>
> (Stanton 2010, 122)

Not long after William's death, his past as a mental health patient was taken up by commentators, some of whom asserted that his freedom walk was an insane attempt to achieve martyrdom. Others assumed a patronizing and condescending posture, including the author of the editorial in the *New York Times*, who referred to William's walk as 'a pitifully naïve pilgrimage' (Stanton 2010, 87). However, his moral conviction and courage also inspired many people, especially those who were themselves involved in the civil rights movement. One of them was the folk singer Phil Ochs, who wrote a song simply entitled 'William Moore' to pay homage to his hero.

William Moore never tried to hide the fact that he had been confined in a mental hospital. He was a man who in a fundamental way was much more sane, and much more virtuous and worthy of our respect, than any of those psychiatrists turned into manipulators we have met in this chapter. The very last words of his book are worth quoting, because they capture something essential about 'normality', 'sanity' and 'madness' in the Cold War era and beyond: 'One ends up wondering: Will an age of reason ever come? Probably not. It wouldn't be "normal"' (Moore 1955, 315).

Bibliography

Applebaum, A. (2003) *Gulag: A History*, New York: Double Day.
Beers, C. (2007) *A Mind that Found Itself*, 1st edn 1907, Milton Keynes: Filiquarian Publishing.
Cameron, E. (1956) 'Psychic driving', *The American Journal of Psychiatry*, 112: 502–9.
Cameron, E. (1960) 'Production of differential amnesia as a factor in the treatment of schizophrenia', *Comprehensive Psychiatry*, 1: 26–34.
Cannon, B.J. and Kramer, L.M. (2011) 'Delusion content across the 20th century in an American psychiatric hospital', *International Journal of Social Psychiatry*, published online doi: 10.1177/0020764010396413
Collins, A. (1988) *In the Sleep Room. The Story of the CIA Brainwashing Experiments in Canada*, Toronto: Lester & Orpen Dennys.
Grob, G.N. (1994) *The Mad Among Us*, New York: The Free Press.
Khlevniuk, O.V. (2004) *The History of the Gulag: From Collectivization to the Great Terror*, trans. V.A. Staklo, New Haven, CT: Yale University Press.
Marks, J. (1979) *In Search of the Manchurian Candidate*, New York: Times Books.
McCoy, A.W. (2007) *A Question of Torture. CIA Interrogation from the Cold War to the War on Terror*, New York: Holt Paperbacks.
McFadden, R.D. (1996) 'Joseph Brodsky, exiled poet who won Nobel, dies at 55' (Obituary), *New York Times*, 29 January.
Medvedev, Z. and Medvedev, R. (1971) *A Question of Madness*, trans. E. de Kadt, London: Macmillan.
Moore, W.L. (1955) *The Mind in Chains: The Autobiography of a Schizophrenic*, New York: Exposition Press.
Munro, R. (2006) *China's Psychiatric Inquisition*, London: Wiley, Simmond & Hill.
Musil, R. (1990) 'On stupidity', in B. Pike and D.S. Luft (eds and trans.) *Precision and Soul. Essays and Addresses*, orig. German edn 1937, Chicago: The University of Chicago Press.
Rhodes, R. (2005) *Dark Sun: The Making of the Hydrogen Bomb*, 1st edn 1995, New York: Simon & Schuster.
Salomon, P., Leiderman, H., Mendelson, J. and Wexler, D. (1957) 'Sensory deprivation. A review', *American Journal of Psychiatry*, 114: 357–63.
Seton-Watson, H. (1967) *The Russian Empire*, Oxford: Oxford University Press.
Silverman, B. (1967) 'Dr. D. Ewen Cameron – an appreciation', *Canadian Medical Association Journal*, 97, October 14: 985–6.
Stanton, M. (2010) *Freedom Walk: Mississippi or Bust*, 1st edn 2003, Jackson: University Press of Mississippi.
Streatfeild, D. (2008) *Brainwash. The Secret History of Mind Control*, New York: Picador.
Tarsis, V. (1965) *Ward 7. An Autobiographical Novel*, trans. K. Brown, London: Collins and Harvill Press.

van Voren, R. (2010) *Cold War in Psychiatry – Human Factors, Secret Actors*, Amsterdam: Rodopi.

van Voren, R. (2013) *Psychiatry as a Tool for Coercion in Post-Soviet Countries*, Brussels: European Parliament.

Weinstein, H.M. (1990) *Psychiatry and the CIA. Victims of Mind Control*, Washington, DC: American Psychiatric Press.

Zajicek, B. (2009) 'Scientific Psychiatry in Stalin's Soviet Union: The Politics of Modern Medicine and the Struggle to Define 'Pavlovian' Psychiatry, 1939–1953', PhD Diss., Chicago, IL: The University of Chicago.

14

THE PSYCHOPHARMACOLOGICAL REVOLUTION

In 1968, the World Health Organization (WHO) initiated a large-scale follow-up study of schizophrenia in nine countries. After five years of data collection, the study revealed that the patients from the three developing countries (India, Nigeria and Colombia) fared much better than the patients in the United States and four other industrial countries, including the UK and the Soviet Union. In the developing countries, patients were much more often (64 per cent) asymptomatic and functioning well. In contrast, only a distinct minority of the patients (18 per cent) in the industrial countries were doing well. WHO researchers concluded that falling ill in a western industrial nation was a 'strong predictor' that a patient suffering from schizophrenia would never *fully* recover (Whitaker 2003, 227–8).

The WHO's International Pilot Study of schizophrenia was embarrassing to the western psychiatric community. Taken aback, psychiatrists began to offer explanations. There must have been a serious flaw in the design of the study! Alternatively, patients in India, Nigeria and Colombia were not really schizophrenic. The WHO investigators responded to the critique by launching a new follow-up study in 1978, in this case in ten countries. This time the researchers targeted schizophrenics who were suffering their first psychotic episodes and who were all diagnosed by the same (western) criteria. The results were the same: after two years, almost two-thirds of the schizophrenics in developing countries had recovered or else fared much better than the patients in the industrialized countries. Apparently, something protected people with schizophrenia in poor countries from becoming chronically ill. What could it be (Leff 1992; Jablensky 1992)?

In the latter follow-up study, the WHO examined the effects of psychiatric medication. Initially, the WHO investigators assumed that patients in the poor countries fared better because, compared to the patients in the industrialized countries, they were swallowing their pills more dutifully. In fact, the reverse was true: only 16 per cent of the patients in the developing countries were even maintained on medication, while 61 per cent of the industrialized countries were kept on psychiatric drugs. The Indian patients in the town of Agra had the most favourable outcome, and only 3 per cent of the patients were maintained on drugs there. By contrast, in Moscow, 88 per cent of the patients were kept continually on medication, yet more than 80 per cent were doing badly at the end of two years (Jablensky 1992, 60). This was a piece of unwelcome news to the western psychiatric community, because it revealed a strong negative correlation between medication and outcomes.

In 1997, the WHO investigators interviewed patients from the two follow-up studies. They found out that in the developing countries the patients continued to fare better than in the industrialized countries. The majority (53 per cent) of the schizophrenic patients were no longer suffering from psychotic symptoms, and almost three-quarters (73 per cent) had returned to work. The message coming from these studies and follow-up interviews was loud and clear: in countries where the patients were *not* maintained on psychiatric drugs during the first schizophrenic episode, most people had recovered from the illness and were doing well 15 years later. How, then, should we deal with this supposedly surprising indicator of the inefficiency or sheer harmfulness of psychotropic drugs? Let us try to unravel the puzzle by examining the history of drug use in mental medicine.

Medicating madness

For millennia, all sorts of herbs, extracts and drugs have been used to treat mental disorders (on the history of 'psychotropic' drugs, see Caldwell 1970; Weber 1999; Healy 2002; Tone 2009; Balz 2010). For example, since antiquity, *Hyoscamus niger* (henbane, also known as black henbane or stinking nightshade) and other extracts from nightshades were used as remedies for all kinds of ailments, including mania and sexual impotence. In the early nineteenth century, Philippe Pinel, who represents a threshold figure between traditional mental medicine and modern psychiatry, made a pertinent remark that is still valid today:

> In diseases of the mind, as well as in all other ailments, it is an art of no little importance to administer medicines properly; but it is an art of much greater and more difficult acquisition to know when to suspend or altogether to omit them.
>
> (Pinel 2009, 26)

Generations of alienists after Pinel have had to deal with the difficult problem of how to use drugs both therapeutically and responsibly. In the nineteenth century, alienists introduced new drugs, some of which have since become illegal. For example, Jacques Moreau (de Tours) (1804–84) brought cannabis back from his travels in the Middle East and Asia Minor at the end of the 1830s. In that part of the world, cannabis had been used for centuries as a drug and stimulant. Moreau himself smoked hashish, and he also offered it to his friends and patients at the

Bicêtre Mental Hospital. In 1845, Moreau published a book in which he claimed that psychologically there was no difference between sleep and the delirium that was common both in mental disturbance and hashish intoxication. On a psychological level, to dream and to be mad were identical processes in Moreau's opinion. Still, he did not believe that hashish was an efficient drug (Dowbiggin 1991, 55–8; Goldstein 1987, 266).

Compared to cannabis, opium, obtained from the opium poppy, had been known and used in Europe since antiquity. Opium produces a pleasant lassitude and drowsiness, and it was the most potent form of pain relief. In antiquity, all known antidotes included opium. In the sixteenth century, the innovative physician Paracelsus described an opium-based tincture that he called 'laudanum', and he recommended that it be used – sparingly, though – as a potent painkiller. The seventeenth-century British doctor Thomas Sydenham praised opium as the most universal and efficacious drug for the relief of suffering, and he compounded a proprietary opium tincture that he also named laudanum (Jones 1983, 39). When the East India Company became involved in the opium trade through India in the late eighteenth century, laudanum became popular among doctors and their patients in Britain.

In 1804, the alkaloid morphine was extracted from the opium poppy plant in Germany. Morphine began to be used as a sedative in German psychiatry (Hodgson 2001). Named after the Greek god Morpheus, morphine was an efficient painkiller, but it was soon noticed that it was more addictive than opium or alcohol. In the 1830s, hyoscyamine was isolated from *Hyoscamus* in Germany, and pharmacological investigations indicated that the drug had hypnotic (sleep-inducing) and sedative properties. Hyoscamine was taken into use in mental asylums, and some alienists even reported patients with chronic forms of mania and alcoholism being cured. Then, in 1874, heroin (diacetylmorphine) was synthesized from morphine. Heroin was the most potent opium-based drug, and also the most addictive. But the latter information was still lacking when the drug company Bayer brought it to market in 1898 as a non-addictive morphine substitute and cough suppressant (Fernandez & Libby 2011).

In the 1880s, hyoscine was isolated from hyoscamine, and the new drug, later named scopolamine, began to be used in asylums to calm agitated patients. The drug also produced confusion, disorientation and incoordination. The German drug company Merck became the leading manufacturer of hyoscine, and the drug was still used in the 1950s, for example in Dutch mental hospitals (Pieters & Snelders 2006, 383–5). As it was thought that individuals under the influence of scopolamine (hyoscine) could not tell lies, scopolamine was also used for a while as a 'truth serum' in the United States. In 1922, the US obstetrician Robert House suggested that the drug be used in the interrogation of suspected criminals, and he himself did one successful experiment with two prisoners from Dallas county jail. For a while, scopolamine was indeed used for police interrogation, but due to its undesirable side effects, it was disqualified as a truth serum in the United States (Bimmerle 1993).

Opium-based drugs were welcomed as painkillers in general medicine, and henbane extracts were useful in dampening manic and nervous excitation. Asylums were also in need of drugs that would put the patients to sleep. One of the first sleeping aids was chloral hydrate, synthesized in 1832 and used as a sedative and hypnotic from 1869 onwards. Chloral hydrate is soluble in both water and alcohol, and it became known as 'knockout drops' when it was mixed with alcohol – it was put into a drink surreptitiously to render the drinker temporarily unconscious so that the victim could then be robbed. As a drug, chloral hydrate was anything but safe, because it could cause rashes, gastric discomfort and severe renal, cardiac and hepatic failure. Overdosage could be fatal. Another widely used sleeping aid or 'hypnotic' was paraldehyde, a bitter-tasting liquid of penetrating odour (Jones 1983, 42–3). Memories of the unpleasant odour of paraldehyde haunted many patients and nurses until the mid-twentieth century, and these olfactory memories were certainly very unlike the French novelist Marcel Proust's evocative memory of a lovely madeleine biscuit that he had tasted as a child.

Opiates were used especially for the treatment of nervous illnesses. Otherwise, physicians did not usually favour medication as a primary treatment for mental disorders until the mid-twentieth century. In 1879, the British psychiatrist Henry Maudsley criticized what he regarded as a reckless use of sedatives, which he called 'chemical restraints'. Some years later, his colleague Daniel Hack Tuke, descendant of the 'anti-medical' Tuke family of the York Retreat fame, was even more critical, claiming that 'while the bromide has slain its thousands, chloral hydrate has slain its tens of thousands' (Jones 1983, 106). Both bromide and chloral hydrate were difficult to administer due to the danger of overdose. No wonder alienists were glad to replace them with the new class of sedatives called barbiturates, which were developed by German chemists at the beginning of the twentieth century. In most mental hospitals in the western hemisphere during the first half of the twentieth century, patients were given barbiturates that had such brand names as *Veronal*, *Somnifem* or *Medinal*. They were less toxic than bromides and free of their bitter aftertaste. A little later, luminal and sodium amytal, both barbiturate derivatives, began to be used at mental hospitals not only to induce sleep, but also to reduce anxiety. In general practice, barbiturates were widely prescribed for anxiety-related conditions. By the mid-twentieth century, pharmaceutical companies had produced around 1,500 variants of barbiturates or 'goofballs', as they were called on the street. Notwithstanding their popularity, they were anything but safe drugs: dangerous overdoses were common, and the drugs were also addictive. Marilyn Monroe died of an overdose of barbiturates in 1962, and the deaths of Judy Garland (in 1969) and Elvis Presley (in 1977) were also barbiturate-related (Tone 2009).

Natural remedy for manic-depression

One of the most extraordinary drugs in the history of psychopharmacology is lithium (see Johnson 1984; Healy 2002, 47–50; Shorter 2009, 65–8). Although a psychotropic drug, it was not produced by a pharmaceutical company. Rather, it is a chemical element (Li), a soft, silver-white metal belonging to the alkali metal group of chemical elements. It is found in minute quantities in bubbling waters fed by underground springs. Today, there is much demand for lithium, because its applications are used in aircraft, lithium batteries and lithium ion batteries in mobile phones and computers. Lithium was isolated in 1817, and it began to be used medically for gout as well as for various nervous afflictions in spas around Europe. At the turn of the twentieth century, lithium was widely marketed as one of the so-called patent medicine products, and later it was the medicinal ingredient of a lemon-lime soft drink. Originally named 'Bib-Label Lithiated Lemon-Lime Soda', its name was soon changed to 7 Up, perhaps with reference to its seven 'refreshing' ingredients (its inventor also boasted that the drink would cure humankind's 'seven hangovers'). This popular lemonade contained lithium citrate until American beverage makers were forced to remove the lithium in 1948.

The therapeutic usefulness of lithium in the treatment of manic-depression was discovered by chance only one year after lithium was removed from 7 Up. In 1949, a previously unknown Australian psychiatrist, John Cade, found out that lithium had psychotropic effects. He then published an article reporting the promising results: lithium produced dramatic therapeutic effects on the mental state of manic patients within days (Cade 1949). Cade's report was received coolly due to lithium's rather bad reputation as a therapeutic substance. When his colleague in Australia reported the first fatality linked to lithium's psychiatric use in 1950, it was bad publicity for Cade, who lost confidence in lithium and began to experiment with a number of other minerals. It was only after the young Danish psychiatrist Mogens Schou (1918–2005) became interested in lithium that it was brought to the attention of the international psychiatric community in the 1950s. Schou decided to embark on a new type of controlled trial to evaluate the effects of lithium (Shorter 2009, 65–6). In the new type of trial, neither the patients, nor the psychiatrists assessing the effects of treatment, nor the nursing staff knew (for sure) whether a particular patient was taking lithium or placebo. The idea of comparing the drug under investigation with a placebo pill had emerged in the late 1930s, and the controlled trial used by Schou began to be known as a *randomized controlled trial* (RCT). Subsequently RCT has a become a standard procedure in medical trials, so much so that other types of trials are hardly used at all.

Schou's trial showed the therapeutic effects of lithium, which had a peculiar effect on manic-depressive patients: the drug made both the highs of mania and the lows of depression disappear (Schou 1959, 65–78). Lithium appeared to have a dual effect on a 'dualistic' illness. Subsequent clinical trials confirmed John Cade's original report on lithium as a therapeutic drug. More precisely, new RCTs suggested that while lithium did not actually cure manic-depressive psychosis, it functioned as a mood-stabilizing drug. Lithium could alleviate the worst symptoms of manic-depressive patients, which is something other drugs failed to do as consistently as lithium. It appeared to be more effective in preventing mania than depression, and it also reduced the risk of suicide in manic-depressive patients. Furthermore, it was more effective than neuroleptics in the prevention of relapse (Shorter 2009, 68).

292 Madness in the Cold War era and beyond

The application of lithium in manic episodes was approved by the US Food and Drug Administration in 1970, and some years later its use was extended to manic-depressive illness. Like other psychotropic drugs, lithium produces a number of side effects, some of which can be very unpleasant and even hazardous to health, including tremor, ataxia (loss of balance), slurred speech, disorientation and, in the final stages, even coma, kidney failure and death. As an alkali metal, lithium is toxic to the human body and especially to the nervous system (Moncrieff 2009, 187).

Magic bullets of psychiatry

The French pharmaceutical company Rhône-Poulenc synthesized antihistamines in the 1940s. One of these antihistamines, promethazine, had a sedative effect, so it began to be used as a sleeping aid. Initially, the executives at Rhône-Poulenc were not interested in psychiatry but in the surgical uses of antihistamines. When the Parisian physician Henri Laborit (1914–95) tested the compound and found that it produced indifference in his patients, he became interested in the usefulness of the compound in surgery. One of the new antihistamine compounds was RP 4560 or chlorpromazine. It affected the sympathetic nervous system and enhanced the sedative effect of barbiturates. When the compound was given to rats, they appeared to become not so much sedated or confused as indifferent to external stimuli. Intrigued by the indifference that the compound produced, Laborit continued his experiments with chlorpromazine. One of his colleagues had said to him that chlorpromazine produced 'a veritable medicinal lobotomy'. Laborit himself reported on both the indifference and 'detachment' induced by the drug – it seemed to induce a mental state in which patients were uninterested in what went on around them (Healy 2002, 80–2; Valenstein 2001, 22–6).

In early 1952, psychiatrist Pierre Deniker (1917–98) took a decisive step by giving chlorpromazine to his patients in the male locked ward in the large Parisian mental hospital Sainte-Anne. The effect of the drug was startling: just like his surgeon colleagues, Deniker noted that, unlike barbiturates, chlorpromazine did not sedate patients so that they became drowsy and lethargic. Instead, the drug produced an attitude of indifference, as if there were an invisible wall between the patients and their environment. Under the influence of chlorpromazine, patients often became motionless and silent *without* becoming unresponsive, inattentive or non-reflective. Better still, some patients appeared to wake up. Some of these awakenings were quite dramatic. One patient at Sainte-Anne was a barber from Lyon, a chronic psychotic who was unresponsive to his environment. When the barber was given chlorpromazine,

> he awoke from this stuporous state and told his doctor, Jean Perrin, that he now knew where he was and who he was, and that he wanted to go home and back to work. Perrin responded by challenging him to give him a shave. The open razor, water, and towels were produced and the patient set about

doing his work perfectly. Either Perrin had considerable nerve or the transformations were truly extraordinary.

(Healy 2002, 91)

In another hospital, chlorpromazine woke up a chronic psychotic patient who was frozen in a series of postures and whose personal history was unknown to everyone. His response to the drug was as dramatic as that of Perrin's barber. He greeted his doctor and the nursing staff and asked them to bring him some billiard balls. When the balls were given to him, he began to juggle them as if he were in a circus. It turned out that the man had been a professional juggler before going mad. In several wards across France, psychiatrists witnessed similar awakenings, which in their eyes were nothing less than miraculous. Patients told about the voices that they had been hearing for years: they were gone. Now they were well and would like to go back home (Healy 2002, 91–2).

No wonder Pierre Deniker and his superior Jean Delay (1907–87) rushed to send reports on these 'magic bullets' to the medical journals. After all, they were the first to have the idea of giving their patients chlorpromazine alone, and not together with other compounds. The main point in their articles was that chlorpromazine appeared to affect the brain and the central nervous system. To emphasize this point, Jean Delay coined the term 'neuroleptic' to refer to the observation that the drug caused neurological motor symptoms that resembled Parkinson's disease. Delay and Deniker inferred that chlorpromazine took hold of the nervous system and dulled its activity. At first, the medical reception to their reports was cool – the received wisdom was that psychosis could not be treated, let alone cured, by drugs. Even the pharmaceutical company Rhône-Poulenc was not keen on marketing chlorpromazine as a psychiatric drug, because it was not considered profitable enough. The very idea that psychiatric drugs could sell well was alien to the pharmaceutical companies in the early 1950s. But this time Rhône-Poulenc decided to start manufacturing chlorpromazine under the trade name *Largactil* and to send samples to more than a hundred researchers in nine different countries for clinical trials (Healy 2002, 92; Valenstein 2001, 25).

Struck by the initial positive responses to chlorpromazine, the French psychiatrists had no idea of the effects of the drug in the long term. It was in the mental hospital in Lyon where psychiatrists first reported the recurrence of psychosis when the rapidly discharged patients returned to the hospital in a few days. It began to dawn on the psychiatrists that chlorpromazine was not like penicillin – it did not kill the 'insanity virus' just like that. Rather than curing mental patients, the drug only alleviated the symptoms of psychosis. This discovery at first discouraged psychiatrists, but it also led to the development of new methods, such as milieu therapy and group psychotherapy, which were designed to rehabilitate and resocialize discharged patients (Healy 2002, 93–5).

In Basel, Switzerland, psychiatrists made the same observation as their French colleagues: chlorpromazine woke up many patients from their stuporous condition, and chronic psychotics seemed to return to their former selves, as if their

294 Madness in the Cold War era and beyond

personalities had been reintegrated. As a result, the locked doors of the wards were opened, staff morale was improved ('we can really help our patients!'), and the need for restraints was almost completely eliminated. In short, the whole atmosphere of the mental hospital became more positive, more therapeutic. At the same time, patients were usually not cured, and the symptoms tended to return as soon as the medication was discontinued and the patients were discharged. What was even worse, a third of the patients relapsed despite ongoing chlorpromazine treatment (Healy 2002, 95–6).

Medical historian Viola Balz has examined the effects of chlorpromazine by looking at the patient records at the Heidelberg psychiatric clinic in Germany. She investigated a clinical trial conducted in 1953 at Heidelberg, where psychiatrists tested *Megaphen*, chlorpromazine manufactured by the pharmaceutical company Bayer. Balz analysed the hospital records of the first patient to be treated with chlorpromazine, and she noticed how the patient and the doctors had strikingly different perspectives on both the diagnosis and the treatment. The patient was a middle-aged, well-educated man by the name of Anton Melchers, who had been an editor of a national-socialistic newspaper and then, when the war broke out in 1939, a war reporter. When the drug trial started, he had been in the Heidelberg clinic for two weeks, and his doctors suspected that he was suffering from schizophrenia. What was striking was that neither Melchers nor any of his relatives gave their consent to the new form of drug therapy – apparently, they were not even asked about it. This was a violation of the 1946 Nuremberg Code, which stipulated that patients had to give their informed consent to treatment. Such a negligence of medical ethics was not unusual in post-war psychiatric practices in western countries; what was quite unusual was that Melchers himself was asked or told to write a self-report on the drug trial.

In his report, Melchers described his symptoms in colloquial language, not in medical jargon. For example, his auditory hallucinations were a sign of 'nervousness', his nerves were 'strained' and his nervous system as a whole was 'oversensitive'. As we have seen, many psychiatric patients preferred to suffer from 'nervousness' rather than mental illness, because nervous people were considered curable. Furthermore, Melchers did not attribute his improvement to the medication, as he was told to do, but instead referred to a sensible lifestyle, avoidance of overwork and, most importantly, to exercise, healthy nutrition and fresh air. Unfortunately, when the medication was discontinued, Melchers' symptoms reappeared. He then received a second *Megaphen* treatment, to no avail: auditory hallucinations bothered Melchers so much that he spent much of his time lying in bed with his hands over his ears. Disappointed, his doctors replaced chlorpromazine with electroshocks and insulin coma therapy. But Melchers was still hearing voices. He was then transferred to another asylum, from where he was released into the charge of his family about five months later (Balz 2011, 190–2).

Melcher was expected to give a detailed description of the (positive) effects of chlorpromazine. Instead, in his self-report he virtually disregarded the significance of the drug. Moreover, he avoided using psychiatric terms when he described his

The psychopharmacological revolution **295**

condition. Basically, Melchers failed to fulfil his role as a good patient. This fundamental discrepancy between the hopes and expectations of physicians and the experiences and perceptions of patients has characterized the history of psychiatry from the very beginning (see Goldberg 1999). Melchers' case is instructive in that when we examine the efficiency of drug therapy or any other type of treatment we have to take into account the experiences and descriptions of the patients. Otherwise, as Viola Balz points out, there is a real danger of historians 'conspiring again with psychiatrists to exclude patients from the history of therapeutic innovation' (Balz 2011, 193). This is especially important in the case of psychiatric therapies, because in clinical psychiatry the evaluation of therapeutic efficiency is largely dependent on the patient's subjective voice. By excluding the sufferers' experiences we distort the truth about the nature of psychiatric treatments.

Thorazine conquers America

In the United States, Rhône-Poulenc licensed chlorpromazine to Smith, Kline & French (today's GlaxoSmithKline), and the drug was named *Thorazine*. In 1954, the first clinical trial of chlorpromazine conducted in the United States was published. In this clinical trial, financed by Smith, Kline & French and lasting for eight months, a group of 142 schizophrenic, manic, psychoneurotic, senile, epileptic and neurologically impaired patients received varying doses of *Thorazine*. In his report, the psychiatrist William Winkelman eulogized chlorpromazine:

> The drug is especially remarkable in that it can reduce severe anxiety, diminish phobias and obsessions, reverse or modify a paranoid psychosis, quiet manic or extremely agitated patients, and change the hostile, agitated, senile patient into a quiet, easily managed patient.
>
> (Valenstein 2001, 32)

Winkelman's conclusion was firm and clear: excluding depression, chlorpromazine was useful in treating almost any type of mental disorder confronted by psychiatrists in their daily practice.

In overcrowded asylums across the United States, the medical staff and administrators pricked up their ears at these startling reports. Could it really be the case that finally there was a remedy that in a cheap and easy way alleviated the symptoms of psychosis and pacified the wards? At first, many psychiatrists thought that *Thorazine* was merely a sedative that would curb the acute symptoms until the psychotic episode remitted. Soon the American asylum doctors noticed the same phenomenon as their French and Swiss colleagues: *Thorazine* seemed to wake psychotic patients from their stuporous or catatonic condition. Once the news of these 'awakenings' spread across American asylums, chlorpromazine began to be valued almost as a miracle drug. In Germany, on the other hand, the reception of chlorpromazine was more lukewarm. There, the effects of the drug were described with terms such as 'cold sleep' (*Kälteschlaf*) and 'hibernation' (*Winterschlaf*), which referred to the state of consciousness between sleep and being awake. German psychiatrists noted that chlorpromazine lowered the circulation, body temperature, oxygen intake and blood pressure, thereby producing a peculiar state resembling artificial hibernation (Balz 2011). There was more enthusiasm for the therapeutic potential of chlorpromazine in the United States than in Germany, where the compound was seen more as a chemical inhibitor.

In the United States, the marketing of *Thorazine* began in spring 1954. Within a year, over 2 million prescriptions were written for the drug, and the sales for the first year were reportedly $75 million (nearly $6.6 billion in today's dollars). Executives at Smith, Kline & French must have been extremely happy. An obvious reason for such a demand was the massive number of 'customers': in 1955, there were 559,000 hospitalized mental patients in the United States (the peak number); in England and Wales too, the number was huge – nearly 150,000 patients in 1954. In some American asylums there were around 15,000 patients. In addition, private practitioners, who initially only wanted to use medication to support the psycho-therapeutic process, gradually began to rely more on drugs and less on intensive talk therapy (Valenstein 2001, 2). Edward Shorter, a historian of psychiatry, has claimed that chlorpromazine 'initiated a revolution in psychiatry, comparable to the introduction of penicillin in general medicine' (Shorter 1997, 255). A less hyberbolic commentator, David Healy, is probably right in calling chlorpromazine the 'single most important breakthrough in psychiatric treatment' (Healy 1997, 46).

Nevertheless, Pierre Deniker and Jean Delay, the two French psychiatrists who were the first to report on the exclusively psychiatric properties of the compound, waited in vain to win the Nobel Prize in Medicine. Instead, for the radical French students of the late 1960s, Delay represented the rigid hierarchical order these 'anti-psychiatric' students wanted to destroy. In the 'crazy year' of 1968, Parisian students invaded and ransacked Delay's office in the Department of Psychiatry and proclaimed that, due to the massive administration of neuroleptics such as chlorpromazine, the new silence reigning in mental hospitals was the silence of the cemetery. When the University of Paris responded to the students' demands by proposing a reorganization, Delay resigned (Healy 2002, 176–7).

Chlorpromazine was quickly taken into clinical use all over the world. Together with other neuroleptics, such as reserpine and haloperidol, it contributed to the transformation of mental health care from asylum-based institutional care to outpatient care, polyclinics, day hospitals, counselling and health care centres. In the United States, the status of chlorpromazine was gradually elevated to that of 'antipsychotic', whereas the more cautious Europeans stuck to the less grandiose term 'neuroleptic'. What also happened in the United States in the late 1960s was that psychiatrists became more impatient with the therapeutic results of *Thorazine*. To speed up the alleged healing process, they increased the doses from 200 to 600 milligrams per day to as much as 2 grams per day. In other words, megadoses of neuroleptics were administered to the patients, whose so-called side effects naturally became more severe.

The psychopharmacological revolution   **297**

FIGURE 14.1 Thorazine advert (1962).

In 1964, the term 'tardive dyskinesia' was coined to refer to the problems of abnormal involuntary movements, such as strange jaw, tongue and cheek movements. It slowly dawned on psychiatrists that long-term drug treatment might cause these 'pseudo-Parkinsonian' symptoms. An even more serious clinical problem was akathisia, which literally means the inability to sit still. Earliest descriptions of this pernicious malady date from the seventeenth century, and it reappeared in Europe with the frightening epidemic of *encephalitis lethargica*, which followed, but was not caused by, the great influenza epidemic of 1918 (Foley 2014). Doctors noticed then that 'while some encephalitis patients went into either vegetative or severe Parkinsonian states, others exhibited just the opposite syndrome: excessive motor restlessness' (Healy 2002, 113). For decades after this mysterious epidemic, akathisia remained in the shadows. It was only in association with the introduction of neuroleptics that akathisia became well-known again. In short, akathisia and tardive dyskinesia impaired the health of a number of patients who were on neuroleptic medication (Healy 2002, 249–50).

298 Madness in the Cold War era and beyond

By the end of the 1950s, chlorpromazine had been followed by other potent psychiatric drugs, such as reserpine and haloperidol, by 'minor tranquillizers', such as *Miltown*, and by imipramine and iproniazid, the first antidepressants. At the beginning of the 1960s, the psychopharmacological front was wider than ever.

LSD and experimental madness

The mental effects of lysergic acid diethylamide (LSD-25) were accidentally discovered by the Swiss chemist Albert Hofmann (1906–2008). Hofmann studied lysergic acid derivatives in the hope of developing a respiratory and circulatory stimulant, and, while synthesizing LSD in his laboratory in 1943, he accidentally absorbed a small quantity through his fingertips. When he returned home, he fell into a dream-like state: 'I perceived an uninterrupted stream of fantastic pictures, extraordinary shapes with intense, kaleidoscopic play of colors' (Hofmann 1980, 15). After two hours or so his strange condition faded away. A few days later, Hofmann intentionally took 0.25 milligrams of LSD and experienced a more intensive and terrifying 'acid trip':

> Everything in the room spun around, and the familiar objects and pieces of furniture assumed grotesque, threatening forms. [. . .] A demon had invaded me, had taken possession of my body, mind, and soul. I jumped up and screamed, trying to free myself from him, but then sank down again and lay helpless on the sofa. The substance, with which I had wanted to experiment, had vanquished me. It was the demon that scornfully triumphed over my will. I was seized by the dreadful fear of going insane. I was taken to another world, another place, another time. My body seemed to be without sensation, lifeless, strange. Was I dying? Was this the transition?
>
> (Hofmann 1980, 15)

After this shattering experience, Hofmann realized that LSD caused artificial hallucinations – it was a hallucinogenic drug, a very, very potent drug.

When Hofmann reported the hallucinogenic properties of LSD, human researchers became intrigued by a substance that had such a dramatic effect on people. Some researchers wondered whether there was a specific site of action or a receptor in the brain in which LSD acted as if it were a chemical key that opened the mental lock shielding behaviour and perceptions. Could it be that LSD released the unconscious and repressed forces of the mind? What was not speculation was that LSD was far superior to mescaline, another hallucinogenic, because in order to have the same effects as LSD, hundreds of milligrams of mescaline had to be administered. Therefore, it was easy to see mescaline as a poison, which in large doses seizes the brain. LSD did not have such 'poisonous' effects. It also differed from cannabis, because it was not considered addictive (Healy 2002, 179–80).

In the early 1950s, LSD began to be used clinically and for research purposes. Based on their mind-altering properties, the British psychiatrist Humphrey

Osmond coined the term 'psychedelic' to describe LSD and mescaline. It was discovered that when chlorpromazine was given to patients beforehand, it blocked the effects of LSD and mescaline. And when it was given afterwards, it helped resolve the conditions induced by these psychedelics. It appeared that LSD could induce and resolve symptoms of insanity within hours. This made LSD a suitable research tool for psychiatrists who had an ambition to turn mental medicine into a true science. If it was possible to build experimental and quantifiable models of madness, in which the manipulation of certain variables would provide accurate data on the biochemistry of the brain and, thereby, on the mechanisms of mental illness, then, who knows, it might open a new, truly scientific chapter in the history of psychiatry (Healy 2002, 181–2).

Physicians also started to administer LSD as a therapeutic agent to patients suffering from neuroses, personality problems and alcohol dependence. Being curious about its effects, they also took LSD themselves, and gave it to their friends and colleagues. In Montreal, psychiatrist Ewen Cameron used LSD and other hallucinogens to break the 'psychic defences' of his neurotic patients (see Chapter 13). In California, a young wanna-be writer Ken Kesey participated in a government-sponsored experiment with psychedelics in 1960. At the local veterans' hospital, Kesey was paid 75 dollars to take LSD, mescaline, amphetamine and psilocybin (naturally occurring compound produced by more than 200 species of mushrooms, collectively known as psilocybin mushrooms). Later in the same year, Kesey worked at the hospital for a while as a psychiatric aide, which made it possible for him to take experimental chemicals while sweeping the floor and doing a little typing on his typewriter that he was allowed to bring onto the ward. Soon after this summer job, Kesey wrote his first novel *One Flew Over the Cuckoo's Nest* (1962), a biting satire of the 'pathology of normality' set in a mental hospital in Oregon (for a perceptive analysis of the novel, see Swirski 2012, 52–89). The book became a sensation, as did the 1975 film version, directed by Milos Forman and starring Jack Nicholson. Kesey became an icon of the 1960s counterculture, giving a middle-finger to the 'establishment' with his experimental lifestyle, which included 'acid tests' that he organized in California together with his like-minded friends, the so-called Merry Pranksters (Kesey 2005, vii–viii; Faggen 2005; Stevens 1987, 225–8).

In the 1960s, LSD was used by writers, artists, musicians, hippies and all sorts of bohemians. Many of them were inspired by the 'psychedelic aristocrat' Aldous Huxley, the famous author of *Brave New World* (1932), who in the early 1950s became so enthusiastic about hallucinogens that he wrote two books about them (*The Doors of Perception*, 1954; and *Heaven and Hell*, 1956). Huxley's well-articulated and yet poetic paeans to psychedelics were read by the young Californian musicians who founded the rock group the Doors in the mid-1960s. Quite fittingly, the first single released by the band in 1967 was *Break on Through (to the Other Side)*. On the other side of the Atlantic, the Beatles were rumoured to boost their creativity with the help of LSD. Whereas chlorpromazine was totally devoid of any sort of Romanticism or countercultural posture, LSD was tinged with

300 Madness in the Cold War era and beyond

spirituality, oriental wisdom and consciousness-expanding mysticism. The most famous prophet of LSD was the Harvard psychologist Timothy Leary, who was ousted from Harvard when he became a fervent evangelic of worldwide psychedelic revolution (Higgs 2006).

A more sinister story of LSD involves children. Until the late 1960s, LSD as well as amphetamines and neuroleptics were given to children. One researcher who experimented with children was the eminent American neuropsychiatrist Lauretta Bender (1897–1987), whose work was funded by a CIA front organization in the early 1960s. Bender also administered numerous electroshocks to children between 3 and 12 years of age. In 1960, she started LSD experiments at the Creedmore State Hospital in New York with her colleagues. The experiments varied, as did the numbers and ages of children who were given LSD and neuroleptics, such as reserpine. In one article, Bender and her co-workers reported on the treatment of schizophrenia and autism with LSD. In some experiments, the youngest children were 6 years old. Bender hoped to find out whether the 'autistic defenses of schizophrenic children might be broken down' (Bender et al. 1966, 464). Her descriptions of the therapeutic effects of LSD are mostly positive. Regarding a group of 11 'autistic' boys between the ages of 7 to 11, LSD produced the following results: boys 'became gay, laughing frequently', their awareness was increased and they were 'more affectionate' and 'more like human beings' (Bender et al. 1966, 469). If signs of mental regression occurred in some of the boys, it was attributed to schizophrenia and not to LSD. She summarizes the treatment as follows: when treated with LSD, schizophrenic or brain-damaged (i.e. autistic) children are 'less anxious, less autistic, less plastic, tend to relate better and in general to act like more concrete, less disturbed, retarded children' (Bender et al. 1966, 471).

Interestingly, Bender cites two teenaged schizophrenic boys whose reaction to LSD was different from that of pre-puberty children. The boys said to Bender, '"You are cheating us out of time. You are trying to make us crazy, make us sad, make us do things." Later one said, "You were making us see green monsters but we wouldn't tell you"' (Bender et al. 1966, 485). This utterance can be compared with the remark made by a certain Miss. B., one of the numerous adult patients to receive LSD for experimental purposes in the 1950s. She told her ward doctor in a resigned tone: 'Dr. X, this is serious business – we are pathetic people, don't play with us' (Cholden, Kurland & Savage 1955, 217). All in all, Bender may have conducted nearly 200 LSD experiments with children. She continued her research until the end of the 1960s, when LSD was made illegal even in medical trials. Many of her test subjects were orphans or raised in institutions (Albarelli & Kaye 2010).

LSD was also given to children in Britain. One of these 'acid children' was Marion, who later became a lawyer and a professor in the United States. Marion, then 13, and her elder sister, then 15, were taken to the Chelsea Clinic in London in 1960. They were both normal, healthy teenagers, but unfortunately their own parents, having experimented with LSD themselves, had a strong faith in the benefits of LSD. The parents volunteered their daughters for ten experimental LSD sessions at the clinic. Marion and her sister were given very vague information about the 'therapy', and nothing, for example, was said about hallucinations or perceptual distortions. They were kept separately in darkened rooms, mostly with some unknown person present in the room. Sometimes their mother was also present in the sessions. This is how Marion remembers the ordeal:

> At times, I was so frightened by the hallucinations that I screamed and tried to escape from the room. I remember once actually reaching the hallway and being forcibly put back into the bedroom by my mother. I saw a wild array of images – nightmarish visions, occasionally provoking hysterical laughter.
>
> (Albarelli & Kaye 2010)

Following the final session, Marion experienced frequent nightmares for weeks – visions of crawling insects, horrible masks and so forth. She could not understand what was happening to her. It was a terrifying experience.

After the LSD sessions, Marion became afraid of the dark, unable to sleep and afraid to shut her eyes. What was worse, the parents showed no compassion for their children. Marion's sister never fully recovered from the ordeal, and she has been on medication since she suffered a nervous breakdown two years after the experiment. In none of the publications reporting on LSD experiments with children are there any indications of concern over the possible codes or statutes regarding patient rights, human rights or human dignity. Today, Bender is still hailed by some psychiatrists as a daring pioneer in the study of childhood schizophrenia.

By the mid-1960s there were more and more media reports on suicides, violence and other incidents of antisocial behaviour incited by the recreational consumption of LSD. This was the first time that drugs became a problem haunting the middle class, especially middle-class parents who became worried about their children's 'drug-crazed' lifestyle and morality on university campuses and in big cities. This prompted the authorities to classify LSD, cannabis and heroin as illegal narcotic drugs. There was also a research-based reason to stigmatize LSD: during 20 years of experimental work the accumulated positive evidence of the therapeutic effects of LSD on mental patients was slim indeed. At the same time, there was a growing number of drug addicts among those patients. By the early 1970s, LSD had become illegal across the western world and it was no longer possible to use it for research purposes either (Dyck 2008).

In the 2000s, there has been some resurgence of the medical interest in psychedelic drugs and especially psilocybin, which already in the early 1960s had shown some initial promise in treating chronic pain and depression in terminally ill patients. In recent years, more rigorous, double-blind research has reopened the doors of (scientific) perception, with reports referring to spiritual effects and the increase of an overall sense of well-being and life satisfaction (Biello 2006). Yet, it is unlikely that hallucinogens will in the near future occupy a role even remotely comparable to the wild years of the 1950s and the 1960s.

Mother's Little Helper: tranquillizing nervousness

Readers may not be surprised to learn that the first anti-anxiety drug was discovered accidentally. The story begins in post-war Britain, where the Czech-born physician and pharmacologist Frank Berger (1913–2008) was doing penicillin research. One day, he was testing a penicillin preservative called mephenesin, which he injected into mice to evaluate its toxicity. He noticed that, in low doses, the compound appeared to make the mice relaxed and calm. Intrigued, Berger continued his tests, which confirmed the initial observations: mephenesin caused muscle relaxation and temporary paralysis without making the mice lose consciousness. Next, Berger's 'mouse relaxer' was successfully tested on humans when it was given intravenously to patients waiting for a surgical operation. The effect of mephenesin began to be described as *tranquillizing*. The main problem with the drug was that its effects lasted only a few hours, which prevented its use except as a muscle relaxant. Another problem was that the drug lost much of its potency in oral form. Berger decided to develop a medicine 'that would be as effective as mephenesin, last longer, and remain as potent in pill form' (Tone 2009, 36).

After moving to the United States, Berger continued his work on drug development in New Jersey. One of the compounds that seemed particularly promising was meprobamate, which had calming effects on the volatile Rhesus and Java monkeys that were kept in the laboratory. Berger and his colleagues hit on the idea of making a short documentary film about the Rhesus monkeys. First, the monkeys were shown in their 'natural' state, in which they were volatile and violent. Then they were featured in two distinct chemical states: unconscious on barbiturates, and calm but alert on meprobamate. Then, when the compound was tested on humans, it had the same effects as it had on monkeys: the drug reduced anxiety without sedation. One last piece of the puzzle was put in place by the young biologically oriented psychiatrist Nathan Kline, whom Berger met in a Manhattan restaurant. Berger was thinking of calling the new drug a sedative, but Kline talked him out of it: "'The world doesn't need new sedatives. What the world really needs is a tranquilizer. The world needs tranquility'" (Tone 2009, 52).

In 1955, meprobamate was put on the market first as *Miltown*, and then (by another company) as *Equanil*. They were marketed as tranquillizers and, to a lesser extent, as muscle relaxants, and the target audience was as wide as possible: anybody with troubled nerves was a potential customer. This marketing strategy worked better than Berger or anyone had dreamed of: the net profit of the first-year sales was $100 million (in today's money, $8.6 *billion*). With the help of marketing campaigns and nationwide media coverage, *Miltown* was turned into an emotional aspirin that belonged in the medicine cabinet of each and every American. Meprobamate became the best-selling drug ever marketed in the United States. It was not devoid of side effects and it could also be mildly addictive. But the overall reactions from physicians were positive: meprobamate was a relatively safe drug, and there was no doubt that it worked for many people (Shorter 2009, 44–5; Tone 2009, 84–5).

The psychopharmacological revolution **303**

Many Hollywood celebrities boosted the sales by praising *Miltown* in public, but Frank Berger himself was less than happy about the media hype. In his mind, the media was parlaying a serious problem – anxiety – into a 'stupid joke'. Berger was a dedicated medical scientist and a European intellectual who admired the rationalist philosophy of Spinoza and saw the importance of the drug in its calming effect on anxiety, which impaired clear thinking and blocked attempts at serious discussion. Besides, he was committed to socialized medicine and disliked drug promotion, marketing and salesmanship (Tone 2009, 48, 67). It is somewhat ironic that his pharmaceutical discovery became the best-selling drug in the most capitalist country in the world.

In the mid-1950s, the United States was becoming an increasingly affluent society, but Americans felt somewhat anxious about the Cold War and the possibility of a devastating nuclear war. The whole society was in flux: the rapidly growing middle class began to move from city centres to suburbs; there was more demand for office workers as the industrial society was gradually becoming more consumer centred and managerial; and the normative codes regulating social life became rather conformist and uniform. Thus there was a social demand for anti-anxiety therapy, just as in the late nineteenth-century era of industralization and urbanization there had been social demand for 'weakness of the nerves' (neurasthenia) and 'nerve pills' that aimed to invigorate the overtaxed and exhausted nervous system (Schuster 2011). In the American society of the 1950s, tranquillizing drugs were commonly perceived as a sign of success in the same way as a house in a fashionable neighbourhood, a credit card, an electric refrigerator, TV-dinners or cosmetics. Furthermore, *Miltown* was a much easier and quicker way to find relief than the then very fashionable Freudian psychotherapy. *Miltown* fitted very well with the American go-getter mentality that favoured a quick fix for society's ills.

Tranquillizers were later associated with women's worries and especially with the anxieties of suburban housewives suffering from unfulfilled lives. In the light of this cliché it is in order to point out that *Miltown* was originally marketed to men and men were also the first consumers of tranquillizers. For instance, President John F. Kennedy, the ultimate alpha male, took painkillers, *Ritalin* as an energizer, barbiturates as a sleeping aid and meprobamate as well as *Librium* as anti-anxiety drugs (*Librium* since 1960) (Tone 2009, xvii, 106–7, 112).

Miltown and other mebrobamates enjoyed an extremely wide popularity until the new generation of anti-anxiety drugs appeared on the scene in the early 1960s. These new drugs belonged to the group of benzodiazepines and they were the result of systematic research and development. The first benzodiazepine to hit the market was *Librium*, which, like mebrobamate, was developed by a European-born researcher, Leo Sternbach (1908–2005), who as a Jew had suffered from anti-Semitism while studying in Poland. Sternbach and other chemists at the pharmaceutical company Hoffmann-La Roche were prompted by its executives to produce a drug that would sell more than *Miltown* or the chlorpromazine *Thorazine*. Sternbach did as he was told, and his success, after many frustrating years of hard work, went beyond the wildest dreams of his employers. Sternbach had created

304 Madness in the Cold War era and beyond

a drug that resembled mebrobamate but was more effective and less sedative and toxic. He had synthesized new kinds of chemicals, benzodiazepines, which were effective as tranquillizers and simultaneously kept the mind clear and intelligence unimpaired. The result was the anti-anxiety drug *Librium*, which was released in 1960 (Tone 2009, 133).

Librium quickly became the most popular tranquillizer in the United States. Three years later Roche brought to the growing pharmaceutical market an even more fast-selling benzodiazepine, *Valium*. It was more effective than *Librium* and it lacked the bitter aftertaste of its predecessor. The sales figures of *Valium* were astronomical and there has been nothing comparable before or since. In 1964, 4 million prescriptions were written for *Valium* in the United States; eight years later (1972), the number of prescriptions had grown to over 50 million. It was *Valium* that inspired the Rolling Stones to write a song about 'benzos': in 'Mother's Little Helper' (1966), a desperate housewife asks her doctor to prescribe more pills to alleviate her existential pain. For the last half century, benzos have been a psychomedical smash hit, with worldwide sales exceeding those of any other medicine in the western world between 1968 and 1981. According to some estimates, 100 million prescriptions were written for benzos in 1975 in the United States alone. The consumption of tranquillizers per capita in France in the 1970s was already greater than in the United States. Whereas the Americans and the British have since become more prohibitionary regarding the use of benzos, France and the rest of the industrial world have been much more faithful to these 'minor tranquillizers', as they began to be called in the 1960s in contrast to 'major tranquillizers', such as chlorpromazine and haloperidol (Tone 2009, 223–4).

The negative side of benzos was brought to light in the 1990s, especially in the United States and Britain. The Food and Drug Agency played a pivotal role in the legal restrictions on the prescription of *Valium* and other hugely popular tranquillizers. There was much public discussion about dependency, withdrawal problems and side effects, such as neurological pain, headache, amnesia and cognitive impairment. In 1979, a research committee led by Senator Edward Kennedy, and especially the public hearings that he convened, contributed to the significant decrease in the number of prescriptions from the late 1970s onwards. In Britain, a similar 'anti-benzo' campaign resulted in a dramatic decrease in the number of prescriptions, which were to be limited to 'short-term use' (Shorter 2009, 121–2). Before such restrictions regarding prescriptions were put in place, 'mother's little helper' calmed the nerves of numerous frustrated, anxious and stressed-out men and women all across the world.

From 'energizers' to 'antidepressants'

Depression was a relatively rare diagnosis until the late 1980s, when *Prozac* and other so-called selective serotonin reuptake inhibitor (SSRI) catapulted depression into diagnostic stardom. Not that there were no antidepressants or 'energizers' at all before *Prozac*. On the contrary, there were a number of drugs, none of which,

The psychopharmacological revolution **305**

however, managed to gain even a fraction of the popularity enjoyed by the tranquillizers *Miltown, Librium* or *Valium.*

As Edward Shorter has pointed out, 'history's first true antidepressants were the amphetamines' (Shorter 2009, 24). Amphetamines were effective for low mood, but at the same time they made anxiety worse. In 1919, methamphetamine was synthesized in Japan, and while this particular drug, being very addictive, is now illegal, it is a very effective antidepressant. During World War II, amphetamine and especially methamphetamine were widely used as energizers; they kept tired pilots and soldiers alert in battle. However, they were also used and abused for recreational purposes, which meant that despite their effectiveness as antidepressants, they were considered potentially dangerous to health. Something else had to be used. The solution was found in an unlikely place.

During World War II, the Germans developed the V-2 rocket, the world's first long-range ballistic missile that during the last year of the war (1944–5) was used to bomb London and some other cities in Britain and on the Continent (especially Antwerp in Belgium). One of the fuels used for the rocket was hydrazine, an inorganic compound that was explosive and highly toxic. But when it was combined with other substances and modified, some of these new compounds appeared to have properties that seemed to be potentially useful in medicine. In 1951, American researchers at the Swiss pharmaceutical company Hoffmann-La Roche developed two hydrazine compounds, isoniazid and iproniazid, which turned out to be effective against the tuberculosis bacterium (Valenstein 2001, 36–7).

The new drugs were quickly taken into use at tuberculosis sanatoria. Soon there were reports of the energizing effects of these drugs. In 1952, *Time* magazine described how tuberculosis patients were dancing with joy, which prompted physicians to ponder on the usefulness of these drugs in the treatment of depression. Several groups began to test isoniazid and iproniazid on psychiatric patients, but the results were disappointing, and their use was curtailed in sanatoria (Whitaker 2010, 53). One might have thought that this would have been the end of iproniazid, but the psychiatrist Nathan Kline rescued the compound in 1957 with his clinical report, in which he claimed that if the depressed patients were kept on medication long enough – at least five weeks – then the drug was, after all, effective. Of the 16 patients in Kline's trial, 14 were relieved of their symptoms, and some of them were totally symptom free. These figures impressed the psychiatric community. Most importantly, Kline's observation was accurate: it took several weeks before iproniazid began to have an antidepressant effect. Kline, who some years earlier had told Frank Berger to call mebrobamate a 'tranquillizer', termed the new drug a 'psychic energizer'. As a result of Kline's report, iproniazid, brand-named *Marsilid*, was released in 1958 as an energizer. The new drug appeared to elicit a 'Mona Lisa smile' in depressed patients (Shorter 2009, 55; Valenstein 2001, 37–8).

Around the same time, another 'psychic energizer' was brought to the growing psychopharmacological market. This drug, imipramine, represented the so-called tricyclic antidepressants, so named because of their tricyclic chemical structure. Imipramine was developed by the Swiss psychiatrist Roland Kuhn, whose systematic search resulted in the discovery of a compound that had a visible effect on so-called 'vital depression', which referred to a form of melancholia with the physical sensations of pain and fatigue. The compound seemed to be a 'magic bullet', as it targeted a specific illness or syndrome. In the United States, investigators decided to call both imipramine and iproniazid *antidepressive* agents, a term that would have staying power. Kuhn himself noted that the action of imipramine 'is always purely symptomatic. As soon as the medicant is discontinued the illness breaks out again, usually with undiminished severity after a few days, and it can be cured again by repeating the medicant' (Kuhn 1958, 460).

In the 1960s pharmaceutical companies considered the market for antidepressants too small to be of interest. However, the drug scene changed dramatically in the late 1980s, when the reputation and sales of *Valium* and other benzodiazepines declined while those of the new class of antidepressants, SSRIs, arrived triumphantly on the psychopharmacological scene (Healy 2004). In recent decades, millions of Americans and other westerners have taken Prozac and other SSRIs, and depression, which was an almost unrecognized illness in the 1970s, has become a contagious diagnosis par excellence. As Allen Frances, a prominent US psychiatrist, has noted, the SRRIs were 'user-friendly' medicines that were designed to appeal to a mass consumer market. They were the 'perfect vehicle – no more effective than their predecessors, but much more easily tolerated and safe in overdose'. On the other hand, for a 'significant percentage of people with mild or transient symptoms, SSRIs are nothing more than very expensive, potentially harmful placebos' (Frances 2013, 92, 157). In the light of such expert evaluations (see also Gøtzsche 2013; Angell 2005; and Healy 2004), it may be safe to say that, during the last half century, Big Pharma has not produced better psychiatric drugs, but it has made huge profits by transforming millions of more or less normal people into mental patients who supposedly need (continuous) medication. This is indeed a success story of sorts, but only from the point of view of cash flow for pharmaceutical companies and doctors writing prescriptions.

The era of psychopharmacology

In the annals of psychiatry, a new chapter was opened in the latter half of the 1950s. Henceforth, psychiatry would to a large extent be drug-based. This drug-centred approach was supported and scientifically legitimized by biochemical research on serotonin, dopamine and other so-called neurotransmitters. Such cutting-edge research seemed to confirm the emerging psychopharmacological consensus, according to which mental disorders were essentially biological afflictions that had their matrix in genetics, biochemistry and metabolism. The excitement felt by many early psychopharmacologists is neatly captured by Nathan Kline, who compared the new psychiatric drugs with something of lesser world historical importance, namely nuclear weapons:

> If these drugs provide the long-awaited key which will unlock the mysteries of the relationship of man's chemical constitution to his psychological behaviour and provide effective means of correcting pathological needs there may no longer be any necessity for turning thermonuclear energy to destructive purposes.
>
> (Tone 2009, 83)

Within the time span of a few years (1954–9) psychiatrists around the western world began to use chlorpromazine and reserpine in mental hospitals and tranquillizers and 'psychic energizers' (antidepressants) to treat both institutionalized patients and 'everyday neurotics' who wanted to have pills to ease their minds or nerves. But it would be misleading to think that from the mid-1950s onwards psychiatry became part of biomedicine. On the contrary, while patients at mental institutions became rather heavily drugged, clinical psychology, psychoanalysis and social psychiatry all influenced post-war psychiatry and gave impetus to the idea and practice of a 'therapeutic community', as well as to the inclusion of various forms of psychotherapy in the therapeutic arsenal, and, lastly, to the emphasis on social programmes and the rehabilitation of mental patients. Social psychiatry emerged from World War II as a specialty, and in the late 1960s it became a fashionable framework for explaining the occurrence of mental disorders (Staub 2011). Sociological and psychological approaches to mental health issues were especially popular in academic psychiatry, whereas asylum doctors remained more attached to somatic explanations and therapies.

Moreover, there were no insurmountable barriers between 'hard-nosed' biological psychiatry and 'soft-hearted' psychosocial psychiatry. Many pioneers of psychopharmacology understood the importance of psychosocial support, particularly following the crucial moment when medication was terminated or decreased and the recovering patients returned to their communities. To some early psychopharmacologists, drugs enabled psychotherapy by removing the disturbing symptoms that prevented discussions between the patient and the doctor. In his later years Heinz Lehmann, who was the first psychiatrist to test chlorpromazine in North America, was concerned about the irresponsible way 'anti-psychotics' were used: these powerful drugs prevented the building of communication and trust between the patient and the doctor. In a presentation he gave in 1987, Lehmann said, 'I am anxiously awaiting the next revolution in psychiatry which, I hope, will be a return to the humanities in psychiatry' (Collins 1988, 187).

During the early years of the psychopharmacological era, drugs were not regarded as some sort of antibiotics of the mind. After the initial surprise at the sudden 'awakenings' that asylum psychiatrists witnessed when chlorpromazine was taken into use, expectations became more realistic and moderate. The *New*

York Times described *Thorazine* and *Miltown* as 'adjuncts to psychotherapy, not the cure', and *Life* magazine noted in a 1956 article that 'the search has only begun' and that the 'bacteria' of mental illnesses had yet to be discovered. But it took only a few more years before caution was thrown to the wind, and wishful thinking and ungrounded exaggerations entered the psychopharmacological scene. In 1958, a statement by an American psychiatrist in the prestigious journal *Science* reflected the new hyberbolic language: he wrote that the new 'psychic energizers' or antidepressants (iproniazid and imipramine) 'may be compared with the advent of insulin, which counteracts symptoms of diabetes'. Psychopharmacological enthusiasts and pharmaceutical companies began to trumpet the message that antidepressants, tranquillizers and neuroleptics ('antipsychotics') were fixing something wrong in the brain (Whitaker 2010, 60). Irresponsible comparisons with insulin also suggested that it might be necessary for mental patients to be on psychiatric medication for a very long time if not for the rest of their lives (Valenstein 2001, 221).

The final step towards the rhetorical 'insulinization' of psychiatric drugs was taken in 1963, when the US National Institute for Mental Health (NIMH) conducted a six-week trial of chlorpromazine and other neuroleptics. This high-profile trial showed that these drugs were more effective than placebo in alleviating psychotic symptoms. Clinical researchers did not waste time in pronouncing that neuroleptics should be considered 'anti-schizophrenic' in the broad sense, and not just as 'tranquillizers'. As the journalist and psychiatric historian Robert Whitaker concludes, 'with this pronouncement by the NIMH, the transformation of the psychiatric drugs was basically complete' (Whitaker 2010, 61). What this transformation meant was that, in the early 1960s, *Thorazine* and other potent drugs were no longer mere neuroleptics or 'major tranquillizers'; they were becoming 'antipsychotics' – drugs that worked like antidotes to specific mental diseases. Thus they were supposed to be comparable to antibiotics; both classes of drugs 'killed microbes', but the 'mental microbes' of schizophrenia and other (non-syphilitic) mental illnesses could not yet be detected even with the most advanced technology.

The only thing that was still missing in this fairytale of psychiatric progress was the biological explanation of mental disorders. What researchers had in the early 1960s were some clues that might be helpful in the construction of biological hypotheses about the causes of insanity (Whitaker 2010, 60–1). These clues suggested that the main culprit of mental illness could be found in the biochemistry of the brain. What happened next was that a large-scale scientific search for this or that neurotransmitter, dopamine and serotonin in particular, was launched. Judging by the expectations and initial statements by biochemical researchers, it was thought to be only a matter of time before the riddle of schizophrenia could be solved. In some respects, great expectations were indeed fulfilled, but they were related to the increasing net profits of drug companies rather than to the scientific elucidation of the mechanisms of madness.

Two paths of psychiatric development can be discerned since the early 1960s. On the one hand, pharmacological treatment and biological research have come more and more to the fore. On the other hand, a growing number of people in the United States and other western countries appeared to suffer from mental health problems. Strangely enough, these two paths did not seem to converge, still less to harmonize with each other. Clearly something was wrong in the way western psychiatry was developing if mental suffering was becoming more common and the number of diagnosed and medicated individuals getting larger and larger.

I will conclude this chapter by citing the neuropsychologist and historian Elliot Valenstein, to whose perceptive analysis of drugs and mental health I fully subscribe. At the end of his book *Blaming the Brain* (2001), Valenstein writes the following:

> There is such a morass of experimental and clinical literature of questionable reliability and validity that it is possible to find studies that can support any theory that someone dreams up and wants to promote [. . .] The claims that complex mental and personality traits can be explained by the balance between a couple of neurotransmitters is no more valid than the Hippocratic theory that claimed many of these same traits are determined by the balance between the four basic humours.
>
> (Valenstein 2001, 234–5)

If, indeed, we have ended up reviving the Hippocratic humoral-pathological doctrine in a new guise, then there is more than a slight irony in our story of the development of psychopharmacology. Nietzsche might have called it the 'myth of the eternal return'.

Bibliography

Albarelli Jr, H.P. and Kaye, J.S. (2010) 'The hidden tragedy of the CIA's experiments on children', *Global Research*, August 15. Online. Available HTTP: <www.globalresearch.ca/index.php?context=va&aid=20634> (accessed 11 November 2011).

Angell, M. (2005) *The Truth About the Drug Companies: How They Deceive Us and What to Do About It*, New York: Random House.

Balz, V. (2010) *Zwischen Wirkung und Erfahrung – eine Geschichte der Psychopharmaka. Neuroleptika in der Bunderepublik Deutschland, 1950–1980*, Bielefeld, Germany: Transcript.

Balz, V. (2011) 'Terra incognita: an historiographic approach to the first chlorpromazine trials using patient records of the psychiatric clinic in Heidelberg', *History of Psychiatry*, 22: 182–200.

Bender, L., Cobrinik, L., Faretra, G. and Sankar, D. (1966) 'The treatment of childhood schizophrenia with LSD and UML', in M. Rinkel (ed.) *Biological Treatment of Mental Illness*, New York: L.C. Page & Co.

Biello, D. (2006) 'Not imagining it – research into hallucinogens cautiously resumes', *Scientific American*, November: 33–5.

Bimmerle, G. (1993) '"Truth" drugs in interrogation', *Studies in Intelligence* 5:2. Online. Available HTTP: <www.cia.gov/library/center-for-the-study-of-intelligence/kent-csi/vol5no2/html/v05i2a09p_0001.htm> (accessed 12 October 2014).

Cade, J.F.J. (1949) 'Lithium salts in the treatment of psychotic excitement', *Medical Journal of Australia*, 2: 349–52.

Caldwell, A.E. (1970) *Origins of Psychopharmacology. From CPZ to LSD*, Springfield, IL: Charles C. Thomas.

Cholden, L.S., Kurland, A. and Savage, C. (1955) 'Clinical reactions and tolerance to LSD in chronic schizophrenia', *The Journal of Nervous and Mental Disease*, 122: 211–21.

Collins, A. (1988) *In the Sleep Room. The Story of the CIA Brainwashing Experiments in Canada*, Toronto: Lester & Orpen Dennys.

Dowbiggin, I. (1991) *Inheriting Madness: Professionalization and Psychiatric Knowledge in Nineteenth-century France*, Berkeley: University of California Press.

Dyck, E. (2008) *Psychedelic Psychiatry: LSD from Clinic to Campus*, Baltimore, MD: The Johns Hopkins University Press.

Faggen, R. (2005) 'Introduction', in K. Kesey, *One Flew Over the Cuckoo's Nest*, London: Penguin.

Fernandez, H. and Libby, T.A. (2011) *Heroin: Its History, Pharmacology & Treatment*, Center City, MN: Hazelden.

Foley, P. (2014) *Encephalitis Lethargica: The Mind and Brain Virus*, Berlin: Springer.

Frances, A. (2013) *Saving Normal. An Insider's Revolt against Out-of-control Psychiatric Diagnosis, DSM-5, Big Pharma, and the Medicalization of Ordinary Life*, New York: William Morrow.

Goldberg, A. (1999) *Sex, Religion and the Making of Modern Madness*, Oxford: Oxford University Press.

Goldstein, J. (1987) *Console and Classify. The French Psychiatric Profession in the Nineteenth Century*, Cambridge: Cambridge University Press.

Gøtzsche, P.C. (2013) *Deadly Medicines and Organised Crime*, London: Radcliffe Publishing.

Healy, D. (1997) *The Antidepressant Era*, Cambridge, MA: Harvard University Press.

Healy, D. (2002) *The Creation of Psychopharmacology*, Cambridge, MA: Harvard University Press.

Healy, D. (2004) *Let Them Eat Prozac*, New York: New York University Press.

Higgs, J. (2006) *I Have America Surrounded: A Biography of Timothy Leary*, London: Friday Books.

Hodgson, B. (2001) *In the Arms of Morpheus: The Tragic History of Laudanum, Morphine, and Patent Medicines*, Buffalo, NY: Firefly Books.

Hofmann, A. (1980) *LSD – My Problem Child*, trans. J. Ott, New York: MacGraw-Hill.

Jablensky, A. (1992) 'Schizophrenia: Manifestations, incidence and course in different cultures, a World Health Organization ten-country study', *Psychological Medicine, Suppl.*, 22: 1–95.

Johnson, F.N. (1984) *The History of Lithium Therapy*, London: Macmillan.

Jones, W.L. (1983) *Ministering to Minds Diseased*, London: William Heinemann Medical Books.

Kesey, K. (2005) *One Flew Over the Cuckoo's Nest*, 1st edn 1962, London: Penguin.

Kuhn, R. (1958) 'The treatment of depressive states with G22355 (imipramine hydrochloride)', *American Journal of Psychiatry*, 115: 459–64.

Leff, J. (1992) 'The international pilot study of schizophrenia: five-year follow-up findings', *Psychological Medicine*, 22: 131–45.

Moncrieff, J. (2009) *Myth of the Chemical Cure*, Basingstoke: Palgrave Macmillan.

Pieters, T. and Snelders, S. (2006) 'Mental ills and the "hidden history" of drug treatment practices', in M. Gijswijt, H. Oosterhuis and J. Vijselaar (eds) *Psychiatric Cultures Compared: Psychiatry and Mental Health Care in the Twentieth Century*, Amsterdam: Amsterdam University Press.

Pinel, P. (2009) *A Treatise on Insanity*, orig. French edn 1801, Milton Keynes: General Books.

Schou, M. (1959) 'Lithium in psychiatric therapy', *Psychopharmacologia*, 1: 65–78.

Schuster, D.G. (2011) *Neurasthenic Nation: America's Search for Health, Happiness, and Comfort, 1869–1920*, New Brunswick, NJ: Rutgers University Press.

Shorter, E. (1997) *A History of Psychiatry*, New York: John Wiley & Sons.

Shorter, E. (2009) *Before Prozac. The Troubled History of Mood Disorders in Psychiatry*, Oxford: Oxford University Press.

Staub, M.E. (2011) *Madness is Civilization: When the Diagnosis Was Social, 1948–1980*, Chicago: University of Chicago Press.

Stevens, J. (1987) *Storming Heaven: LSD and the American Dream*, New York: Grove Press.

Swirski, P. (2012) *American Utopia and Social Engineering in Literature, Social Thought, and Political History*, New York: Routledge.

Tone, A. (2009) *The Age of Anxiety*, New York: Basic Books.

Valenstein, E.S. (2001) *Blaming the Brain*, New York: The Free Press.

Weber, M.M. (1999) *Die Entwicklung der Psychopharmakologie im Zeitalter der naturwissenschaftlichen Medizin: Ideengeschichte eines psychiatrischen Therapiesystems*, Munich: Urban und Vogel.

Whitaker, R. (2003) *Mad in America*, New York: Basic Books.

Whitaker, R. (2010) *Anatomy of an Epidemic*, New York: Crown.

15

MADNESS BETWEEN SANITY AND NORMALITY

Political psychiatry became more systematic and repressive in the Soviet Union during the 1960s, but in the Western bloc it was psychiatry *itself* that came under attack. As we will see in this chapter, while the principal target of such anti-psychiatric assault was mental medicine, radical critics of psychiatry did not spare the political and economic establishment either. However, by the end of the 1970s radical psychiatry was already yesterday's papers to the younger generation of mental health experts, and the medical model of madness was re-emerging with a vengeance. This chapter gives an account of the twists and turns in the theories and management of madness from the 1960s to the end of the century.

'Coercion as cure': anti-psychiatry and the madness of normality

In a book published in 1961, the Hungarian-born American psychiatrist Thomas Szasz (1920–2012) made a startling statement about mental illness: it did not exist! In his *Myth of Mental Illness*, Szasz argued that the concept of mental illness was 'scientifically worthless and socially harmful' (Szasz 1974, xiii). He justified his extravagant claim by referring to the fact that there is no medically reliable way of verifying illnesses of the mind. Hence, rather than talk about mental illness as if it were an objective disease entity, we should talk about the *myth* of mental illness. What is common to all myths is that while they are imaginative stories, people have tended to believe them, at least for a while, because they seem to say something important about the gods and other supernatural entities as well as about the human condition. The myth of mental illness is a myth precisely because we are inclined to believe in it 'half-instinctively' and uncritically. Szasz himself could only accept the reality of somatic diseases that could be verified by objective means (such as X-ray or blood test). By contrast, something that cannot be seen or measured objectively – the mind – cannot fall ill. Szasz was a philosophical realist who argued that since diseases are by definition something that affect only the body or soma, mental illness can only exist as a metaphor. Minds can only be 'sick' in the same way that 'jokes are "sick" or economies are "sick"' (Szasz 1974, 267). While modern medicine discovers diseases, modern psychiatry *invents* them. To Szasz, hysteria and schizophrenia are good examples of invented diseases. What follows from this line of reasoning is that mental patients do not have medical but *moral* problems (Szasz 1974, xi, 12).

Szasz was not content with his denial of the objective reality of mental illness, he also maintained that in psychiatry there is an inbuilt drive to change mental patients regardless of their own will. For this reason, psychiatry is not a medical specialty but a form of moral and psychological suggestion. As a profession, psychiatry resembles the work of pastors, priests and policemen more than that of physicians (Szasz 2007). Szasz's take-no-prisoners approach is unmistakable in his evaluation of psychiatric diagnoses as well: they do more harm than good to people. This was the anti-psychiatric message Szasz proclaimed with enviable vigour and energy from the early 1960s until his death in 2012. In his numerous writings during these 50 years, he was especially fierce and uncompromising in his attack on psychiatric treatment methods and on what he saw as deprivation of freedom without the informed consent of individuals. According to Szasz, when therapeutic interventions are carried out without informed consent, they are 'crimes against humanity' (Szasz 1974, 268). His bold and provocative arguments and assertions made Szasz famous both among friends and critics of psychiatry. In the latter group, the Church of Scientology has become a tireless accuser of psychiatry from the vantage point of human rights, and Szasz, a libertarian rationalist, found common ground with scientologists on this particular point. In 1969, they co-founded the Citizens Commission for Human Rights (CCHR), which makes extremely extravagant statements about psychiatry, including allegations about psychiatry's long-standing 'master plan' for world domination (Gumbel 2006).

As the 1960s drew to a close, Szasz found that he was associated with other critics of psychiatry, some of whom were politically radical or left-wing. One of them was the Canadian-American sociologist Erving Goffman, whose study of 'total institutions' inspired many social scientists to do critical research on mental health issues (*Asylums*, 1961; on Goffman's concept of total institution, see Chapter 7). His 1963 work on stigma, in which he studied the ways in which people managed their 'spoiled identity' and how they tried to control information about it, also found a receptive audience among critics of psychiatry (Goffman 1963). Goffman's American colleague Thomas Scheff (b. 1929) in turn developed the labelling theory of mental illness, which inspired Szasz. Scheff argued quite persuasively that psychiatric diagnoses are stigmatizing labels that mark deviant people as disordered and legitimize their incarceration in mental institutes. Scheff's critique of the questionable legal justifications of involuntary treatment had an impact on the reforms of American mental health legislation. He later conceded that his labelling theory is only one of many possible perspectives on mental illness (Scheff 1999).

314 Madness in the Cold War era and beyond

Alongside Szasz, perhaps the most important critic of psychiatry was Michel Foucault, Professor of the History of Systems of Thought at the Collège de France (on Foucault's idea of 'the great confinement', see Chapter 5). In 1961, the same year that Szasz's *Myth of Mental Illness* as well as Goffman's *Asylums* were published, Foucault defended his extensive doctoral dissertation on the history of madness (*Folie et Déraison. Histoire de la folie à l'âge classique*). In his dissertation, the English translation of which was published in its entirety only in 2006 as *History of Madness*, he casts a shadow of doubt on the whole medical 'discourse on madness'. To Foucault and his ever-growing academic disciples, madness or 'unreason' (*déraison*) appeared to be some sort of existential authenticity, as if the mad had chosen their unconventional lifestyle, which then caused them suffering and misery. Foucault was instrumental in establishing a vantage point on the history of madness that was critical, philosophical and suspicious of all that seemed self-evident and unproblematic in such a history (many of his later writings also deal with psychiatry and medicine). His influence is still very visible, and most historians of psychiatry or madness cannot avoid referring to him and his ideas, and the tone in the commentaries is mostly either positive or negative, seldom neutral.

Although there never was anything like an 'anti-psychiatric movement', what united the radical critics of psychiatry was their assumption that psychiatry is a form of social control rather than a robust medical or psychological science (see e.g. Szasz 1974, 66–9). This common point of view notwithstanding, the ideas and arguments of 'anti-psychiatrists' diverged and sometimes even conflicted with one another. Thomas Szasz, the most outspoken critic of psychiatry as a medical specialty, had a very critical if not hostile attitude towards two of his radical colleagues who, in a way, stole the limelight in the latter half of the 1960s.

Mad, bad and dangerous

Szasz could hardly stomach the ideas and therapeutic practices of R.D. Laing (1927–89) and David Cooper (1931–86), who (mostly) lived and worked in Britain (Kotowicz 1997). These two men could be seen as playing a similar role in the field of psychiatry as the Rolling Stones did in the field of popular music: they were mad, bad and dangerous. Laing was a Scottish psychiatrist and psychoanalyst who first gained a reputation with his empathetic and tolerant approach to disturbed patients. His enemy was biological psychiatry with its brutal shock methods, mind-clouding pills and uniform white coats (A. Laing 1996, 53). David Cooper, in turn, moved in the 1950s from South Africa to England, where he assumed the role of psychiatric contrarian. He opposed almost anything that smacked of the 'establishment', including hospitals, universities, schools, prisons, racial segregation, social conventions, the family and – of course – psychiatry. It was Cooper who coined the term 'anti-psychiatry' in his 1967 book *Psychiatry and Anti-Psychiatry*.

Laing and Cooper did not like 'pill psychiatry', but LSD was an altogether different kind of chemical compound. Both used 'acid' recreationally as well as part of their therapy. Obviously, their own acid trips shaped their ideas of madness and normality. In *The Death of the Family* (1971), Cooper describes how, during one of his trips, 'I died out of the existence of David Cooper who till then had been alive and well and working in London, and I became a Mongolian sage from about the middle of the nineteenth century' (Cooper 1971, 120). Some of Laing's former patients have warm recollections of their LSD therapy sessions with him. Some ex-patients have said that one six-hour LSD session with Laing was more therapeutic than years of psychoanalytic therapy (A. Laing 1996, 71). Once, when he was delivering a speech to a prestigious audience, Laing praised the therapeutic effects of LSD, denied the existence of schizophrenia as an illness and emphasized doctors' need to heal themselves before they try to heal others. This is how he talked about therapy:

> The aim of therapy will be to enhance consciousness rather than to diminish it. Drugs of choice, if any are to be used, will be predominantly consciousness expanding drugs, rather than consciousness constrictors – the psychic energizers, not the tranquillisers.
>
> (A. Laing 1996, 121)

Laing had received positive attention with his 1959 book *The Divided Self,* in which he approached schizophrenia from an existential perspective as a form of personal alienation (Laing 1959). In the 1960s, he began to study the possible influences of the family constellation on the outbreak of mental illness. He was simultaneously a psychoanalyst in private practice and, between 1965 and 1969, a primus motor behind an experimental therapeutic community at Kingsley Hall in London. Laing belonged to the group of therapists who wanted to replace traditional institutional care with small-scale treatment that avoided drugs, white coats and somatic therapy. At the same time, he was turning traditional assumptions about madness upside down. His most controversial idea concerned mental illness as an escape from the 'madness of normality'. Laing contended that if individuals cannot stand the pathology of normality, including conformism, aggression, competition and greed, they may use schizophrenia as a strategy for coping with unbearable reality. As a consequence, they are declared mentally disordered, while the so-called well-adjusted, normal people go on living their 'one-dimensional' lives in a sick society. Laing saw madness in a double light:

> Madness need not be all breakdown. It may also be breakthrough. It is potentially liberation and renewal as well as enslavement and existential death.
>
> (Laing 1983, 133)

With his therapy, Laing wanted to test the idea that mental illness was in itself a healing process, in which outsiders should not get involved (A. Laing 1996, 102). In his view, schizophrenics could teach psychiatrists about the inner world more than psychiatrists their patients (Laing 1983, 109). As a remedy to the alienation of 'normal people', Laing offered the psychocultural doctrine of self-knowledge, which

316 Madness in the Cold War era and beyond

he adorned with existential philosophy and a romanticized ethics of authenticity. The Laingian mode of thinking about self and society stood in stark contrast to the American psychiatry of adjustment that had given medical, psychological and social legitimation to various tools of re-adjustment, such as shock methods, neuroleptics and lobotomy. With his mindset Laing represented the radical generation of the 1960s for whom the norms of social adjustment might as well signify adjustment not necessarily to the liberal-democratic value system but to the authoritarian and violent values of fascism. There is no doubt that the Nazi bureaucrat Adolf Eichmann, whose trial in Jerusalem caught the attention of international media in the early 1960s, was well-adjusted to the social reality of the Third Reich. To Laing and other radical psychiatrists,

> social adaptation to a dysfunctional society may be very dangerous. The perfectly adjusted bomber pilot may be a greater threat to species survival than the hospitalized schizophrenic deluded that the Bomb is inside him. Our society may itself have become biologically dysfunctional, and some forms of schizophrenic alienation from the alienation of society may have a sociobiological function that we have not recognized.
>
> (Laing 1983, 120)

Laing held the family responsible for alienation. Parents teach their children to adopt the values of 'normality' that may very well be sick and alienating (money, career, reputation, respectability, conformism). David Cooper, Laing's colleague and friend in the 1960s, agreed with Laing, but he was more extremist in his views. In his own way, Cooper was a full-blooded, romantic-utopian revolutionary, who regarded the death of the (bourgeois) family as the most important step towards creating a better society and a better human being. He attacked the patriarchal-capitalistic family system, but in his own attitude towards women and children he displayed an unmistakable sign of chauvinism: he charged mothers with the principal if not sole responsibility of raising children. It is the mother's duty to 'generate the field of reciprocal action so that the infant learns how to affect her as another', which is the 'precondition for the realization of his personal autonomy'. If the mother fails in producing a 'field of possibilities in which her child may become someone else, another person', the child will remain 'a thing, an appendage, something not quite human, a perfectly animated doll', devoid of autonomous personality (Cooper 1967, 21). Like mainstream psychoanalysts, Cooper was monitoring – and blaming – mothers, while fathers conveniently slipped under his radar. He was also a typical utopian in his disparaging attitude towards family ties: 'Blood is thicker than water only in the sense of being the vitalizing stream of a certain social stupidity' (Cooper 1971, 27). The family becomes moronic, and the 'bourgeois state is a tranquilizer pill with lethal side effects' (Cooper 1971, 33). In the film *Family Life* (1971), the British director Ken Loach clearly drew on the writings of Laing and Cooper in his depiction of an emotional and existential crisis of a young woman who was alienated from her 'normal' household, which drove her to fear and anguish. The 'misbehaving' protagonist of the film was a tragic victim of the tyranny of her family, her doctors and the whole capitalist society. The psychiatric message of *Family Life* was clear: in many if not most families, there is a lack of communication between parents and children, and schizophrenia can be caused by poor parenting and by self-righteous physicians who are lackeys of the capitalist system.

Like Laing, Cooper talked a great deal about alienation, which he conceptualized first in terms of Marxism and then also through the lens of oriental philosophy. When a schizophrenic has a psychotic episode, it can be an attempt to break free from the alienating social system. This means that a schizophrenic is 'in some sense less "ill" or at least less alienated than the "normal" offspring of "normal" families'. Cooper believed it was 'about time that we, who would be healers, took our hands off their [schizophrenics'] throats' (Cooper 1967, 37, 109). He dreamed of a 'Madness Revolution that reinvents our selves' (Cooper 1971, 113). To Cooper and Laing, mental disorders were strategies, patterns of behaviour or escape mechanisms rather than illnesses in the medical sense of the term. Small wonder, then, that radical psychiatrists were deeply suspicious of medication, physical methods of treatment and biological explanations of madness. Instead, they usually favoured psychotherapy, not least because they often made their living as psychotherapists (as both Laing and Cooper did). Szasz, who had tenure in the State University of New York, Syracuse, was of the opinion that psychotherapy was useful because it helps individuals to learn about themselves and their lives, not because it cures their ills (Szasz 1974, xvi).

Unlike Laing and especially Cooper, Szasz was not a socialist but a libertarian who maintained that the government should intervene in the lives of citizens as little as possible. And he strongly rejected the suggestion that he would belong to any sort of anti-psychiatric movement. In one of his last books (*Coercion as Cure*, 2007), he made no bones about his dislike of Laing, who did not deny the existence of mental illness and who in Szasz's view mistreated his patients (one of whom wrote a critical book about his therapy with Laing). To Szasz, so-called radical psychiatrists did not really fight for their patients' rights or human rights in general. In their own way, claimed Szasz, Laing and his cronies wanted to control the lives and minds of people diagnosed as mentally ill, and Laing 'sought establishment approval as a medical doctor' while cultivating the 'image of anti-establishment guru' (Szasz 2007, 217). Obviously, Szasz regarded Laing as a fake guru:

> Lotus-sitting, long-haired, bare-footed Laing made a sport of betraying every promise and trust, explicit and implicit – to wives, children, friends, and patients [. . .] With his LSD-laced 'therapy', Indian junket, faux meditation, and alcohol-fueled lecture-theatrics, Laing managed, for a while, to con people into believing that his boorish behavior was a badge of superior wisdom. Then, as quickly as he built it, his house of cards collapsed of its own featherweight.
>
> (Szasz 2007, 216)

318 Madness in the Cold War era and beyond

With the benefit of hindsight, Szasz could conclude that Laing's and Cooper's visions remained unfulfilled. As Laing's son Adrian wrote in his sympathetic biography of his father, in the 1970s Laing's popularity declined together with his charismatic power: 'Ronnie's "stuff" was brilliant and exciting the first time around; listening to his views more than once made them seem platitudinous, bordering on the self-indulgent. Only the die-hards stuck with Ronnie through the sixties and seventies' (A. Laing 1996, 116).

There was to be no Madness Revolution à la Cooper and Laing. Instead, both men became heavy drinkers and marginalized figures in academic psychiatry, while biological, brain-centred psychiatry began to occupy the centre stage in the 1970s and the 1980s. But from the mid-1960s to the mid-1970s 'anti-psychiatric' and critical views of psychiatry as an instrument of social control became part of leftist student movements, thereby influencing the attitudes of these future policy makers, academics and public officials. In academic psychiatry, 'anti-psychiatry' began to be referred to as a passing phase, a mere ideological fad that revealed the unrealistic naïvety of the 1960s counterculture. Still, I believe Laing and the whole 'anti-psychiatric' set of ideas and practices has a lasting legacy, which is the human-centred and critical approach to madness and its treatment that is badly needed in today's drug-centred psychiatry of adjustment. Obviously, 'anti-psychiatry' was scientifically inadequate and vague, but in the clinical face-to-face situations it was in principle a valiant attempt to understand what Laing called the 'divided self'. In the management of madness, there is no need for egocentric gurus or prophets, but neither is there much need for mere technicians who know how to measure the biochemical ingredients in the brain but who have no understanding of what it is like to become crazy, and how crazy people can be helped and supported not just by prescribing drugs, but also by social support and by having (sometimes) lengthy discussions with them and their nearest and dearest. If, as I believe, madness is to a large extent a communication problem, it can only be solved when we try to communicate with the people deemed to be mad, crazy or – in today's clinical language – mentally disordered. Management of madness requires time and patience.

'On being sane in insane places': Rosenhan's pseudopatient study

In the late 1960s and early 1970s, attitudes towards psychiatry and institutional mental health care were more severe than ever before. Fuelled by the provocative statements of critics who were inspired by Laing, Cooper, Szasz, Foucault, Scheff and Goffman, psychiatrists were in the line of fire, and the widely published accusations of involuntary incarceration of deviant individuals, inhumane treatment of patients and unscientific theories all tarnished the reputation of psychiatry as a medical science and clinical practice. In 1973, the American psychologist Daniel Rosenhan (1929–2012) published a study that further undermined the status of psychiatry and contributed to radical reform in the classification of mental disorders in the United States.

Inspired by the critics of psychiatry, Rosenhan wondered how to distinguish between sanity and insanity. In particular, he wanted to know how well psychiatrists were able to detect insanity. To find an empirical answer to this question, he devised an experiment in which a number of pseudopatients would try to get into mental hospitals and, once they were accepted as patients, to act completely normally. Would the individuals with faked symptoms fool psychiatrists into believing they were mentally ill? And would the staff in the wards notice that they were not mentally ill at all? Rosenhan called eight people he knew personally – psychologists, physicians, a painter and a housewife – and asked them to join the experiment. These pseudopatients, Rosenhan himself among them, went to the admission offices of 12 different mental hospitals with false names, vocations and employment. In the interview with the psychiatrist on duty, they all said that they had been hearing voices. The voices had said 'empty', 'hollow' and 'thud'. The point in choosing these three words was that they appeared to be 'existential symptoms' that seemed to say, 'my life is empty and hollow' (Rosenhan 1973, 251). This auditory hallucination was the only symptom they feigned, and they all told their real life histories, which did not include any episodes of mental problems. On the basis of this single symptom, all the pseudopatients were admitted to hospital. In 11 cases they were diagnosed as schizophrenics; only once was the patient admitted with a different diagnosis (manic-depression, which was given by the psychiatrist in the only private hospital in the study). The length of their hospitalization ranged from one week to 52 days, with an average of 19 days – less than three weeks. With the exception of Rosenhan himself, none of the medical staff or administration at the hospitals were aware of the presence of pseudopatients in their establishments (Rosenhan 1973, 252).

Once the pseudopatients were admitted to hospital, they began to act and behave normally, at least if normality in such circumstances included making copious notes in public and without any concern about the staff or other patients. How long would it take before they would be pronounced sane and released from the hospital? This remained an unanswered question, because there was not a single member of staff in any of these 12 hospitals who noticed that they were not 'real' patients. By contrast, other patients often realized that the pseudopatients were sane. They might say, 'You're not crazy. You're a journalist, or a professor'. The observations of the pseudopatients were rather unflattering to the staff: patients were treated as if they were inanimate objects; they were subjected to physical and verbal violence; they were given an enormous amount of pills (all in all nearly 2,100!); they had very little contact with the nurses, physicians or psychologists; and their words and deeds were systematically seen as symptoms, no matter what they did or said. In short, the pseudopatients had a strong sense of depersonalization and invisibility – they were 'things' rather than human beings, and this experience of depersonalization was aggravated by the minimal amount of personal privacy. Furthermore, only rarely was the 'aberrant' behaviour of patients interpreted in the context of their immediate surroundings and the peculiar circumstances prevailing in a 'total institution'. For example, there was a group

320 Madness in the Cold War era and beyond

of patients sitting outside the cafeteria entrance well before lunchtime. Nearby, one psychiatrist explained in psychoanalytic jargon to junior doctors accompanying him that the oral-acquisitive aspect of the disorder triggered such 'aberrant' behaviour in these patients. It seemed not to have occurred to the psychiatrist that eating was one of the very few highlights of the day in the dull ambience of a psychiatric hospital. Once, when a pseudopatient was pacing the long hospital corridors, a nurse who was watching him asked him, 'Nervous, Mr. X?' He replied: 'No, bored' (Rosenhan 1973, 253).

What took most pseudopatients by surprise was the intensity of the psychological stress they began to experience in the wards. All but one of them wanted to get out of the hospital almost as soon as they were admitted (Rosenhan 1973, 252). When they were discharged, none of the 'schizophrenics' was declared sane or cured. Rather, they had a diagnosis of schizophrenia 'in remission', which indicated that their essential sanity was not detected.

The staff at one research and teaching hospital heard about Rosenhan's study and voiced their doubt that such an error could occur in their psychiatric hospital. Rosenhan took the challenge and informed the staff that:

> in the next three months he would send an undisclosed number of pseudopatients to this particular hospital, and the staff were to judge, in a sort of experimental reverse, not who was insane, but who was sane. One month passed. Two months passed. At the end of three months the hospital staff reported to Rosenhan that they had detected with a high degree of confidence forty-one of Rosenhan's pseudopatients. Rosenhan had, in fact, sent none.
>
> (Slater 2005, 76)

Rosenhan added insult to injury by publishing the results of his study in the prestigious journal *Science*, which guaranteed that the experiment would receive a maximum amount of scientific attention. It must have been painful for the leading lights of American psychiatry to read the following conclusions in Rosenhan's article 'On Being Sane in Insane Places'. First, when individuals constantly experience depersonalization in a psychiatric hospital, they are overwhelmed by a sense of powerlessness. Second, psychiatrists, like all physicians, believe that it is more dangerous to misdiagnose disease than health. Therefore, they are more inclined to give diagnosis to a healthy person than pronounce an ill person healthy. Finally, and most damagingly to psychiatry, '[i]t is clear that we cannot distinguish the sane from the insane in psychiatric hospitals [. . .] How many people, one wonders, are sane but not recognized as such in our psychiatric institutions?' (Rosenhan 1973, 252–7).

Rosenhan's conclusions were too disturbing and too much discussed to be ignored by the psychiatric establishment. One who took it upon himself not only to reply to Rosenhan but also to reform American psychiatry was Robert L. Spitzer from the New York State Department of Mental Hygiene. In his rebuttal of Rosenhan's study, Spitzer called it 'pseudoscience presented as science' (Spitzer 1975, 442). Spitzer defended the use of schizophrenia as the only proper diagnosis in cases of auditory hallucinations of longer duration (Rosenhan had told Spitzer personally what he did not mention in his article, namely that the pseudopatients had heard voices for three weeks). More importantly to the future of psychiatry, Spitzer raised the question of the reliability of psychiatric diagnosis. Dissatisfied with the prevailing diagnostic criteria, he had begun to cooperate with his like-minded colleagues in the so-called St Louis group associated with the Department of Psychiatry at Washington University in St Louis. Together, they had an ambition to develop a totally new and more scientific classification of mental disorders based on empirical evidence and stringent diagnostic criteria rather than on sloppy and frustratingly vague psychodynamic speculations that were at least partly to be blamed for the weaknesses and problems that Rosenhan's study had exposed. Another major change was going to happen in the institutional form of mental health care: large hospitals were to be replaced by outpatient care, clinics and 'community psychiatry' that would help mental patients in their own social environment.

Before I move on to the realization of Spitzer's and his associate's diagnostic vision, I want to give the last word to David L. Rosenhan. His ground-breaking study is far from perfect in its design and in its inordinately generalizing conclusions, but it has deservedly become one of the classic social psychological experiments. In his commentary to Spitzer's rebuttal, Rosenhan refers to a problem that in my view has haunted patients since the beginning of institutional mental health care: it is no use trying to convince the staff that you are (now) sane and that you should be discharged on account of your sanity. When Rosenhan and other pseudopatients asked real patients, 'How do you get out of hospital?', they were never advised simply to tell the staff they were fine now, and that they wanted to go home. Such a straightforward request would not be taken seriously. Instead,

> [the patients] encouraged us to be cooperative, patient, and not make waves. Sometimes they recommended a special kind of indirection: 'Don't tell them you're well. They won't believe you. Tell them you're sick, but getting better. That's called insight, and they'll discharge you!'
>
> (Rosenhan 1975, 472)

No wonder Rosenhan and other pseudopatients were discharged with the diagnosis 'schizophrenia in remission' – they must have had 'insight' into their condition.

The new diagnosis makers

Over the past 200 years, there have been hundreds of different classificatory systems in world psychiatry. Such a proliferation of psychiatric classifications created a confusion of diagnoses and disease entities that at worst resembled the confusion

322 Madness in the Cold War era and beyond

of tongues in the biblical story of the tower of Babel (in Genesis 11:1–9). More concerted efforts at creating an international system of classification were undertaken only in the latter half of the twentieth century. The most important system was created by the WHO, which was itself a newly founded organization when it included mental illnesses in its International Classification of Diseases (ICD) in 1949. Another, increasingly important system was created by the American Psychiatric Association (APA), which published its first, rather modest and insignificant *Diagnostic and Statistical Manual* (DSM-I) in 1952. The publication of DSM-II in 1968 was not a major improvement, suffused as it was with ungrounded psychoanalytical assumptions, assertions and theories that revolved around the large and vague array of neuroses.

In a comparative study of the uses of diagnostic categories in the early 1970s, a group of British and American psychiatrists watched a video tape in which a patient was interviewed by a psychiatrist. On the basis of the interview, more than two-thirds of the American psychiatrists (69 per cent) diagnosed the patient as schizophrenic, whereas only 2 per cent of the British psychiatrists did the same. This was not only an academic or theoretical problem, because the prescription of a proper psychiatric drug was dependent on the diagnosis – there were different drugs for people suffering from schizophrenia, anxiety or depression (Valenstein 2001, 157). It became painfully obvious to mental health experts that there was a great disparity in the recognition and diagnosis of schizophrenia between countries and even between hospitals within a country. For Robert L. Spitzer, one embarrassing discovery was that American patients were diagnosed with schizophrenia much more frequently than patients in most European countries. At the time when Rosenhan's pseudopatient study was published in 1973, Spitzer and his colleagues at Washington University were totally fed up with the neuroses, psychoanalytic speculations and general disregard for scientific rigour in American psychiatry. The efforts of Spitzer and his group ('Task Force') resulted in the publication of DSM-III in 1980 (Decker 2013).

DSM-III was designed to elevate the scientific status of American psychiatry by making the recognition and classification of mental illness as reliable as possible. To achieve this goal, DSM-III focused on the classification of symptoms, strict use of diagnostic criteria, increase of disease entities and avoidance of all conjectures about the causes of mental disorders. The proliferation of diagnoses was to some extent the result of the deletion of the category of Psychoneurotic Disorders (DSM-I) and Neuroses (DSM-II) from the manual, but at the same time it created a broad new category of mental disorders, Anxiety Disorders, which was partly a small concession to psychoanalysis that had dominated American psychiatry for three decades, and partly old wine in new bottles, because it relabelled and fine-tuned some of the popular neuroses. While the psychoanalytic Anxiety Neurosis was dropped, what was taken aboard was Generalized Anxiety Disorder, Panic Disorder and five types of Phobic Disorder. There were also new diagnoses that were meant for children; one of them was Attention Deficit Disorder (ADD), which in the revised edition in 1987 was changed to Attention

Deficit Hyperactivity Disorder (ADHD). ADHD has become a controversial disease entity, just like Post-traumatic Stress Disorder that appeared for the first time in DSM-III (Kutchins & Kirk 1999, 24–5, 45).

One far-reaching consequence of DSM-III was that the social, economic and existential context of mental suffering disappeared from view. The only situationally bound mental state that remained in the new manual was grief resulting from the death of a loved one. Other than that, no attention was given to the life situation of patients, to the varying circumstances and adversities in the context of which mental symptoms were traditionally seen. The new DSM symbolized the transformation of (American) psychiatry, which amounted to what the American researchers Allan Horwitz and Jerome Wakefield have called the 'loss of sadness'. Such a loss was most evident in the emergence of depression as a major disorder in the western world in the 1980s. This new, post-DSM-III depression was a strange, almost free-floating affliction that hardly ever escaped the narrow confines of biochemical explanation, according to which depression resulted from low levels of the neurotransmitter serotonin in the brain (Horwitz & Wakefield 2007). Eschewing psychological and sociological explanations in favour of medical ones, DSM-III boosted the influence of biological, drug-centred psychiatry that has dominated mental medicine since the 1980s.

In its pragmatic, atheoretical approach to mental disorders, DSM-III became popular and much used by the international psychiatric community. What increased its relevancy was its usefulness for health insurance companies, which required clear-cut diagnostic categories on insurance claim forms. At the same time, the new DSM failed to fulfil the partly conflicting expectations regarding its scientific validity and reliability. For example, there were no references to any scientific studies that would have supported the claims made in the manual. A creation of the revised edition of the manual appeared on the agenda of the APA only a few years after the publication of DSM-III, and it appeared in 1987 (DSM-III TR). In the revised edition, more than 30 new diagnostic categories were added. Seven years later (1994), it was time for DSM-IV to appear. Like its predecessor, DSM-IV is a purely descriptive work, not a scientific document. An inclusion of more theoretical and uncertain issues would have made DSM a much more controversial work, which in turn could have revealed the tensions, conflicts and rivalries within the psychiatric community. Once belittled and ignored, the DSM has grown to be such an important work that the WHO's International Classification of Diseases largely follows its model of classification. Although the ICD remains the official classificatory system in world psychiatry, the DSM has become the leading model, the 'psychiatric bible', not least because of the global dominance or at least influence of American psychiatry (Kutchins & Kirk 1999; Decker 2013).

One distinctive feature of the DSM is the increase in disorders from one edition to another. In DSM-I (1952), there were 106 illnesses or 'reactions' as they were called in post-war American psychiatry. In DSM-II (1968), the number of diagnoses was 182, and the paradigmatic DSM-III (1980) listed no fewer than 265 diagnoses.

324 Madness in the Cold War era and beyond

Finally, the 'diagnostic climax' was reached with the more than 300 diagnoses described in the 886-page DSM-IV (1994). Naturally, such an avalanche of new diagnoses in a time span of a few decades prompted a number of critics to voice concern at the increasing medicalization of human life (Conrad 2007). Could the increase of diagnoses be explained by the employment of more accurate diagnostic tools, or was DSM a product of massive pathologization of deviant or unusual behaviour? What about the role of the pharmaceutical industry and the requirements of insurance companies? DSM is obviously a very complex product that aims to satisfy the needs of many different interest groups, but those who are suspicious of the active role of drug companies in the construction of the DSM are not necessarily paranoiac: more than half of the 170 authors of DSM-IV had economic ties with the pharmaceutical industry. This majority included each and every psychiatrist who wrote about mood disorders and schizophrenia in the manual (Angell 2009, 10).

The most recent edition, the DSM-5, was published in 2013, and it continued the pattern created by DSM-III, with some modifications. As could be predicted, DSM-5 has also stirred up debates in medical and academic communities as well in social media (www.dsm5.org). Apparently, there are many people in the world today who want to express their opinion about this medical, social and cultural innovation, the mastermind of which was Robert L. Spitzer. Incidentally (or not), Spitzer, who was also instrumental in the construction of DSM-IV, has turned critical towards the DSM, protesting about what he saw as secrecy surrounding the production of DSM-5 (Spitzer 2009). Another eminent advocate-turned-critic, Allen Frances, Chair of the DSM-IV Task Force, has noted that 'except for [the partly de-medicalized] autism, all the DSM 5 changes loosen diagnosis and threaten to turn our current diagnostic inflation into diagnostic hyperinflation' (Frances 2012).

Dorothy Rowe, a renowned clinical psychologist and researcher on depression, summarizes the multidimensional reality included in this diagnostic juggernaut in her introduction to a critical study of the DSM:

> This book [*Making Us Crazy* by Herb Kutchins and Stuart A. Kirk] [. . .] shows how the DSM makes it possible for victims to be blamed, ordinary behaviour to be turned into pathology, homosexuality to be changed from being a disorder to not being a disorder, the effects of trauma to be ignored and then turned into a pathology, modest, compliant women to be diagnosed as mentally ill for being what society expects them to be, aggressive, sexist men to be protected from the stigma of mental illness, difficult patients to be punished, and racial prejudice to masquerade as science.
>
> (Rowe 1999, xii)

The history of DSM can be compared to the story of Pandora's Box in Greek mythology: whereas Pandora releases all sorts of evils that spread over the earth, DSM releases all sorts of diagnoses, syndromes and disease entities that spread all over the world. One thing, however, remains lying at the bottom of the box (actually, a jar): the Spirit of Hope. Maybe the same spirit, called Elpis in the ancient Greek myth, remains on the pages of the DSM. Or maybe I am suffering from a DSM disorder called Delusional Optimism.

From back wards to back streets: the decline of institutional mental health care

In western Europe and North America, the dismantling of large-scale institutional mental health care began in the 1960s. To some extent, the so-called psychopharmacological revolution of the 1950s had pacified the psychiatric wards, and the increasing emphasis on community care, rehabilitation and the negative effects of 'total institutions' on mental patients all created a momentum for broad mental health reforms. Following President Kennedy's Community Mental Health Centers Act of 1963, American mental health administration began to establish mental health centres. Partly funded by the federal government, these centres paved the way for a new type of care: instead of incarcerating masses of patients in mental hospitals, the new programme assumed optimistically that a community-oriented mental health policy could overcome the persistent defects of mental hospitals and that mentally disordered people could live in their homes with their families while they underwent rehabilitation. Even though the reality was less rosy – many patients had no home or family – the new non-institutional model of mental health care was to some degree adopted in all western countries. Today, Americans still follow the model that was designed and implemented by the Kennedy administration and his successor Lyndon B. Johnson, who forcefully implemented his progressive Great Society programme in the mid-1960s. Despite the reforms, public mental hospitals continued to care for persons who were more severely and chronically ill throughout the 1960s and the 1970s, while mental health centres treated individuals for a variety of problems from social maladjustment and substance addiction to depression and marital problems (Grob 1994, 249–68).

The next radical turn away from hospital-based mental health care occurred in the 1980s, when the neoliberal governments of Margaret Thatcher in the UK and Ronald Reagan in the United States began to dismantle the Keynesian welfare state that was still strong, even if weakened by the worldwide energy crisis of the mid-1970s. Inspired by Thatcher's policy, the goal of which was to weaken the structures of the public sector and to support privatization and entrepreneurship, the Reagan administration started to implement policies aimed to remove all structural barriers to the free operation of market forces. If the 1960s and the 1970s had been an era of the welfare state and Keynesian economics, in the 1980s the tide was turning as the 'market was held out as the realm of freedom, choice, and reason' (Rodgers 2011, 42). Adopting the neoliberal policy agenda, Reagan's administration made drastic cuts in health care programmes and social services, with the result that federal support for the chronically mentally ill declined sharply. Unfortunately, this occurred at the same time as the states had to struggle with serious

326 Madness in the Cold War era and beyond

social and economic problems that had detrimental effects on mental health care in the United States (Grob 1994, 287).

In England and Wales, there were nearly 150,000 institutionalized mental health patients in 1954; by the end of the 1980s, the number had decreased to fewer than 60,000. In the United States, deinstitutionalization had started at a slow pace in the mid-1950s, when the staggering number of 559,000 patients were confined in mental institutions. It was only during the Reagan administration that the number of hospital beds in state and county institutions declined rapidly at the same time as the length of stay was reduced to days or weeks. In 1986, the number of inpatient beds was 119,000; by 2007, the number had declined to fewer than 60,000, with around 240,000 admissions annually. Deinstitutionalization was most extreme in Italy, where a law enacted in 1978 decreed that mental hospitals were to be replaced by a radically new model of territorial services. It was a law that abolished psychiatric hospitals, plain and simple. The primus motor behind this law was a group of reformist mental health experts, the most well-known of whom was the sociologically oriented psychiatrist Franco Basaglia (1924–80). Inspired by Laing, Foucault and other critics of traditional psychiatry, Basaglia was an anti-authoritarian psychiatrist who regarded economic factors as the major cause of deviant behaviour (he wrote a book on the 'deviant majority' in the early 1970s). He became convinced that traditional institutional mental health care had no future, and that the psychiatric hospital had to destroy its social function, which was to forcibly incarcerate deviant individuals (Basaglia 1987).

Basaglia and his like-minded colleagues succeeded in making Italian politicians promote their goals, and in persuading the psychiatric community to implement them. The result was Law 180, one of the most radical laws in the history of mental health care. The implementation of this law was tantamount to a large-scale, anti-institutional project of emancipation. At the end of the 1970s, Italy began to develop community-based mental health services, with small psychiatric units for acute cases established in large general hospitals. Follow-up studies of Italian mental patients report a fairly high degree of satisfaction with their quality of life, whereas patients' families are often less satisfied, because they have to bear a heavy burden in providing care for mentally disorganized family members. An enduring problem in Italy as well as in other western countries that experienced deinstitutionalization has been a lack of resources: the majority of public funding is directed at general hospitals, so community mental health centres and other forms of outpatient care have developed painfully slowly (Palermo 1991; de Girolamo et al. 2007).

The avoidable tragedy with 'the great anti-confinement', laudable in itself, was that as more and more mentally disordered people began to live in the community rather than in public hospitals, the system of community care proved to be grossly inadequate – there were not enough day hospitals, outpatient clinics, shelters and other forms of medical, psychological and social support. It is no exaggeration to say that too many mentally ill persons were left to their own devices by the Reagan administration. Since the triumph of the neoliberal political economy and the ensuing return of dramatic socio-economic inequalities in the 1980s, mental health care has hardly improved anywhere in the western world, not even in countries that have been less affected by cuts in social spending. In the United States, the increasing number of homeless people with a severe mental disorder began to be called 'sidewalk psychotics', many of whom had to cope with multiple problems in their lives, such as substance abuse, poverty, physical ill health and racism. In New York, for example, they lived 'in subway tunnels and on steam grates, and die[d] in cardboard boxes on windswept street corners' (Grob 1994, 1). Too many were also confined in penal and correctional institutions, which also happened in Italy after the implementation of Law 180.

In the early 2000s, more than 100,000 Americans with mental health problems lived in group homes or board-and-care facilities, large buildings often located in run-down neigbourhoods. In addition, about 300,000 non-demented people with psychiatric diagnoses lived in nursing homes, and more than 1,250,000 of the prisoners and local jail inmates in 2006 suffered from severe mental health problems. In these circumstances, a reintegration into society is difficult, which is also seen in the unemployment rates: in the United States, 'people with psychiatric disabilities have a staggering national unemployment rate of 90 percent, despite research showing that the vast majority are ready and eager to work' (Penney & Stastny 2009, 187). For mentally ill persons, the risk of social exclusion is very real even in today's affluent west. The inefficiency of (long-term) institutional care is crystal-clear to all concerned, but the main problem is the weakness of the alternative, non-institutional forms of mental health services, with the result that too many people fell through the cracks of the safety net system. (On contemporary mental health care across Europe, see Knapp et al. 2007.)

An alternative perspective to deinstitutionalization is offered by the historian Barbara Taylor, who in the late 1980s was herself a mental patient in the Friern Mental Hospital in north London (established as Colney Hatch in the mid-nineteenth century). Taylor was an inmate at a time when the remaining old Victorian asylums were about to be closed down (this happened to Friern in the early 1990s), and she writes about the chequered past of Friern, which includes public scandals when regular occurrences of patient coercion and abuse became known to the authorities and media in the 1960s and the 1970s. Yet, she also writes about the humanity and camaraderie of the 'bin'. Taylor ends her memoir about her illness and the treatment she received with these words:

> The mental health system I entered in the 1980s was deeply flawed, but at least it recognized needs – for ongoing care, for asylum, for someone to rely upon when self-reliance is no option – that the present system pretends do not exist, offering in their stead individualist pieties and self-help prescriptions that are a mockery of people's sufferings. The story of the Asylum Age is not a happy one. But if the death of the asylum means the demise of effective and humane mental health care, then this will be more than a bad ending to the story: it will be a tragedy.
>
> (Taylor 2014, 264)

328 Madness in the Cold War era and beyond

I wonder where we should look to find madness in today's world – could it be the case that there is more madness in the mental health care system than in the mentally disordered individuals?

Happiness, unhappiness and madness

There is a lesson to be learned from the history of madness: times change, theories of disordered brain and mind change, diagnoses change and forms of mental health care certainly change, but the mad, the lunatics, the insane and the mentally ill, in short, the mental sufferers always have to struggle for justice and defend their basic human rights in the face of indifference, mismanagement or, in extreme cases, sheer adversity and racial hygienic persecution. Fortunately, there is also some good news on this front. One is the development of the patients' rights groups and peer support organizations since the 1960s. Today, these groups and organizations constitute a political force that to some extent, at least, is able to reduce prejudice and discrimination, and to promote and protect the human rights of people with mental disabilities. Another piece of good news is that, if we are to believe a study conducted in the Netherlands, the majority of people with a diagnosed mental disorder feel happy most of the time. Among these people, those with substance abuse and anxiety disorders were happier than the depressed individuals (Bergsma & Veenhoven 2011).

The happiness of mentally disordered Dutch people implies that mental illness is not necessarily associated with unhappiness. Indeed, the fact that there are probably very many happy people with mild or even severe mental disorders in modern society is a useful reminder to all of us who like to think that we are experts in the field of mental illness. We must be on our guard lest we create new, presumably humanitarian prejudices and stereotypes about people with mental disabilities – that they are supposedly 'unhappy', 'helpless', 'discontent', 'victims of society' and so forth. One way to respect the autonomy and self-determination of these individuals is for the behaviour experts to stop believing that they 'understand' the reality of these people and that the experts know what is good and what is bad for them. To define someone in medical, psychological and social terms is to exert power, and to exert expert power is to influence the person's self-understanding and potentially cultivate a culture of vulnerability, no matter if it is done with a benevolent purpose.

I am not arguing that we leave the mentally ill persons alone, simply because I am well aware that they often need psychosocial support and rehabilitation. What I *am* arguing is that we should not ascribe powerlessness, helplessness and unhappiness to mentally disorganized persons. They should not become passive subjects of our psychocultural tendency to victimize people and to impose a new conformity through therapeutic intervention, management and well-meaning acts of 'understanding' (see Furedi 2004). With good reason, we abhor a society in which citizens are surveilled and controlled by the Orwellian Thought Police; I believe we should also be wary of the Therapeutic Police who want to monitor and control citizens with the help of psychological expertise, diagnostic categories and a culturally sanctioned encouragement of individuals to expose their innermost feelings and thoughts. In his short story 'The Academy' (1954), the American science fiction writer Robert Sheckley (1928–2005) describes a society where everyone's mental health is constantly monitored by the authorities. Thanks to the technical innovation called the Sanity Meter, each individual's exact level of mental health can be measured, and when the indicator of the gadget stops between four and ten, then the individual is mentally disordered to a lesser or greater extent.

In his short story, Sheckley portrays a totalitarian society where the value of individuals is measured by their levels of sanity, and where sanity is defined as the individual's level of adjustment to their social environment. Those who are not willing or able to accept the inevitable and fully conform to the demands of the State are by definition 'unsane' and therefore a threat to the social order. In short, the authorities maintain law and order by normalizing deviation with the help of mental health experts. Apparently, Sheckley was mocking the 1950s American society with its increasing preoccupation with psychiatric, psychological and therapeutic expertise, on the one hand, and with the question of adjustment and maladjustment, on the other (Sheckley 1959).

Now, more than half a century later, the mental health totalitarianism satirized by Robert Sheckley is still affecting our lives. In fact, long before Sheckley, contemporary obsession with health and mental health was uncannily predicted by the German national poet Johann Wolfgang von Goethe. In the 1780s, Goethe made the following observation on the future of humanity: 'Speaking for myself, I too believe that humanity will win in the long run; I am only afraid that at the same time the world will have turned into one huge hospital where everyone is everybody else's humane nurse' (Goethe 1962, 312). Today, western societies are preoccupied with healthism, which can be defined as a belief system that revolves around the imperative of a healthy lifestyle and that prescribes normative codes to citizens whose political consciousness and moral sense are being pushed aside by an individualized theology of health: you are required to stay fit, pursue well-being and constantly monitor your health and mental health (on healthism, see Skrabanek 1994 and Rose 1999). Contemporary 'mental healthism' cannot be considered a pure blessing to the mentally ill, because such health ideology reaches and stimulates the worried well rather those who are seriously afflicted by mental health problems. The latter group is truly in need of help and support, but they are the ones who appear to be neglected by the public health system, while the members of the educated middle classes receive treatment and care for their neuroses as well as for their tennis elbows. A sobering indication of the sorry state of mental health care is that the life expectancy of patients with serious mental health problems has declined in the western world (Scull 2011, 123) – this decline is a unique phenomenon.

Still, I am not sure whether persons with mental afflictions appreciate finding themselves defined in terms of dependence and vulnerability. Maybe we 'normal ones' feel more secure when we attribute unhappiness to people with mental

330 Madness in the Cold War era and beyond

disabilities and assume that we are by definition unlike them on an emotional and existential level. But as Alan Watts (1915–73), the maverick writer and advocate of eastern philosophy, wrote in the early 1960s, 'no one is more dangerously insane than one who is sane all the time: he is like a steel bridge without flexibility, and the order of his life is rigid and brittle' (Watts 2013, 84).

Just like someone without mental illness

The American paediatrician Mark Vonnegut is in many ways a typical mental patient of our era; his two psychotic episodes in the 1970s and the 1980s required hospitalization, but since then he has been relatively well. What is unusual about Vonnegut is that he has written two books about his life and his illness. It is no coincidence that he has literary gifts; his father was the famous writer Kurt Vonnegut. His episodes of schizophrenia/bipolar disorder were also not that surprising, since there are several family members with mental health problems on both his father's and his mother's sides of the family. His mother's auditory and visual hallucinations did not turn her into a mental patient, because 'she always managed to make friends with them [voices and visions] and was much too charming to hospitalize even at her craziest' (Vonnegut 2010, 6).

Obviously, Mark Vonnegut's childhood and youth were not exactly average (whatever 'average' means). He himself sees the careless disregard of the pressure to be normal as the greatest blessing in his mental illness. Perhaps his unusual childhood environment and the many eccentric, mad and half-mad family members have endowed him with an exceptional ability to understand mental deviancies and symptoms such as hearing voices. Vonnegut's message to us, 'normal people', is that mental illness is not such an exceptional state of mind, something very unusual, strange or alien. In fact, he believes that wherever you go you find people with some sort of mental illness or affliction: 'It all depends on where you set the bar and how hard you look. What is a myth is that we are mostly mentally well most of the time' (Vonnegut 2010, 166). In the light of these words it is instructive to ponder on the report of the recent European-wide epidemiological research, which concluded that almost 40 per cent (38.2 per cent) of the EU population suffer from a mental disorder in every year (Wittchen et al. 2011). These are colossal figures (and, based on an over-inclusive concept of mental disorder), but if we take a 'Vonnegutian' approach to the question of mental health we could just as well wonder whether it is indeed possible that more than half of Europeans do *not* have any sort of mental problem annually. Is this not a desperate attempt to underpin the myth of mental health?

In 1935, a Finnish woman published an account of her experience in a mental asylum. Aino Manner, like many other patients in asylums around the world, endured harsh treatment. What strikes the reader most about Aino's account is the description of her 'episodes'. She compares her illness to a dream, a dream which at first appeared as a strange and frightening nightmare, but which eventually changed its meaning after she had 'recapitulated to the conqueror'. Aino's subsequent episodes were dream-like, 'magnificent experiences' that did not frighten her; all she had to do was to let the dreaming continue to its end and not fight it. Analogous to the dream that ends when you wake up, mental illness can also end (Manner 1935). Indeed, many people often recover from mental illness and live happy productive lives. According to Mark Vonnegut, someone with mental illness is 'just like someone without mental illness, only more so' (Vonnegut 2010). The possibility of recovery, this fundamental fact attending the phenomena of mental illness, provides us with a hopeful ending to this journey into the history of madness.

Bibliography

Angell, M. (2009) 'Drug companies and doctors: a story of corruption', *New York Review of Books*, 15 January.

Basaglia, F. (1987) *Psychiatry Inside Out: Selected Writings of Franco Basaglia*, eds N. Scheper-Hughes and A.M. Lovell, New York: Columbia University Press.

Bergsma, A. and Veenhoven, R. (2011) 'The happiness of people with a mental disorder in modern society', *Psychology of Well-Being: Theory, Research and Practice*, 1. Online. Available HTTP: <www.psywb.com/content/1/1/2> (accessed 14 August 2014).

Conrad, P. (2007) *The Medicalization of Society: On the Transformation of Human Conditions into Treatable Disorders*, Baltimore, MD: Johns Hopkins University Press.

Cooper, D. (1967) *Psychiatry and Anti-Psychiatry*, London: Tavistock Publications.

Cooper, D. (1971) *The Death of the Family*, New York: Random House.

Decker, H.S. (2013) *The Making of DSM-III: A Diagnostic Manual's Conquest of American Psychiatry*, Oxford: Oxford University Press.

Frances, A. (2012) 'DSM 5 is guide not Bible – ignore its ten worst changes', *Psychology Today*. Online. Available HTTP: <www.psychologytoday.com/blog/dsm5-in-distress/201212/dsm-5-is- guide-not-bible-ignore-its-ten-worst-changes> (accessed 18 May 2014).

Furedi, F. (2004) *Therapy Culture*, London: Routledge.

de Girolamo, G. Bassi, M., Neri, G., Ruggeri, M., Santone, G. and Picardi, A. (2007) 'The current state of mental health care in Italy: problems, perspectives, and lessons to learn', *European Archives of Psychiatry and Clinical Neuroscience* 257: 83–91.

Goethe, J.W. (1962) *Italian Journey*, trans. W.H. Auden and E. Mayer, orig. German edn 1817, London: Collins.

Goffman, E. (1963) *Stigma. Notes on the Management of Spoiled Identity*, New York: Simon & Schuster.

Grob, G.N. (1994) *The Mad Among Us*, New York: The Free Press.

Gumbel, A. (2006) 'Scientology vs. Science', *Los Angeles City Beat*, 12 January.

Horwitz, A.V. and Wakefield, J.C. (2007) *The Loss of Sadness*, Oxford: Oxford University Press.

Knapp, M., McDaid, D., Mossialos, E. and Thornicroft, G. (2007) *Mental Health Policy and Practice Across Europe*, Maidenhead: Open University Press.

Kotowicz, Z. (1997) *R.D. Laing and the Paths of Anti-Psychiatry*, London: Routledge.

Kutchins, H. and Kirk, S.A. (1999) *Making Us Crazy. DSM: The Psychiatric Bible and the Creation of Mental Disorders*, London: Constable.

Laing, A. (1996) *R.D. Laing – A Biography*, New York: Thunder's Mouth Press.

Laing, R.D. (1959) *The Divided Self*, London: Tavistock Publications.

332 Madness in the Cold War era and beyond

Laing, R.D. (1983) *The Politics of Experience*, 1st edn 1967, New York: Pantheon Books.

Manner, A. (1935) *Viesti yöstä. Mielisairaalakokemuksia*, Porvoo, Finland: WSOY.

Palermo, J.B. (1991) 'The 1978 Italian mental health law – a personal evaluation. A review', *Journal of the Royal Society of Medicine*, 84: 99–102.

Penney, D. and Stastny, P. (2009) *The Lives They Left Behind*, New York: Bellevue Literary Press.

Rodgers, D.T. (2011) *Age of Fracture*, Cambridge, MA: Belknap Press.

Rose, N. (1999) *Powers of Freedom: Reframing Political Thought*, Cambridge: Cambridge University Press.

Rosenhan, D.L. (1973) 'On being sane in insane places', *Science*, 179 (January): 250–8.

Rosenhan, D.L. (1975) 'The contextual nature of psychiatric diagnosis', *Journal of Abnormal Psychology*, 84: 462–74.

Rowe, D. (1999) 'Introduction', in H. Kutchins and S.A. Kirk, *Making Us Crazy. DSM: The Psychiatric Bible and the Creation of Mental Disorders*, London: Constable.

Scheff, T. (1999) *Being Mentally Ill: A Sociological Theory*, 1st edn 1966, New York: Aldine Press.

Scull, A. (2011) *Madness – A Very Short Introduction*, Oxford: Oxford University Press.

Sheckley, R. (1959) 'The academy', in *Pilgrimage to Earth*, London: Corgi Books.

Skrabanek, P. (1994) *The Death of Humane Medicine and the Rise of Coercive Healthism*, Bury St Edmunds, Suffolk: The Social Affairs Unit.

Slater, L. (2005) *Opening Skinner's Box. Great Psychological Experiments of the Twentieth Century*, New York: W.W. Norton.

Spitzer, R.L. (1975) 'On pseudoscience in science, logic in remission, and psychiatric diagnosis: a critique of Rosenhan's "On being sane in insane places"', *Journal of Abnormal Psychology*, 84: 442–52.

Spitzer, R.L. (2009) 'DSM-V transparency: fact or rhetoric?', *Psychiatric Times*, March 6. Online. Available HTTP: <www.psychiatrictimes.com/articles/dsm-v-transparency-fact-or- rhetoric/page/0/1> (accessed 2 May 2014).

Szasz, T. (1974) *Myth of Mental Illness*, 1st edn 1961, New York: Harper & Row.

Szasz, T. (2007) *Coercion as Cure*, New Brunswick, NJ: Transaction Publishers.

Taylor, B. (2014) *The Last Asylum. A Memoir of Madness in Our Times*, London: Hamish Hamilton.

Valenstein, E. S. (2001) *Blaming the Brain*, New York: The Free Press.

Vonnegut, M. (2010) *Just Like Someone Without Mental Illness, Only More So*, New York: Delacorte Press.

Watts, A. (2013) *The Joyous Cosmology: Adventures in the Chemistry of Consciousness*, 1st edn 1962, Novato, CA: New World Library.

Wittchen, H.U. et al. (2011) 'The size and burden of mental disorders and other disorders of the brain', *European Neuropsychopharmacology*, 21: 655–79.

EPILOGUE

In modern times, the management of madness has oscillated between hope and despair, Utopia and dystopia. In the early nineteenth century, when Philippe Pinel was developing psychiatry on the basis of the humane principles of the Enlightenment and moral treatment, we can see how he and other pioneer psychiatrists were inspired by the vision of the Therapeutic Society. In this better world of the future, the insane would be taken care of, and maybe even cured, by the new scientists and physicians of the soul. The idea and practice of early nineteenth-century moral treatment tried to implement this therapeutic vision with the new type of mental asylums where the insane would regain their senses and be restored to a form of citizenship required in a society bent towards political freedom and democratization. Some scholars have seen the mental asylum in early nineteenth-century France as a laboratory of democracy, where alienists tried to save the glimmer of sanity left in mental patients in order to restore their ability as social beings and autonomous persons (Gauchet & Swain 1999). This short epilogue catalogues the hopes and promises in mental health care and how they remain unfulfilled.

Promises unfulfilled

As the years passed and the initial therapeutic optimism turned to pessimism if not nihilism, nineteenth-century asylums started to resemble vast human warehouses rather than places of cure. The transformation of asylums from houses of cure into custodial institutions signified a grand promise that remained unfulfilled. From the late nineteenth century onwards, the introduction of a number of psychological and somatic therapies seemed to promise a turn for the better: maybe, after all, mental illness can be remedied with the help of psychotherapy, psychoanalysis, various shock methods and, as a 'last resort', psychosurgery. Psychological therapies were mostly administered to those whose mental afflictions

334 Epilogue

were less severe and who could afford to pay for individual psychotherapeutic sessions. True, in many European countries (e.g. the UK), public health care systems started to provide psychotherapeutic services for patients after World War II, but such services were mostly restricted to the patients treated in out-patient facilities, while institutionalized, more severely ill patients were more or less out of reach of psychotherapy. Moreover, while it was obvious that talk therapy helped some people, to some extent, it was also evident that its therapeutic effect did not often last long, if it had any effect in the first place. As for the somatic therapies, such as insulin coma therapy and electroshocks, their therapeutic effect proved to be transitory. And psychosurgery caused brain damage, which in turn caused a personality change of some degree. Thus, the promise that the new methods of treatment would restore the mental health of patients remained unfulfilled.

The so-called psychopharmacological revolution of the 1950s raised new therapeutic hopes as *Thorazine* and other neuroleptics seemed to alleviate the condition of institutionalized patients around the world. But it was soon discovered that instead of curing patients the way aspirin cures a headache or antibiotics kill harmful bacteria, *Thorazine* and other 'major tranquillizers' act as mental stabilizers that, at least in the short term, remove the disturbing symptoms and help the patients cope with the demands of everyday life. The flip side of this psychopharmaceutical coin is that, for too many people, these so-called 'anti-psychotics' impair mental functioning and lessen the quality of life. Moreover, pills create dependence and cause side effects that can be detrimental to both physical and mental health. While psychiatric medications are certainly effective for many people, for many others they are much less so, and for a large minority they do more harm and good. There is accumulating evidence that drugs are much less effective and helpful than has been claimed for decades (Gøtzsche 2013; Frances 2013; Healy 2012; Angell 2005). Now that western psychiatry has been drug-centred for half a century, it is relatively safe to conclude that something has gone wrong if more and more people swallow pills and yet there seem to be more and more people with mental illness in the western world. If we are to believe the report published by the US Centers for Disease Control and Prevention, in 2011 a quarter (25 per cent) of the US population suffered from mental illness (Reeves et al. 2011). The psychopharmacological revolution was another promise that remained unfulfilled.

From the late 1950s onwards, so-called deinstitutionalization has turned hospital-based institutional care into community-based (open) care. The therapeutic vision behind this transformation was laudable: let us keep the mentally ill in our communities rather than incarcerating them in large, inhumane institutions; and let us establish outpatient clinics, psychiatric wards in general hospitals, day hospitals and social support rather than locked wards, lobotomies and a numb existence in loony bins. What actually happened between 1960 and 2000 was the reverse of 'the great confinement' of the Asylum Age: the whole structure of the asylum system was disassembled as the number of mental hospital beds was reduced to one-tenth or so of what it had been during the heyday of asylums. It is a contested issue whether national governments and the states in the United States had any intention of investing in mental health care beyond what was necessary to keep up the appearance of organized care. Closing down asylums was economically beneficial to the public authorities, but to what extent were they prepared to *spend* money to create 'community services' for mental patients, the great majority of whom were no longer sheltered and cared for in hospitals? Sadly, not much, and a solid infrastructure of mental health services is still missing in most if not all western countries. As a consequence of deinstitutionalization, homelessness skyrocketed, for example in the UK and the United States, and a growing number of mental patients ended up on the streets, in jails or in shelters for the homeless. A leading figure in the UK mental health politics, Baroness Elaine Murphy, 'titled her account of community care between 1962 and 1990 "The Disaster Years"' (Taylor 2014, 116). To speak of the mental health care system is to speak of the most recent unfulfilled promise.

If the mentally ill do not have a safe place to go and receive treatment – other than pills – then how does 'community care' differ from systematic negligence? Large asylums were hardly an ideal solution to the problem of mental illness, but community care without resources is no solution at all. Nevertheless, as Andrew Scull points out, the 'consensus on the desirability of community care has become as overwhelming as the Victorians' convictions about the merits of the asylum' (Scull 2011, 114). Historian Barbara Taylor reminds us that, with all its faults, the mental hospital was a place where the patients socialized with each other and protected each other, and where they were not discharged as quickly as possible, which is the case in today's psychiatric clinics and emergency wards in general hospitals with their *über*-fast turnover of patients. Above all, asylums were places of safety for people who often desperately needed shelter, security and care (Taylor 2014, 243–64).

In a way, we have returned to the pre-asylum days when families and local communities were in charge of the mentally ill. We have gone around full circle and are back in a world that has uncanny resemblances with the 'pre-confinement' era, with the exception of psychiatric pills, patient organizations and the individualist ethos of self-management. According to a recent report in *USA Today*, there is a huge number of Americans with mental illness who are homeless and who often find themselves in city streets, emergency rooms and county jails (Szabo 2014). When I look at this world and all the developments in it, I am tempted to employ the term 'madness' not so much to describe mental illnesses, afflictions and disorders themselves as to characterize all the medical, psychological, eugenic, social-political, structural, economic and ideological tools, methods and approaches that have been used to solve the problem of madness. In short, 'madness' in this book has referred to the management of madness at least as much as it has referred to mental illness. And who knows, maybe some of you readers will be inspired by this history of madness to embark on another book project: History of Sanity is yet to be written.

336 Epilogue

Bibliography

Angell, M. (2005) *The Truth about the Drug Companies: How They Deceive Us and What to Do About It*, New York: Random House.

Frances, A. (2013) *Saving Normal. An Insider's Revolt Against Out-of-control Psychiatric Diagnosis, DSM-5, Big Pharma, and the Medicalization of Ordinary Life*, New York: William Morrow.

Gauchet, M. and Swain, G. (1999) *Madness and Democracy*, trans. C. Porter, orig. French edn 1980, Princeton, NJ: Princeton University Press.

Gøtzsche, P.C. (2013) *Deadly Medicines and Organised Crime*, London: Radcliffe Publishing.

Healy, D. (2012) *Pharmageddon*, Berkeley: University of California Press.

Reeves, W.C. et al. (2011) 'Mental illness surveillance among adults in the United States', *Morbidity and Mortality Weekly Report*, 60, Supplement, September 2, Atlanta, GA: Centres for Disease Control and Prevention.

Scull, A. (2011) *Madness – A Very Short Introduction*, Oxford: Oxford University Press.

Szabo, L. (2014) 'The cost of not caring: Nowhere to go', *USA Today*. Online. Available HTTP: <www.usatoday.com/longform/news/nation/2014/05/12/mental-health-system-crisis/7746535/> (accessed 20 August 2014).

Taylor, B. (2014) *The Last Asylum. A Memoir of Madness in Our Times*, London: Hamish Hamilton.

INDEX

1st Earl of Shaftesbury (Lord Anthony Ashley Cooper) 70
7 Up 291

Ablard, J. 101
aboulia 178–9
Abraham, K. 190
adjustment 8, 135, 153, 204–5, 277, 316, 318, 325, 329
Adler, A. 220
Aetius of Amida 164
Afghanistan 239, 270
Age of the Enlightenment 5, 22, 55, 57, 71, 79
aggression 149, 206, 225, 315
Agnew, A. 82
akathisia 297
alcoholism 81, 96, 98, 125–8, 204, 214, 234, 262, 282, 289
Alexander, F. 224–5
Algeria 99–100; Algerian War of Independence 100; Algiers School of French psychiatry 99
alienation 46, 107–12, 126, 142, 159, 163, 206, 264, 315–17
alienism 103
American Psychiatric Association 93, 193, 201, 207, 239, 322
amphetamine 299–300, 305; methamphetamine 305
Andropov, Y. 279
Angst, J. 201
animal magnetism 172, 212–13
Anna O. (Bertha Pappenheim) 217

anorexia nervosa 224–5
anthropometry 123
anti-psychiatry 5, 136, 196, 205, 261, 296, 312–18
anti-Semitism 102, 303
anxiety, anxiety neurosis, anxiety disorders 43, 47, 96, 98, 120, 140, 149, 160, 170–1, 176, 208, 216, 220, 228, 230, 239, 244, 249, 257, 260, 273–4, 290, 295, 302–3, 305, 322, 328
aphasia 116
Arataeus of Cappadocia 162
Argentina 4, 97, 100–3, 281
Aristotelian philosophy 32
Arlidge, J.T. 147
Arnold, T. 165
Asclepiades 20–1, 23
Assisi, St Francis of 29
asthma 127, 223–5
astrology 26, 30, 32
asylums see mental hospitals
attention deficit disorder (ADD) 207, 322
attention deficit hyperactivity disorder (ADHD) 207, 323
Augustine, St 29
Aurelanius, C. 108
Aurelius, M. 21
Australia 4, 97–8, 117, 239, 291
autism 159, 191, 300, 324

Baillarger, J. 199
Ballets Russes 196
Baltic countries 50
Balz, V. 288, 294–6

338 Index

Balzac, H. 117
Barham, P. 231
Bartholomew, R.E. 43
Basaglia, F. 326
Battie, W. 72, 124–5, 175
Bayle, A.-L. 112, 123
Beard, G. 175–6, 250
Beatles, the 299
Beers, C. 282–3
Beethoven, L. van 166, 200
Belgium 31, 141, 305; the village of Gheel 31
Bender, L. 300–1
Bentall, R. 192
Berger, F. 302–3, 305
Bernheim, H. 174–5, 215
Berrios, G. 158, 162
Bible, the 15, 17, 91; New Testament 17, 28; Old Testament 16–18
Bini, L. 251–2
Binswanger, L. 190
biological psychiatry 5, 102, 244, 307, 314
bipolar disorder 201, 330
Black Death, the (plague epidemic) 15, 33–6
Bleuler, E. 186, 188–93, 195–6, 198, 220
Bleuler, M. 192
Blom, J.D. 165
Boccaccio, G. 33
Borch-Jacobsen, M. 217, 219
Bosch, H. 54
Bourne, H. 247–8
Brahe, T. 58
Braid, J. 214
brainwashing 5, 33, 269–75, 281; see also mind control
Brandt, K. 232, 235
Brant, S. 53–4
Brazil 257, 262
Breivik, A. 202
Breuer, J. 217
Brezhnev, L. 279
Brill, A. 190
Briquet, P. 173
Britain, England 4, 33, 44, 50, 58, 61, 63, 65–6, 69, 71, 78–80, 83, 85–91, 93, 95, 98, 101, 108, 114, 117, 127, 130–1, 138, 147, 150, 155, 162, 172, 192, 202, 214, 231, 246–7, 289, 296, 300, 302, 304–5, 314, 326; Act for Regulating Private Madhouses (1774) 87; Act of Parliament of (1808) 87; The Mad House Act (1828) 88; The County Asylums Act and the Lunacy Act (1845) 88
Broca P. 116, 123

Brodsky, J. 144, 280
Brown, J. 16
Buckholtz, J. 207
Burton, R. 61–5, 162, 165; *Anatomy of Melancholy* 61–5, 162, 165
Butler, S. 207
Byron, Lord 63
Byzantine 25

Cade, J. 291
Cameron, E. 270–5, 281
Canada 194, 262, 271–2
cannabis 288–9, 298, 301
capitalism 36, 39, 80, 156, 205, 303, 316–17
Capone, A. 166
carbon dioxide treatment 250
Cartesian philosophy 66–8, 70
Cartwright, S.E. 94
castration 130, 192, 220, 243, 254
catalepsy 174, 187
catatonia 4, 24, 150, 159, 187–8, 193, 244, 249, 295
Catel, W. 235
Catholic Church 3, 25, 27, 29, 43, 47–8, 50, 60, 66, 102, 155
Celsus, A.C. 23
Cerletti, U. 251–2
Cervantes, M.de 64
Chaadayev, P. 276
Chaplin, C. 6
Charcot, J.-M. 120, 172–5
Charlemagne 26
Charles VI (King of France) 64
Charles, R. 94
Cheyne, G. 162
Chiarugi, V. 91
Chile 281
China 43, 225, 270–1, 275, 281
Christianity 16–7, 25–6, 115
Churchill, W. 71
CIA, the (Central Intelligence Agency) 5, 270–3, 275
Citizens Commission for Human Rights (CCHR) 313
classification of madness and mental illness 5, 20, 72, 96–7, 151, 159–62, 177, 186, 189, 206, 232, 318, 321–3
Cleckley, H. 204–5
cognitive behavioural therapy (CBT) 221
Coleborne, C. 97–8
colonialism 97–100, 128, 156
Columbia 287
Combe, G. 121
communism 26, 205, 269–71, 275–6, 279, 281

compulsion 169–71, 178–9, 200
Comte, A. 124
Condillac, É.B. 109
Conolly, J. 140
Constantine (Emperor) 25
convulsive shock therapy (Cardiazol, Metrazol) 242, 248–50
Cooper, D. 314–18
Copernicus 58
Cotton, H. 254–5
Cox, J.M. 143–4
craniology 120, 123
Crichton-Browne, J. 120
criminology 101, 123, 203
Cullen, W. 162, 177
Custance, J. 195–6
Cyprus 238

d'Holbach, Baron (P.-H. Thiry) 67–8
Dadas, A. 178
dancing mania 5, 38, 40–3
Dante, A. 245
de Puységur, Marquis C. 212–13
Dean, J. 205
deep brain stimulation (DBS) 263
degeneration, degenerationism, degeneracy theory 27, 98, 101, 126–9, 136, 150–1, 169–70, 203
deinstitutionalization 5, 326–7, 334–5
Delay, J. 293, 296
delusions 3, 43, 45, 64
dementia 97, 123, 160, 163, 166, 168
dementia praecox 163, 186–90, 192, 194, 199–200
Democritus 20
Deniker, P. 292–3, 296
depersonalization 165, 319–20
depression 7, 24, 68, 95, 145, 159, 163–4, 166, 178, 198–9, 201, 207–8, 219, 226, 228, 238, 250, 252–3, 258, 260, 263, 291, 295, 301, 304–6, 322–5
Descartes, R. 57, 66–8
deviance 1, 3, 8, 81, 97, 101, 113, 277
devil, demons, demonology 3, 6, 16–18, 26–7, 29–31, 34, 39–41, 43–9, 51–2, 55, 57–63, 67–9, 83, 195, 237
Devine, H. 192
Diagnostic and Statistical Manual of the American Psychiatric Association (DSM) 193, 206, 322–5; DSM-I 322–3; DSM-II 322–3; DSM-III 201, 229, 239, 322–3; DSM-IV 207, 323–4; DSM-5 193, 207, 325
Diamond, H.W. 118, 120
Dickens, C. 200

Diderot, D. 67–8
dislocation 98, 152, 177, 205, 249
Dix, D. 93
Dols, M.W. 17, 22, 27–30, 164, 169
Doors, the 205, 299
Doré, G. 245
Dörner, K. 77
Dr Caligari's Cabinet (movie) 214
'drowning therapy' 141
drugs: antidepressants, imipramine, iproniazid, isoniazid, 'psychic energizers', tricyclic 239, 298, 302, 304–8, 315; antihistamines 292; barbiturates, sodium amytal 233, 235, 242, 271, 290, 292, 302–3; benzodiazepines, Librium, Valium 303–6; bromides 290; chloral hydrate 290; chlorpromazine, Largactil, Megaphen, Thorazine 278, 292–6, 298–9, 303–4, 307–8; hyoscyamine, hyoscine 288–9; lithium 290–2; luminal 290; mephenesin 302; meprobamate, Miltown, Equanil 298, 302–3, 305, 308; neuroleptics 239, 280, 291, 296–7, 300, 308, 316, 334; paraldehyde 290; reserpine 296, 298, 300, 307; Ritalin 303; Salvarsan 167; scopolamine 289; selective serotonin reuptake inhibitors (SSRIs), Prozac 304, 306; *see also* psychopharmacology
Dubois, P. 176, 216
Dulles, A. 271
Dully, H. 260–1
Dunner, D. 201

Egypt 27, 28, 168–9
Ehrlich, P. 167
Eichmann, A. 316
Eitinger, L. 237–8
electroconvulsive therapy (ECT), electroshocks 144, 236, 250–3, 271, 273–4, 278, 294, 300, 334
Ellenberger, H. 128
encephalitis lethargica 297
England *see* Britain
Enlightenment 66–8, 79–80, 84–5, 106, 109, 333
epilepsy 16, 19, 29, 127, 173, 248, 250, 262
Erasmus of Rotterdam 52–4
Ervin, F. 264
Esquirol, J.-É. D. 111–13, 115, 117, 125, 163, 165, 170
eugenics 120, 123, 129–31, 161, 233; euthanasia programme in the Third

340 Index

Reich (Germany) 232–5; *see also* racial hygiene

Euripides 18–19

evolution, biological 7–8, 120, 124–8, 130, 158, 217

exorcism 17, 29, 43–5, 48, 59, 68, 211

Falret, J.-P. 199

Fanon, F. 99–100

fascism 26, 316

Faust, J. 60; the legend of Faust 60–1

feeblemindedness, the feebleminded 81, 83, 92, 96, 117, 126–7, 129–30, 136, 161, 192, 228, 232, 236

Ferguson, A. 156

Feuchtersleben, E. von 202, 216–17

feudalism 35

Feynman, R. 1–4

Finland 4, 50, 130, 144, 148–9, 154, 185, 206, 244, 261

flagellants 34–5

Fliess, Wilhelm 218, 222

focal sepsis, the doctrine of 254

folie à deux 145

folly 38, 52–4, 161, 275; court fools 5, 53, 55; holy fools 29–30, 53, 69, 72, 83

Forel, A. 192

forensic psychiatry 113, 279

Forman, M. 299

Foucault, M. 5, 9, 77–81, 83–4, 89, 136, 156, 314, 318, 326; concept of the great confinement 77–82

Fournier, J.A. 167

France 125–8, 165, 167, 170, 172, 175–6, 178, 187, 207, 212–3, 229, 231, 293, 304, 333; French colonial psychiatry 4, 99–100

Frances, A. 324

Franco-Prussian War 127, 170

Franklin, B. 91

Freeman, H. 87–9

Freeman, W. 256–61

Freud, S. 59, 102, 171, 176, 189–90, 214–23, 231

fugue 6, 178–9

Fulton, J. 255

Gadelius, B. 9

Galen (Claudius Galenus) 21

Galileo Galilei 58

Gall, F.J. 120–3

Galt, J.M. 94

Galton, F. 120, 130

Gamwell, L. 77, 92–4

Garland, J. 290

general paresis of the insane 112, 123, 173; *see also* neurosyphilis

Geoffrey of Monmouth 29

Georget, É.-J. 112–13

Géricault, T. 118

Germany 1, 4, 6, 30, 34–5, 40–1, 44, 50, 60, 66, 79–80, 83, 95–7, 112, 114–16, 126–7, 130–1, 134, 137, 142, 149, 161, 176, 187, 213, 228, 232–5, 289, 294–6

glass delusion 64–5

Goethe, J.W. von 329

Goffman, E. 8–9, 153–4, 156, 313–14, 318; *Asylums* 153–4, 313, 314; *see also* total institutions

van Gogh, V. 63, 166, 198, 200

Goldberger, J. 169

Gorbachov, M. 281

Gottlieb, S. 275

Gould, G. 65

Great War (1914–18) 228–31, 236

Greece 15, 17–19, 22–3, 211

Greek mythology 17–18, 23, 324

Griesinger, W. 115–16

Grob, G. 283

Groddeck, G. 224

Guislain, J. 141–2

Gutenberg, J. 53

gynaecology 254

habeas corpus 138

Haber, F. 230

Habsburg Empire 65, 121

Hacking, I. 179

Hahnemann, S. 213

Haizmann, C. 59–61

hallucinations 47, 51, 58–9, 147, 159, 185–6, 189, 191–4, 237, 256, 274, 294, 298, 301, 321, 330

Hare, R.D. 207

hashish 288–9

Haslam, J. 125, 146

Hata, S. 167

healthism 329

Healy, D. 239, 244, 251–3

Hebb, D. 273–4

hebephrenia 187–8

Hecker, E. 187

Heinroth, J. 115, 165

Herlihy, D. 34, 36

heroin 289, 291

Hippocrates 19–20, 171; Hippocratic medicine 15, 19–23, 71, 159

Hitler, A. 131, 166, 232

Hobbes, T. 57, 64, 68–70

Hobsbawm, E. 240

Hofer, J. 177
Hofmann, A. 298
Holocaust, the Final Solution 35, 234
homeopathy 213
homosexuality 78, 176, 203–5, 224, 234, 324
Hopkins, A. 201
Horace (Quintus Horatius Flaccus) 23–4
Horowitz, V. 65
Horwitz, A. 323
House, R. 289
Huizinga, J. 39
Hume, D. 109
Hungary 169, 248–9, 312
Hunter, E. 59, 60
Huxley, A. 299
hypnosis, hypnotism, hypnotherapy 5, 119, 172–5, 212–6, 272
hypochondriasis 162, 171, 175
hysteria 41–2, 127, 171–7, 212, 214–19, 223, 229–30, 313; conversion hysteria 223

Ibn Sīnā (Avicenna) 27, 164
idiocy, idiotia, idiotism 70, 97, 117, 126, 160–1
immigration 101
imperialism 97, 128, 239
India 225, 287–9, 317
Indians, Native Americans 94, 123, 131
industrialization, Industrial Revolution 66, 141, 151–2
insulin coma therapy (ICT) 242–8, 294, 334
International Classification of Diseases (ICD) 206, 322–3
Iraq 27, 239
Ireland 50, 80, 94, 98, 117, 155–6, 194
Islam, Islamic Near East, Islamic culture 4, 15, 26–8, 30, 80, 82
Israel 237–9
Italy 4, 26–7, 32–4, 43, 67, 91, 123–4, 127, 169, 250, 326–7; Law 180, 326–7

Jacobsen, C. 255
James, W. 156
Janet, P. 170–1, 175–6, 215–16, 220
Japan 262, 305
Jarvis, E. 151
Jaspers, K. 178, 186
Jesuits 48
Jesus Christ 17, 26, 28, 30, 60
Jews, Judaism 16, 26, 28, 34–5, 66, 102, 117, 234, 237–8
Johannisson, K. 65

Johnson, R. 61
Johnson, L.B. 325
Joseph, S. 239
Joyce, J. 166
Jung, C.G. 1, 30, 166, 190, 220–1

Kahlbaum, K. 187, 199
Kandel, E. 168
Kanner, L. 191
Kaptchuk, T. 211
Keller, R.C. 99–100
Kennedy, E. 304
Kennedy, J.F. 263, 283–4, 303, 325
Kennedy, R. 263
Kepler, J. 58
Kesey, K. 299
KGB (the Soviet Committee for State Security) 277–80
Khrushchev, N. 276, 279–80
Kiehl, K. 207
King, M.L. 283
Kivimäki, V. 236–7
Klaesi, J. 242
Kleinman, A. 225
Kline, N. 302, 305–6
Koch, J.L. 202–4
Koch, R. 176
Korean War 270
Kraepelin, E. 128, 163, 186–93, 198–201, 203
Krafft-Ebing, R. 169
Kramer, H. (Henricus Institoris) 48
Kropotkin, P. 77
Ku Klux Klan 283–4
Kubrick, S. 231
Kuhn, R. 190, 306

La Mettrie, J.O. 68
Laborit, H. 292
Laing, A. 314–15, 318
Laing, R.D. 314–18, 326
Lamarck, J.-B. 126, 128; Lamarckism 128–9, 217–8
Lang, F. 63
laudanum 289
Lavater, J.K. 117
Leary, T. 300
Lec, S.J. 144
Lederer, D. 6, 31, 40, 44–5, 47–8, 52, 58, 91
Lehmann, H. 30
Leibniz, G.W. 66
Lemnius, L. 64
leprosy 78, 82
Lincoln, A. 94, 166, 192

342 Index

Lindren, R. 205
Linnaeus, C. (von Linné) 160, 177
Lipowski, Z. 225
Loach, K. 316
lobotomy, transorbital lobotomy,
    leucotomy 144, 254–62, 316; *see also*
    psychosurgery
localization theory 124
Locke, J. 66, 70–1
Lombroso, C. 203
London, J. 200
Louis XIV (King of France) 83
LSD 271–2, 298–301
lunacy 6, 7, 72, 147, 155
Luther, M. 39, 42
Lysenko, T.D. 277; Lysenkoism 277

MacDonald, M. 47–8
Machiavelli, N. 39
magic 16, 29, 40, 47, 49, 57, 60–2, 165
magnetic sleep 213
majnūn ('madman' or 'possessed') 27
maladjustment *see* adjustment
malaria fever therapy 168, 231
Mandela, N. 192
mania 18, 20, 24–5, 29, 34, 38–40, 57, 97,
    107, 288–9, 291
manic-depression 5, 9, 165, 179, 186,
    198–200, 201, 218, 290–1, 319
Mann, T. 61
Manner, A. 330–1
Maori people 98
marabouts (spiritual healers) 99
Marcuse, H. 205
maristans (hospices for the mentally ill)
    99, 100
Mark, V. 264
Marlowe, C. 60
Marx, K. 102, 115, 161
Massa, N. 67
materialism 67–9, 106, 114
Maudsley, H. 290
Maupassant, G. de 166
McCissock, W. 261
medicalization 9, 71, 92, 103, 106, 109,
    151, 207, 239, 324
Meduna, L. von 248–51
Medvedev, R. 277–9
Medvedev, Z. 276–9
melancholy, melancholia 19–20, 24–5, 40,
    46–7, 61–5, 69, 72, 107, 125, 159–60,
    162–65, 199
Melchers, A. 294–5
Mengele, J. 234

Mental hospitals: Establishment of 82–3;
    overcrowding at 100, 102–3, 150–1;
    in different countries:
Algeria: Hôpital Psychiatrique de Blida
    (Centre Hospitalier Universitaire
    Frantz Fanon) 99
Argentina: Casa de Dementes 101;
    Convalecencia 101
Australia: Gladesville Hospital for the
    Insane 97
Austria: Bellevue Sanatorium 196;
    Psychiatric University Clinic in
    Vienna 167
Britain: Bethlem hospital 71, 82,
    85; Colney Hatch/Friern Mental
    Hospital 79, 327; Lincoln Asylum 140;
    Middlesex County Asylum 140; St
    Luke's Hospital 72, 124; St Patrick's
    88; West Riding Asylum in Wakefield
    120; York Asylum 89; York Retreat
    89–91, 140, 290
Canada: Allan Memorial Institute 271
Denmark: Schleswig Asylum 137;
    Vordingborg 250
Egypt: Mansūri Hospital 80
Finland: Nikkilä Mental Hospital 149;
    Pitkäniemi Hospital 244; Oulu
    District Mental Hospital 4, 149, 154,
    185, 194, 200, 206
France: Bicêtre Mental Hospital 9, 289,
    Charenton Asylum 165; Hôtel-Dieu
    80, 84, 107, 110; La Salpêtrière 106,
    108, 174; Sainte-Anne 292
Germany: Charité clinic 116; Heidelberg
    psychiatric clinic 294; Mental hospital
    in Jena 137; Meseritz-Obrawalde
    Hospital 235
Iraq: Dār al-Māristān 27
Italy: Bonifacio Hospital 91
New Zealand: Auckland Mental Hospital
    97
Poland: Mental hospital in Kocborowo
    (Conradstein) 232
Soviet Union: Kaluga Psychiatric
    Hospital 277; Psychiatric Hospital
    No. 2 (Leningrad) 280
Switzerland: Burghölzli Mental Hospital
    166, 189, 196, 220
Spain: Casa de Orates 82
USA: Asylum for the Relief of
    Friends Deprived of Their Reason
    93; Bloomingdale Asylum 135;
    Boston Psychopathic Hospital 202;
    Connecticut Retreat for the Insane

(known as the Hartford Retreat) 93; Creedmore State Hospital, New York 300; Eastern Lunatic Asylum of Virginia 93; Government Hospital for the Insane in Washington, DC (St. Elizabeth's Hospital) 93; Ionia State Hospital for the Criminally Insane 193; Maryland Hospital 93; Massachusetts State Lunatic Hospital 93; McLean Asylum 93; New York Hospital 93; Ohio Lunatic Asylum 135; Pennsylvania Hospital 91–2, 269; Trenton State Hospital, New Jersey 254; Utica State Hospital 138; Veterans' Administration Hospital in Albany, NY 274; Worcester Hospital 135
mental hygiene movement 144
mescaline 271, 298–9
Mesmer, F.A. 212–13; mesmerism 212
Metcalf, U. 85–6
Metzl, J.M. 193
Meyer, A. 283
Micale, M. 171–2, 175
Michel, A. 68
Michelangelo 200
Midelfort, E. 30–1, 39–40
Mills, C.W. 205
mind control 5, 269–75, 281; MKULTRA 271, 275, 281; *see also* brainwashing
Möbius, P.J. 127
Moniz, E. 255
monomanias 97, 112, 202; erotomania 112; homicidal monomania 112, 202, 207; kleptomania 112; nymphomania 112, 160; pyromania 112
Monro, T. 87
Monroe, M. 200, 290
mood swings 4, 198, 200, 259
Moore, W. 147–8, 253, 281–2, 284–5
moral insanity 202
moral treatment 83, 89–90, 93, 108–9, 111, 135, 140, 145, 333
Moreau, J.-J. (de Tours) 127, 288–9
Morel, B.A. 126–7
Morocco 27, 99
Morozov, G. 279
morphine 230, 233, 289
Morselli, E. 123
Muhammed 28
multiple personality disorder 42, 190, 216
Munch, E. 200
Munthe, A. 173, 222–3
Murnau, F.W. 61
Murphy, Baroness E. 335

Musil, R. 275
mutually assured destruction (MAD), the doctrine of 270
Myers, C.S. 229

Nadezhdin, N.L. 276
Naess, A. 196
Napier, R. 47, 85
Napoleon Bonaparte 166, 172
Narr, C. 55
nasal reflex neurosis 218, 222
Nash, J.F. 63, 94
National Socialism 130, 228, 232, 235, 294
Nebuchadnezzar, king of Babel (Babylon) 16–17
nervousness 6, 260, 294, 302
Netherlands, the 4, 34, 41, 61, 66, 78, 80, 176, 328
neurasthenia 170, 175–8, 214, 218, 230, 250, 303
neurosis 59, 127, 129, 170–3, 176, 178, 201, 208, 216, 218
neurosyphilis 123, 128–9, 158, 165–8, 199, 231, 242; *see also* general paresis of the insane
neurotransmitters, dopamine, serotonin 304, 306, 308, 309, 323
New Zealand 4, 97–8, 158, 177, 262
Newton, I. 58, 67, 200
Nicholas I, Tsar 276
Nicholson, J. 299
Nider, J. 49
Nietzsche, F. 63, 166, 309
Nigeria 287
Nijinsky, R. 196–7
Nijinsky, V. 196–8
Nikitin, A. 281
Noë, A. 8
non compos mentis ('not of sound mind'), the principle of 52, 112
Nordic countries 4, 6, 31, 81, 85, 97, 127, 130–1, 189, 261–3
Norway 130, 196, 202, 237
nostalgia 6, 98, 160, 177–8

obsession 6, 18, 47, 64, 110–11, 169–71, 179, 239, 295, 329
obsessive-compulsory disorder 7
Ochs, P. 284
One Flew Over the Cuckoo's Nest (novel and movie) 221, 299
opium 289–90
Oribasius of Pergamon 164
Origen (Origen Adamantius) 17

344 Index

Orlikow, V. ('Val') 272
Osmond, H. 299
Ottoman Empire 66

Padel, R. 18–9
Palestine 238
panic disorder 208, 322
Paracelsus (Theophrastus Philippus Aureolus Bombastus von Hohenheim) 44, 289
paralysis agitans 127, 173; *see also* Parkinson's disease
paranoia 23–4, 113, 187–8, 273–4
parapsychology 213
Parkinson's disease 127, 173, 224, 263, 293; *see also* paralysis agitans
Pasteur, L. 176
Paths of Glory (movie) 231
pellagra 158, 168–9
Perceval, J. 145
Perón, J. 102
Perrin, J. 292–3
Persia 27
Petrarch 27
phobia, phobic disorder 4, 7, 160, 170–1, 219, 295, 322
phrenetis 24
phrenology 120–3
physiognomy 117–18, 120
pilgrimage 30–1, 284
Pinel, P. 9, 89, 91, 99, 106–12, 114, 117, 125, 159–63, 199, 288, 333
placebo 211, 213–14, 248, 291, 306, 308
Plath, S. 94
Plato 94
Platter, F. 46
Poe, E.A. 63, 117, 200
Poland 80, 144, 196, 225, 231, 237, 303
political psychiatry 269–75, 312
Polybus 20
Pope Clement VI 35
Porot, A. 99
Porter, R. 5, 15, 32, 58, 71, 79–80, 87, 91, 144, 146–7, 154, 159, 176, 195, 198
Portugal 26, 50, 255, 257
positivism 124, 219
possession, demonic 6–7, 17, 19, 29, 31, 40, 43–8, 58–9, 68, 298
post-traumatic stress disorder (PTSD) 229, 239, 323
poverty 23, 32, 38–9, 62, 65, 78, 125–6, 129, 152, 169, 327
Presley, E. 205, 290
Pressman, J. 3, 149, 248, 253, 256, 263

Prichard, J.C. 202
'primitive mentality' 99
prostitution, prostitutes 84, 96, 126–7, 166–7, 203, 234
Proust, M. 290
Prussia 114, 150, 235
pseudopatient study 318–21; *see also* Rosenhan, David
psilocybin 299, 301
psychasthenia 170, 176–8
psychoanalysis 5, 10, 102, 129, 211, 216–22, 225, 307, 322, 333
psychoneurosis, psychoneurotic disorders 176, 216, 322
psychopathy 5, 113, 179, 186, 201–7, 217; anti-social personality disorder 206; *see also* sociopathy
psychopharmacology 5, 287–311, 325, 334; *see also* drugs
psychosis 3, 8, 129, 159, 169–70, 186–8, 193, 197–7, 202, 217, 228, 244, 257, 291, 293, 295
psychosomatic medicine 222–6
psychosurgery 3, 5, 99, 211, 248, 254–9, 261–4, 333–4; *see also* lobotomy
psychotherapy 206, 215–17, 219–21, 252, 256, 263, 293, 303, 307, 317, 333–4
Puerto Rico 131
Pussy Riot, the 281
Putin, V. 281

Quakers 58, 89, 91
Qur'ān 28

Rabbi Benjamin 27
racial hygiene 81, 129–30, 161, 168, 192, 232; sterilization laws 130–1; *see also* eugenics
racism, racialism 99, 100, 123, 131, 283, 327
randomized controlled trial (RCT) 291
Ray, I. 141
Reagan, R. 325–6
Rebel without a Cause (book and movie) 205
reflex neurosis 222
Reformation 38–9, 50
Reil, J. 107, 114–15, 125, 161
religious fanaticism 52, 58, 61, 65
religious madness 15, 33–5, 62, 69
Renaissance 25–7, 35, 53, 63
restraints 87, 90, 91, 116, 137–140
Ribot, T. 178
Richer, P. 174

Rituale Romanum (the Roman Ritual) 45
Rockefeller Foundation 130–1
Rolling Stones, the 205, 304
Roma people 238
Romania 281
Romanticism 114, 299
Rosen, J. 216
Rosenhan, D. 318–22; *see also*
    pseudopatient study
Rousseau, J.-J. 109, 171–2
Rowe, D. 324
Rush, B. 92, 143, 202
Russia 50, 65, 80, 276
Rüdin, E. 232
Rylander, G. 259

Sakel, M. 197, 243–5, 248–9
Sakharov, A. 278
Sami people 123
Satan 17, 26, 28, 48
Saul, the first king of Israel 16–17
Scandinavia 50, 72, 80
Scheff, T. 8, 313, 318
schizophrenia 5–6, 8–9, 24, 59, 113, 147,
    150, 158, 163, 165, 179, 186, 189–98,
    200, 203, 207, 220–1, 232, 237,
    242–4, 247–50, 252–3, 257–9, 262,
    273, 278, 280, 282, 287–8, 294–5,
    300–1, 308, 313, 315–17, 319–22,
    324, 330; Bleuler's invention of
    the diagnosis 189–93; the WHO's
    International Pilot Study of
    schizophrenia 287
Schneider, C. 234
Schneider, K. 192–3, 203–4
Schott, H. 134
Schou, M. 291
Schumann, R. 198
scientology 313
Scotland 65–6, 109, 121, 162, 177, 270, 314
Scull, A. 140, 171, 254–5, 329, 335
sensory deprivation, the method of 143,
    273–4
Shakespeare, W. 63
Sheckley, R. 329
Ship of Fools (*Narrenschiff*) 53–4
Shorter, E. 5, 125, 175, 177, 192, 197, 222,
    225, 244, 251–53, 290–1, 296, 302,
    304–5
Simpson, F. 283–4
Sirola, H. 208, 252
slavery 23, 39, 65, 92, 94; *drapetomania* 94
sleep treatment 242, 273
Slovenia 269

Snake Pit, The (novel and movie) 146
Snezhnevsky, A. 280
social engineering 100, 131
socialism 71, 101, 127, 131, 189, 279, 281, 317
sociopathy 204–5; *see also* psychopathy
Socrates 22–3
Solzhenitsyn, A. 278–9
somatization 20, 223, 225
somnambulism 174, 213–14
Sophocles 18–19
Soranus 24
South Africa 281, 314
Soviet Union 5, 144, 205, 232, 235,
    262, 269–70, 275–80, 287, 312;
    Gulag labour camps 276; political
    psychiatry in 276–81
Spain 26, 50, 80, 82, 169
spinal irritation 175, 177, 222
Spinoza, B. 57, 66, 303
spiritual affliction 14, 40, 47
spiritual physic(k) 15, 31, 44, 47, 58, 83, 91
Spitzer, R.L. 320–2, 324
Sprenger, J. 48–9
Spurzheim, J. 121
SS (the *Schutzstaffel*) 232, 238
Stalin, J. 221, 276
Stekel, W. 223–5
Sternbach, L. 303
stigma, stigmatization 8, 31, 77, 152, 155,
    205, 236, 301, 313, 324
straitjacket 6, 87–8, 116, 134, 137, 143–4
Stravinsky, I. 196–7
stupor 24, 159, 163, 187, 199, 292–3, 295
suicide 16, 82, 127, 149, 162, 185–6, 194,
    196, 206, 219, 239, 250, 252, 257,
    291, 301
Sweden 9, 33, 66, 82–3, 118, 130–1, 160,
    163, 173, 176, 222, 259
Switzerland 45, 50, 112, 117, 130, 151, 166,
    176–7, 186, 189, 192, 196, 216, 220,
    242, 293, 295, 298, 305–6
Sydenham, T. 171, 289
Syria 27–8
Szasz, T. 9, 312–14, 317–18

Tanzania (Tanganyika) 42
tardive dyskinesia 297
Tarsis, V. 279–80
Taylor, B. 327, 335
Taylor, J. 94
Thatcher, M. 325
Thelmar, Ms. 194, 196
Theophrastus 202
'therapeutic community' 149, 307, 315

346 Index

Thirty Years' War 38, 51, 57–8, 65, 77
Tölle, R. 134
Tomes, N. 92
torture 50, 60, 102, 144, 147, 231, 240,
    270–1, 274–5, 281
total institutions, Goffman's concept of
    153–6, 313, 325
'trade in lunacy' 80, 88
tranquilizer chair 143
traumatic neurosis 176, 229–30
tuberculosis 305
Tuke, D.H. 290
Tuke, S. 90
Tuke, W. 89
Tunisia 99
Turkey 25, 27, 66

Ukraine 279, 281
United Kingdom *see* Britain
United States 8, 83, 90–5, 101–2, 107, 117,
    130–1, 135, 138, 141, 143–4, 154, 169,
    176, 190, 193, 204–5, 216, 219, 221,
    236, 239, 244, 248–9, 260–2, 270–1,
    274, 277, 281, 287, 289, 295–6, 300,
    302–4, 306, 309, 318, 325–7, 335;
    American Civil War 177, 229; civil
    rights movement 8, 283–4; National
    Committee for Mental Hygiene 283;
    National Institute for Mental Health
    (NIMH) 308
Uruguay 196

Valenstein, E. 245, 305, 309
Venezuela 262
Vietnam War 205, 229, 236, 239, 270
Virchow, R. 124
Vonnegut, K. 330
Vonnegut, M. 330–1

Wagner-Jauregg, J. 167–8, 231, 242
Wakefield, J. 323
Wales 89, 296, 326
Wallace, G. 284
Waller, J. 41–2
war neurosis 5, 129, 221, 228–9, 231,
    236–7
Ward, M.J. 146
Watts, A. 330
Watts, J. 187, 256–60
Weismann, A. 128
Werlinder, H. 206–7
Wernicke, H. 235
wet packs 144, 278
Weyer, J. 51–2
Whitaker, R. 308
Wiene, R. 214
Wilde, O. 117, 166
Wiley, L. 195–6
Willis, T. 58, 171
Wilson, B. 63
Winkelman, W. 295
witchcraft, witch-hunts 26, 38–9, 44–5,
    48–53, 58, 65–6; *Malleus maleficarum*
    ('Hammer of the Witches') 48–9
Wittgenstein, L. 10
Wolf-madness (*lycantrophy*) 164–5
workhouses 78–9, 84, 88–9, 95
World Health Organization (WHO)
    287–8, 322–3
World Medical Association 274
Wortis, J. 247
Wundt, W. 116–17, 189

Yugoslavia 281

Zambia 158
Zweig, S. 167